THEODORE ROOSEVELT AND THE AMERICAN POLITICAL TRADITION

American Political Thought
Wilson Carey McWilliams and Lance Banning
Founding Editors

THEODORE ROOSEVELT AND THE AMERICAN POLITICAL TRADITION

Jean M. Yarbrough

University Press of Kansas

Published by the University Press of Kansas (Lawrence, Kansas 66045), which was organized by the Kansas Board of Regents and is operated and funded by Emporia State University, Fort Hays State University, Kansas State University, Pittsburg State University, the University of Kansas, and Wichita State University

Library of Congress Cataloging-in-Publication Data

Yarbrough, Jean M.
Theodore Roosevelt and the American political tradition / Jean M. Yarbrough.
p. cm. — (American political thought)
Includes bibliographical references and index.
ISBN 978-0-7006-1968-9 (pbk : alk. paper)
1. Roosevelt, Theodore, 1858–1919—Political and social views. 2. United States—Politics and government—1901–1909. 3. Executive power—United States—History—20th century. 4. Republicanism—United States—History—20th century. 5. Political culture—United States. I. Title.
E757.Y37 2012
973.91'1092—dc23
[B]

2012019762

British Library Cataloguing in Publication Data is available.

Printed in the United States of America

10 9 8 7 6 5 4 3 2 1

The paper used in this publication is recycled and contains 30 percent postconsumer waste. It is acid free and meets the minimum requirements of the American National Standard for Permanence of Paper for Printed Library Materials z39.48-1992.

For Dick

Read The Federalist—*it is one of the greatest—I hardly know whether it would not be right to say that it is on the whole the greatest book dealing with applied politics there has ever been.*

Theodore Roosevelt, Address to the Liberal Club of Buffalo, September 1895

Now, and here, let me guard a little against being misunderstood. I do not mean to say that we are bound to follow implicitly in whatever our fathers did. To do so, would be to discard all the lights of current experience—to reject all progress—all improvement. What I do say is, that if we would supplant the opinions and policy of our fathers in any case, we should do so on evidence so conclusive, and argument so clear, that even their great authority, fairly considered and weighed, cannot stand; and most surely not in a case whereof we ourselves declare they understood the question better than we.

Abraham Lincoln, Address at Cooper Institute, February 1860

Contents

Acknowledgments

During the twelve years that I have been at work on this book, I have accumulated many debts that I am—at long last—delighted to acknowledge. Bowdoin College made it possible for me to take three full years off during my sabbatical leaves by generously funding additional semesters. I am especially grateful to Charles R. Beitz, now at Princeton, who, when he was dean of faculty affairs, supported my application for a William R. Kenan Research Fellowship. Among other things, the grant enabled me to spend time in Cambridge, making good use of the Theodore Roosevelt Collection and the Harvard College Archives. Craig McEwen, who served as acting dean during my second sabbatical, oversaw a second grant and supported my project in important ways at a difficult time. Cristle Collins Judd, the present dean of faculty affairs, came up with a creative solution that made possible my most recent sabbatical and the completion of this book. The Earhart Foundation provided additional funding during my sabbaticals in 1999 and again in 2005, and I am grateful for their generous support. Once again, it is a pleasure to acknowledge the National Endowment for the Humanities, which provided support for this project in 2006 under its "We the People" initiative.

I am happy to join the legions of Roosevelt scholars who are indebted to Wallace Finley Dailey, curator of the Roosevelt Collection, at Harvard College. Mr. Dailey provided me with materials relating to Roosevelt's legal education and when, near the end of my research, technology failed, sent me photocopies of hard-to-find Roosevelt essays. I am also grateful to Tim Driscoll, senior reference archivist at Harvard, and to Robin Carlaw and Barbara Maloney in the Harvard Archives, all of whom responded to queries about Roosevelt's undergraduate years. Adrienne Fischer, librarian at the Harvard Club of New York, allowed me to examine the Harvard College catalogs from 1875 to 1880. Susan Sarna, museum specialist at Sagamore Hill, helpfully provided a copy of the probate list of Roosevelt's library and answered questions about these holdings.

Over the last decade, numerous Bowdoin students have served as research assistants, among them Jamie Quinn ('06), Brandon Mazer ('08), Dustin Brooks ('08), Christina Curtin, ('12), Louisa Diaz ('13), and Judah Isseroff ('13).

I must single out for special mention Taylor Washburn ('04), who, while a law student at Columbia, did research on Roosevelt's time there, and Eric Penley ('05), who tracked down unpublished letters between TR and John W. Burgess in the Library of Congress while working in Washington, D.C. To the students in my Advanced Seminars on The Idea of Progress and Tocqueville, a collective thanks. As always, I am grateful for the support of Virginia Hopcroft and Carmen Greenlee, research librarians at Bowdoin College. It is impossible to recount all the ways in which Lynne Atkinson, our indispensable government department coordinator, assisted me on this project, from unsnarling the copier, to supervising the student assistants and preparing the index. On the home front, Pam Geroux has for many years made life run more smoothly, and I thank her. My dear friend, Linda B. Bell, of Stonington, Connecticut, applied her creative talents to this project as only she could do.

My colleague and friend, Paul Franco, read the Introduction and Epilogue, as well as Chapters 1 and 6, making substantive suggestions and serving as my able guide on all things Hegelian. I have also benefited from the advice of Jeff Selinger, who offered feedback on Chapter 5, and alerted me to the most recent work in his subfield of American Political Development. On a lighter note, my dear friend and colleague William C. Watterson never failed to delight me with amusing bits of TR memorabilia.

Colleagues at other institutions also have been generous with their time and advice. Jeremy Rabkin, at the George Mason School of Law, provided assistance on legal questions as well as offering detailed comments (on very short notice) on Chapters 3 and 5. James R. Stoner of Louisiana State University also responded to my legal queries and provided helpful comments on Chapter 1, as did Michael Zuckert at Notre Dame. Marc Landy at Boston College offered feedback—and constructive criticism—on Chapter 5. On innumerable occasions, Michael Uhlmann, of Claremont Graduate University, walked me through the labyrinthine workings of the administrative state. Over the years, James W. Ceaser at the University of Virginia extended numerous invitations to lecture on Roosevelt. On two visits to Charlottesville, Sid Milkis proved, as always, a lively sparring partner. Special thanks also to the Fellows at the Program on Constitutionalism and Democracy at the University of Virginia, especially Keegan Callanan (Bowdoin '03), Matt Sitman, and Daniel Doneson, for their intellectual stimulation and hospitality during my visits. The Jack Miller Center for Teaching American Founding Principles and History, which Jim Ceaser heads with Bill McClay, provided me with additional opportunities to discuss my work with graduate students and junior scholars in Charlottesville, Chicago, and Pasadena. I am grateful also to Robbie George at the James Madison Program in American Ideals and Institutions at Princeton University for inviting me to deliver an earlier version of Chapter 2 on Roosevelt as historian. Bradley C. S. Watson, at St. Vincent's College, and Mark Blitz, at Claremont McKenna College, invited me to deliver talks on parts of this manuscript. Thanks, also, to Charles Kesler, for opportunities to review the latest books on TR and the progressives in the *Claremont Review of Books.*

John Milton Cooper, Jr. generously read the entire manuscript and offered sage advice on every chapter. Some years back, Bill McClay, at the University of Tennessee at Chattanooga, promised he would help me with this book, and I can only say that he has more than delivered on that promise. He has read and commented on countless iterations of every chapter, and it would be an understatement to say that my book is better because of him. More than a colleague, Bill has shown himself to be the best kind of friend.

Throughout this long gestation period, Fred Woodward, director of the University Press of Kansas, never lost confidence in me, and I thank him for his constancy. Thanks also to Larisa Martin, Martha Whitt, and Susan Schott, Fred's able staff, as well as two reviewers for the press who provided careful and detailed comments on the manuscript.

It is, finally, a pleasure to acknowledge the debts closest to home. Many years ago, my parents, Mary and Ralph Yarbrough, presented me with a twenty-dollar "Liberty" gold coin, designed by Augustus Saint-Gaudens during Roosevelt's presidency, and it has served as a talisman during my labors. I regret that my father did not live to see the publication of this book. My older son, James Yarbrough Stern, helped track down unpublished letters in the Library of Congress while working in Washington, D.C., last year, offered assistance on legal fine points, and helped me make several of my arguments clearer. After years of my reading (and criticizing) his papers, my younger son, John Francis Sutherlin Stern, returned the favor with interest. During this last year, while himself a busy graduate student, he read portions of the manuscript, providing valuable editorial advice that I was by turns pleased and humbled to accept. But my greatest debt is to my husband and colleague, Richard E. Morgan, who, for more than a decade, whiskey in hand, has listened nightly to dramatic readings of these chapters. With unfailing good humor and superb judgment, he has showered me with love and support. I could not ask for more.

Jean M. Yarbrough
Brunswick, Maine
January 12, 2012

Introduction

There he is, with George Washington, Thomas Jefferson, and Abraham Lincoln, atop Mount Rushmore, their colossal faces chiseled into the South Dakota granite, looking out on America. For Theodore Roosevelt, the only one of the four presidents to have lived in the Dakota Territory and whose histories sang the glories of westward expansion and Manifest Destiny, the site seems especially fitting. The monument, the cornerstone of which was dedicated in 1927 by President Calvin Coolidge, was the work of Gutzon Borglum, an Idaho-born artist working in the tradition of heroic nationalism. Borglum, the son of Danish immigrants, had already sculpted a giant marble bust of Lincoln that Roosevelt displayed while in the White House and won the competition to create a statue of General Philip Sheridan for the nation's capital. For Mount Rushmore, the artist chose to memorialize those presidents who had founded, unified, and preserved the American republic, while extending its territorial reach. Borglum, who knew and admired Roosevelt, selected TR because he thought that the Panama Canal fulfilled the dream of Manifest Destiny and made the United States into a world power. Along with the four sculptures, the artist envisioned a Hall of Records, containing the most important documents of the republic so that thousands of years hence posterity would understand what "manner of men" the Americans were and why they had carved these gigantic faces on Mount Rushmore.

Borglum's decision to include Roosevelt provoked criticism and controversy, with many complaining that not enough time had elapsed to allow the country to place Roosevelt's presidency in historical perspective.[1] But today, it seems fair to say that, of the four, Roosevelt has become, as he once observed of Lincoln, "the most real of the dead presidents."[2] During the decade or more that I have been at work on this book, I have been amazed at how familiar Americans are with TR, though mostly what they know are the highlights of his action-packed, adventure-filled life—Rough Rider, trust-buster, big-game hunter, explorer, Bull Moose—episodes gleaned from an endless stream of crisp, fast-paced biographies. With so colorful a subject, it is not surprising that his biographers have tended to

1

shy away from his political thought. When, on those rare occasions they do wade into his ideas, they either mangle them or retail the standard progressive narrative. Without actually discussing the theories underlying his policies, they assure readers that his actions were necessary to rein in the "robber barons." They fail to take the full measure of the New Nationalism and *a fortiori* the Bull Moose campaign. Withal, they accept at face value Roosevelt's insistence that he remained at heart a "conservative," who sought to avert all-out class warfare by adapting American institutions to a changed political environment. But, for biographers, ideas clearly take a backseat to Roosevelt, the man of action. For different reasons, academic historians also have not regarded Roosevelt's thought as worthy of serious consideration. Richard Hofstadter set the tone in 1948 with *The American Political Tradition and the Men Who Made It*. In his chapter, "The Conservative as Progressive," Hofstadter conceded an "occasional insight," but dismissed Roosevelt's collected writings as "a bundle of philistine conventionalities, the intellectual fiber of a muscular and combative Polonius."[3] For Hofstadter, a man of the left, Roosevelt's belated embrace of progressive ideals smacked too much of opportunism and compromise to be taken seriously. TR had no positive impulses; he did not "bleed" for exploited workers, but merely sought to avoid mob violence. There could be no more damning assessment than to brand Roosevelt's politics "conservative," his thought superficial. The charges stuck.

The publication of Roosevelt's *Letters* helped to restore TR's reputation as a forceful president after it had fallen into disrepute following the domestic and wartime successes of TR's distant cousin, Franklin.[4] Nevertheless, in his introduction to Volume 5 of the series, the principal editor, Elting E. Morison, wondered whether the Rough Rider would be "cast into oblivion" as his age faded from historical memory. Roosevelt's presidency, Morison concluded, "did not contribute any of the massive formulations, either of intellect or spirit, that appear in the national heritage." In part, this was because TR was by temperament a "conservative," and conservatives lacked "a body of principled theory" that might serve as a guide to political action. In contrast to liberals, Roosevelt offered no "very cheerful or reassuring notions about the meaning of life itself."[5]

Despite these shortcomings, the associate editor of his *Letters*, John Morton Blum, made his own reputation by attempting to rehabilitate TR's in *The Republican Roosevelt*. But he did so by shifting the focus toward his use of power to maintain stability and order. Assessing his political career, Blum concluded that Roosevelt developed no new ideas after the age of forty, that is, before he became president. Along with Morison (and Hofstadter, up to a point), Blum argued that Roosevelt was essentially a "conservative," who concerned himself very little with "happiness." Indeed, by the end of his study he complained that Roosevelt had, among other sins, allowed his "viable conservatism" to degenerate "to a creed akin to fascism" (ignoring that fascism started out on the left as national socialism). Yet there he was in the preface to the second edition in 1962, conceding that his original characterization of Roosevelt as a "conservative" was "arbitrary," and agreeing with Eric F. Goldman and George E. Mowry that Roosevelt was a "progressive," in fact, "the most compelling" progressive of his day. This was not a recipe for intellectual clarity.[6]

By contrast, Mowry's two books were models of clear thinking: Roosevelt was a progressive, and progressivism was good. Mowry did not so much argue this point as assert it.[7] Nor did he have to make an argument, for as David M. Kennedy has perceptively noted, "most American academic historians have thought of themselves as the political heirs of the Progressive tradition." Now, of course, historians can (and do) work themselves up into a lather debating whether progressivism ever existed, or if so, what it meant and who belongs to it, but Kennedy's broad point is that "academic historical writing" has "been largely monopolized by liberals," or those on the left.[8] That said, I have learned much from Kathleen Dalton, Martin J. Sklar, and John Milton Cooper, Jr., although I should quickly add that I have used their research to advance an argument they would not endorse. Dalton argued convincingly that Roosevelt continued to press for radical economic reforms after World War I broke out and he returned to the Republican fold. Sklar's detailed examination of the regulatory policies Roosevelt supported, beginning in 1907 and continuing after he stepped down from the presidency, laid bare just how "statist" Roosevelt's proposed policies actually were. Cooper's insightful comparisons of the "warrior" and the "priest" offer a useful starting point for understanding the differences between Woodrow Wilson and TR.[9]

Nevertheless, it is time to revisit the historiography of the progressive era and to hold it up to critical scrutiny. As a guild, academic historians have prided themselves on their openness to revisionist interpretations, yet the one subject that they have not been willing to reconsider is the progressive narrative itself. Most of the studies of this period, and of Roosevelt, start from the assumption that the political arrangements put in place at the time of the founding were inadequate to solve the problems of industrialization, urbanization, and mass immigration. Common law understandings and entrenched legal precedents, federalism, the separation of powers—to say nothing of the relatively unfettered operation of the markets—prevented the United States from dealing effectively with the social and industrial problems it faced at the end of the nineteenth century. What America needed, as Herbert Croly argued in 1909, was not reform, but wholesale reconstruction. With few exceptions, this view has not been seriously challenged.[10]

The discipline of political science is somewhat less monolithic, with American Political Development and political theory providing competing frameworks of analysis, and divisions among theorists offering additional food for thought. Here, too, I have profited from the work of colleagues in American Political Development, though the very nature of the subfield is that it studies, well, "development." As with academic historians, scholars of APD generally assume that the founders' constitutional arrangements embody no special wisdom, though they do help to explain the particular ways in which American institutions have evolved to meet new challenges. In this vein, Stephen Skowronek and Sidney M. Milkis, two of the leading scholars in this field, have further added to our understanding of American politics by highlighting the shift of power away from Congress and the courts to the executive and administrative agencies. Their studies focus, respectively, on "transformational" presidencies, or as in the case of 1912, a transformational election, where questions of direct democracy, the living constitution, the rhetorical presidency, the shape of the administrative state, and the nature of political parties were all up for debate. Milkis especially deserves praise for incorporating questions of political theory into his analysis, but they are not his central focus.[11]

In my own subfield of political theory, I have profited from Eldon Eisenach's study of the core beliefs of leading academic progressives, as well as from James T. Kloppenberg's exploration of its trans-Atlantic dimension.[12] Bridging APD and political theory, James W. Ceaser has traced the use of nature and history as competing foundational ideas in American Political Development and offered insightful reflections on the role of "public philosophy" in shaping institutional change.[13] There has also been renewed interest in Woodrow Wilson by political theorists.[14] But surprisingly, for one whose hold on the popular imagination is as great as his is, there have been almost no studies of the political thought of Theodore Roosevelt.[15]

Outside of the academy, Roosevelt does not lack for critics on the right. In recent years, his ideas have come in for scathing critiques from libertarians, of which Jim Powell's *Bully Boy* provides an extended polemic.[16] As such, it offers a provocative counterpoint to much of the existing academic literature, but Powell's approach is not mine. Although I am a critic of progressivism and its relentless push toward greater equality in the name of social justice, I am not a libertarian. I believe that *The Federalist* makes a persuasive case for "limited but energetic" national government, and especially a vigorous executive. There is a useful, indeed even necessary, place for regulation, at both the state and federal levels. But—with the exception of traditional state police powers operating at the margins—those regulations should serve the purpose of making free markets function more smoothly, not strangling them, or worse, attempting vainly to redeem human nature. The first object of republican government should be, as Jefferson announced in the Declaration, the protection of individual rights. At the same time, there are other goods—among them, greatness and excellence—with which the more thoughtful friends of democracy have concerned themselves, and these do not always fit together smoothly with the core commitment to equal rights. To his credit, Roosevelt sought to promote national greatness, though his conception of greatness tended to lay too much stress on conquest and "expansion." As for domestic affairs, one need not be a libertarian to see that Roosevelt begins to go seriously astray from the economic principles of Alexander Hamilton and Abraham Lincoln during his presidency, and certainly afterwards. That is my point. My book is informed by the idea that the founders Roosevelt most admired provided political principles, suitably adapted, that were still useful in his day, as they remain in ours, had he seriously considered them. But for all his energy and intelligence—and Roosevelt possessed both in abundance—he seems not to have weighed this possibility. Perhaps that is because he never encountered a thoughtful treatment of American political principles in college or law school, and the ideas to which he was introduced (Teutonic "germ theory," Darwinism, historicism, German idealism) could not easily be reconciled with the ideals of his heroes. So, even before he became a progressive, his views, while reflecting the main intellectual currents of the day, diverged in key respects from the views of the nationalistic founders he admired and Lincoln. In this most "Lincoln-like" sense, Theodore Roosevelt was never a "conservative."

Nevertheless, Roosevelt talked a good game. Consequently, he has for too long been given a "pass" by political theorists and students of American Political Development who have been inclined to take his admiring references to the more nationalistic founders and Lincoln at face value.[17] Here, the contrast with Woodrow Wilson is especially striking. Unlike the Princeton professor, Roosevelt offered no scholarly critiques of the Declaration or the Constitution.[18] At the very moment when Wilson was urging Americans to move toward a British-style parliamentary democracy, Roosevelt dismissed such calls as an "un-American" colonial throwback and instead exhorted college graduates to "Read *The Federalist.*" His biography of *Gouverneur*

Morris pronounced the Constitution that emerged in Philadelphia the best possible arrangement for America. As president, he turned to the writings of Lincoln for guidance and inspiration. Yet, these principles meshed uneasily with the competing intellectual arguments swimming around in his head. How did these conflicting stands play out at various stages of his long political career? What does his thought add up to, where does it fit in the American political tradition, and what is his legacy today? I am not offering an intellectual biography, but rather an analysis of Roosevelt's political thought and what it means for republican self-government.

Chapter 1 examines the influence of Roosevelt's education on his political thought. Although in his *Autobiography* TR famously insisted that "very little" of what he learned in college would be of use to him in later life, in fact, some of the ideas he was introduced to helped shape his political thought for years to come. Consulting the Harvard College catalogues from 1876 to 1880, I have gone back to school with Roosevelt, reading his course assignments and examining the views of his professors to gain further insight into his early political ideas. At Harvard, Theodore took only the one required sophomore course in history, where he was introduced to the Teutonic "germ theory" that would find its way into the histories that he himself would write only a few years later. He took two courses in political economy from a classical liberal perspective, but soon discovered that the Republican Party of the 1880s and 1890s had other ideas. He read classical Greek and German texts and studied evolutionary biology, all of which, at different times, would also shape his political thought. Most scholars pass over his brief stint at the Columbia Law School, but the courses Roosevelt took with John W. Burgess helped shape his intellectual horizon. Although Burgess and Roosevelt would diverge politically, Burgess's ideas would find their way, first, into Roosevelt's histories, and then later, during the heyday of his progressivism, in his references to a more "ethical state."

Chapter 2 looks at Roosevelt's political thought as it emerges in his historical writings, beginning with *The Naval War of 1812*, then moving on to his biographies of *Thomas Hart Benton* and *Gouverneur Morris*, and culminating in his epic *Winning of the West*. Although his biography of Morris was effusive in its praise of the Constitution, Roosevelt was far more interested in the growth and expansion of America than in its "founding." The chapter compares the narrative that emerges in *Thomas Hart Benton* and *The Winning of the West* with the political thought of the founders he admired. Whereas Hamilton in *The Federalist* had emphasized the capacity of individuals to establish good government based on "reflection and choice," Roosevelt chose to stress the three-hundred-year unplanned movement of

the English-speaking peoples as they spread out across America, unconsciously replicating their medieval Teutonic "folk moots." In place of compact and consent in the service of individual rights, his was a narrative that
focused on conquest and expansion for the sake of national greatness. In
Roosevelt's account, history, rather than nature, supplies the moral ground
against which political action must be judged.

Chapter 3 considers Roosevelt's early political career as a Republican reformer, beginning with his election to the New York Assembly in 1882 and
ending with his election to the governorship of the state in 1898. I focus
on Roosevelt's political thought as he dealt with the practical problems of
immigration, machine politics, civil service reform, and foreign policy. I
also consider his role as a public intellectual reviewing important books of
the day. Although during these years Roosevelt was outspoken in defense
of the Framers' Constitution, his political thought diverged from theirs in
important respects. In contrast to the view of human nature that emerges
in *The Federalist*, Roosevelt already showed signs of believing that individuals could act from disinterested motives, even as he conceived of the "law of
nature" in harsh Darwinian terms. Roosevelt was also more hostile to the
commercial republic and to the notion of commercial greatness than was
Hamilton. After the official closing of the frontier in 1890, Roosevelt would
seek national greatness in building up the navy, a vigorous defense of the
Monroe Doctrine, support for war with Spain, and "expansion" abroad.

Chapter 4 examines Roosevelt's brief stint as governor of New York,
where for the first time he had the opportunity to wield executive power.
Very quickly, he began to develop a theory of justice that would inform his
exercise of power. Following the advice of Aristotle, whose works he had
read and now quoted, Roosevelt would seek to avoid the extremes of mob
rule and plutocracy, striking a "just balance" between competing political and economic demands. His biography of *Oliver Cromwell*—in many
ways the most interesting of his historical studies—provided him with the
opportunity to reflect further on the role of executive power in revolutionary times and the need, especially in republics, to cabin this power within
a larger constitutional framework. Roosevelt's assessment of Cromwell's
failings provides important insights into the problems with his own view of
executive power as it unfolded during his presidency and afterward.

Chapter 5 considers Roosevelt's gradual embrace of progressive thought
during his presidential years. It focuses on his handling of the anthracite
coal strike, his attempts to assert control over the corporations through antitrust and regulatory policy, his support for railroad regulation, conservation, and foreign policy. For most of his presidency, Roosevelt continued to

seek a "balance" between competing social classes and economic interests, though his understanding of where the balance should be struck changed dramatically during his last two years. In addition, he now had to consider the place of executive power within the republican constitutional order. In the coal strike, Roosevelt experimented with the idea that the emergency justified his use of extraordinary powers, invoking old common law doctrines as well as Lincoln's actions during the Civil War as precedents. Later, emboldened by his landslide reelection and pushed leftward by insurgents within his own party, Roosevelt floated the idea that the nation possessed "inherent power" to fill in whatever gaps existed between federal and state power. When that argument failed to develop traction, he would offer his "stewardship" theory of presidential power. The chapter concludes with a comparison of Hamilton's arguments in *The Federalist* and in the "Pacificus" papers in defense of energetic executive power and Roosevelt's still more expansive views as he embraced the progressive agenda.

Chapter 6 explores Roosevelt's bid to lead the progressive cause in his postpresidential years. Roosevelt returned from his European tour convinced that America must now catch up with "the world movement." After he read Herbert Croly's *Promise of American Life,* his policy prescriptions took on a sharper theoretical edge. The New Nationalism reflects this shift, effectively discarding the idea of balance in favor of the notion that government must discriminate in favor of its friends. Moreover, Roosevelt here fleshes out what he means when he says that property rights can only be justified by "service to the nation." As the former president considers a primary challenge to Taft, he embraces the idea of direct democracy and supports the initiative, referendum, and recall, arguing that these mechanisms do not undermine constitutional government but are in fact necessary to restore it. As a corollary, he insists that these reforms make it all the more imperative for Americans to cultivate the right kind of virtues. Finally, in bolting the Republican Party and running on the Progressive Party ticket, Roosevelt comes out in favor of social security in the form of old age, unemployment, and health insurance. In defending these policies, Roosevelt asserts that he is acting in the "spirit" of Lincoln, a claim I challenge. The chapter concludes with an analysis of Roosevelt's political thought in his final years, arguing that he viewed the American entry into World War I as a catalyst for even more far-reaching progressive reforms that would move the United States toward the social democratic model he thought was the wave of the future.

The Epilogue takes its inspiration from Roosevelt's 1913 essay, "The Heirs of Abraham Lincoln," tracing Roosevelt's various "heirs" over the last hundred years and assessing the intended and unintended consequences of the reforms he supported. Far from being "consigned to oblivion," as Elting E. Morison speculated in the 1950s, Roosevelt's political thought continues to resonate across the political spectrum as his "heirs" battle each other for a part of his legacy. The centennial of Theodore Roosevelt's Progressive Party run for the presidency provides a fitting opportunity to assess his political thought and to compare it with the American political tradition represented by his heroes on Mount Rushmore.

1. The Education of Theodore Roosevelt

In the fall of 1876 a not quite eighteen-year-old Theodore Roosevelt arrived in Cambridge to begin his formal education at Harvard College. As it happened, his matriculation coincided, in a way that now seems telling, with an event of considerable significance in the history of the republic. From May through November of 1876 the attention of much of the United States was riveted on the great Centennial Exhibition then being mounted in Philadelphia. The first of the nation's world's fairs, this grand spectacle was organized to commemorate the 100th anniversary of American independence and succeeded in attracting more than 10 million visitors from across the United States and around the world.

But the Philadelphia exposition was more than a centennial celebration. The International Exhibition of Arts, Manufactures, and Products of the Soil and Mine, as it was officially called, gave vivid expression to the scientific and technological aspirations of a newly reunified and energized America—a nation eager to leave behind the divisions of the Civil War and itching to take its place among the great powers of the world, a message the exposition quietly reinforced by placing the United States at the center of the show and arranging the foreign exhibitions by their distance from it, with China and Japan furthest away.[1] Overall, the Centennial offered powerful testimony to Americans' faith in progress and their growing confidence in the material bounty awaiting them in the near future. Visitors to the sprawling fairgrounds in Fairmount Park could forget for a while about the scandal-ridden Grant administration and the divisive politics of Reconstruction, and instead wander from exhibit to exhibit, imagining a future with such modern conveniences as Alexander Graham Bell's telephone, Remington's typewriter, and the Singer sewing machine while sampling such novelties as Heinz Ketchup and Hire's Root Beer.

Yet amidst all this forward-looking bustle and energy, the Exposition seemed to lose sight of what Abraham Lincoln regarded as the signal achievement of American independence: the timeless truths enshrined in the Declaration. Of course, on the Fourth of July, that document would take center stage, as it was read aloud by Richard Henry Lee, namesake of the Virginia signer, with the vice president of the United States presiding over the festivities. But this event, intended to pay homage to the nation's founding principles, was not without its ironies. For a delegation of women suffragists, inspired and emboldened by Declaration's commitment to equality and natural rights, had requested permission from the Centennial Commission to read their protest bill of rights at the close of the reading and had been politely, but firmly, refused. After Richard Henry Lee had concluded, the women, led by Susan B. Anthony, marched to the stage and presented officials with their declaration. They then withdrew to a platform that had been erected in front of old Independence Hall and read their protest aloud.[2]

In an even worse affront, the distinguished black orator Frederick Douglass, who had been invited to join the dignitaries at the opening-day ceremonies, was refused permission to the platform. Only after the personal intervention of New York Senator Roscoe Conkling was he finally allowed to mount the stage. And although arguably the most magnificent orator of the period, he was not invited to address the crowd.[3] As in 1776, and again in the 1850s (and as it would during the civil rights marches in the 1960s), the Declaration spoke most powerfully to those who believed they were denied its full blessings.

Nor were the protesting suffragists and the treatment of Douglass the only discordant notes. The organizers of the Exposition, like an increasing number of educated Americans, seemed less interested in the Declaration's understanding of limited government than they were captivated by the powerful model of the newly unified German state and the cutting-edge ideas emanating from the German university system. One small, but revealing, indication of the American fascination with Germany was that the organizers commissioned the German operatic composer Richard Wagner to write the "Grand Inaugural March" for the opening ceremony on May 10, attended by the President and Mrs. Grant.

But the German influence went much further and suggested an idea of progress at odds with the political principles the Exposition was at least nominally celebrating.[4] Working closely with ethnologists from the Smithsonian, the organizers arranged the exhibits in the Main Hall according to race, with the United States as the hub, and Britain, France, and Germany given the most prominent locations. Thus, Britain and her colonies were grouped together as Anglo-Saxons, France and her colonies, Latins, and the German Empire, along with Austria-Hungary, the Teutonic races.

Within the American exhibit, the Indian displays were organized according to the German idea of *Kulturgeschichte* (history of culture), developed by Gustav Klemm, which in turn was part of his larger classification of mankind into "active" and "passive" races based on temperament and mentality.[5] According to this framework, the Indians belonged to the dawn of human history, with, in the words of one critic, "their worth as human beings" being "determined by their usefulness as counterpoint to the unfolding progress of the ages."[6] Needless to say, the use of these crude racial categories could not be reconciled with the Declaration's insistence that every human being was created equal and endowed with certain inalienable rights.

The Centennial Exposition, therefore, reflected a growing conflict at the heart of America's self-understanding as the nation moved into its second century: should the United States continue to revere—and act upon—the principles of the Declaration or should Americans throw their lot in with the emerging progressive worldview? And if so, which understanding of progress should they choose? As such, the Philadelphia exposition captured the same dilemma that would soon face the young Theodore Roosevelt, as he navigated the intellectual currents swirling about him when he arrived in Cambridge that fall.

Roosevelt was an instinctive patriot, whose upbringing and childhood reading had instilled a deep pride in the principles and practices of his country. He yielded to no one in his esteem for the valiant deeds of the men of 1776.[7] Yet at Harvard, he would be introduced to new ideas from Europe that would challenge his received views of American history, American government, and the proper aims of politics. Over the next few decades, these arguments would pull both the country and Roosevelt toward opposite extremes: first, toward an intense, competitive individualism that marched under the banner of Social Darwinism, and then toward a more cooperative, collective vision that in time would become the ideological basis of progressivism.

Roosevelt's intellectual development, rife with inconsistencies, tensions, and reversals, is best understood against this backdrop. Accordingly, his formal education takes on particular importance, in fact, a good deal more importance than he was willing to admit. Looking back on his college years later in his *Autobiography* after his failed Progressive run for the presidency in 1912, Roosevelt would claim that "very little" of what he had learned at Harvard had prepared him for the great role he would play in American politics.[8] But that was clearly not true, for at various points in his public life Theodore flirted with many of the ideas he had absorbed in college, incorporating them into his historical studies and applying them to practical political problems during the 1880s and 1890s. Moreover, although he said nothing in the *Autobiography* about his courses at the Columbia Law School, dwelling instead on what he considered the defects of the legal profession,[9] in fact, his classes with John W. Burgess would introduce him to Hegelian state theory, important elements of which would find their way into Roosevelt's later progressivism.

In short, Roosevelt would exhibit in his own life the same contradiction that lay at the heart of the Centennial Exposition. He never ceased to insist that George Washington and Abraham Lincoln were his heroes, and that *The Federalist* was the best book on political theory and practice ever written. He did so even though the new ideas he would come to embrace posed a fundamental challenge to the principles for which his heroes stood.

EVOLUTIONARY BIOLOGY AND SOCIAL DARWINISM

For a budding natural scientist such as Roosevelt, the first and most immediately influential of these was evolutionary biology. In 1859 Charles Darwin had published *The Origin of the Species*, which set in motion a scientific revolution that would throw into question the founders' understanding of human nature and natural rights. Darwin did not, as is popularly supposed, discover evolution. What he did was offer a more compelling account of how evolution worked, displacing the earlier Lamarckian explanation that organisms evolved through adaptation that they then passed on to their offspring. Instead, Darwin argued that evolution occurred through a process of natural selection, that is, a brutal competition in which only the fittest survived. *The Origin* quietly unseated God as the Author of creation, substituting chance and relentless random mutations that favored one species over another in the unceasing struggle for food and place.

Although Darwin deliberately declined to discuss the evolution of man in the *Origin of the Species,* there could be little doubt where his argument was pointing. However, Theodore, who first read the book at the age of fourteen, may well have missed its larger implications.[10] But if human beings had also evolved randomly, through struggle, it made no sense to speak of "the laws of nature and nature's God" in any moral sense. In like manner, there was no room in Darwin's theory for a "Creator" who endowed all men with certain inalienable rights, since evolution depended on chance. Indeed, it was no longer possible to speak intelligibly of natural rights because Darwin's evolutionary breakthrough implied that there was no such thing as a fixed human nature. It is, however, one of history's little ironies that Darwin was born on February 12, 1809, the same day as Abraham Lincoln, America's most brilliant defender of those very truths and one of Roosevelt's greatest American heroes. In still another remarkable coincidence, the same year that *The Origin of the Species* appeared Lincoln was hailing the author of the Declaration for going beyond the original purpose of the document and including the "abstract truth" that all men were created equal and endowed with certain inalienable rights.[11]

As Darwin himself emphasized, the "struggle for existence" was only meant to explain how species had evolved; by his own admission, it had never occurred to him to apply the principle of natural selection to the dynamics of social life. Nevertheless, it did not take sociologists long to make the connection. Indeed, even before Darwin had published *The Origin of the Species,* the English thinker Herbert Spencer had already sketched out the social logic of "the survival of the fittest," a term he first employed in 1851 in his *Social Statics*.[12] That work, which would find its way into American constitutional law during Roosevelt's presidency when Oliver Wendell Holmes protested that the Fourteenth Amendment did not enact Mr. Spencer's *Social Statics,* was the first to link limited government with evolutionary progress.

Unlike Darwin, Spencer regarded evolution as the working out of a grand cosmological design that would eventuate in "the ideal man" living in the "ideal civilization." For the sake of that progress, government must refrain from interfering with the liberty of the individual. Taxation, he argued, should be only for the purpose of protecting the individual; it should not be used to fund education, the established church, or empire building. For the same reason, he opposed government efforts to regulate commerce. Each individual must be free to enter into whatever contract arrangement he wished. It was not the duty of the state to regulate hours, wages, or workplace conditions; nor should it legislate tariffs, regulate currency, establish national banks, administer a postal system, or undertake public works. Public charity was out of the question, though he did support private charity, principally for its salutary effect on the giver. Spencer also conceded that the state might punish those who unnecessarily polluted the environment, making it "detrimental to health or disagreeable to the senses," but this was because such actions impinged on the rights of others.[13]

At the same time, he resisted all efforts to make the government responsible in any way for maintaining the physical or moral health of its citizenry. To attempt to regulate the sale of drugs or to license those who practiced medicine would interfere with the right of the individual to buy what he deemed necessary and to seek advice from whom he pleased; it would also restrict the right of the unlicensed practitioner to sell to whomever wanted to purchase his goods or services. Moreover, once the principle that the state was responsible for securing the health of the citizenry was admitted, it would be impossible to set any limitations to its power. Government, he warned, would then become responsible for ensuring that all the conditions essential to good health were fulfilled, including prescribing the proper diet, amount of exercise, hours of sleep, and so on—in short, "a universal supervision" of what was and should be private conduct.[14]

To the objection that the people, and especially the poorer classes, were too ignorant or incompetent to make informed decisions and would therefore suffer if government did not intervene to protect them, Spencer appealed to the severe, but in his view, ultimately benign, discipline of nature:

> Nature just as much insists on fitness between mental character and circumstances, as between physical character and circumstances; and radical defects are as much causes of death in one case as in the other. He on whom his own stupidity, or vice, or idleness entails loss of life, must, in the generalizations of philosophy, be classed with the victims of weak viscera or malformed limbs. In his case, as in the others, there exists a fatal non-adaptation; and it matters not in the abstract whether it be a moral, an intellectual, or a corporeal one. Beings thus imperfect are Nature's failures, and are recalled by her when found to be such. Along with the rest they are put on trial. If they are sufficiently complete to live, they *do* live, and it is well they should live. If they are not sufficiently complete to live, they die, and it is best they should die.[15]

Spencer conceded that it might be harsh that the artisan lacking in skills should go hungry, that the laborer incapacitated by illness should suffer, or that widows and orphans should be left to struggle to survive, but this was to look at the problem from the perspective of particular individuals. When considered from the perspective of "universal humanity," these "harsh fatalities" were actually beneficent, since they weeded out the "unhealthy, imbecile, slow, vacillating, faithless members" of society and encouraged the multiplication of the competent and provident. This process was both natural and necessary; consequently, its "sufferings *must* be endured." There was nothing that statesmen, reformers, revolutionaries, or philanthropists could do to repeal the workings of nature. Nor should they try, since doing so would only retard the "purifying process" on which progress depended.[16]

Yet intertwined with this fatalism was a curious optimism, for Spencer was confident that nature was gradually bringing about a new human being. As human beings entered the industrial age, the peaceful and cooperative virtues were gaining over the older martial and competitive ideals. Benevolence was on the rise so that as people adapted to this new altruistic environment, the interests of the individual and the interests of society would eventually converge. In the meantime, nature would continue to inflict its "salutary sufferings" upon the sick, the incompetent, the feeble, and the lazy, weeding out these weaker specimens to prepare for the "ultimate perfection."[17] The brand of Social "Darwinism" that emerged in Spencer's *Social Statics* was a strange amalgam of misery and pain in the service of its own vision of progress and perfection.

In America, Social Darwinism was most closely associated with the sociologist William Graham Sumner.[18] Roosevelt would meet the Yale professor in the winter of 1879 when Sumner journeyed to Cambridge to deliver a talk on the subject of "The Relation of Legislation to Money" before the newly formed Finance Club, of which Theodore was an officer.[19] An avid free trader and supporter of sound currency, Sumner ranged widely over the nature and history of money, setting forth the "abuses of legislation in regard to money."[20] Afterward, the Harvard *Advocate* praised the club for its enterprise in turning out "a larger body of students . . . than we have seen on such an occasion in Sanders for years."[21]

Although Sumner is often described by both his supporters and critics as a "classical liberal" in the tradition of John Locke and the founders, this characterization is misleading because it focuses exclusively on Sumner's defense of limited government and individual liberty, while ignoring the Darwinian ground of his argument. In contrast to the founders, the only "laws of nature" Sumner acknowledged were those of competition and survival of the fittest. In the American context, Sumner was particularly keen to dispel the notion that human beings were endowed with natural rights. In keeping with his historicist approach, he was willing to grant that the appeal to natural rights had once played a valuable role in overthrowing feudal constraints and establishing the principle that all individuals were free and equal. But whatever constructive purpose the doctrine had once served was now long past. Those who argued for natural rights in the present day had expanded their meaning beyond all recognition, so that they became rights to whatever anyone wanted or needed. Acting on this "vicious social dogma," they had turned the right to pursue happiness into a right to happiness itself and construed the necessity to labor to mean a "right" to set the terms of employment and the scale of wages in defiance of the natural operations of the market. Moreover, the same logic was at work in the ever more expansive demands for equality.[22] Since nature could not deliver on these claims, society would be forced to do so; natural rights would lead inevitably to socialism.

Yet Sumner's objection was not simply that natural rights had strayed too far from their eighteenth-century moorings. His Darwinian view of nature was fundamentally at odds with the founders' moral understanding of the "laws of nature and Nature's God." Consequently, Sumner argued, instead of securing natural rights, republican government should aim to protect civil liberty, which, unlike natural rights, was grounded in the evolving mores of a particular people as ratified by history and tradition. For Americans, civil liberty meant the freedom of each individual to use his energies to subdue nature and enjoy the fruits of his labor without being compelled to share them with others. Where civil liberty flourished, however, inequality resulted, and in an industrial society the inequalities would necessarily be great. Wealth was not wicked or evil, but rather the reward for self-denial and effort. As Sumner saw it, society had only two choices: liberty, inequality, and survival of the fittest or equality, the destruction of liberty, and the survival of the unfit.[23] There was no third way.

The Yale sociologist had no use for social reformers and "sentimental philanthropists" who refused to look these "facts" squarely in the face. Instead, their first response was to ask what they could do about the problem, or more precisely, what the taxpayer could do about it.[24] Elsewhere, he described the taxpayer as "The Forgotten Man."[25] All this reforming zeal Sumner traced to German *Socialpolitik,* which argued that the state should intervene to regulate the economy and redistribute wealth. But Sumner, who had himself studied in Germany, retorted, "the cruelest blow that can be aimed at one of these German phrases is to translate it into English, for then all the flatulency is let out of it. . . . It is astonishing how often what seemed a profound piece of philosophy turned out to be a bathos. 'Social policy' in English does not mean anything."[26] On similar grounds, he rejected the notion of the state as an "ethical person," endowed with a higher cultural mission. For if the state could not add to the ethical energy individuals needed in times of social stress, then the "ethical state" was simply an empty phrase. At most, it meant nothing more than "the general advantage of the association and co-operation of men with each other."[27] On social matters, the proper government response was laissez-faire. Nevertheless, Sumner was at pains to distinguish between the "struggle with Nature for existence," where interference was futile and counterproductive, and certain political ills, such as lynch-law, which resulted from the imperfections and errors of social institutions or the malice of men. In the latter case, government interference on behalf of the aggrieved class was indeed justi-fied. The problem was that people often confused the two classes of ills, concluding that because intervention was called for in the one instance it was also appropriate in the other. But, Sumner insisted, the remedy for natural ills was "manly effort and energy," not social action.[28]

In economic matters, too, government should follow a policy of laissez-faire, though here again Sumner was careful to clear up any misconcep-tions. Laissez-faire emphatically did not mean that individuals should never interfere with the spontaneous workings of the economy. Business-men and merchants, he thought, should certainly apply their minds "to trade and industry so as to develop and improve them." What he objected to was having politicians meddle in their operations. Even if statesmen con-sulted with businessmen and tried to work cooperatively with them, the rules they laid down would necessarily "be rigid, arbitrary, hard to change, dictated by some dogma or ideal, and not such as the development of trade and industry would from time to time call for" if left to their own devices. He was particularly scornful of reformers who, acknowledging the com-plexity of the problem, nevertheless welcomed legislation as an experiment. The whole idea of experimentation displayed an astounding ignorance of how societies actually worked. For once the experiment entered the life of society it would be impossible to eradicate. In short, laissez-faire meant: "Do not meddle; wait and observe. Do not regulate; study. Do not give orders; be teachable. Do not enter upon any rash experiments; be patient until you see how it will work out." The last thing to do was legislate.[29]

Recalling his Harvard education in his *Autobiography*, Roosevelt em-phasized that his professors of political economy embraced the doctrines of robust individualism and laissez-faire that were "then accepted as ca-nonical."[30] Indeed, as he now saw it, the defect of his education both at home and in college was that it had placed too great an emphasis on indi-vidual character and personal responsibility, a view he would later regard as inadequate because it ignored each man's "collective responsibility" for the well-being of the whole. "Consciously or unconsciously," he had been taught that the "whole duty" of a man was to make the best of himself and not to bother with improving the lot of others, except perhaps through old-fashioned charity (as his father had done). But Roosevelt's character-ization of his formative years was misleading in two respects: first, it played down how important these ideas had been for much longer than he was willing to admit, and second, it failed to distinguish between the individual responsibility he had been taught at home and the more radical Darwinian underpinning of these ideas that he later adopted. Like Sumner, the young Roosevelt all too often viewed American history and public policy through the distorting lens of natural selection and survival of the fittest. If anything, given his longstanding interest in natural science, he was even more likely to see the political world in this light.

The challenge to the political philosophy of the founders came not just from Darwin and evolutionary biology, however. Since the end of the Civil War, a growing number of Americans had gone abroad to study. Even before the war, Europe had served as a magnet for southerners seeking a conservative alternative to the natural rights philosophy that predominated in America, but after 1865, northerners, too, began to flock to its universities. Indeed, because the United States had no graduate schools of its own, those Americans who wished to pursue advanced degrees were compelled to study abroad, with the overwhelming number of them enrolling at German universities, principally Heidelberg and Berlin. As Roosevelt himself would later note in a letter of congratulations to his former law professor, John W. Burgess, on the occasion of his inauguration as the first Theodore Roosevelt Professor at the University of Berlin in 1906, "Since the Civil War one of the marked features of our intellectual life has been the great exodus of students from our northern states to the German universities, together with the fact that these very men now control the higher education of the United States."[31] Roosevelt, who had been served up a hefty portion of Hegelian philosophy while Burgess's student at Columbia, knew whereof he spoke. And although he himself had not studied abroad, many of the men and women who formed the intellectual base of the progressive movement and who later became his friends and associates had.

To be sure, Hegel was not all these Americans read, since after his death a reaction against his speculative philosophy had set in, favoring a new scientific spirit aimed at the analysis of practical social and economic problems (*Socialpolitik*). But Hegel's turn from nature to history and his description of the state as the embodiment of the ethical life of the nation spoke powerfully to the generation of scholars that came of age after the Civil War.[32] Hegelian philosophy, stressing the progressive unfolding of freedom in history, seemed to offer these Americans a way to make sense out of their own experience. With Hegel as their guide, they now saw the Civil War as a dialectical clash between the southern slaveholders' "abstract right" and the northern abolitionists' "abstract morality," through which the United States emerged at last a unified nation.[33] Carrying this logic forward, they were convinced that it was time for America to advance toward a new synthesis: an "ethical state" that would satisfy the spiritual as well as material needs of the nation. The poet Walt Whitman captured these sentiments perfectly when he wrote, "Only Hegel is fit for America—is large enough and free enough."[34]

Beyond providing Americans with an interpretive framework for understanding their own troubled history, Hegel offered a comprehensive critique of Lockean liberalism that men such as Burgess, witnessing the rapid development of Bismarckian Germany, found compelling. To begin with, liberal political philosophy looked at "man" in the abstract as he existed in a "state of nature," apart from all social and political influences. It then went on to construct a model of legitimate government for human beings everywhere, based on the idea that all men were equal with respect to certain inalienable rights. All legitimate government rested on the consent of the governed and existed solely to secure their rights.

In his *Introduction to the Philosophy of History*, Hegel sought to rectify this error by focusing on the development of particular peoples in their concrete historical circumstances. By history, Hegel did not mean the record of random and contingent events; rather, history was the movement of the spirit or reason, directing the actions of individuals and leading them toward a greater consciousness and realization of freedom. His magisterial survey, starting with oriental despotism then moving on to the Greeks and the Romans and concluding with the Germanic peoples, added new layers of philosophical depth to the argument that the Teutonic peoples were the modern heirs of the Greeks and the Romans, uniquely qualified by culture and history for political rule.

Freedom was not, then, as the social compact philosophers argued, the natural condition of all individuals everywhere, but emerged only historically as men became conscious of their freedom and acted on it. Far from being the gift of nature, freedom had to "be achieved and won through an endless process involving the discipline of knowledge and will." The state of nature was not a state of freedom, but a "condition of injustice, of violence, of untamed natural drives, of inhuman acts, and emotions." Man "by nature" was free only in the sense that freedom was his "implicit destiny," not his actual primitive condition.[35]

Just as freedom emerged only historically, so too did the state. Once again, the social compact theorists had erred by allowing too great a role for human agency in the establishment of government. *The Federalist*'s proud claim that it had been left to the people of America to determine whether good government could be established by "reflection and choice" was not only exaggerated but also mistaken. All states had to pass through a necessary process of development, moving from primitive authoritarian rule to the gradual recognition of individuality. In Hegel's telling, the state had advanced to its final form under the leadership of the German peoples. "This progression is a necessary one, such that each form of government in the sequence is not a matter of choice, but rather is such as to conform to the Spirit of the people."[36]

In addition to his philosophy of history, Hegel sought to develop new principles of political right that would synthesize the classical and modern understandings of politics, restoring the moral grandeur of the *polis* while simultaneously acknowledging the sphere of civil society in which private rights flourished. Although Hegel sought to protect the rights to life, liberty, and property, he differed from the social compact theorists, first by insisting that these "subjective" rights did not naturally belong to the individual, but were the gift of the state. Moreover, he argued that securing these rights could never be the sole or highest end of government because they were merely "negative" liberties, too closely linked with necessity to constitute true freedom. True freedom was rational freedom, where individuals chose not what was good simply for them, but what was good for its own sake; they then universalized these choices by making them laws that were binding on everyone. Such freedom required a willingness to sacrifice personal freedom and economic gain for the sake of something nobler and grander, which could only be achieved by and through the state. In his view, the state was much more than the sum of private interests; consequently, liberal abstract right necessarily pointed beyond itself to the individual as a spiritual being, sustained and supported in his free choice of moral action by the thick web of institutions and associations in the "ethical state."

Above all, it was war that brought out the ethical difference between civil society and the state. The state could demand that individuals sacrifice their private property and even their lives only because it stood for something higher than the protection of individual rights. War preserved "the ethical health of peoples" by giving them the opportunity to display their manly virtues and show their indifference to "the vanity of temporal goods and concerns"[37] for the sake of defending something nobler. In this sense, Hegel maintained, the state was truly "the divine Idea, as it exists on earth."[38]

The state was divine in another sense as well. Whereas liberalism had sought to resolve the tension between revelation and reason by separating church from state, Hegel argued that the Protestant Reformation made it possible to overcome the theological-political problem without diminishing the organic unity of the state. Unlike Catholicism, which refused to recognize the "divine" character of the state, Protestantism refocused its concern toward this world, in effect abolishing the difference between the temporal and the eternal. The result, as Pierre Hassner has argued, was that "religion is done away with while being fulfilled; Protestantism signifies both the Christianization of the *saeculum* and the secularization of Christianity."[39] In short, religion became simply another aspect of the "ethical state," an expression of its subjective consciousness, rather than its chief competitor for the souls of its members. From here, it would be only a short step to the Social Gospel preached by the progressives.[40]

In the *Philosophy of Right*, Hegel set out the various institutional arrangements that supported the "ethical state," each of which attempted to redress the individualistic and limited conception of the liberal state, while at the same time providing for security to these "negative" rights. His model was the Prussian monarchy, and although many of its features remain time-bound, two of his recommendations were especially attractive to his American students. First, because the state sought to promote rational freedom, it was dangerous to assume that only the people could know what was right. The people tended to act on the basis of their particular needs and wishes, and there was no way that the state could achieve its divine ends if all it consulted were "subjective" wills. What a state required was, rather, "trained intelligence," or a "rational will,"[41] and this did not come from consent. Accordingly, Hegel argued that the class of civil servants, comprising the third or "universal" estate, should apply its rational intelligence to solving the pressing social and economic problems of the time. In keeping with its universal mission, membership in the civil service was open to all, regardless of status or birth, on the basis of competitive examinations, and civil servants would receive a salary. These trained professionals would be organized into different departments, each with jurisdiction over a particular policy area. In contrast to laissez-faire theorists, who saw a minimal role for the state in these matters, or to *The Federalist*, which subordinated administration to politics in the service of limited but energetic government, Hegel sought to give trained bureaucrats considerably more independence in regulating industry and commerce and addressing social problems such as poverty. In the complex modern economy that was already emerging, poverty could not simply be blamed on an unwillingness or inability to work, but arose as a consequence of industrial conditions. The task of impartial civil servants was to mitigate this hardship, and to do so efficiently, without undue interference from the people or their elected representatives. Although Hegel was concerned that bureaucrats not become too remote from the people or abuse their power and proposed steps to prevent this, the whole thrust of his argument assumed it was possible to create a class of civil servants that was capable of rising above partisan divisions and political differences to govern impartially.[42]

Second, Hegel sought to promote rational freedom by overcoming what he considered the excessive rigidity of the separation of powers. Although he was willing to grant the necessity of some sort of division of powers, Hegel saw in its classical liberal formulation

> the false doctrine of the absolute self-subsistence of each of the powers against the others . . . [which] then one-sidedly interprets their relation to each other as negative, as a mutual restriction. This view implies that the attitude adopted by each power to the others is hostile and apprehensive, as if the others were evils, and that their function is to oppose one another and as a result of this counterpoise to effect an equilibrium on the whole, but never a living unity.[43]

Such a mechanistic understanding, he thought, might very well serve the ends of limited government, where the aim was to check competing passions and interests, but it fell short of promoting the ethical needs of the state as an organic whole. Instead, Hegel held up the biological sciences to suggest how the powers of government might work together to achieve such unity. "The limbs and organs . . . of an organic body are not merely parts of it: it is only in their unity that they are what they are, and they are unquestionably affected by that unity, as they also in turn affect it."[44] Practically speaking, Hegel sought to combine his criticism of the separation of powers with his faith in disinterested bureaucrats to allow civil servants in the executive branch to participate in the legislature, either as ex officio members or elected representatives. By this means, he hoped to ensure that the bureaucracy would meet no serious obstacle in formulating and carrying out the rational will, or divine idea, of the state.

After this heady experience, it was only natural that American intellectuals, reading Hegel and observing firsthand a unified and rising Germany, should wonder what all this meant for the United States. In the *Philosophy of History*, Hegel had portrayed America as the "land of the future," raising the question of whether he thought that history might continue to unfold and whether the extended democratic and commercial republic had introduced something altogether new into the world. Certainly Madison had thought so when in *Federalist* No. 14, he exhorted his countrymen to hearken not "to the voice that tells you the form of government recommended for your adoption is a novelty in the political world; that it has never yet had a place in the theories of the wildest projectors; that it rashly attempts what it is impossible to accomplish." Americans, he rejoiced, had "accomplished a revolution which has no parallel in the annals of human society." But this was not Hegel's view.[45]

Although conceding that Americans enjoyed a prosperity that was the fruit of their labor, civil order, and freedom, Hegel thought that something was lacking. "The substance of the totality comprised of the need, peace, civil rights, security, and a community arose from the aggregation of atomic individuals, so that the state was only an external institution, set up for the protection of property." In the United States, the protection of property and near absence of taxes revealed the basic character of the society: "it is marked by the private person's striving for acquisition and profit and by the predominance of a private interest which devotes itself to the community for personal benefit alone."[46]

Anticipating the thesis of Frederick Jackson Turner, but viewing it in a more optimistic light, Hegel argued that only after the frontier closed would the United States feel the need to develop a "coherent" political structure. For the present, the absorption of the population by the West would keep society from becoming socially stratified and guarantee the "continuation of the present civil condition." But once the population was pressed back upon itself into the cities, and the United States became divided between the rich and the poor, with the great mass of people unable to satisfy their needs, Americans would be compelled to think about civil society and to develop "an organized state."[47] For the rising generation of Americans reading Hegel in Germany and in America after the Civil War, that time seemed to be fast approaching. The progress of America towards the "ethical state" appeared not only desirable, but also inevitable. "The land of the future" would merely confirm what the world-spirit had foretold.

FAIR HARVARD

As America resumed its relations with Europe after the Civil War, it was forced to confront the challenges posed by these intellectual developments. Indeed, by the time Theodore Roosevelt arrived at Harvard in the fall of 1876, the college itself was in the throes of a major upheaval. For the first time in its history, Harvard in 1869 had appointed a natural scientist, Charles William Eliot, as president, and he had rapidly set about to transform the provincial New England college into a major research institution. Eliot, who graduated from Harvard in 1853, had spent several years touring Europe and was favorably impressed by its educational institutions. Unlike American colleges, which saw their mission as the preparation of young men for careers in the ministry and teaching, European universities were turning out graduates equipped with the practical skills to contribute to their nations' social and economic development. Following their example, Eliot was determined to introduce a curriculum that would serve the economic needs of a rising industrial America. To that end, he appointed his classmate Charles F. Dunbar the first professor of political economy anywhere in the United States and recruited another Harvardian, Adams Sherman Hill, who had earned a law degree in 1855 and become a newspaperman, to teach writing. Not content with revamping the undergraduate curriculum, Eliot also laid the foundation for homegrown doctoral programs. During Roosevelt's freshman year, Henry Cabot Lodge, G. Stanley Hall, and J. Laurence Laughlin would be among the first to be awarded Harvard Ph.D.'s.[48]

Among Eliot's curricular innovations was the elimination of many of the prescribed courses and the introduction of electives. The reform, immediately popular with students, met with resistance from faculty who doubted that students would choose wisely.[49] But Eliot, whose own views combined Yankee practicality and Emersonian individualism, believed that each student should be free to follow his own bent rather than be forced into a prescribed curriculum for four years.[50]

Nevertheless, freshmen in Roosevelt's day were still required to follow a prescribed program of study that combined elements of the older classical curriculum with more modern subjects. During his first year, Theodore took both Greek and Latin, as well as a third course in classical literature, reading parts of the *Odyssey*, Plato's *Apology* and *Crito*, as well as selections from Livy, Horace, and Cicero. Freshmen were also required to continue their study of either French or German, with young Roosevelt opting for German. Courses in mathematics, physics, and chemistry rounded out his freshman program. At that time, the passing grade was 50, with 75 being an honor grade in required courses.[51] Theodore barely scraped by in Greek with a 58, did solid work in the sciences, and earned his best grade in German. At the end of his freshman year, he stood midway in his class.

Over the next three years, Roosevelt would dabble in modern languages, choosing French and Italian as electives in his junior and senior years, in addition to three more courses in German, where he studied scientific prose, German composition, as well as Goethe and German lyrics. As he would later recall, he had developed a deep affinity for German culture dating back to the summer he had spent in Dresden in 1873, when, among other things, the German "capacity for hard work, the sense of duty, the delight in studying literature and science, the pride in the new Germany" had made a deep and lasting impression upon him. Throughout his life, he remained fascinated with the *Nibelungenlied* and Germany poetry, which he confessed he loved as much as the poetry of his native tongue.[52]

When he entered Harvard, Roosevelt had fully expected to become a natural scientist in the manner of Audubon or Hart Merriam, happily spending his days in the field. As a youngster he had shown a precocious interest in natural history dating back to his discovery of a dead seal in a market near his home. The seal haunted his imagination, causing him to return daily, taking "useless" measurements, which he then recorded in his notebook. This adventure then led him to establish the "Roosevelt Museum of Natural History" in his room, where he displayed his collection until the servants complained and it was moved to an upstairs hall. Around the age of thirteen, the budding zoologist began to take taxidermy lessons, and that summer was given his first gun. On his second trip to Europe and the Holy Lands the next year, he began seriously to collect natural history specimens in Egypt for the first time and acquired his first knowledge of Latin by learning the scientific names of the birds and mammals he identified. His boyhood diaries record his ornithological observations at home and abroad, testifying to his impressive knowledge of the natural world.[53]

Ironically, it was another of President Eliot's reforms that dampened Roosevelt's enthusiasm for a career in natural science. Determined to make the science curriculum more practically rigorous, the Harvard president had introduced the seminar method, then prevalent in Germany, in which students carried out experiments in the laboratory and presented their research in class.[54] For an outdoor naturalist like himself, who much preferred fieldwork to being stuck in a lab, Roosevelt found the new system deeply frustrating and chafed at the suggestion that work carried on out of doors was not scientifically serious. Nevertheless, he signed up for Elementary Botany and Comparative Anatomy and Physiology of Vertebrates, taught by the young William James in his sophomore year.

Theodore clearly had mixed feelings about another of Eliot's innovations, which aimed at improving the writing skills of the students. As part of his program to make a Harvard education useful to the new industrial economy, Eliot laid great stress on the proper use of the English language. Whether the study of Greek and Latin helped young men to write better was a question much debated at the time, and Eliot was determined to see that the students could express themselves in clear and serviceable prose. Of the eight prescribed courses that remained after the freshman year, five were in writing. As a sophomore, Theodore was required to take two such courses, one in rhetoric and another in themes. Although the title of the first course suggested that it would deal with the art of persuasion, in fact, as the assigned texts (Abbot's *How to Write Clearly* and Hill's *The Principles of Rhetoric and Their Application, with an Appendix Comprising General Rules for Punctuation*) make clear, it was essentially a course in English composition. Hill was Harvard's own Adams Sherman Hill, the famously acerbic critic of student writing, who would transform the teaching of English at Harvard. In keeping with Eliot's practical mission, Hill's book focused mostly on the mechanics of writing. But it is worth noting that the Boylston Professor of Rhetoric and Oratory couched the entire subject in terms of "Grammatical Purity" and, in one section entitled "Barbarisms," instructed students to avoid the unnecessary importation of foreign words.[55] Whether by accident or design, Hill's preference for words of English origin would reinforce a message of Anglo-Saxon superiority.

In the sophomore and junior themes courses, students were expected to demonstrate their command of the principles they had learned in Rhetoric by producing six essays each year. Forensics, the second of the required junior writing courses, and the only required course in the senior year, differed from the more elementary themes in that these compositions focused on argument rather than style. Prescribed courses in logic and metaphysics in the junior year would presumably help students think more clearly and strengthen their arguments.[56] Roosevelt, who had Professor Hill for Forensics his senior year, later claimed he "owed much" to him, even though at the time he was incensed because Hill had announced before the entire class that "he could not write English."[57]

In his *Autobiography*, Roosevelt mostly blamed himself for his poor performance, observing that he "ought to have gained much more" from his themes and Forensics assignments than he did. His failure, in part, was that he had "no interest in the subjects" and was "not sufficiently developed" to make himself consider intelligently such topics as "the character of the Gracchi." As Roosevelt charmingly confessed, "I worked drearily at the Gracchi because I had to; my conscientious and much-to-be-pitied professor dragging me through the theme by main strength, with my feet firmly planted in idea-proof resistance."[58] That the character of these two Romans, who attempted to remain in office beyond their constitutional term limits to carry out a program of land reform, failed to spark his imagination is an irony that Roosevelt, even in 1913, did not seem to appreciate.[59]

Far more than the character of the Gracchi (whose principal fault Plutarch judged to be their "excessive desire for glory and honors"), the young Roosevelt had discovered a subject more to his taste. During his senior year he began to research the naval war of 1812 and drafted part of what two years later would be his first highly acclaimed history. It is, therefore, worth noting that although Roosevelt would go on to establish a considerable reputation as an amateur historian in the decades following his graduation, the only history course he took at Harvard was the required sophomore class on Anglo-American constitutional history.[60]

Roosevelt's instructor in this class was Silas Marcus Macvane (Harvard 1873), who put together a syllabus that by contemporary standards can only be described as bizarre. According to the Harvard catalog, the course began with the English historian Edward Augustus Freeman's *Outlines of General History,* which students were instructed to read "to p. 272."[61] Freeman, whose outline was specifically intended for use in the schools, sought to trace the origins of the English constitution back to its Aryan roots at the dawn of European history and, as we shall see, Roosevelt's histories would follow Freeman's narrative in important respects. By Aryan, Freeman explained, he meant principally the common language spoken by the Aryan peoples of Europe and Asia, though he added that the Aryan peoples had made "advances in civilization which placed them far above mere savages."[62]

Aryans were further divided into different subgroups, whose distinctive qualities could best be understood by means of historical comparisons or what in more academic works he called the historical-comparative method. As the *Outline* made clear, Freeman was principally concerned with that subgroup known as the Teutons, since this was the branch of the Aryan family to which the English, the Germans, and the Scandinavians belonged.[63] Although Freeman claimed his history was scientific, adopting as it did the comparative method of the natural sciences, in fact there was more than a touch of the romantic in his effort to discover the origins of the English constitution in the primitive past. And beneath this romantic variation on the theme of the "noble savage" was the darker suggestion that the Teutons were a superior race whose political genius was transmitted by blood.[64]

In the *Outline* Freeman pointed out that not every branch of this noble race remained pure, as some tribes were absorbed into the remains of the decaying Roman Empire. However, the Low Dutch, living near the sea by the Rhine, the Elbe, and Weser Rivers, had escaped Roman domination and preserved their ancient Teutonic constitution, consisting of a king elected by the people, a council of nobles, and assemblies of the whole people.[65] As his narrative continued, Britain, which had been partially conquered by the Romans, then fell prey to these Low Dutch tribes of Saxons, Angles, and Jutes, "our own forefathers," who invaded the island and "swept away all Roman institutions more utterly than was done in any part of the mainland."[66] Apparently they swept away more than Roman institutions, since the native Britons were either killed, enslaved, or forced to flee to the west, allowing the Low Dutch invaders to plant their ancient constitution on English soil. Still later, in the ninth century the Danes, another branch of the Teutons untouched by Rome, invaded England. Despite the Norman Conquest, Freeman insisted that the old Teutonic assemblies had never completely died out in England. In time, the old constitution was transported to America by the Anglo-Saxon settlers, who retained the "germ" of the Teutonic folk moot in their town meetings. Although the assigned reading ended in 1648 with the Treaty of Westphalia, it was difficult to miss the point of Freeman's narrative: the English and the Americans were descendants of the same proud racial family, united in their common Teutonic inheritance.[67] Accordingly, Freeman had nothing to say about the differences between the unwritten British constitution and the American document, or the British monarchy and the American republic, which must have struck him as mere distractions or at best minor variations on the deep continuities he discovered in the misty past.

After this sweeping introduction, students then moved on to *The Crown and Its Advisers* by Alexander Charles Ewald. That book, which was originally a series of lectures delivered to conservative workingmen in England, attempted to lay out "the leading *facts* and principles" of the British constitution so that its audience might be able to arrive at informed opinions on political questions. Although a conservative, the author tried to avoid too partisan a tone, and proudly noted that liberals in attendance also approved the lectures. In anodyne terms, the author praised the merits of modern parliamentary government, which he averred was admirably suited to the character and temperament of the British people. Over four successive chapters, Ewald then explained how modern parliamentary government divided power among the crown, the ministry, and the two houses of Parliament, establishing "the most perfect plan of government that could possibly be adopted."[68] For Harvard students, who now presumably viewed the rise of parliamentary government through Freeman's Teutonic lens, the contemporary British constitution emerged in a most favorable light.

Only then did the class at last turn its attention to the U.S. Constitution. Here the assigned reading was Henry Flanders's updated *Exposition of the Constitution of the United States*, which aimed, like Freeman, to serve as a manual of instruction for the youth of the nation.[69] But in contrast to Freeman, Flanders, the author of works on the laws of fire insurance and other technical legal subjects, said nothing about the "germ theory" or the Teutons. Rather, his approach was to go through the Constitution article by article, drawing on established practice and authoritative court decisions, anticipating the formal and legalistic analysis that Edward S. Corwin would make famous in *The Constitution and What It Means Today*.[70] His was a moderate nationalism that tilted republicanism toward legislative predominance and reflected the actual state of affairs in post–Civil War America. It had become, he wrote, "an axiom in republican states that the representatives should be directly responsible to the people, and this responsibility is ensured by the frequency of election."[71] Then, turning to the upper house, he quoted Edmund Burke approvingly that the Senate seemed to be the "very essence of republican government," which, he then added authoritatively, was also "the opinion of the framers of the Constitution of the United States."[72]

Although his revised edition was published in 1874, Flanders (who in 1863 had published an essay setting forth the reasons why the Civil War must go on) was loath to recognize the extent to which military necessity had compelled Lincoln to expand presidential powers. Accordingly, he passed over the power that Lincoln discovered in the presidential oath, said nothing about Lincoln's invocation of his powers as commander-in-chief to issue the Emancipation Proclamation, and flatly declared that the president had no power to suspend the writ of habeas corpus. "The power of the president is limited to executing the laws; he has no power to suspend them."[73] In so doing, Flanders was no longer simply explicating the Constitution, but suggesting ever so gently that Lincoln had violated the intentions of the Framers and exceeded his constitutional authority.

Yet there is no more authoritative explication of the Framers' intentions than *The Federalist*, and it is instructive to compare the two. Unlike Flanders, who seemed far more certain that the spirit of republicanism resided in the legislature, Publius was more measured. In *Federalist* No. 37, he acknowledged that this was the widespread view: "the genius of republican government *seems* to demand . . . not only that all power should be derived from the people, but that those entrusted with it should be kept in dependence on the people by a short duration of their appointments; and that even then the trust should be placed not in a few but a number of hands."[74] For Publius, however, the problem was precisely how to make republican government *good* government, and this required that responsiveness be counterbalanced by energy, which in turn might call forth courage and magnanimity. Accordingly, the president could never be merely an executive carrying out orders but must have "the constitutional means and personal motives" to use the extensive powers of his office, especially in times of emergency or peril, for the good of the country. Properly understood, the separation of powers would create a dynamic contest between the legislative and executive branches that both sides might try to exploit to the best of their ability and ambition. As Publius explained, the separation of powers did more than merely restrain government (though it did that, too); it also encouraged those qualities or virtues that were essential to good government and yet frequently missing in republics. It was precisely this far more supple understanding of the interplay of powers and motives that Flanders missed.[75] Roosevelt, who as a Republican reformer would urge college men to read *The Federalist,* would have to discover that work on his own.

In his junior year, Roosevelt enrolled in a course that would change the direction of his life, though as is so often the case, not in the way that his professors had hoped. The class was Philosophy 6, taught by one of President Eliot's star recruits, Professor Charles F. Dunbar, with the assistance of J. Laurence Laughlin, a newly minted Harvard Ph.D. The title of the class, however, was misleading: Philosophy 6 was in fact a course on political economy, but because Harvard at that time had no Department of Political Economy, the class was officially listed with the philosophy offerings. Unlike the required sophomore history class, political economy dealt with subjects of more immediate import, though it, too, seemed an odd combination of the practical and the theoretical. While Professor Dunbar lectured on the public finance of the Civil War, his assistant led students through recitations and discussions of John Stuart Mill's *Political Economy.*[76] In a letter to his mother, Theodore confided that he found his courses in Political Economy and the required Metaphysics "rather hard, requiring a good deal of work," but "even more interesting than my Natural History courses," especially since he "radically" disagreed "on many points" with the men whose books he was reading, mentioning Mill and Ferrier (the author of his text in Metaphysics) by name.[77] Roosevelt gave no hint of what precisely he disagreed with in Mill, but one possibility, given Laughlin's general orientation, might have been Mill's quite sympathetic treatment of socialism.[78] In any case, one classmate of his recalled that before Roosevelt "the courses in Political Economy were cold and uninteresting. . . . With his appearance and questionings, things livened up."[79]

To stimulate his students' interest in political economy, Laughlin asked

Roosevelt and a group of classmates to help start a finance club that would invite outside speakers to address contemporary economic issues. At the inaugural meeting of the club, Roosevelt and his classmate Robert Bacon presented a paper of their own on municipal taxation. Of that event, Laughlin later recalled, "We little supposed that evening that we were being addressed by a future President of the United States and his Secretary of State."[80] In addition to William Graham Sumner, outside speakers included Henry George, whose *Progress and Poverty* was published in 1879, and Abram S. Hewitt, who (along with Henry George and Roosevelt) would run for mayor of New York City in 1886, and Francis A. Walker, who spoke on "The Principles of Taxation." But perhaps the lecture that generated the most excitement was that of Colonel Thomas Wentworth Higginson on "Young Men in Politics," a subject that could not but appeal to Roosevelt.[81]

His interest piqued, Theodore received an 89, the highest grade in the class,[82] which understandably made him wonder whether he should switch his focus to political economy. As Laughlin recounted, Roosevelt visited him in his office sometime during his junior year to explore precisely this question. The young instructor advised his student that "the country at that time especially needed men trained to think correctly on public questions and that these questions were nine-tenths economic."[83] In the end, Roosevelt signed up for Political Economy 3 his senior year, where he read Cairnes's *Principles of Political Economy*, McLeod's *Elements of Banking*, and Bastiat's *Harmonies Economiques* with Professor Dunbar. But since economic questions as such never really interested Roosevelt, it is perhaps not surprising that he did not do as well in this course as he had in the joint class with Dunbar and Laughlin the previous semester.[84]

Even as he branched out into political economy, Roosevelt maintained his interest in the natural sciences. During his senior year, he took two courses, including one in geology with Professor Shaler. In one contemporary account, Nathaniel Southgate Shaler showed "a distinct fondness" for his enthusiastic pupil, whom he already knew from the Natural History Society, where Roosevelt served as vice-president, and whose antics had richly amused him.[85] Perhaps it was from Shaler that Theodore learned to combine Darwinian natural selection with a Lamarckian optimism regarding the inheritance of acquired characteristics, although the course touched only glancingly on this subject.[86] In any case, it was a position that both men would share. Whether or not he ever heard Shaler give voice to his belief in the superiority of the Anglo-Saxons, whose supposed political genius seemed to confirm Lamarck's theories, those views were by no means unusual in the Harvard of Roosevelt's day.

DECISIONS

Despite his strong showing in the natural sciences, Theodore, with Laughlin's encouragement, was beginning to consider other career possibilities. For one thing, he had fallen in love with Alice Hathaway Lee, who did not relish sharing a home with the specimens of the latest Roosevelt Museum.[87] For another, Professor Hill's low opinion of his writing notwithstanding, Roosevelt was enjoying considerable success as an editor of the *Advocate* and briefly considered becoming a journalist.[88] And finally, the fighter in him wanted to avenge the injustice done to his father by the corrupt New York party machine.

After the 1876 election, President Rutherford B. Hayes had named the senior Roosevelt, a prominent philanthropist and champion of civil service reform, to serve as Collector of Customs for the Port of New York. The nomination was correctly seen as a direct challenge to the New York Republican machine, whose own choice was Chester A. Arthur. When Roosevelt's name came before the Senate Committee for confirmation, New York Senator Roscoe Conkling opposed him and succeeded in sinking the nomination. Roosevelt's death from cancer later that winter left his son shattered and with a bitter taste in his mouth about machine politics. Now, as a senior thinking seriously about what he would do after graduation, he was haunted by the idea that he should somehow try to carry on his father's legacy. In a talk before the O.K. Society, Theodore delivered a paper on "The Machine in Politics."[89] As Edmund Morris has noted, the topic was highly symbolic. Machine politics had crushed his father, and Roosevelt himself would take on the New York machine two years later.[90]

Further evidence of his growing interest in politics may be seen in Roosevelt's involvement in the upcoming presidential election of 1880. Taking to heart Colonel Higginson's advice to college men to become involved in politics, Roosevelt organized a poll to determine student opinion and encourage his classmates to vote. An editorial in the *Advocate*, where Theodore served as an editor, reminded Harvard men, who were in his day inclined toward a studied indifference,[91] that representative democracy depended on the views of all its citizens, and that the opinions of the intelligent and good men might very well help to ensure the nomination of the best type of men. The editorial went on to assure its readers that "the gentleman in charge of the polls is proof that the movement is not one of idle curiosity, but of earnest purpose."[92]

Although Republicans outnumbered Democrats on campus, the *Advocate* emphasized that "intelligent and conservative men will not allow party affiliation to rule their better judgement and force them to support an unfit or corrupt candidate" or one who was seeking a third term.[93] With the actions of the corrupt New York Republican machine still clearly in his mind, Roosevelt favored Senator Thomas F. Bayard, a Democrat, over the three leading Republican contenders Ulysses S. Grant, James G. Blaine, and John Sherman. In striking contrast to a similar poll at Yale, where Grant emerged the clear winner, Bayard carried the day at Harvard, a testimony to Roosevelt's influence. Yet four years later, Roosevelt, who by that time had served in the New York Assembly as a reform Republican, would take a principled stand in favor of party loyalty even though he once again opposed the nominee. His political education was just beginning.

His mind now focused on public affairs, Theodore chose as the topic for his Commencement Day Dissertation "The Practicability of Equalizing Men and Women before the Law."[94] At the outset, Roosevelt conceded that, "in the abstract, women should have equal rights with men." But since the world as it actually existed was still stuck in its "semi-barbarous state," Roosevelt would focus his remarks not on the justice of the idea, but on its practicality. The principal difference between the sexes was that men were physically stronger and therefore able to fight in defense of their rights. Although he hastened to qualify this point, and held out the possibility that women might be effective fighters in a society "radically different" from his own, their present inability to defend the right to vote remained a powerful argument against woman suffrage (a position he would continue to hold until 1912, by which time he had begun to reconceive rights less as something to be defended and more as entitlements).

In all other matters, however, Roosevelt insisted that women be treated equally before the law. But this bifurcation of voting rights and civil rights suggested that he was confused about whether to take into account the biological differences between men and women or to treat them as equals— even though they were physically weaker. Here, too, his Darwinism clouded his views. Moreover, without perhaps realizing it, Theodore then went on to suggest that women were perhaps not the most rational creatures, for he added, "A cripple or a consumptive in the eye of the law is equal to the strongest athlete *or the deepest thinker*; and the same justice should be shown to a woman, whether she is, or is not, the equal of man" [emphasis added]. And although this was perfectly consistent with the Declaration's understanding of equal rights, which Jefferson insisted applied no less to the meanest intellect than to Sir Isaac Newton,[95] rhetorically, it left something to be desired.

Whatever his intellectual confusions about women's equality as a general matter, on a more personal level the soon-to-be bridegroom was emphatic that marriage laws should preserve "the most absolute equality" between the husband and wife. *"I do not think the woman should assume the man's name,"* he wrote, underlining the sentence. The word "obey" should be taken out of the marriage vows. Women should have an equal, if not greater, voice in the rearing of children, and husbands should have no more right over their wives' person or property than wives have over husbands'. Roosevelt did not believe that women needed men to stand up for their interests; they were perfectly capable of doing this themselves (though he made no effort to square this with his earlier assertion that women were too weak to defend their rights in public).

To put teeth into the idea of equal rights, women should be allowed to attend law school, though this by itself was not enough. Public opinion would also need to change, especially among women, so that they were willing to engage lawyers of their own sex to defend their rights. To ensure that they got a fair hearing, women should also be allowed to serve on juries. At this point, however, Roosevelt seemed overwhelmed by the social changes that would be necessary to bring about women's equality and concluded lamely that until women were allowed to become lawyers and serve on juries, "I doubt if it is practicable to put both sexes on a footing of equality."[96] Amidst this muddle, it was perhaps fortunate that he did not deliver his "dissertation" at commencement.[97]

Although Roosevelt confessed that he "thoroughly enjoyed" his undergraduate years, the few short pages devoted to his studies in the *Autobiography* were mostly filled with frustrations and regrets, tempered by a due acknowledgment of his own inadequacies. Not knowing then that he would pursue a public career, Roosevelt saw no need to practice debating, the omission of which was already clear in his Commencement Day Dissertation. In retrospect, Theodore was sorry he had not learned how to debate, though he disapproved of the prevailing technique that arbitrarily assigned each team a particular position to defend on important questions such as "Our Colonial Policy," "The Need of a Navy," and "The Proper Position of the Courts in Constitutional Questions," regardless of whether they believed in it. These would all later become issues about which Roosevelt cared deeply.[98] It was, therefore, the duty of a college to turn out young men who had "ardent convictions on the side of the right," not merely to teach them how to win an argument. All this style of debate did was teach them to talk "glibly" about their assigned topic; it did nothing to harness their convictions to their arguments. Public speaking, however, was a different matter. After a lifetime of public service, Roosevelt regretted that he had not studied elocution.[99]

A LEGAL EDUCATION AND MORE

Upon graduation, Roosevelt headed back to New York, where he enrolled in the Columbia Law School that fall. For reasons not altogether clear, he never completed his studies and did not earn a law degree. In his *Autobiography*, Roosevelt attributed this to the excessively legalistic approach he encountered in his law books and in the classroom, which as a full-blown progressive struck him as being an obstacle to social justice. When Roosevelt was at Columbia, law was taught using "the Dwight method," in which students were first instructed in broad legal principles and then asked to deduce rules for them in particular cases. In retrospect, Theodore much preferred the case method employed at Harvard, where students reasoned inductively from the particular case to general principles. Had he studied law with James Bradley Thayer at Harvard, Roosevelt believed he would have developed a deeper appreciation of how lawyers might advance the cause of social justice.[100] As it was, he found his legal education too much in thrall to the "big corporation lawyers" whose standards he found "incompatible with the idealism I suppose every high-minded man is apt to feel." Roosevelt was especially repelled by "the *caveat emptor* side of the law," in which one side engaged in "sharp practice" for its own advantage, rather than seeking a solution that redounded to the benefit of both.[101]

However much this may fit with Roosevelt's progressive narrative, there is nothing in the contemporary accounts to suggest that he thought this way at the time. It is true that he brought with him a high sense of moral earnestness, but entries in his private diary suggest that he was enjoying his legal studies, as do letters to his mother and sister. Far more plausible an explanation for why he failed to complete his legal education was the decision by New York State to change its rules for entering private practice. When Roosevelt entered law school in 1880, the state had required only two years of legal training and a passing grade on Columbia's two-year comprehensive exam to practice law. As of 1882, New York would require a third year, either in law school or as clerk in a law office. In addition, the state withdrew its "diploma privilege" to graduates of the Columbia Law School, requiring them for the first time to pass the state bar exam before they could practice law. Roosevelt, who had joined the Twenty-first District Republican Association at the same time that he entered Columbia and been elected in his second year of law school to the lower house of the New York legislature, was already launched on his political career and might not have seen the need, at least at that time, to spend an additional year to earn the degree and then prepare for the bar exam. Thus, it seems likely that Roosevelt's comments in the *Autobiography* more accurately reflected his later experiences when he tangled with these corporate lawyers in his battles against the trusts, rather than his views of the legal profession at the time. Indeed, even in the *Autobiography,* he admitted that if he had had to earn all of his living, he might very well have stuck with the law.[102]

What is also curious—at least at first sight—was that Roosevelt said nothing about John W. Burgess, either in the *Autobiography* or anywhere else. Yet during his time at the Columbia Law School, Roosevelt took several courses with Burgess, who introduced him to elements of the German state theory that underlay much of progressive thought. What we know of Roosevelt's days at Columbia comes chiefly from Burgess's memoirs, though it is perhaps not surprising that the professor would wish to take credit for helping to shape the mind of the future president.

In his *Reminiscences of an American Scholar,* published long after Roosevelt's death, Burgess boasted that Roosevelt "registered for *all* the courses in political history, public law, and political science and appeared to be more interested in these than in the topics of municipal law"[103] taught by his senior colleague Theodore Woolsey Dwight, a point borne out by the doodles in the margins of his municipal law notebooks.[104] As Burgess recalled, Roosevelt's "mental activity was simply prodigious." Sitting in the front row, he was able "by his superior preparedness" to take down everything the professor said. Thus, it is a pity that although seven of Roosevelt's law school notebooks have been discovered, they include none from Burgess's classes.[105] For Burgess remembered him as being "very quick and correct in comprehension, very accurate in examination, and the most rapid and voluminous reader of references in the school. He was exceedingly industrious, and his power of work was outrun only by his zeal in application." Elsewhere, he added that the future president "asked very pertinent questions, and gave very enlightened answers." In Burgess's recollection, this most promising student volunteered that he was "tremendously interested" in the subjects of the professor's lectures and hoped to "devote . . . [his] life to the investigation and realization of them." No wonder that the professor "marked him for a future colleague."[106] At the time, Burgess was eagerly recruiting future faculty for his brainchild, the School of Political Science, a hybrid of the French and German university systems, which he hoped would transform Columbia into a great research university, much as Eliot in his own way was doing at Harvard.

JOHN W. BURGESS AND THE GERMAN CONNECTION

John W. Burgess was a Southern Whig, who fought with the Union Army and experienced at close range the horrors of the Civil War. In 1863 in the midst of battle, he vowed that if he survived, he would devote his life "to teaching men how to live by reason and compromise instead of by bloodshed and destruction."[107] When the war ended, he enrolled at Amherst College, where Professor Julius H. Seelye introduced him to Hegel and German idealism. After graduation, Burgess traveled to Germany to continue his studies and there met the American historian and diplomat George Bancroft, who advised him on a plan of studies. The year was 1871. Taking time off from his courses, Burgess witnessed the triumphant entry of the Prussian army into Berlin, which he proclaimed the "most magnificent manifestation of power which the world had ever furnished," truly a "world-historic" event.[108] Thus began the lifelong infatuation with German theory and practice, reason and power that would inform his political science.[109]

Although he took no degree, Burgess, following Bancroft's advice, studied at Göttingen, Leipzig, and Berlin. Of the three, Berlin was the most influential. Established in 1810, it had risen in prominence along with Prussia and was now the very model of the modern research university. Faculty were free to pursue their own teaching and research programs, and Burgess soon found himself working in the Prussian archives for the historian Johann Gustav Droysen, whom he credited with having taught him the methods of historical research and construction and to whom he dedicated his first book. By his own admission, however, the professor who had the most lasting influence on him was Rudolf von Gniest, who taught public law and served as legal counsel to Bismarck. What Burgess especially admired was the way von Gniest combined elements of English common law and Roman law in the new imperial legal codes, using his research to serve his country. Burgess credited his historical and comparative studies with teaching him to think internationally and vowed that he would never again be "provincial or chauvinistic."[110] Following his mentor, he would attempt to weave elements of German state theory into the post–Civil War Constitution in order to serve his country.

Returning to America, the young instructor was courted by Theodore W. Dwight at the Columbia Law School, but chose instead to return to Amherst. There, he ran into stiff resistance from faculty who did not share his view that the traditional college curriculum was obsolete and who resented his efforts to set up an informal "graduate" program to promote the scientific study of history, ethics, sociology, and philosophy.[111] When Dwight renewed his offer in 1876, Burgess left his *alma mater* to join the Columbia Law School, where he hoped to "develop the 'science of jurisprudence' in the fashion of the German universities."[112] "Instead of the monotonous maintenance of so-called established truth," he vowed to make "the progressive development of truth" his "guiding principle."[113]

Quickly shedding his obligations to undergraduate education at Columbia College, Burgess focused his efforts entirely on the law school, where he developed a two-year sequence of courses, starting with a general survey of political and constitutional history from ancient Rome to "the realization of the constitutional idea in the nineteenth century," and followed by a course in the comparative public law of England, France, Germany, and the United States. He also offered International Law from the Peace of Westphalia in 1648 to the Treaty of Berlin in 1878 and a more general course in international law. As a capstone, Burgess developed a course examining "the fundamental principles of political science as a generalization from the foregoing investigations." A man of boundless energy and ambition, he also conducted an intensive weekly seminar in political science methodology for "volunteers" from both the first- and second-year classes. Because that course required a knowledge of Latin, French, and German, Burgess boasted that his classes attracted only the brightest and best-educated students.[114]

Although the Columbia archives do not indicate what courses TR took from Burgess in 1880–1882, or what Burgess taught in them, we do know that Burgess had been developing his ideas about jurisprudence and political science since his "graduate" courses at Amherst and had been teaching at Columbia for four years before Roosevelt arrived.[115] Eventually, Burgess's lectures were compiled and published in his two-volume *Political Science and Comparative Constitutional Law* (1890), which was followed by a trilogy of American constitutional history (1897–1902). These books, along with articles published in the *Political Science Quarterly*, which Burgess helped found in 1886 to provide a platform for the new political science, provide some insight into what Roosevelt might have learned while sitting attentively in the front row.

By Burgess's own admission, the great "peculiarity" of his work was its methodology. Like Freeman, Burgess took his cue from the comparative method that had proven so fruitful in the natural sciences, adapting it to the study of politics and constitutional law. Just as natural scientists studied comparative anatomy for glimpses into how the species had evolved, Burgess traced the origin and development of the nation-state in Germany, England, France, and America, "in order to learn the meaning of our legal, political, and economic institutions and principles."[116] Nevertheless, two important differences emerged between the methods of natural science and Burgess's historical-comparative approach. For one thing, although the historical-comparative method claimed to be inductive, in fact Burgess (again like Freeman) started from the assumption that the "germ" of free institutions could be traced back to the Teutonic past.[117] For another, unlike natural science, which tried to explain only how the species had evolved so far and left open the question of where evolution was going, Burgess believed that history was moving toward a definite end.[118] Although humanity was still a long way from reaching this end-state, Burgess was certain he knew where it was leading. For all his pretenses to be scientific, Burgess remained in thrall to the Hegelian idea of historical progress.[119]

Burgess began by considering the nation, which he defined as a group of people living in a particular territory, with a shared understanding of right and wrong, and belonging to a particular "race." He recognized that America was a "cosmopolitan" nation, made up of several different races, but the "dominant factor" was "an amalgamated Teutonic race." What distinguished the Teutonic race was that it alone among the modern races displayed a genius for politics, rivaled only by the Romans of yore. But where the Romans had created a universal empire, the Teutonic genius manifested itself in the creation of the nation-state, which for Burgess represented the most perfect form of political organization so far developed. The professor lost no time in drawing out the policy implications of this racial superiority, and Roosevelt was quick to grasp his lessons.[120]

First, nations must carefully supervise their immigration policies to make sure that they admitted only immigrants who would preserve their language, customs and institutions. Since it was difficult, if not impossible, for most races to "amalgamate" with the predominant Anglo-American branch of the Teutonic race, they should be kept out of the United States. Burgess particularly worried about the Slavs, those ancient enemies of the Teutons, whose political "incapacity" fitted them only for Caesarism.[121] Rejecting any notion that America was, even in part, a creedal nation, in which citizenship might be extended to all those who accepted its fundamental principles regardless of race or ethnicity, Burgess insisted that the "highest duty" of the nation-state was "to preserve, strengthen, and develop its own national character."[122] As a rising Republican reformer, Roosevelt would soften Burgess's policy, holding out the (Lamarckian) possibility that these European immigrants might (indeed, must be made to) adapt to their political environment, but he drew the line with Asian peoples, whose cultures he thought could never be assimilated to that of the United States.

Second, in what was clearly a jab at the Radical Reconstructionists, Burgess, the Kentucky Union-man, argued that where the majority of a nation belonged to the Teutonic race, it must never surrender its political power. His meaning only thinly veiled, Burgess insisted that "under certain circumstances" a nation was justified in denying "other ethnical elements" any share in political power if doing so would prevent "corruption and confusion" harmful to the rights of all and to civilization as a whole. "The Teutonic nations can never regard the exercise of political power as a right of man." The right to vote should be conferred only when these other groups had demonstrated their capacity to discharge their political duties. In the meantime, the ruling Teutonic race must exercise its political power with justice and moderation, displaying those virtues that established their political superiority.[123] Although Roosevelt never went so far as to support the disenfranchisement of blacks in the South and publicly insisted that each black be judged on his merits as an individual, he would defend the "Lily White" strategy of excluding southern black delegates from the Progressive nominating convention of 1912 with much the same argument.

Third, and perhaps most important, Burgess argued that Teutonic nations had a duty to civilize the "unpolitical" and barbaric races of the world. Burgess was keenly aware that his countrymen tended to view such involvement as an "unwarrantable interference in the affairs of other states," but this, he insisted, was shortsighted. Lacking the political genius of the Teutons, these benighted populations had no way to advance unless the "political nations" undertook to organize them. There was "no human right to the status of barbarism": backward nations must be forced to become civilized. Accordingly, he counseled, the Teutonic races "must have a colonial policy," a view Roosevelt strenuously endorsed.[124]

In what was clearly a reference to the policy of the United States toward the Indians, Burgess insisted that the civilized state "may righteously *go still further* than the exercise of force in imposing organization." Should these barbaric peoples refuse to be civilized, "the civilized state may *clear the territory of their presence* and make it the abode of civilized man." Of course, the civilized nation must once again exercise those virtues for which it was renowned, "but it should not be troubled in its conscience" about its actions. Compared to the "transcendent right and duty to establish political and legal order everywhere," savages had no real rights. "The fact that a politically unorganized population roves through the wilderness, or camps within it, does not create rights, either public or private, which a civilized state, pursuing its great world-mission, is under any obligations, legal or moral, to respect."[125] Within the space of a few years after he had left Columbia, Roosevelt would make the same argument in almost identical words in his histories.

Finally, Teutonic nations were justified in interfering in nations that had made some progress toward forming a state and were no longer "wholly barbaric." They did not need to wait for an invitation to intervene, though when they did, it should be for the good of the subjected population to move them along the path to civilization and to their "incorporation in the world society." Political science—as Burgess understood it—confirmed that the duty and the interest of the Teutonic nations coincided in pursuing this policy of benevolent intervention. As president, Roosevelt would offer a similar rationale to justify his policies towards Latin America, and especially his actions involving the Panama Canal.

For nations to distinguish themselves on the world stage, however, they had first to organize themselves politically into states. Above all, this meant confronting the question of sovereignty, which Burgess defined as "original, absolute, unlimited, universal power over the individual subject and over all associations of subjects."[126] Burgess understood that so sweeping a grant of power was sure to set off alarms for Americans, who, although unfamiliar with German state theory, would immediately see the specter of Hobbes's Leviathan looming over his argument. But he insisted that because the modern state embodied the unified will of the nation, united in a shared understanding of right and wrong, especially about liberty, it had little inclination to infringe upon the rights of its citizens. Indeed, he went so far as to insist that sovereignty was "not only not inimical to individual liberty and individual rights, but it is their only solid foundation and guaranty."[127] In support of his statement, he argued that it was in fact the failure of the United States in 1787 to solve the problem of sovereignty that led to the Civil War.[128]

At the same time, Burgess (now sounding more like Rousseau) was at pains to correct those German theorists who failed to distinguish between the state, as the political embodiment of the unified nation, and the government, which was merely the agent of the state. Burgess readily admitted that the government might encroach upon the liberties of the people (which is why, despite his infatuation with both German state theory and Prussian power, he defended the separation of powers, modern federalism, and the notion of limited government).[129] But if the government did threaten the liberties of the people, he was confident that the sovereign state would come to the rescue. Americans, he thought, could more readily grasp the distinction between state and government because public law was more highly developed there than in the European states. The signal triumph of the United States was that it was restrained by a written constitution, enforceable in the courts.[130] So far, so good, but Burgess then went on to add that in back of the Constitution was the sovereign state, rather than the looser and more familiar notion of the sovereign people, a confusion that Roosevelt, developing his theory of "inherent powers," would later echo.

Even stranger to American ears was his insistence that the state was not only the source of government, but also of liberty. Burgess recognized that the notion of the state as the source of all liberty flew in the face of the founders' dedication to natural rights, but he did not regard this as a serious problem and thought that when presented with scientific evidence to the contrary, Americans, at least the educated classes, would at last give up their "cherished" principle. In keeping with his historical approach, Burgess was willing to grant (as Sumner was) that the doctrine had served a "practical" role in mobilizing the people against tyrannical states that disregarded the "ethical feelings of the nation." But now that the state had become democratic, the natural rights doctrine could only be seen as "unscientific, erroneous and harmful." Or, as he put it in an earlier essay in the *Political Science Quarterly*, "every student of political and legal science should divest himself, at the outset of this pernicious doctrine of natural rights."[131]

The doctrine of natural rights was "unscientific" and "erroneous" because it was based on a mistaken understanding of human nature. It assumed that liberty belonged to the individual as a human being, when in fact men became free only *after* they established a state. Until then, natural rights were nothing more than the "mere ideas" of a particular people about what should be free from government control. Such rights had no legal force; nor was there anything timeless or universal about them. Liberty meant different things to different people, and even to the same people at different stages of civilization. Strictly speaking, rights only became "truly rights" when the state was able to enforce them, and it was the state that determined what they were.[132] Roosevelt, of course, would never come out and flatly deny the truth of natural rights, but his insistence in New Nationalism that the state could determine the extent of property rights, and later, that the rights announced in the Declaration should be revised in light of changing historical circumstances, owed much to the wholesale attack on natural rights that he learned at Harvard and Columbia.

The doctrine of natural rights was also "harmful" and "pernicious" because it inflamed the most destructive political passions. If the state did not clearly establish the limits of individual freedom, then individuals would interpret their rights for themselves, and anarchy would follow, as the French Revolutionaries clearly demonstrated. In this assessment, too,

Roosevelt seemed to be channeling his old professor. Speaking in Berlin in 1910, the former president would describe the passions that so often accompanied natural rights as "rancorous and evil."

Moreover, the idea of natural rights served as a brake on the power of the state and prevented it from achieving its highest ends. For over and above its police functions, the state was "a moral conception of the highest order," representing the shared understanding of the nation regarding right and wrong at a particular historical moment.[133] Here again, Roosevelt would echo the sentiments of his teacher, when in his high progressive phase he insisted on pursuing not merely "legal justice," but "ethical justice," a variation on Hegel's ideal of the "ethical state."

Against the ahistorical and unscientific approach of the natural rights school, Burgess insisted that the state was best understood as the "product of the progressive revelation of the human reason in history."[134] Accordingly, he rejected the social compact theorists' account of its origins. The trouble with this view (as Hegel had argued) was that it presupposed a highly developed political life in which the idea of the state was already present in the minds of men, along with a disposition to obey the law. But these conditions existed only *after* the state had passed through several stages of development. America did not suddenly become a nation-state in 1776, or even in 1789; historical forces had been preparing that ground for over a century. In *The Winning of the West*, Roosevelt would go even farther than his Columbia professor, asserting that the forces leading up to the American Revolution had been building for the past three centuries. The social compact theory announced in the Declaration would play second fiddle to the "unconscious" race memory of the "folk moot."

Turning from the origins of the state to its ends, Burgess argued that the state had three ends, which emerged historically in successive order. The first was to give the government sufficient power to guard against internal and external dangers while at the same time securing individual liberty. Although Burgess (this time in contrast to Hegel) viewed America as the most advanced of the four states in protecting liberty, he nevertheless emphasized the imperfections of the original constitutional design. Especially after 1815, the idea that America was a confederacy of sovereign states gained force, with the states claiming primary responsibility for protecting individual liberty. That experiment ended in dismal failure. "If the political history of the United States from 1790 to 1860 taught anything, it was this: That the so-called States were not sufficient guarantors, to say the least, of individual liberty, and that the United States government must be authorized to change its position from a passive non-infringer of individual liberty to an active defender of the same against the tyranny of the commonwealths themselves." The Civil War showed decisively that something was wrong with the original Constitution, though the amendment process allowed Americans to correct their initial error by strengthening the powers of the national government.[135] The nationalist in Roosevelt heartily assented.

In the interests of genuine reconciliation, Burgess, the Southern Whig, urged the North to put aside further thoughts of retribution. Seen from a "scientific" (i.e., historicist) perspective, neither side was to blame. Both the North and the South were simply working out "half-consciously" their solutions to the problem of sovereignty, and trying to square it with individual liberty. To punish southern leaders would mean they were personally responsible, when in fact they were simply caught up in the process of political development. Past errors were not crimes or wrongs, but imperfections, which got worked out in history as human reason unfolded.[136] Roosevelt, too, would take a conciliatory approach toward the South, though given his mother's southern roots and the fact that two of his Bulloch uncles had fought on the Confederate side, Burgess simply provided the rationale for what he was already disposed to believe.

Once the state had accomplished its first end, it could then move on to the second, which was the perfection of its national genius through the development of individual liberty. Adopting the language of Hegel, though not his meaning, Burgess argued that liberty had both a negative and a positive aspect. Negative liberty referred to immunities or constitutional safeguards against encroachments by the federal or state governments; it was the public law side of liberty. Positive liberty referred to those rights that the state granted to the individual and which it empowered the government to protect against encroachments by others; it was the private law side of liberty.[137] And this is where Burgess, following the example of von Gniest, attempted to graft Hegelian principles onto the Constitution. Starting with Hegel's claim that the state had a higher ethical purpose, Burgess then shifted the focus back to the individual. The signal triumph of the modern state was that it carved out an area in which the individual was free to exercise his liberty for his own highest development and the highest development of his society and state. (And although this was consistent with Hegel's political philosophy, the Framers of the Constitution had not conceived of the state in higher "ethical" terms.) What is more, Burgess expected that as the nation advanced in civilization, the tendency would be for the state to expand the sphere of private rights (as it did with the ratification of the Thirteenth and Fourteenth Amendments, as well as the Civil Rights Act of 1866).[138] By permitting individuals to work in concert for certain common goals, and even assisting them in their projects so that they did not have to rely on government, the State would enable them to "accomplish the more spiritual as well as material ends of civilization." It was, Burgess thought, characteristic of the modern state to work through both government and liberty to achieve its highest spiritual and political aims.[139]

Only when the national genius of the different states had been "developed and perfected and made objective in customs, laws, and institutions," could the state then advance to its ultimate and universal end, which Burgess grandly described as "the perfection of humanity; the civilization of the world; the perfect development of human reason, and its attainment to universal command over individualism; the apotheosis of man. This end is wholly spiritual; and in it, mankind, as spirit, triumphs over all fleshly weakness, error, and sin." Leaving no doubt about the provenance of this argument, Burgess immediately added, "This is what Hegel meant by his doctrine that morality (*Sittlichkeit*) is the end of the state."[140] It was surely no accident that Roosevelt, in his speech at the University of Berlin in 1910, would hold out his "dream" in almost identical language, though it was impossible to reconcile such a vision with the political thought of the Framers.

WHEN THEORY MEETS PRACTICE

Shortly after Roosevelt succeeded to the presidency in 1901, he received a letter of congratulations from his old law school professor in which Burgess expressed his pride in Roosevelt's "great career," adding shamelessly that he hoped that he had "played some little part" in forming the mind and character of so admirable a world figure. For good measure, he sent along his "little book" on *The Civil War and the Constitution* and offered his support to the administration "if ever wanted." Responding the next day to Burgess's overture, the president wrote: "The simple truth is that your teaching was one of the formative influences in my life. You impressed me more than you will ever know."[141] Doubtless Roosevelt was being polite, for later in his presidency he confided to a friend that "some" of Burgess's historical work was "bright and suggestive, but much of it . . . hopelessly wrongheaded."[142] Yet these two statements are not as far apart as they may at first appear. For at one point or another in his long political career, Roosevelt did echo many of Burgess's arguments. And although most of these points of convergence occurred before 1898, Roosevelt's dream of an "ethical state," outlined in Berlin in 1910, was surprisingly similar to the end-state Burgess had sketched in his textbook.

At the same time, however, Burgess used German state theory in ways that were inimical to the progressive program, which would have made it impossible for Roosevelt, when he thought about Burgess's classes later on, to regard him as a mentor. Whereas progressives embraced the Hegelian idea of the "ethical state," they could never agree to limit the powers of government, as Burgess insisted upon doing.[143] Indeed, the progressives wished to use the power of an expanded national government to create a disinterested bureaucracy that would regulate and redistribute private property in the name of social justice. Burgess, too, welcomed the Civil War Amendments that increased the power of the national government over the states, but in contrast to the progressives, he sought to use the Due Process Clause of the Fourteenth Amendment to protect the rights of property against what he considered undue interference from the state legislatures.

In his criticism of the *Slaughterhouse Cases* (1873), one of the earliest attempts by the Supreme Court to interpret the Fourteenth Amendment, Burgess argued that the Court had shown an "extravagant" deference to the state's police powers at the expense of property rights (or what he considered positive liberty). Although he acknowledged that Louisiana had the right to make laws regulating the health, safety, and morals of its citizens, he insisted that this power was not unlimited and should not be allowed to interfere with what he thought was a federal common law right to pursue a legitimate occupation. When the Court rejected the argument that the Fourteenth Amendment protected the butchers' right to sustain their lives through their labor, Burgess thundered that it effectively "threw away the gains made by appeal to arms."[144] Ironically, Burgess used German state theory, suitably modified to fit American circumstances, to defend the classical liberal order that Roosevelt and his Progressive allies would attack.[145]

A second reason why Roosevelt might not have thought much about the professor's influence in his later life is that, although Burgess had early on argued that the Teutonic races had a duty to impose civilization on the less developed parts of the world, he bitterly opposed the Spanish-American War and used the *Political Science Quarterly* to rally opposition against it. On a personal level, the war put paid to his Civil War vow to find a rational solution to political problems, while on a national level, it proved "disastrous to American political civilization." In arguments similar to those of William Graham Sumner,[146] Burgess protested that America would have to exercise despotic rule over its newly acquired colonies, and this would eventually undermine the liberties of its citizens at home. Only the special interests would profit. Moreover, once started down the road to imperialism, it would be impossible to turn back. Americans would become a different people, no longer capable of defending their liberty and independence.[147]

In his *Reminiscences,* published in 1934, after World War I had shattered his dreams of a grand Teutonic coalition and dashed his academic ambitions,[148] Burgess gave full vent to his fury, singling out his former student for special criticism. Roosevelt was merely the most visible representative of "a large class of ambitious men thirsting for glory and the chance of political advancement through the fortunes of war." He was not, in Burgess's estimation, "a great man," and nothing he did during the war altered that view. "As lieutenant colonel and then as colonel of the 'Rough Riders,' he bustled around noisily, even boisterously, and finally in a little battle which we old soldiers of the Civil War considered only a skirmish, he won the laurel crown which made him governor of New York and then President of the United States. It was a small thing for such mighty results."[149] But while Roosevelt lived, and especially after he became president, Burgess made a great effort to ingratiate himself with his former student. Yet despite his overtures, the two no longer saw eye-to-eye on questions of practical politics.

A final and amusing incident, omitted from Burgess's memoirs, suggests a third reason why TR no longer thought so highly of his former professor. With the backing of Columbia's president and Roosevelt's old law school classmate, Nicholas Murray Butler, Columbia in 1906 endowed the Theodore Roosevelt Professorship at the University of Berlin and named Burgess as its first occupant. The chair fulfilled Burgess's longtime ambition to establish an exchange program between these two branches of the Teutonic peoples. In his Inaugural Address, delivered on Roosevelt's birthday, Burgess emphasized that the holder of the chair would not be constrained by diplomatic niceties from discussing freely and fully, i.e., "scientifically," all aspects of American politics, without fear of "arousing the hostility of the Union." To illustrate this principle, he thought that America's self-appointed ambassador of "peace and culture" might explore the question of whether the Monroe Doctrine had outlived its usefulness. Exercising this freedom of speech, he then suggested that America no longer had an interest in keeping Europeans out but, on the contrary, should now welcome the "large Teutonic immigration into South America, so that the colonization of that giant continent through people capable of a high culture would be assured."[150]

Coming on the heels of the "Roosevelt Corollary" to the Monroe Doctrine (1904), in which the United States announced its intention to intervene militarily in South American affairs to keep the Europeans from doing so, Burgess's remarks caused quite a diplomatic stir. His comments were widely covered in the American press, and Roosevelt lost no time in conveying his displeasure to the freelance cultural ambassador. After several abject apologies from Burgess, the president advised him simply to drop the matter.[151] Although the Theodore Roosevelt Professor had volunteered to place his political science at the service of his country, the president made it clear that he had no interest in the offer. This incident alone was enough to sour Roosevelt on his former professor, though if Roosevelt had followed his scholarly writings in defense of substantive due process and opposing the Spanish-American War, he would have had other reasons to consider him a "political opponent" as well.[152]

Although Burgess shared with the progressives a deep admiration for German theory and practice that Roosevelt found attractive, his peculiar combination of German idealism in the service of individual liberty, together with his visceral aversion to the use of force—at least of American force—and his love for all things German even at the expense of America's *national* interest, meant that Burgess's influence, however "formative" and "suggestive," would not be decisive as Roosevelt searched, as he would later insist all great statesmen must, for a theory to undergird his progressive politics. But progressivism was off in Roosevelt's future. For the moment, and for longer than he wanted to remember, he would draw heavily on what he had learned at Harvard and Columbia.

2. History Lessons: Roosevelt's America

Theodore Roosevelt took only the one required history course at Harvard, and in his senior year, his Forensics professor had embarrassed him in front of the class by telling him that he could not write. Certainly, it was true that he had not been able to make much headway on assignments such as "the character of the Gracchi." But on his own he had begun to develop "a serious interest" in "the frigate and sloop actions between the American and British sea-tigers in 1812,"[1] sketching out several chapters before leaving Cambridge, and completing the project while a law student at Columbia. Published in 1882, when Roosevelt was just twenty-three, *The Naval War of 1812* was an immediate success, winning praise on both sides of the Atlantic for its accuracy, thoroughness, and impartiality.

Remarkably, for one so young and lacking in formal training, Roosevelt displayed an impressive grasp of the responsibilities of the historian. Unlike the standard accounts on both sides, which were prejudiced in favor of their country, Roosevelt vowed to examine the evidence impartially in order to arrive at "the exact truth."[2] In so doing, he would avoid the deliberate deceptions and false pride that marred the existing studies, while avoiding the dull statistical analyses that made some of the more reliable accounts useless to the general reader. Whether by accident or design, he would emulate Tacitus, telling the story *sine ira et studio*, neither magnifying the failings of the British, nor exaggerating the virtues of his countrymen.

To be impartial, however, did not mean that he would refrain from judgment, especially where the Americans were concerned. "History has not yet done justice to the ludicrous and painful folly and stupidity of which the government founded by Jefferson, and carried on by Madison, was guilty, both in its preparations for, and in its way of carrying on this war."[3] In his concluding chapter on the Battle of New Orleans, the only land combat he discussed, Roosevelt was scathing. Jefferson's election in 1800 had seen the country's ability to maintain order at home and defend her honor abroad steadily dwindle. "Twelve years' nerveless reign of Doctrinaire Democracy had left us impotent for attack and almost as feeble for defense." In Roosevelt's judgment, Jefferson was "perhaps the most incapable executive that ever filled the presidential chair." Certainly, he was supremely unqualified "to guide the State with honor and safety through the stormy times that marked the opening of the present century."[4]

Jefferson had grand theories, one of which was that he could avoid war by clamping a trade embargo on Britain; but he had so weakened the navy that he was unable to carry out this policy successfully. All he managed to do was antagonize Britain, making war inevitable. Roosevelt did not blame Jefferson and his party for the war, which in his view was "eminently justifiable,"[5] but rather for their indecision, weakness, and incompetence. "Without the prudence to avoid war or the forethought to prepare for it, the Administration drifted helplessly into a conflict in which only the navy prepared by the Federalists twelve years before, and weakened rather than strengthened during the intervening time, saved us from complete and shameful defeat."[6]

Another misguided idea of Jefferson's was that republican governments should rely on a citizen militia rather than a regular army for their land defense. The Battle of New Orleans, won by Andrew Jackson after the war had officially ended, proved that the militia "*could* fight superbly." Unfortunately, the other battles during the war showed that they generally "*would not* fight at all," but "ran like sheep whenever brought into the field."[7] Roosevelt could not forgive Jefferson for holding the country hostage to his visionary theories and putting in jeopardy America's westward expansion. If, as he would later write, the best kind of statesman was the man who combined theory and practice, the worst was the man who had nothing but theories and no will to back them up. And yet, Roosevelt lamented, Jefferson's views and theories had exercised a "profound influence on our national life."[8]

Roosevelt's interest in the War of 1812 was not merely antiquarian, however. Although he thrilled to the story of how the fledgling American navy was able to prevail against the colossus of the sea, the future Secretary of the Navy saw useful lessons for America in 1882. For despite the "criminal folly" of Jefferson and Madison, the United States then possessed a small but excellent fleet. Now, the navy was "the exact reverse" of what it had been in 1812. By studying that period of American history when "our navy stood at the highest pitch of its fame," Roosevelt hoped to awaken his countrymen to the present danger of relying on a navy "composed partly of antiquated hulks and partly of new vessels rather more worthless than the old."[9] Northerners especially, he would later insist, should not be lulled into a false sense of security by their recent victory over the South.[10] In any serious naval encounter, American ships would be found wanting, even though her personnel remained excellent. Rather than waste money maintaining the current fleet, the future assistant secretary of the navy recommended that the United States construct "half a dozen ships on the most effective model."[11] As an emerging industrial nation spanning two oceans, America must begin to build a first-class navy, if not in size, at least in quality. Here, Roosevelt pointed to one other development that strengthened the case for a naval buildup: America had less need of a regular army now than it did in 1812. Spanish power had declined, and British forces in Canada no longer posed a threat to American interests. The Indian tribes that had once terrorized white settlers were "broken and scattered," and Mexico was weak.[12] With no serious ground threat, America must now focus its attention on the sea.

Still, Roosevelt's understanding of history was not simply utilitarian or policy-driven, either. In focusing on the great naval battles that took place both on the ocean and on the inland lakes, he reached toward the monumental, holding up for future generations models to emulate. Many years later, addressing the American Historical Association, to which he had been elected president, Roosevelt would insist that there would always be a place for the study of the heroic.[13] Although modern historians might properly investigate the living conditions of ordinary men and women, they should not go to the extreme of dismissing war and greatness as proper subjects of historical inquiry, provided they were "scientific," and made use of all the available facts. Using charts, tables, and sketches, *The Naval War of 1812* paid homage to the courage and skill of the great captains on both sides of the conflict. Moreover, for one who only two years earlier had thrashed about trying to explain "the character of the Gracchi," Roosevelt here showed considerable insight into human nature, at one point observing that "courage is only one of the many elements which go to make up the character of a first-rate commander; something more than bravery is needed before a leader can really be called great."[14]

Yet for all its insights, the narrative was not without its peculiarities. Drawing on what he had learned at Harvard and Columbia, Roosevelt insisted that the lessons of the war could not be understood unless the reader kept in mind the common racial characteristics of the two combatants. English blood was just as "pure" along the New England coast as it was in Britain, and to the extent that America had received an infusion of new blood, it had come from the same sources in roughly the same proportions as had mixed with the original English stock. Both the combatants were descended from the Dutch, and following Freeman, "nearer to the true old English of Alfred and Harold than are, for example, the thoroughly Anglicized Welsh of Cornwall," making the contest "practically a civil war."[15]

Why all this talk of race and blood was crucial for understanding the outcome of the war was unclear, since Roosevelt concluded that what gave America the advantage was her politics. Owing to her "freer" republican institutions, Americans were more intelligent and self-reliant and showed better judgment than their English cousins.[16] Nevertheless, this tendency to examine politics in terms of race, blood, and stock, in other words, to dwell on those characteristics over which a people had little or no control, would, if anything, become even stronger in Roosevelt's later historical writings.

Over the next decade or so, while serving in the New York legislature, running (unsuccessfully) for mayor of New York City, moving to Washington to serve on the Civil Service Commission, and then back to New York as Police Commissioner, he would churn out an impressive number of historical studies, including two early biographies of Americans and a later study of Oliver Cromwell; a book of hero tales (with Henry Cabot Lodge) aimed at providing American youth with models of patriotism, courage, and self-sacrifice; a history of New York; and his six-volume *Winning of the West*. Taken as a whole, the histories lay bare the grounds of TR's vigorous Americanism, making clear the sometimes subtle but always significant ways in which the young Roosevelt was at odds with the political principles of the men he claimed most to admire.

BIOGRAPHY AND "AUTOBIOGRAPHY":
THOMAS HART BENTON AND *GOUVERNEUR MORRIS*

On the strength of *The Naval War of 1812*, which had run through three editions in one year, Roosevelt was commissioned to prepare a biography of the Missouri senator Thomas Hart Benton (1782–1858) for the prestigious American Statesmen Series at Houghton Mifflin. Unlike *The Naval War*, which Roosevelt spent two years laboriously researching, and which he later confessed was "so dry" that it made a dictionary seem like "light reading," his first biography was dashed off in five action-packed months while cow punching in the Dakota Badlands in the spring of 1886. Roosevelt had fled to the West in 1884 after the deaths of his mother and young wife on the same day, shuttling back and forth between his cattle ranch in Medora and New York and attempting to overcome his grief through sheer physical activity of a particularly manly sort. This latest chapter in his life seemed to make him the perfect candidate to write the biography of the western senator, but there were important differences between *The Naval War* and *Benton*.

In a revealing letter written to Henry Cabot Lodge, who had contributed several volumes to the American Statesmen Series and had helped get him the commission, Theodore displayed a rather more cavalier attitude toward the writing of history than in the carefully documented *Naval War of 1812*. After four months of writing, Roosevelt now reported that he had almost completed Benton, but since books were scarce on the range, he had taken a different tack, "mainly evolving him from my inner consciousness." He knew nothing of Benton's life after he left the Senate in 1850, not even the date of his death. He had no idea what the issues were when Benton ran for Congress, or why he was defeated. Nor did he know anything about his failed run for the Missouri governorship. Adopting a jocular tone, Roosevelt described himself as a "timid man," but also "on occasions, by choice a truthful man," who preferred "to have some foundation of fact, no matter how slender on which to build the airy and arabesque superstructure of my fancy," especially since he was "writing a history." If it was not too much trouble, could Lodge, who was now the president of the *Boston Advertiser,* hire one of his minions, at Roosevelt's expense, "of course," to research these details, since the young historian was reluctant to "invent all of the work of his later years." Still, Roosevelt hated to impose on his friend and told him not to bother if it would be too much trouble.[17] Lodge obliged, and TR completed the project that summer, though after he sent the manuscript off, he confessed that he "had been troubled with dreadful misgivings."[18]

Light on facts, Roosevelt's first biographical study is of interest chiefly because it shows how Roosevelt here used history less to get at "the exact truth" than to advance his own pet theories and political views. In another earlier letter to Lodge, Roosevelt indicated that he had started writing and had "some good ideas in the first chapter," but he worried they were not "worked up properly."[19] One "good idea" perhaps, plucked straight from Freeman, was that the method of settlement closely resembled "the tribe movements of the Germanic peoples in time past." In particular, Roosevelt saw certain similarities between the frontiersmen and "the Jutish and Low Dutch sea-thieves on the coast of Britain," which he would then weave through the later chapters.[20]

Possibly another "good idea" floated in the first chapter was the distinctive influence of the West on the American character. Although Missouri was largely settled by southerners, these frontiersmen had evolved into "a peculiar and characteristically American type." Of necessity, they were a "warlike race," possessed of great virtues and equally strong vices. They loved their country with a fierce, though "perhaps ignorant" devotion, and, being "a race of masterful spirit," considered the lands bordering the United States as territory that should one day belong to them or their children. "Courage, loyalty, truth, and patriotism" were the virtues they prized above all others. At the same time, they were neither thrifty nor industrious and tended to disregard both their financial obligations and the rights of others. Their character, the distinctive western character, was "stern, rude, and hard, like the lives they led"; indeed, there was something almost savage about these frontiersmen.[21]

Roosevelt was not altogether wrong to have "misgivings" about the project, since the "good ideas" he tossed into the first chapter did not quite cohere. For if the westerners were in fact the descendents of the Teutonic raiders, then there was nothing distinctive about the western character. Conversely, if the frontier fundamentally shaped the American character then the Teutonic "germ theory" made little sense. Moreover, if the frontier tended to bring out the savage in civilized men (rather than make them more democratic as Frederick Jackson Turner would later argue), then, as John Jay had warned, there might be something deeply problematic about westward expansion.[22]

Of these possible explanations, Roosevelt seemed to place greater emphasis on the effect of the frontier. Benton was "the most typical representative" of the "Western and ultra-American" spirit that itself was "a most healthy sign of the virile strength of a young community." Above all, he stood for Manifest Destiny, which, "reduced to its simplest terms, was: that it was our manifest destiny to swallow up the land of all adjoining nations who were too weak to with stand us." This included the territories of the original Indian inhabitants, the Spanish lands to the west and southwest, and the British possessions to the north. It would also have included French Louisiana, if that territory had not already been obtained through purchase. Roosevelt conceded that at the root of this doctrine was a "belligerent, indeed piratical, way of looking at territory," but he embraced it just the same. Unlike the effete northeasterners, whose commercial policies had turned them into a "timid bourgeoisie," oriented more toward Europe than the West, the Missouri statesman understood the significance of territorial expansion for national greatness.[23]

Manifest Destiny meant first that the frontiersman, in his relentless drive forward, would continue to encroach upon Indian lands. As a westerner, Benton took "the frontier view of the Indian question," introducing into the

Senate measures to remove the southern and western Indian tribes beyond the immediate reach of the white man. Benton tried to carry out this policy "kindly and humanely," but inevitably it led to "much injustice and wrong." Still, Roosevelt was convinced that, whatever its shortcomings, the western approach was preferable to the "so-called humanitarian or Eastern view." The Indians occupied more than 60 million acres of desirable territory and harried the white men who coveted their lands. It was "out of the question" to let them remain where they were, since these sovereign tribes did not come under the jurisdiction of the states where they lived. Nor could they be brought up to the level of the westerners' civilization quickly enough to accommodate themselves to their changed circumstances. Even the Cherokees, the most civilized of the tribes, could not be allowed to remain. Although it was "a cruel grief and wrong to take them away from their homes," the only "alternative" was gradually to accord them the rights of state citizenship in exchange for their lands. But the times were not then ripe for such assimilation and, Roosevelt added, unfortunately, still were not.[24]

Warming to his subject, the young historian then went on to condemn as "maudlin nonsense" protests that the white men had robbed the Indians of their land, citing Benton's arguments that the United States had paid the Indians handsomely.[25] Indeed, Roosevelt seemed to go farther: even though the United States purchased the land from them, the "simple truth" was that the Indians had "no possible title to most of the lands we took, not even that of occupancy, and at the most were in possession merely by virtue of having butchered the previous occupants."[26] Here, Roosevelt was clearly echoing Burgess's argument that the savages had no legal or moral rights that the civilized nations, pursuing their world-historic mission, were bound to respect. It was "petty morality indeed" for masterful Teutonic peoples to enter into contracts for the purpose of obtaining Indian lands.[27] Although Roosevelt was at least willing to grant that Benton's support for the removal of the Indians was harsh and caused "a certain amount of temporary suffering," he nevertheless seemed satisfied that this policy was "more just and merciful" toward the Indians than the utopian schemes put forward by the "sentimental philanthropists."[28] Here, too, Roosevelt followed Burgess, who decried the "weak sentimentality" that reflexively took the side of the Indians.[29]

Roosevelt's comments suggest that he saw only two alternatives for dealing with the Indians: either a full-throated defense of Manifest Destiny that denied the native tribes any rightful claims to their lands or a "maudlin sentimentality" that had no basis in fact. But this stark choice overlooked a third position held by those American statesmen Roosevelt claimed most to admire. George Washington, who had begun his military career battling the French and Indians on the western frontier and who then faced hostile tribes allied with the British during the Revolutionary War, nevertheless insisted that American policy be guided to the extent possible by certain fixed moral principles. Thus, as John Marshall, another of Roosevelt's heroes, pointed out in his *Life of George Washington,* the first president sought to resolve disputes with the Indians by negotiation, rather than force. Although Marshall noted that Washington's policy was to some extent driven by necessity, since the army was too small to impose settlements by the sword, unlike the western position Roosevelt defended, Washington also acted out of "real respect for the natives."[30] Over time, as it became clear that the Americans would ultimately prevail, Washington went on to counsel good faith and magnanimity. "A System corresponding with the mild principles of Religion and Philanthropy towards an unenlightened race of Men, whose happiness materially depends on the conduct of the United States, would be as honorable to the national character as conformable to the dictates of sound policy."[31] And John Marshall himself, who as chief justice of the United States wrote three opinions on the Indian cases in the 1830s, also entreated Americans to exercise "humanity and justice" when dealing with "a helpless people" who depended on the "magnanimity and justice" of the white man for his continued existence. Having made a careful study of these arguments, Ralph Lerner has concluded, "It is to the enduring credit of the new national government that its leading figures concerned with Indian affairs chose to regard themselves as charged with delicate moral responsibilities."[32]

That the federal government in the early years of the republic was too weak to carry out this policy in the face of opposition from both the states and the frontiersmen does not, however, detract from the nobility of these principles. For Washington, acutely aware of the precedents he was laying down, established a standard by which future administrations, more powerful than his, might be judged. Yet this is what Roosevelt, who admired Washington and Marshall, but followed Burgess, failed to see. In lumping these statesmen's calls for magnanimity and justice together with sentimental Eastern humanitarianism of the worst kind, Roosevelt traduced the very ideals to which these men had pledged their "sacred honor" and on which the American republic was founded.

Turning his attention to the Southwest, Roosevelt cast the struggle between the English-speaking settlers and the Mexicans in stark Darwinian terms. It was both inevitable and desirable that these raw, pushing, brawling westerners animated by "bitter race prejudices" should covet the lands occupied by peoples too weak to resist. In Texas, the Mexicans proved no match for the frontiersmen who, "flushed with the pride of strength and self-confidence," were "utterly careless of the rights of others, looking upon the possessions of all weaker races as simply their natural prey." The Mexicans were absolutely unfit to govern themselves, much less rule over the "warlike, reckless, and overbearing" Texans. Whatever international morality in the abstract might dictate, it was "out of the question" that the Texans should continue to "submit to the mastery of the weaker race, which they were supplanting."[33]

Dilating on this last point, Roosevelt maintained that the standards of "highly civilized nations" could not be applied on the frontier. In saying this, he did not mean that allowances had to be made for necessity, or that the moral principles set forth in the Declaration should be applied prudently as circumstances permitted. Rather, Roosevelt seemed to be rejecting the idea that "abstract right" should ever govern American policy, substituting for it the view that justice was relative to the stage of historical development. This was a contest between two very different races, in which Americans like Sam Houston had not advanced beyond the "old-world Viking"[34] stage of development a thousand years ago and the Mexicans were even further behind. History alone provided the standard by which the two races should be judged; the only comparison was with how other peoples had acted at similar stages of development. In Roosevelt's view, "the conquest of Texas should properly be classed with the conquests like those of the Norse sea-rovers" and judged accordingly rather than by the standards of the civilized world.[35]

As a westerner, Benton's vision of Manifest Destiny went beyond conquering the more backward or weaker races and laying claim to their lands. Where American expansion was concerned, the Democratic senator from Missouri yielded to no one, including the "civilized" British. Roosevelt called Benton's patriotism "violent and aggressive" but thought it "more than justified by the destiny of the great Republic; and it would have been well for all America if we had insisted even more than we did upon the extension northward of our boundaries." Going even beyond Benton, Roosevelt thundered, "No foot of soil to which we had any title in the Northwest should have been given up; we were the people who could use it best, and we ought to have taken it all."[36]

In this case, however, his rationale was different. The extension northward of the American boundary into what is now western Canada was at least as much for the sake of the settlers, who were, after all, a branch of the English-speaking people, as it was for America's national greatness. As part of the United States, Columbia, Saskatchewan, and Manitoba would attain a greater dignity and grandeur than they could "ever hope to reach either as independent communities or as provincial dependents of a foreign power that treats them with a kindly tolerance somewhat akin to contemptuous indifference." And, going well beyond what the Monroe Doctrine announced, Roosevelt insisted that it was not in the interest of the "western hemisphere" that European nations exercise any colonial dominion over extensive territory between the two oceans. "By right we should have given ourselves the benefit of every doubt in all territorial questions, and have shown ourselves ready to make prompt appeal to the sword whenever it became necessary in the last resort."[37]

Nevertheless, Roosevelt conceded that the time to have acted was before the territories were settled. Rather than compromise with Britain as the Whigs proposed, and the Ashburton Treaty (negotiated by that northeasterner Daniel Webster) ratified, America should have claimed all the lands in the Oregon Territory and (as Machiavelli advised in *The Prince*) sent armed citizens to occupy them. Faced with a fait accompli, the British would have been in no position to resist, and the United States could have claimed the entire Northwest as its prize. Roosevelt made no secret of his disappointment that national policy for this region was shaped largely by the wealthy and educated classes of the Northeast who were "more cautious and timid" when it came to the prospect of foreign wars and had "never felt much of the spirit which made the West stretch out impatiently for new lands."[38]

In defending Manifest Destiny, Roosevelt was at great pains to refute the argument that American expansion was driven principally by slavery. He was willing to concede that this was the position of southern leaders such as John C. Calhoun but westerners on both sides of the slavery debate acted out of a different motive: "greed for the conquest of new lands." The men of the West sincerely believed they were "created the heirs of the earth," or at least of North America, and were prepared to risk any danger to lay claim to their "heritage."[39] Benton himself, Roosevelt thought, seemed to lend support to this view. A slaveholder, the Missourian nevertheless opposed its spread, initially speaking out against the Mexican War and then later refusing to back the Compromise of 1850 because it held the admission of California as a free state hostage to the politics of slavery. For western statesmen such as Benton, animated by a grand vision of a continental America, Manifest Destiny had little or nothing to do with slavery. And with the benefit of hindsight, Roosevelt could affirm this view, minimizing the threat that southern, pro-slavery expansionists posed to the preservation of republican self-government.

When he began the Benton biography, Roosevelt had no idea that the Missourian's outspoken opposition to the spread of slavery would in the end cost him his Senate seat, and then, after one term, his House seat, followed by his failed run for governor. But apparently with the help of Lodge's researcher, Roosevelt was able to conclude the biography by hailing his speech in opposition to the Kansas-Nebraska Act as one of the "best and greatest he ever made"[40] and praising him for his stand against *Dred Scott.* For a slaveholding Democrat, Benton's views on slavery closely tracked those of Lincoln, whom Roosevelt in this biography lauded as "the greatest man of the nineteenth century."[41]

Like Benton, and his hero, Abraham Lincoln, Roosevelt hated slavery, but ironically the arguments he used to defend Manifest Destiny, resting on assumptions of racial superiority and Darwinian survival of the fittest, bear a striking resemblance to the arguments advanced by the supporters of slavery. For if the westerners, as Roosevelt described them, viewed Mexicans as a weaker race and thought that they had a "right" to treat their possessions as "natural prey," what would prevent them from throwing their lot in with those southerners who used precisely such arguments to justify the expansion of slavery into Mexico and beyond to enslave those races they considered inferior? Once again, Roosevelt failed to see the contradiction between the racialist/Darwinian rhetoric he employed and the principles of the men he most admired.

Aside from Roosevelt's vigorous defense of Manifest Destiny, *Thomas Hart Benton* is most notable as a barometer for Roosevelt's own political views. Although Roosevelt had backed the Democratic presidential candidate while a senior at Harvard, he had made the fateful decision to throw his lot in with the Republicans in the 1884 election, refusing to jump ship with the mugwumps in support of the Democratic candidate, Grover Cleveland. Accordingly, when Roosevelt declared that "a healthy party spirit is a prerequisite to the performance of effective work in American political life," he was not only criticizing John Quincy Adams for his excessive nonpartisanship, but also praising himself for sticking with the Republican Party.[42] At the same time, Roosevelt again showed considerable insight and prospectively shed light on his own motives in 1912 when he observed of Calhoun that he "seceded from his party, and was sore with disappointed ambition."[43]

As a loyal Republican, Roosevelt was also forced to reconsider his position on the tariff. In a nod to his Harvard professors, he observed that "political economists have pretty generally agreed that protection is vicious in theory and harmful in practice," but in fact, he now regarded the tariff as "purely a business matter" that should be "decided solely on grounds of expediency," a position he would reiterate while president. In a preview of his later position, he now maintained that the question of whether to impose a protective tariff was "open," but if one were adopted, the duties should be "certain and steady."[44] He also applauded Benton's opposition to Jackson on the spoils system.[45]

Roosevelt also used the Benton biography to interject his own views on citizenship. As he had in his Commencement Day Dissertation, he connected full membership in the political community with a willingness to bear arms and to fight for one's rights, this time taking aim at the Quakers and suggesting that because they were pacifists they were not "entitled to the privilege of living in a free community." He also lashed out at the "emotional" philanthropists of his own day who supported unlimited Chinese immigration. It was, he thundered, "incredible" that anyone of "even moderate intelligence" could not see what a great calamity" it would be for America to have the West coast filled up with "a Mongolian population."[46] As with the Indians, Asians could never be assimilated into American culture, first because of their racial differences, and second because they lagged behind their American counterparts by centuries if not longer.

Finally, *Thomas Hart Benton* is notable for the light that it sheds on the young Roosevelt's understanding of the Constitution and for laying down a marker for how far he would have to travel before he emerged as a full-blown progressive. In the Bull Moose Campaign of 1912, Roosevelt would insist that majority tyranny no longer posed a danger to American democracy, and therefore that constitutional checks on the power of the people, especially by an independent judiciary, were unnecessary. In 1886, by contrast, the historian found much to praise in the original constitutional design.

As a Republican, Roosevelt took a critical view of Andrew Jackson, whom Benton wholeheartedly supported, both in his failed presidential bid in 1824 and in his successful attempt four years later. In the 1824 election, a four-way race in which Jackson won the popular vote but failed to secure a majority of the Electoral College, Benton insisted that the House of Representatives had a duty to make Jackson president because he had won a plurality of the electoral vote. Roosevelt delighted in pointing out that, on matters of states' rights and internal improvements, Benton took a strict constructionist view of the Constitution. But in this case, the Missouri senator thought that the Constitution, which did not mandate how the representatives should vote when the presidential election was thrown into the House, should be disregarded on the "ridiculous" and "absurd" theory that in any conflict between the Constitution and the democratic principle, the people should ultimately rule.[47]

In contrast to Benton, and to the progressive he would later become, the young Roosevelt was far more wary of appeals to raw democratic power. As he saw it, the election of Old Hickory in 1828 was notable chiefly for the class antagonisms it unleashed. For the first time since the Constitution was established, the people had voted to put into high office someone not drawn from the educated, social elite on the theory that such leaders were too far removed from the personal feelings and habits of the great mass of the citizens. Benton actively inflamed this class warfare, fanning hopes of "retrieving the country from the deplorable condition in which the enlightened classes had sunk it." But from Roosevelt's perspective, the election of Andrew Jackson, an "ignorant, headstrong, and straight-forward soldier," gave the lie to the democratic dogma that the people were always right.[48]

Although Roosevelt awarded Jackson and Benton high marks for standing up to Calhoun in the nullification crisis, he thought that the controversy over rechartering the bank brought out the worst in both men. As Roosevelt observed, in a remark that could later be applied equally well to him, an attack on "the money power" was likely to be popular in a democratic republic, "partly on account of the vague fear with which the poorer and more ignorant voters regard a powerful institution whose workings they do not understand and partly on account of the jealousy they feel toward those who are better off than themselves." When earnest men, "convinced of the justice and wisdom of their course," stirred up these passions, they could become powerful weapons in any political battle. But to Roosevelt, Benton's assault on the bank was nothing more than "pure demagogic pyrotechnics."[49]

Roosevelt lost no opportunity to take another swipe at the founder of the Democratic Party, whom he branded a "scholarly, timid, and shifty doctrinaire." Benton's great failing was that he was an "enthusiastic believer in the extreme Jeffersonian doctrinaire views as to the will of the majority being always right, and as to the moral perfection of the average voter." Secure in his conviction that the voice of the people was the voice of God, Benton could not see that the majority had no right to tyrannize over the minority.[50] Although Roosevelt agreed that where the interests of the whole community were concerned, the majority was the best judge, he nevertheless insisted that the distinctive feature of the American constitutional order was its concern with personal independence and individual freedom. So far as possible, the Constitution guaranteed to each man "his right to live as he chooses and to regulate his own private affairs as he wishes, without

being interfered with or tyrannized over by an individual, or by an oligarchic minority, or by a Democratic majority." In contrast to the "democratic
principle" Benton worshipped, the young Roosevelt heartily approved of
the governmental checks that made the constitutional system "eminently
conservative."[51]

From the standpoint of the progressive Roosevelt would later become,
two other of his observations in *Benton* merit mention. First, he took a
dim view of Jackson's idea, later revived by Henry Clay, that "when the
people elect a President they thereby mark with the seal of approval any
and every measure with which that favored mortal or his advisers may
consider themselves identified." The danger with assuming that the people
supported everything the president proposed was that it emboldened him
to push his favorite "hobbies," to which a majority of the people had never
given a second thought. Along the same lines, Roosevelt criticized Benton
for equating the function of the president with that of the Roman tribunes.
Unlike the tribunes of old, the president was not charged with the responsibility of defending the people's interests in the legislature. In the American system, legislators, too, were elected by the people to represent their
interests, something the Missouri senator should have known.[52] And second, Roosevelt lavished praise on Benton for opposing the pension system,
"which in our own day threatens to become a really crying evil." In speaking against the measure, Benton "showed that he would not let himself, by
any specious plea of exceptional suffering or need for charity, be led into
vicious special legislation, sure in the end to bring about the breaking down
of some of the most important principles of government."[53]

The following year, on the strength of favorable reviews of *Thomas Hart
Benton*, Roosevelt, now returned from the West, was commissioned to prepare a biography of Gouverneur Morris for the same American Statesmen
Series. Morris (1752–1816), a native New Yorker who served as Pennsylvania
delegate to the Federal Convention, was by temperament and situation disposed to look at politics from a national perspective. It was he who penned
the lines of the Preamble, emphasizing that Americans, regardless of their
state affiliations, were now one people. As a member of the all-important
Committee of Style, Morris was part of the select working group that produced the final draft of the Constitution. A colorful figure whose peg-leg
and dashing manner made him irresistible to the ladies, Morris later served
as Minister to France from 1792 to 1794, where he engaged in intrigues both
sexual and political. For the next few years, he traveled throughout Europe,
returning to America just in time to become embroiled in presidential politics. With Alexander Hamilton, he backed the doomed effort to dump John

Adams in favor of Charles C. Pinckney of South Carolina, effectively dividing his party and helping the Republicans. In 1800, just as the Federalists were going down to defeat, Morris was selected to fill an unexpired three-year term in the Senate. As senator from New York, he gave his support for the Louisiana Purchase. But owing to Jefferson's incompetence during his second term, Morris gradually became disillusioned with republican government. So disgusted was he with Jefferson and Madison that during the War of 1812 he threw his lot in with the northern secessionists who preferred to break up the Union rather than remain under the control of the feckless Virginia republicans. In short, the life of Gouverneur Morris provided Roosevelt with another opportunity to applaud the friends of a strong national government and to attack their enemies, especially Jefferson, with his characteristic brio.

Roosevelt's appraisal of Morris was mixed. Although he had served his country well at several points, his later embrace of secession had tarnished his reputation. (In *Thomas Hart Benton,* Roosevelt had called secession a "perversion and distortion of the defiant and self-reliant independence of spirit which is one of the chief of the race virtues.")[54] Overall, Roosevelt judged Morris a brilliant but erratic statesman, whose principal claim to greatness lay in his service to the Union at the Federal Convention.[55] But even there, his character was marred by an "incurable cynicism and deep-rooted distrust of mankind," a refusal to credit the more "generous and unselfish passions" that kept him from rising to the ranks of the truly great.[56]

In preparing the biography, Roosevelt had expected to consult Morris's unpublished papers, but when the Morris family denied him access to these materials, he was compelled to fall back on public documents, including James Madison's notes on "Debates."[57] Although this meant that Roosevelt would not have much to go on in sketching Morris's early life, once he arrived at the Federal Convention, the notes would supply a treasure trove of information. Given that all he read in college was Flanders' textbook, Roosevelt found Madison's notes invaluable, since they supplied him with firsthand accounts of the arguments underlying the Constitution. (Nevertheless, the full contours of the executive would not become clear until Hamilton explored them, first in *The Federalist* and then in the "Pacificus" papers.)

Of all his historical studies, *Gouverneur Morris* was the only one to focus on the work of the Framers, and Roosevelt was effusive in his praise. Not only was the charter they produced "the best possible one for America at that time, but it was also, in spite of its shortcomings," most in accord with "the principles of abstract right" and "probably the best that any nation has ever had." It was certainly better than the ancient constitutions produced by a single lawgiver. Although it did not go as far as the most ardent nationalists like Morris wished, its compromises were better suited to the "proud, liberty-loving, and essentially democratic" American character.[58]

At every turn, Morris, who brought with him no sentimental theories or "ideal" political principles, argued in favor of scrapping a loose federal league and replacing it with a strong national government. Roosevelt praised him for his utter lack of regard for states' rights and for his opposition to the Connecticut Compromise that accorded the small states equal representation in the Senate. In one memorable speech before the Convention, Morris cast himself not as a delegate from Pennsylvania, but "as a representative of America—a representative in some degree of the whole human race." Morris, Roosevelt noted approvingly, had no patience with the small-minded demagogues who wished to preserve the political privileges of their states at the expense of the people. A robust nationalist, Roosevelt agreed with Morris that there was no "good argument" to be made for the equal representation of the states, though he conceded that so far it had done no harm.[59]

If Morris was correct in arguing for proportional representation in the Senate, Roosevelt thought he was wrong in trying to give that body a more aristocratic cast. But Morris was convinced that there "never was or would be a civilized society without an aristocracy." Aristocracy tended to grow up in civilized society because the great object of civilization was not liberty, which Morris dryly added, "was sufficiently guaranteed even by savagery," but the protection of property. It was the better part of political wisdom to recognize that aristocracy was inevitable and take the necessary precautions to keep that body from doing mischief. To that end, he put forth a "wild plan," in which an aristocratic upper house, representing property as well as numbers, would act as a check on the democratic lower house, based on population alone. To insure that the Senate would have the personal motives to check the more democratic House, Morris proposed that the senators be drawn from the wealthy "aristocratic" class and serve for life. He had no illusions that the rich were any better than the poor, but thought that at least they could check each other. If, on the other hand, the rich and the poor were thrown together in the legislature, the result would be either oligarchy or democratic despotism.[60]

Although Morris regarded the protection of property as the end of society, he was a staunch antislavery man who opposed southern efforts to increase their representation in the House by counting slaves and spoke out against the slave trade. In a speech before the Convention, Morris declared that, given the choice between doing injustice to the southern states or to human nature, he would rather offend the South. When the measures he supported failed, he at first thought that the North and the South should go their separate ways. He then thought the better of it, realizing that the best hope for the abolition of slavery lay with the establishment and preservation of a firm Union. Roosevelt also approved of Morris's willingness "to call things by their proper names" and have slavery mentioned outright in the Constitution, "instead of being characterized with cowardly circumlocution, as was actually done."[61]

Again, in view of the progressive he would later become, Roosevelt pronounced Morris's views on the judiciary "sound."[62] Both men looked to the courts to defend society against encroachments from the more popular branch of government, "the one from which the danger was to be feared."[63] On the executive, too, Roosevelt considered Morris's proposals "in the main sound." From his early experiences in New York, Morris had long supported a powerful executive, arguing that there was nothing to fear, so long as he was accountable to the people, though he was quick to add that accountability did not mean demagogic obeisance to their every wish. At the Federal Convention, Morris at first proposed that the president hold office during good behavior, but when this failed, backed the plan for indefinite re-eligibility. He led the fight to give the president a qualified veto over legislation, to have him serve as commander-in-chief of the armed forces, and to exercise broad appointment powers. To ensure that the executive, armed with such extensive powers, would remain faithful to the Constitution, Morris relied on the impeachment provision.

Morris's "especial service," however, was his last-minute plan to have the executive chosen by the people through electors they had picked, rather than by the legislature as the Virginia Plan originally provided. Entrusting the legislature with the power to choose the executive would detract from the dignity of the office, Morris feared, opening it up to legislative intrigue and cabal, and giving greater scope to "designing demagogues and tricksters." By contrast, having him chosen indirectly by the people would guarantee that only a man of "continental reputation" would be selected. Morris's proposal, slipped into the final revisions of the Committee of Style, created a presidential rather than a parliamentary system of government in which the executive was not beholden to the legislature in carrying out his constitutional duties.[64]

A far-seeing statesman and patriot, Morris nevertheless had one narrow sectional blind spot. Like many of the eastern Federalists, he was basically satisfied with the present size of the United States, and saw no need for western expansion. At the Convention, Morris sought to convince the delegates to "commit the criminal folly" of keeping the West in permanent subordination to the Atlantic states. To his everlasting discredit, he repeatedly insisted that the compacting states should reserve the right to place conditions on future western states so that they might retain a preponderance of power. He warned of the dangers of power shifting to the most ignorant members of the population, who could be counted on to oppose all sensible proposals.[65]

What Morris failed to see was that, in providing for future states to enter into the Union on an equal footing with the original states, the Constitution avoided the mistake of the Roman Empire, which treated its provinces as subordinates. Article IV, section 3, imposing no qualifications or restrictions on new states, which Morris opposed and about which even *The Federalist* had little to say, proved one of its most significant provisions. Having spent some time in the Dakotas, Roosevelt knew firsthand the importance of an ever-expanding West that stood on a par with the seaboard states. He had tentatively explored this theme in *Benton* and it was to this subject that he would again return in his most ambitious historical study, *The Winning of the West.*

THE WINNING OF THE WEST

At the time when Roosevelt first began to think about his next history project, his political career had stalled. After a promising two-year stint in the New York Assembly, where he had risen to Minority Leader, and serving as a delegate to the Republican Nominating Convention in 1884, Roosevelt had dropped out of politics after the death of his wife and taken up the life of a rancher. Returning to New York in 1886, Roosevelt agreed at the last minute to stand as the Republican candidate in a three-way race for mayor, losing badly to the Democrat, Abram S. Hewitt, and trailing even the third-party challenger, Henry George. It was suddenly unclear to him whether he had a political future. With his acclaimed naval history, his biography of Benton about to appear, and a new biography of Gouverneur Morris in the works, Roosevelt confided to Lodge that if he did undertake another historical study, his "dream" would be to make it his "*magnum opus.*" This, however, would mean taking "more time," and doing it more "carefully and thoroughly, so as to avoid the roughness and interruption of the Benton." As *The Winning of the West* took shape, Roosevelt began to nurture the hope that this would be the "first class" work that might win him respect as a serious historian.[66]

Roosevelt's ambitions were complicated, however, by the transformation then taking place within the historical profession. During the 1880s the writing of history was passing from gifted amateurs, such as George Bancroft and Francis Parkman, to a new generation of academic historians who wrote not for the reading public, but for each other in the newly established graduate departments of history. Trained mostly in Germany, these scholars were part of a reaction against the more speculative, philosophic histories inspired by Hegel. Adopting a more scientific approach, these academic historians buried themselves in archives, ferreting out neglected documents and preparing specialized monographs of interest mostly to their guild. Up to a point, Roosevelt, who would later be elected president of the American Historical Association, agreed with the new scientific thrust. Historians must not indulge in "self-communion," or ponder "the soul of mankind," but neither should they be deadly dull, or of use only to the specialized reader. The best historical studies, while based on painstaking and laborious research, should also be animated by a "vision" that was "wide and lofty." Although striving for impartiality, the great historian was perforce "a great moralist," who treated his subject with both justice and sympathy.[67]

The Winning of the West, which traced the westward extension of the American frontier from the Alleghenies to the Mississippi and beyond during the period from 1769 to 1796, was dedicated to Francis Parkman, whose style Roosevelt hoped to emulate. Writing to the historian to request his permission for the dedication, Roosevelt was effusive in his praise of the seven-volume *History of France and England in North America.* Parkman's works were without equal, and must serve as "models for all historical treatment of the founding of new communities and the growth of the frontier."[68] When, after the first two volumes of *The Winning of the West* were published in 1889, and Roosevelt received an admiring note from his hero, he reciprocated in a review essay praising Parkman as "the greatest historian whom the United States has yet produced."[69] In Roosevelt's estimation, Parkman not only grasped the significance of the struggle between the French and the English for control of the "destiny" of North America, he also captured the romance of the conflict between these mighty European powers: the French, medieval in their religious absolutism and feudal politics; the English, infused with a new spirit of religious and political liberty that would reach its greatest fulfillment in America.

Parkman's tale also focused on the dramatic contest between the white men and the "original red lords of the land." What made his narrative superior was that Parkman, fresh out of Harvard, had traveled to the Rockies and learned about the Indians and the frontiersmen firsthand. Avoiding the sentimentality that marred so many treatments of the Indians, Parkman had grasped the true character of both parties: the fickleness, treachery, and inhuman cruelty of the Indians; the lawlessness, greed, and brutality of the whites. In the end, Parkman sided with his countrymen, but Roosevelt concluded that he had succeeded as a great moralist, who treated both races fairly and honestly. It added immeasurably to his achievement that Parkman was not one of those "hysterical beings," who thought it was wrong for the white man to spread across the continent because there was no way to do this justly.[70]

Like Parkman, Roosevelt felt a kinship with his subject because he too had lived on the frontier (even if his sojourn was sporadic). And again like Parkman, Roosevelt was interested in the larger meaning of the events. As he explained to the historian, he had sketched out these ideas in the opening chapter of *Benton*, and now intended to flesh them out in greater detail. In a sweeping first chapter, "The Spread of the English-Speaking Peoples," Roosevelt once again drew on Edward Augustus Freeman's Teutonic narrative to place the story of America's westward push in a larger, indeed world-historic, context.

Over the last three hundred years the English-speaking peoples had undergone a great period of race expansion as they spread out into Australia, New Zealand, India, South Africa, Canada, and the United States.[71] This race expansion was itself the result of earlier historical developments that could be traced back to the "half-mythical" exploits of the Germanic tribes. Of all the European peoples, only the Germans were able to resist being absorbed into the "all-conquering" Roman Empire and to retain their distinctive laws, language, and habits of thought. Although these Teutonic tribes conquered most of Europe, they failed to impose their culture on the Latin peoples of the south and were eventually absorbed by them. Only in England did these Low Dutch "sea rovers" succeed in slaying, driving off, or assimilating the native population and imposing their customs, creed, and laws on them. As a result, England "was destined to be of more importance in the future of the Germanic peoples than all their continental possessions, original and acquired, put together."[72]

In time, the Germanic people of England mixed their blood with that of the Celts and Scandinavians, producing a distinct English nationality that spread around the globe, spawning further variations and adaptations. Roosevelt hastened to assure his reader that this proud racial inheritance was "not foreign to American history. The vast movement by which this continent was conquered and peopled cannot be rightly understood if considered solely by itself. It was the crowning and greatest achievement in a series of mighty movements, and it must be taken in connection with them. Its true significance will be lost unless we grasp, however roughly, the past race-history of the nations that took part therein."[73] *The Winning of the West* was simply the latest and most glorious chapter in this drama, pitting two great branches of the English-speaking peoples against each other and following the victorious Americans as they battled the native Indian tribes for control of the continent.

Having established the "race-importance" of westward expansion, Roosevelt then turned to the events themselves, drawing on "hitherto unused material, both from the unpublished mss. of the State Department and from old diaries, letters, and memoranda in various private libraries at Louisville, Nashville, Lexington, etc."[74] In making use of these archival materials, Roosevelt sought to infuse his narrative with greater scientific precision, and thereby establish his reputation as a serious historian.[75] And unlike most histories of the revolutionary era, which tended to focus on the war between the British and the American colonies along the eastern seaboard, Roosevelt chose to tell the story of a second, lesser known, wilderness war between the backwoodsmen and the various Indian tribes, whose savage raids received the quiet blessing of the British.

Roosevelt began his story in 1769, the year Daniel Boone left his home in North Carolina to explore the Kentucky wilderness, and another group of pioneers established the first settlement west of the Alleghenies at Watauga, in what is now eastern Tennessee. That settlement would surely have been annihilated had it not been for Lord Dunmore's War (1774), which held the Indians at bay for the first two years of the Revolution. During that time, Boone was also able to plant a settlement in Kentucky in 1775, adding a second transmontane outpost. Roosevelt rightly emphasized the long-term significance of this now largely forgotten conflict. At the outset of the Revolutionary War, the westernmost boundary of the United States was the Alleghenies, but by the end of the conflict, thanks to the fearless backwoodsmen who crossed the mountains for the "perilous pleasure" of discovering remote Indian hunting grounds and staking out lands for their descendants, the United States could claim the Mississippi as its western border.[76] Nevertheless, the war for the lands between the Alleghenies and the Mississippi was itself only "a stage." After the Revolution, not even the mighty Mississippi could restrain the advance of this "vigorous and aggressive race" as they continued their conquest of the continent.[77]

As in *Thomas Hart Benton*, Roosevelt moved back and forth between competing theories to explain the significance of America's westward expansion. In "The Spread of the English-Speaking Peoples," as well as subsequent chapters, notably, "The Indian Wars, 1784–1787" and "St. Clair's Defeat," Roosevelt, following Freeman (as well as Burgess), emphasized the Teutonic racial inheritance as it was transmitted by the English and carried to America. But elsewhere, especially in "Kentucky's Struggle for Statehood, 1784–1790," Roosevelt stressed the importance of the frontier in shaping a distinct American character. This second account was further complicated in two ways. First, in contrast to *Benton*, where these backwoodsmen were depicted as semi-barbarians no more morally advanced than the Teutonic sea-rovers of the fifth century, Roosevelt, who had read Frederick Jackson Turner's influential essay on the frontier and promised the author that he would make use of it in the second volume of his work, offered a more nuanced account of the influence of the frontier on the American character. Rather than treat only the primitive backwoodsmen who first ventured into the wilds, Roosevelt now depicted the conquest of the west as proceeding in stages.[78] First came the solitary hunters and trappers, of which Daniel Boone and his descendants were prime examples, forever pressing westward to escape encroaching civilization. Close behind were the rude hunter-settlers, from whom Abraham Lincoln was descended. These were the rough men and women who, facing perils on the frontier, gave America its distinctive character. But just "as the frontiersman conquered and transformed the wilderness," so too did that encounter spell his own doom. Inevitably, these backwoodsmen passed away, succeeded by a third stage of thrifty and industrious settlers, men and women who ventured west to lay claim to the land and pass it on to their children. They had no wish to remain lifelong pioneers, but settled down to raise large families and form "the backbone and body of the State." Finally, they were joined by well-to-do planters, merchants, and lawyers of "good blood," who felt a "pride of race" that spurred them on to greater efforts. Thus did the frontiersman give way to an ever more civilized way of life whose "advance guard" he had been, even though somehow "much of his blood" remained and helped shape "the development of the land."[79]

Second, when discussing the way in which the frontier helped to shape the western, and characteristically American, character, Roosevelt further distinguished between the settlements of the Southwest and those in the Northwest.[80] The southern outposts, one in Kentucky and two in Tennessee, were established by backwoodsmen from Virginia and North Carolina, who acted on their own initiative with no help from the government. Life on the frontier, especially in the early stages, appealed to and reinforced their unbridled individualism, where, as in Israel of old, "each man did what seemed best in his own eyes."[81]

Having crossed the Alleghenies on their own, these pioneers felt no allegiance to the weak central government and little for the state governments they had left behind. Only once during the Revolutionary War did they cross back over the mountains to help their brethren in North Carolina prevail against Cornwallis at the battle of Kings Mountain, which proved to be the turning point of the war in the South. Although Roosevelt applauded their performance, he could not help but note that these backwoodsmen were much too impatient with authority to be effective in a more protracted campaign. In such contests the regular army proved far superior to the battle-loving, but undisciplined, militia.

Once the war was over, their "extreme and defiant individualism" fanned the fires of separatism throughout the West, creating divisions that the European powers were only too happy to exploit. The breakaway state of Franklin in eastern Tennessee (1784–1788) was but the first of a series of episodes that threatened the future of the Union. Had the Constitution failed to create a more perfect Union, Roosevelt predicted that the West would have splintered into countless petty states and fallen prey to revolutions, wars, and foreign intrigue, much as South America had done.

By contrast, the settlement of the Northwest occurred later and "sprang directly from the action of the Federal Government," assisted by the regular army. Unlike the territories of Kentucky and Tennessee, which were explored and settled (however spottily) by backwoodsmen from Virginia and North Carolina before the Revolution, the Northwest remained largely unexplored before the war. Thus, Roosevelt could say: "The Northwest played no part in our country as it originally stood; it had no portion in the Declaration of Independence. It did not revolt, it was conquered."[82] It was true that many of the newly independent states laid claim to the territory under their old colonial charters, but these claims were not "substantial" as long as the lands remained unoccupied.[83] Roosevelt singled out the exploits of George Rogers Clark during the Revolution as critical to the settlement of the American boundary in the Northwest, but it was not until General Wayne's victory at Fallen Timbers (1794) that the nation was finally able to assert control over the region, paving the way for its eventual settlement.

At the end of the war, the British surrendered their territorial claims to the United States, and Congress set about getting the individual states to cede their claims to the nation. Recognizing that the issue could not be decided by a consideration of "abstract rights," Congress appealed to their patriotism and common sense. Virginia, which held the most substantial claims, ceded her territory to the United States in 1784, paving the way for the others. In each case, Congress prudently accepted the lands as a gift from the states, instead of claiming them as an unconditional right. It then applied its "collective power" to survey and dispose of the territory, thereby averting the problem of contested property titles that plagued the Southwest.[84] Again, in contrast to the "spirit of intense individualism" of the Southwest, Revolutionary War soldiers established the settlements of the Northwest, giving them a more "national" character. Roosevelt hailed the Miami Company, in which the settlers "all marshaled together in a company instead of moving freely by themselves" as a "triumph of collectivism."[85]

Most important, Congress in 1787 drew up the Northwest Ordinance, providing for the government of these territories. Roosevelt rightly regarded the Northwest Ordinance, enacted by the Confederation Congress and re-enacted by the first Congress of the United States, as one of the most important American state papers, on a par with the Declaration of Independence, the Constitution, Washington's Farewell Address, the Emancipation Proclamation, and Lincoln's Second Inaugural. For one thing, the Northwest Ordinance reversed the relation between the original thirteen states and the Union, laying the foundation for a more perfect Union. Unlike the Articles of Confederation, which was a creation of the states, the states that were eventually carved out of the Northwest Territory were "creatures of the nation," acquired through conquest, and "by the compact declared forever inseparable from it."[86] At the same time, the Northwest Ordinance provided that these territories, when they became states, would enter the Union on an equal footing with the original states, thereby establishing a precedent for how to deal with future westward expansion. And finally, in keeping with its more "collectivist" approach, Congress forever banned slavery in the Northwest Territory, whereas in the "individualistic" Southwest, North Carolina gave up its claim to its western territory only on condition that Tennessee not outlaw slavery.

Although Roosevelt had originally planned to cover the history of the entire Southwest, including the annexation of Texas, the Mexican War, from which the United States acquired New Mexico, Arizona, and California, as well as the Gold Rush, by 1896 he was back in the thick of politics and decided to wind up the project. Roosevelt had managed to complete the second half of the study while serving as a member of the Civil Service Commission in Washington, D.C., a position he held from 1889 when the first volume was published until 1895, when he resigned to become president of the Board of Police Commissioners in New York City. Now with the presidential race heating up, Roosevelt sensed a new opportunity. *The Winning of the West* effectively concluded with General Wayne's victory over the Northwest Indians at Fallen Timbers in 1794. The Louisiana Purchase, together with the expeditions of Lewis and Clark and Zebulon Pike to the far West, hastily tacked on, brought the narrative to a close.[87]

The Winning of the West was an immediate success, bringing Roosevelt the professional recognition he sought. Not only did Francis Parkman write him an appreciative letter, but the work as a whole received generally positive reviews, including one from Frederick Jackson Turner. Unlike the hastily thrown together *Thomas Hart Benton,* Roosevelt had managed to combine a certain flare for the dramatic with careful and extensive research.[88] Yet, on closer inspection, the history introduced several themes that were not only foreign but also antithetical to the principles of the founders Roosevelt claimed to admire.

RACE

The most striking difference was the weight Roosevelt attached to race. From its opening pages, *The Winning of the West* cast westward expansion as a grand racial epic, though Roosevelt was hardly precise in his use of the term.[89] At various points in the narrative, he used "race" in at least five different ways. First, and most obviously, it referred to the basic color groups, especially red and white, and occasionally black and yellow. But as the opening chapter suggested, Roosevelt also linked race with language, grouping diverse nationalities under the same rubric, as in the "English-speaking race." In this sense, Roosevelt sometimes referred to the Americans as part of the English race, though it might be more accurate to speak of a common Anglo-American culture. Third, Roosevelt spoke of a distinctive "American race" (or what we today would call nationality), formed by language, customs, creed, and "blood." Yet as Roosevelt's narrative clearly recognized, there was no one blood that flowed in American veins. Along the seaboard, English "blood" predominated, though it was mixed. (Roosevelt's own "blood" on his father's side was Dutch.) And in the Southwest, where much of the narrative is set, Scots-Irish Presbyterians prevailed. Not only did these Celts have no English (or Anglo-Saxon) blood, they also had no love for England and its vaunted liberties. Yet it was this "race" of frontiersmen whom Roosevelt considered "characteristically American." In still other places, Roosevelt used "race" to mean ethnic groups or tribes, such as the Scots-Irish or Cherokees. And finally, he occasionally used it to refer to a particular group, most notably, the Kentucky "race." Given this imprecision, it might seem that the best strategy would be simply to ignore the term and focus on the history.

But upon reflection, this is not possible for two reasons. First, *The Winning of the West*, for all its sloppy terminology, abounds with invidious racial distinctions and racial judgments. The Indians were a "weaker and wholly alien race," the Negro belonged to one of "the inferior races," the French were an alien race, "utterly unsuited for liberty as the Americans understand it." Elsewhere, Roosevelt warned against the dangers of conquests by "barbarians of low racial characteristics," notably the Turks and the Tartars.[90]

Even more important, one of the central themes of *The Winning of the West* was the necessity of race expansion and "race-supremacy" for national greatness. In a long digression, prompted by St. Clair's humiliating defeat at the hands of the Miamis and Shawnees,[91] Roosevelt insisted that only "a mighty race, in its vigorous and masterful prime," could extend its sway over the weaker and alien races. What he had in mind was not merely the *conquest* of territory, but, following the example of the Germanic tribes in England, the removal or annihilation of the Indian tribes. Assimilation was not a serious alternative, both because the Indians were a weaker race and because they were separated from the whites by "untold ages."[92]

Having made his bones with *The Naval War of 1812* and more recently reviewed Admiral Alfred Thayer Mahan's treatise on the importance of sea power, Roosevelt was especially keen to emphasize the importance of "power on the ocean" to race expansion.[93] Of the nations that pursued this aim, Spain, Portugal, France, Holland, and, above all, England, every one of them depended upon their naval forces. But even then, most of them failed to carry the project through successfully because too often they allowed their policy to be guided by the selfish interests of individuals, rather than focusing on the "interest of the race as a whole." Thus, the Dutch preferred the immediate gains from their Spice Island trade to the more long-range goal of taking possession of Australia and New Zealand. The French, too, chose to spend their blood and treasure fighting for small gains against the Germans and the Italians, rather than focusing their efforts on America. Only England took advantage of the opportunities to expand the dominion of the English-speaking race by settling the "waste spaces" of the New World. Eventually, it too stumbled, led by statesmen who cared only about preserving their valuable fur trade. With American independence from Britain, the "supremacy" of the English-speaking race passed to the United States. Here again, Roosevelt excoriated the shortsighted statesmen of the Northeast who, out of a "cold selfishness," remained blind to "the grandeur of their race's imperial destiny."[94] Only belatedly and grudgingly did they come to support the western backwoodsmen and eastern speculators who "hungered" after Indian lands.

Although elsewhere in *The Winning of the West* Roosevelt had expressed his admiration for the Northwest Ordinance, he said nothing about its provision enjoining the government to act with "utmost good faith" in its dealings with the Indians, declaring that "their property, rights, and liberty" should "never be invaded or disturbed," unless in a just and lawful war, and urging that laws "founded in justice and humanity" be made for the purpose of preventing wrongs from being done to them. On the contrary, he made clear his disagreement with those "governmental authorities," who sought to do "strict justice" to the Indians and who carried out their treaty obligations with "scrupulous fairness." More than once, Roosevelt derided Secretary of War Henry Knox for advising President Washington to observe the treaties with the Indians in an effort to conciliate and attach them to the United States. Roosevelt could barely contain his scorn at Knox's suggestion that a "philosophic mind" would take pleasure in imparting to the Indians a knowledge of cultivation and the arts, "thus preserving and civilizing," rather than removing or exterminating them. Such "large, though vague, beneficence" showed no real knowledge of the Indians, who were "many centuries" away from being civilized. Knox was no better than the sentimental humanitarians he decried. By contrast, "the most far-seeing and high-minded statesman" was the one who grasped "the race-importance" of the conquest and settlement of the continent.[95] As in *Benton*, these were the only two alternatives.

In another chapter on "The Indian Wars," Roosevelt expanded on this theme. Whenever two races at different stages of civilization clashed, the only way to resolve their differences was by force. War with savages was "the most ultimately righteous of all wars," though it was also likely to be the "most terrible and inhuman. The rude fierce settler *who drives the savage from the land* lays all civilized mankind under a debt to him." This was true not only in America, but all over the world. Far more important than the petty territorial squabbles between the civilized nations of Europe were the merciless wars that took place between Boer and Zulu, Cossack and Tartar, New Zealander and Maori, ensuring that "America, Australia, and Siberia should pass out of the hands of their red, black, and yellow aboriginal owners, and become the heritage of the dominant world races."[96]

How this was accomplished, whether by purchase, treaty, or most likely, war, was ultimately of little consequence. No treaty was binding in perpetuity, and Roosevelt left the reader in no doubt that breaking a treaty to advance the claims of civilization and the "dominant race" was "not only expedient, but imperative and honorable." From the "race standpoint" all that mattered was that the land was won:

> It is, indeed, a warped, perverse, and silly morality which would forbid a course of conquest that has turned whole continents into the seats of mighty and flourishing civilized nations. All men of sane and wholesome thought must dismiss with impatient contempt the plea that these continents should be reserved for the use of scattered savage tribes, whose life was but a few degrees less meaningless, squalid, and ferocious than that of the wild beasts with whom they held joint ownership.[97]

But Roosevelt was not content merely to insist that the end (race expansion) justified the means (removal or annihilation). As in *Benton,* he tried to excuse the means by arguing that the savages and the frontiersmen who defeated them could not be held to the same rules of morality as civilized nations. Assimilation worked for the English and the Scandinavians; the Scots-Irish and the French Huguenots, who mingled their blood to create a new American "race"; it would not work with the Indians because at best they had only reached the "savage" stage of development. And besides, they were "a weaker and wholly alien race." Here, the Teutonic conquest of Britain in the fifth century, where the invaders largely annihilated or drove out the local population, provided a more appropriate model. Fortunately, Roosevelt thought, the men who did the "rough pioneer work of civilization in barbarous lands" understood this instinctively, and certainly better than those statesmen whose "abstract morality" and "philosophic minds" provided no practical guidance on the frontier. Missing from his account, as it was in *Benton,* was any recognition that these moral principles of the founders might be applied prudently as circumstances dictated, rather than simply dismissed out of hand as "abstract" and unworkable.

THE FOUNDING

There is no question that the founding of the American republic was unique in the annals of political history. As Publius recounted in *The Federalist,* previous republics had all relied on a single lawgiver, called in from outside and often regarded as divinely inspired, to establish a frame of government. Only in America did the people first proclaim the timeless, universal principles on which all legitimate government should rest, and then authorize their delegates to deliberate about the form of government that would best secure those ends. In so doing, the Americans not only established a standard by which all governments should be judged, they also raised a question for future generations. Should those who came after be bound back to the work of the fathers, accepting as authoritative the principles and practices declared by their ancestors, or should they regard the founding as but one moment in the life of the republic, without any special significance for later generations? Indeed, perhaps wrong or mistaken in crucial respects? Writing in *The Federalist*, Publius had made the case for venerating the Constitution, while Thomas Jefferson responded by insisting that reverence would militate against progress. Even Jefferson, however, insisted that the principles underlying the Constitution, that is, "the inherent and unalienable rights of man" remained "unchangeable."[98] A half century later, Abraham Lincoln revisited that debate and reaffirmed the centrality of the Declaration. "All honor to Jefferson," he wrote, for having had the political "forecast" to include in a "merely revolutionary document, an abstract truth, applicable to all men and all times" that would forever stand as a rebuke to tyranny and oppression. And although Lincoln acknowledged the possibility of progress, both moral and political, beyond what the Framers of the Constitution envisioned, from his earliest days he counseled making "reverence for the laws" the "*political religion* of the nation" and supplanting the policies of the fathers only when the arguments against them were clear and overwhelming.[99]

By contrast, Roosevelt's treatment of the founding in his histories is at best equivocal. Although he admired the work of the Framers (at least the more national-minded of them) and at this point in his political career, warmly supported the Constitution, there is no evidence that Roosevelt had ever read John Locke or given much thought to the philosophical underpinnings of classical liberalism. Everything in his education, from his concentration in the natural sciences to the courses he took at Harvard and Columbia in history, political economy, and law disposed him to look at politics from a developmental and evolutionary perspective, distilled through racial categories inimical to the Declaration's emphasis on individual rights. Freeman's outline of history, from which his own studies drew, located the "germ" of Anglo-Saxon liberty in the semi-mythic past and passed over the founding altogether. Burgess at Columbia went even further, rejecting the Declaration's appeal to natural rights as pernicious. In his view, there were no rights apart from those that the state chose to grant its citizens, and these developed historically over time. Moreover, Burgess argued, even the Framers' Constitution was flawed, since it had failed to solve the fundamental question of sovereignty. To recur to the founding as a guide for political action then would have been, as Wilfred M. McClay has observed, "to challenge the idea that the development of a nation should be understood instead as a process of slow accretion and organic adaptation." It would have meant substituting "an architectural and engineering metaphor of foundations for a biological metaphor of evolution,"[100] and this at the very moment when the biological sciences were establishing their supremacy. What is more, Darwinian evolution found a powerful ally in the German historicism to which Roosevelt had been introduced. It should not, therefore, be surprising that long before he became a progressive, Roosevelt's moral compass pointed away from the natural rights philosophy of the founders.

To be sure, *The Winning of the West* paid lip service to the Declaration of Independence, including it among the great state papers, but only once in its thousand-plus pages did Roosevelt refer to its moral principles. In this instance, the historian excoriated creoles in Illinois who, with "at least" the acquiescence of a Catholic priest, had sentenced a slave to be burned and hanged for witchcraft three years after the Declaration had been signed. But it is likely that Roosevelt was here using the Declaration as a rhetorical weapon to attack French (and Catholic) culture, rather than to affirm the universality and eternal rightness of its principles.[101]

Even more telling was that, in contrast to Lincoln, Roosevelt never invoked the principles of the Declaration to condemn slavery. To be sure, Roosevelt denounced slavery as a "moral evil," but he did so by calling it an offense against "the true standards of humanity and Christianity,"[102] not a violation of natural right. This was because, unlike his heroes, Roosevelt did not see nature as a source of moral principle. His understanding of nature was derived from science, not philosophy. If nature taught anything, it was the survival of the fittest, viewed collectively in terms of "race."[103] To look to nature for moral guidance was to fall prey to sentimentality and useless abstraction. Following the example of his teachers, Roosevelt repeatedly warned against taking one's bearings from "abstract rights," or "abstract morality."

As in *Benton*, history, not nature, provided the standard of right.[104] Throughout *The Winning of the West* Roosevelt emphasized that human beings should only be judged by the standards appropriate to their "stage" of development. Most of the Indian tribes remained stuck at the lowest, "savage" stage of development, centuries behind the white man; a few had "progressed" to the "barbarous" stage. The backwoodsmen who themselves regressed to a state of semi-barbarism could not be judged by "contemporary" standards; nor should they be held to the same moral principles as their more "civilized" brethren. "All that can be asked is that they be judged as other wilderness conquerors, as other slayers and quellers of savage peoples, are judged."[105] Here again, the "Low Dutch sea-thieves" who ravaged England provided a more appropriate standard of comparison.[106] Roosevelt's antipathy to what he called "abstract right," together with his insistence that peoples be judged by the standards appropriate to their historical stage of development, tacitly departed from the founders' appeal to natural right, which Lincoln considered the "sheet anchor of American republicanism."[107]

Roosevelt's histories not only gave short shrift to the natural rights philosophy in the Declaration, they also implicitly challenged one of the critical assumptions underlying the Constitution. In keeping with social compact theory, *The Federalist* had emphasized the signal importance of "reflection and choice" in establishing good government. Yet, as Roosevelt had suggested in *Gouverneur Morris*, too many of the statesmen who framed the Constitution and filled the seats of government in the early years of the republic failed to grasp the significance of the West, or to foresee how rapidly and completely it would be subjugated. Far greater than the events in Philadelphia was the unplanned westward movement of the pioneers, which began with Daniel Boone in 1769 and ended a mere seventy-five years later on the Pacific coast. Compared with this, "all other questions, save those of the preservation of the Union itself and of the emancipation of the blacks, have been of subordinate importance."[108]

Moreover, *The Winning of the West* was primarily a tale of conquest and only secondarily about compact. And even then, Roosevelt tended to play down the importance of deliberation and choice, focusing instead on the "racial" makeup of the pioneers. That frontier leaders like Andrew Jackson, Sam Houston, Davy Crockett, James Robertson, and James Campbell were descended from Scots-Irish Presbyterian "stock" was at times almost sufficient to explain their success. In Roosevelt's romantic imagination, these backwoodsmen were the heirs of Cromwell; the West was won by "the Roundheads of the South."[109]

In his enthusiasm to establish the backwoodsmen's "racial" pedigree, Roosevelt elsewhere turned these Celts into Saxons, linking them through time to the mythical Anglo-Saxon (and ultimately Teutonic) tradition of ancient liberty.[110] Roosevelt devoted an entire chapter to the Watauga Commonwealth, which in 1772 drew up a written constitution, the first ever adopted west of the Alleghenies, and the first anywhere "by a community composed of American-born free-men." But in calling their primitive leg-islature a "witanagemot," Roosevelt was suggesting, implausibly, that these frontiersmen were somehow reaching back to their medieval Anglo-Saxon past. Moreover, although he praised the backwoodsmen's rough practical common sense and their swift execution of justice, he did so by empha-sizing that they avoided those "high-sounding abstractions" that would, beginning with the Declaration, supply the moral foundation for American republicanism.[111]

In another chapter on the Cumberland Settlement, which based its writ-ten constitution partly on the Watauga Articles, Roosevelt made the con-nection to their Anglo-Saxon roots even more explicit. Describing the set-tlers' efforts to set up a self-governing commonwealth in 1780, Roosevelt gushed, "Their compact was thus in some sort of an unconscious repro-duction of the laws and customs of the old-time court-leet, profoundly modified to suit the peculiar needs of backwoods life, the intensely demo-cratic temper of the pioneers, and above all, the military necessities of their existence."[112] That Roosevelt discovered the origins of American liberty in the Anglo-Saxon past is perhaps not altogether surprising, as Edward A. Freeman, whose text was required reading in the only history course Roosevelt took at Harvard and who edited the Historic Towns series in which Roosevelt in 1891 would publish his history of New York, subscribed to the "germ theory" of liberty. So did John W. Burgess, Roosevelt's for-mer law professor. According to this view, free institutions could be traced back to the Teutonic genius for self-government, the "germ" of which was transmitted to the "Germanic" peoples of England (the Anglo-Saxons) and thence to America. In suggesting that these Scots-Irish pioneers (who were in fact Celts) "unconsciously" recalled their ancient Anglo-Saxon heritage, Roosevelt erroneously emphasized a fictitious racial "memory" over the ca-pacity for deliberate choice.[113]

It is possible, of course, that the founders overestimated the extent to which political liberty could be established simply by "reflection and choice," while failing to recognize the role that habits and manners, or mo-res, played in constituting and preserving free governments. Surely culture counts for something. Nevertheless, *The Winning of the West* went too far in the other direction, emphasizing the importance of racial characteris-tics over which a people had no control as the chief determinant of the American character and the guarantor of American liberty.[114] Moreover, as Richard Boyd, who otherwise praises the nineteenth-century "insight that political liberty is not the conscious, deliberate product of human design but instead is given by the traditions, spirit, or mores of the nation," has observed, it was precisely this turn toward political sociology (of sorts) that made possible "the convergence" between later nineteenth-century liberalism and imperialism, which Roosevelt embraced under the more innocuous "expansion."[115]

PROGRESS OF LIBERTY VS. PROGRESS OF GROWTH AND EXPANSION

Not only did Roosevelt look to history rather than nature to discover a standard by which to judge the actions of the pioneers, but he also shifted the narrative focus of the story.[116] Whereas the founders had emphasized the struggle for rights and debated what institutional arrangements would best secure them, Roosevelt showed little interest in these matters. Instead, in these sections he drew on the work of Frederick Jackson Turner, emphasizing how the "absolute democracy" of the frontier compelled the backwoodsmen to adapt their political institutions to their environment. Roosevelt took for granted that the frontiersmen's sense of fair play would protect the minority against the injustice of the many. Manly virtue, meaning a refusal to tolerate majority tyranny, would more than offset their primitive constitution making.[117]

Instead of charting the progress of liberty, Roosevelt fashioned a narrative of progress, understood primarily as the growth and development of a distinctive American "race." As the opening chapter of *The Winning of the West* made clear, this narrative did not begin in 1787 with the Constitution, or even in 1776. Roosevelt began the story in 1769, but the events he related were meant to be understood in the context of a larger narrative of race expansion by the English-speaking people that had been going on for 300 years. Against this backdrop of "racial destiny," the founding narrative of the progress of liberty receded in significance.

Although nature no longer served as a standard of right, it was by no means absent in *The Winning of the West*. Rather Roosevelt reinterpreted it in harsh Darwinian terms that then became part of the narrative. Nature no longer served as a standard by which to judge history, but was instead folded into it. The mighty frontiersmen vanquished their foes: one by one the Indian tribes fell, the Spanish receded, the French sold out, and the British gave up. The fittest race survived and flourished. Indeed, Roosevelt made it clear that the American people had no choice but to expand. To live was to grow. Territorial expansion was "a process as natural as it is desirable"; it was "part of the order of our political nature."[118]

Running alongside the narrative of growth and expansion was a second theme that charted the progress of civilization. This was the movement, captured in its earliest stages by the Indians, from savagery to barbarism and then to civilization. The mark of the savage was his "inhuman love of cruelty for cruelty's sake," while civilization was distinguished by an understanding of justice as something other than the right of the stronger as well as pity and generosity toward the weaker.[119] *The Winning of the West* placed the frontiersman at the mid-point on this spectrum. His lawless hunger for Indian lands provoked merciless outrages that were met with fierce hatred and a desire for revenge. But this regression to semi-barbarism was temporary. The rude pioneer who transformed the wilderness was himself transformed by it. Both disappeared together.[120]

Roosevelt labored under no romantic illusions about "the noble savage"; indeed, he took a certain pleasure in pointing out that those who sentimentalized the way of life of the Indians have usually lived beyond the reach of the tomahawk. It is difficult not to applaud the tough common sense with which he insisted that civilization indeed represented progress over the savage state of nature. But all too often, Roosevelt linked the progress of civilization with explicitly racial themes, and this is what makes his narrative objectionable. His was not an inclusive view of civilization: the Indians were to be killed, or removed from the reach of the ever-expanding "dominant race." He scoffed at suggestions put forth by some of America's early statesmen that civilization would mean treating the vanquished Indians with magnanimity, even as he insisted that generosity and pity were the marks of a civilized state. Sometimes even justice, in the form of observing treaties, was too much of a stretch.[121]

And so, even as he admired the work of Washington and Lincoln and praised the achievements of the more national-minded founders, Roosevelt's histories quietly repudiated the political principles for which they stood. Race-talk replaced rights at the center of the national narrative, while conquest and expansion rather than the spread of liberty set the standards for future greatness. At the same time, the blind, unconscious movement of a whole people supplanted the founders' emphasis on deliberation and choice, and history, rather than natural right, came to supply the moral ground on which political actions were to be judged.

3. Republican Reformer

When he first arrived on the political scene in 1881, Theodore Roosevelt gave no hint of the progressive that he would later become. Nothing in his background—not his family, his upbringing, or his education—had disposed him to the progressive program that would begin to catch on in parts of the academy by the middle of the decade.[1] He had grown up reading youth magazines and adventure tales that emphasized the importance of individual initiative, self-reliance, and personal responsibility, lessons he had taken to heart as he overcame his childhood infirmities through physical exercise and sheer determination. His father, Theodore Roosevelt, Sr., had set the standard for gentlemanly civic engagement, contributing to numerous philanthropic causes and winning national recognition as an early supporter of civil service reform. At Harvard, he had nibbled around the edges of politics and economics, taking courses and meeting speakers who favored limited government and laissez-faire economics and who emphasized the importance of individual character. Nothing during his time at Columbia would unsettle these opinions. Thus, it was not surprising that when, little more than a year out of college and still a law student, Roosevelt decided to run for the New York State Assembly from the "silk-stocking" district of Manhattan, he did so primarily to prove something to himself. He wanted to show that, like his political heroes, he was manly enough to fight for American ideals.[2]

During the 1880s and 1890s, as he served in various elective and appointed offices at both the state and federal level, Roosevelt considered himself nothing more (and nothing less) than a Republican reformer, following in the tradition of national-minded statesmen such as Washington, Hamilton, Webster, Clay, and of course, Lincoln. As Roosevelt then saw it, the task now before the nation was not nearly as momentous as those that faced Washington or Lincoln, but it was work that needed to be done. He fought for municipal reform and exhorted Americans to end the corruption of the spoils system by rallying behind civil service reform. He affirmed the national agenda of the Republican Party in domestic policy and supported measures to assimilate the vast influx of European immigrants. In foreign affairs, he cast himself as a follower of Washington, making the case for military preparedness in pursuit of national greatness.

As he sought to attract a younger generation of college-educated men to political careers, Roosevelt had one bit of advice: "Read *The Federalist*—it is one of the greatest—I hardly know whether it would not be right to say that it is on the whole the greatest book dealing with applied politics there has ever been." What Roosevelt admired about Hamilton, Madison, and Jay was that although they had studied history and political theory, they were also practicing politicians. Aspiring politicians could no more afford to ignore theory than could theorists divorce themselves from the actual experiences of governing. "You have got to have the theory; you have got to have the book-learning," Roosevelt told the members of the Liberal Club in Buffalo, but "if you have nothing else, you will be hopeless and useless."[3] From the standpoint of statesmanship, the best men were those who combined theory and practice; without a theoretical understanding of politics, a politician might do useful work, but never ascend to the highest rank as the authors of *The Federalist* had done.

Yet for all his praise of *The Federalist*, it is worth noting that Roosevelt himself had little to say about the particular theory of republicanism it expounded. He had not read the work in college, and it is not clear when he first sat down with it, or how carefully he had considered its arguments. Indeed, his various comments recommending the work suggest that, as with *Thomas Hart Benton*, Roosevelt largely evolved its theory of government "from his own consciousness," filtering its arguments through the lens of Darwinian struggle that colored his political views. After praising the authors for their political engagement, Roosevelt told his audience, "You have got to go out and rub up with the men who do not think as you do; with the men with different ideas; with the men who are doing the practical work; men who are running the machines. You have got to go up and rub with them, if only for the sake of beating them."[4] For Roosevelt, theory was the armor that reformers put on when they entered the political arena to do battle against their foes. *The Federalist* was great not only because it had a "theory," but also because the men who wrote it had struggled against their adversaries and prevailed.

RUBBING UP AGAINST THE MACHINE

Making his way to Albany in January 1882, Roosevelt was determined to do his part to restore honesty and good government to New York. Almost immediately, he made news by exposing the rampant bribery and extortion in the legislature. He called for an investigation into the actions of Judge Westbrook in connection with the fraudulent Manhattan Elevated Railroad run by Jay Gould. Reelected the following year by a wide margin, Roosevelt, now minority leader, worked to secure passage of a law prohibiting the manufacture of cigars in tenement houses.[5] Following in the footsteps of his late father, Theodore also took up the cause of civil service reform and worked with the reform Democratic governor, Grover Cleveland, to enact legislation modeled on the federal civil service act passed earlier that year. During his final term in the Assembly, Roosevelt provided a baseline for how far he would travel over the course of his political career when he insisted there was "not the least chance" that an aristocracy, "or to speak more precisely, a plutocracy," could ever grow up in America.[6]

After three sessions in the legislature, Roosevelt scored a major victory at the New York Republican Convention in 1884, capturing the state's delegates for Senator George F. Edmunds of Vermont. This victory, however, was purely symbolic, as Edmunds had no chance of winning the nomination. Later that year at the Republican Nominating Convention, Roosevelt joined forces with Henry Cabot Lodge of Massachusetts in an effort to block the nomination of James G. Blaine, whom they considered unworthy to represent the party of Lincoln. But when Blaine emerged victorious, Roosevelt, along with Lodge, made the fateful decision to stick with the party rather than join the mugwumps that had bolted in support of the reform-minded Democratic nominee, Grover Cleveland.[7]

Speaking publicly for the first time about his decision to support the Republican presidential ticket, Roosevelt declared, "I am by inheritance and by education a Republican; whatever good I have been able to accomplish in public life has been accomplished through the Republican party; I have acted with it in the past, and wish to act with it in the future."[8] As Roosevelt explained, Blaine had prevailed fairly and honestly (something he would later argue that could not be said about the nomination of Taft in 1912) and was now the Republican standard-bearer. Ever since the election of Abraham Lincoln in 1860, the Republican Party had occupied the moral high ground in American politics, fighting to preserve the Union, free the slaves, and promote sound economic and foreign policies. No matter how attractive the Democratic candidate was (as assemblyman, Roosevelt had worked well with Cleveland when he was governor of New York), it was the party that mattered most. And the Democratic Party was tainted by its support for secession, slavery, and easy money.

Looking ahead to the future, Roosevelt observed that the next president would in all probability have the opportunity to name a new justice to the Supreme Court. The party loyalist was not about to let the country forget that Democrats had been responsible for the appointment of Roger B. Taney, author of the infamous *Dred Scott* decision. By contrast, the Republicans could be counted on to affirm the nationalist vision of John Marshall and Joseph Story. The choice was not simply between two men; political parties and their traditions also mattered. If backers from the independent wing were unhappy with the nomination of Blaine, the only alternative was to elect men of upright character who would work to restore the moral luster of the Republican Party.[9]

In calling for good men to take up the cause of political reform, Roosevelt was bucking powerful cultural trends. The decades following the Civil War had seen a period of enormous wealth creation and consolidation, in which capitalist entrepreneurs such as Cornelius Vanderbilt, J. P. Morgan, and John D. Rockefeller easily outshone the second-rate politicians of the day. For men with high animal spirits the risks and rewards of building a financial empire proved far more exciting than a seat in Congress or a post in some backwater state capital. Roosevelt's early essays took aim at those wealthy individuals stuck at what he dismissively called the "bourgeois stage of development," who, although upright in their personal lives, devoted all their efforts to moneymaking and ignored their civic responsibilities. But in contrast to the theory of *The Federalist*, which relied principally on self-interest and the selfish passions (ambition, avarice, and the love of fame) to prod men to do what was right, the earnest reformer urged well-to-do businessmen to become involved in public affairs "for the sake of abstract duty."[10]

It was not only self-made entrepreneurs who preferred to remain on the political sidelines. Well-bred young men from "old money" families also tended to stay away, though in this case it was because they regarded the rough-and-tumble of democratic politics as beneath them. In the 1870s and 1880s, few men of the upper class concerned themselves with politics at all, and those that did were largely regarded as well meaning, but ineffectual. They were genteel reformers, "cultivated, refined men of high ideals," who thought that they had done their civic duty when they met with others like themselves to discuss the concerns of the day. In Roosevelt's view, it was "sheer unmanliness and cowardice" to "shrink" from political battle because the work was "difficult or repulsive."[11] Later, recalling the advice he was given by "nice people" on Fifth Avenue to avoid politics because it was filled with "saloon-keepers, horse-car conductors," and other "low" types, rather than "gentlemen" like himself, Roosevelt replied that he wanted to see if he could hold his own with the "rough men" who ruled, and warned that he would join the "muckers" in governing those of his own class if they were "too weak" do it themselves. As he put it, "I intended to be one of the class that governs, not one of the class that is governed."[12]

By standing up to the machine politicians and "special interests" that dominated the state house, the young Roosevelt helped make politics respectable again for a rising generation of reformers. And by rubbing shoulders with men from outside his social class and holding his own with them, he gained new respect and increased the effectiveness of the reform wing of his party. In an era of laissez-faire individualism and crooked political machines, Roosevelt thought that there was a case to be made for the best men to go into politics, and he had a rollicking time making it.[13]

GEOGRAPHY AND THE AMERICAN CHARACTER

Even as Roosevelt celebrated a new national spirit that rose above sectional divisions, he continued to emphasize the effect of regional differences on the American character. As a wealthy New Yorker and admirer of Alexander Hamilton, Roosevelt might have been expected to take a sympathetic view of the East. But in numerous speeches and essays during the 1880s and 1890s, as well as in his histories, Roosevelt depicted the region as the symbol of all that was decadent and effeminate in post–Civil War America. Eastern statesmen had failed to grasp the importance of westward expansion before the war, and now its millionaires were undermining America's moral fiber by pursuing their narrow, selfish interests to the neglect of the more "virile virtues."

Although Roosevelt regarded Brooks Adams's *Law of Civilization and Decay* as a "melancholy book," he shared the author's disgust with the rise of "economic man" in modern times, objecting only that "the disease" was not as all-consuming as Adams believed.[14] "Purely commercial ideals," Roosevelt warned, were "mean and sordid," producing timid and fearful men, "incapable of the thrill of generous emotion" and lacking the capacity for nobility and greatness.[15] Making money, or spending it on frivolous pleasures, held no charms for him. Ranching, hunting big game, exploring the wilderness, waging political combat, leading troops in battle, and of course, fathering many healthy children—these were the things that built the American character and contributed to national greatness—not piling up millions.

Roosevelt was right to despise the vulgar excesses of the Gilded Age and to investigate businessmen who amassed their fortunes by unscrupulous means. But he moved all too easily from condemning these wrongdoers to looking down on any entrepreneur who devoted himself primarily to his commercial activities and did not share his passion for political reform. Some of his disdain was rooted in the snobbery that old money has always felt toward the *nouveau riche*. On more than one occasion, Roosevelt, whose own ranching investment (paid for with inherited wealth) had failed, confessed that businessmen bored him. But especially for one who professed to admire *The Federalist*, Roosevelt failed to appreciate the ways in which America's commercial spirit might contribute to a distinctive form of democratic greatness and encourage the "capable, masterful, and efficient" qualities he most admired.[16] Roosevelt's pulse throbbed to the deeds of "statesmen, patriots, warriors, and poets" but remained curiously unmoved by the post–Civil War captains of industry and finance who helped lay the foundations for a prosperous and free America.

Indeed, the seeds of Roosevelt's later hostility to capitalism could already be seen in his 1895 essay "American Ideals," where he grumbled: "There is not in the world a more ignoble character than the mere money-getting American, insensible to every duty, regardless of every principle, bent only on amassing a fortune, and putting his fortune to the basest uses," such as stock speculation, ruthless competition, vulgar displays of wealth, and shameless social-climbing. He then added that the wealthy businessman who spent part of his fortune to found a college or endow a church was even "more dangerous" because his supposed philanthropy made "those good people who are also foolish forget his real iniquity." But, as we shall see in Chapter 5, some of these so-called iniquities (such as rebates) were nothing more than the consequences of competitive markets and not "iniquities" at all. Nor in making such charges was Roosevelt consistent: he could not seem to decide whether commercial ideals made businessmen timid and fearful or overly masterful. And finally, at least in this essay, he refused to credit the full extent of entrepreneurial philanthropy. For not only did these successful businessmen endow churches and colleges, museums and hospitals, but they also lowered prices, discovered new technologies, and introduced new products that raised the standard of living for average Americans. Yet Roosevelt saw no heroism in their dogged pursuit of material success and little virtue in their triumphs. For him, the only good businessmen were those who did not "shirk" their duty to the state, who rose above shortsightedness and indifference to work for justice and "the right." American ideals must rest on "nobler grounds" than what he dismissed as "mere business expediency."[17]

By contrast, the South (where two of Roosevelt's maternal uncles, James and Irvine Bulloch, had served as officers in the Confederate Navy) fared somewhat better in his estimation. Roosevelt freely conceded that the region had betrayed the democratic principle by continuing the enslavement of the Negro and threatened the preservation of the republic with its doctrines of secession and nullification, but he admired the courage and love of honor it had displayed during the Civil War. Of perhaps greater importance, the South continued to cultivate the martial virtues even after the war, reaching for something higher and nobler than "mere material prosperity."[18]

Not surprisingly, however, it was the West that represented all that was best in the American character. For Roosevelt, it was no accident that both George Washington and Abraham Lincoln had either spent some time on the frontier or were descended from hardy pioneer stock. And Ulysses S. Grant, the greatest of the Civil War generals, hailed from what was then the "western" state of Illinois.[19] Roosevelt fully expected that the West would continue to shape the destiny of the republic in the future, accentuating the "peculiarly American characteristics of its people."[20]

From his own adventures chasing down horse rustlers and roping steers in the Dakota Badlands, Roosevelt had learned firsthand how the West could train the soft easterner in the "virile virtues," while teaching the proud southerner valuable lessons about democratic equality. In his essay on the "Manly Virtues and Practical Politics," published in 1894 and inspired by his time in "cowboy land," Roosevelt insisted that American men must "be vigorous in mind and body, able to hold our own in rough combat with our fellows, able to suffer punishment without flinching, and, at need, be able to repay it in kind with full interest."[21] The proper response to insult or injury was not to be hurt, but to get angry.[22] Manly men did not "flinch," "shirk," or "shrink."[23] Living in a more dangerous age, pioneers and backwoodsmen instinctively knew that they must cultivate the manly virtues of strength, courage, and unwavering resolution, or perish. Yet, it was precisely these virile virtues that a "peaceful and commercial civilization," rendered "cautious and timid" by too much attention to moneymaking or by an excess of intellectual refinement, was inclined to dismiss or, if not dismiss, then to distort.

Roosevelt continued to brood about the effect of wealth and luxury on the American character for the rest of his life. Still, he took some comfort from the fact wealthy eastern boys no longer amused themselves playing billiards, as they had at the outbreak of the Civil War, but now felt peer pressure to develop their bodies, and to some extent their characters, by engaging in strenuous exercise and contact sports that required "pluck, endurance and physical address." As president, Roosevelt would take an active interest in intercollegiate sports programs and praise rough contact sports for turning out vigorous men and not "mollycoddles." In life, as in football, the principle was to "hit the line hard; don't foul and don't shirk, but hit the line hard."[24]

Yet for all his talk of the manly virtues, there was, as Harvey Mansfield has observed, something decidedly juvenile about Roosevelt's treatment of them. Perhaps this should not be surprising. As his friend Cecil Spring-Rice once quipped, Theodore was really only about six years old. He was, observed another, "essentially a boy's man."[25] His was a boyish enthusiasm that focused, as boys do, on bodily notions of manly excellence: physical strength, physical fitness, physical endurance, and physical combat. It brimmed with energy and exuberance in the service of righteousness. Manly virtue, as Roosevelt not only preached, but also practiced it, tended to be self-dramatizing, overly idealistic, and occasionally foolhardy.[26]

Still, even if there was something exaggerated and slightly ridiculous about his conception of the manly virtues, at some basic level, Roosevelt was right. The manly virtues were and always would be an essential part of the character of free men. Although Roosevelt fully accepted the doctrine of evolution, he never seriously considered that men would "evolve" to the point where the manly virtues would become obsolete.[27] Societies might become so over-refined that these virtues atrophied, but this would spell decline, not progress. Whatever else progress might mean, it did not signal an end to a need for the "iron" virtues the pioneers had perfected. But after the frontier was officially declared closed by the census of 1890, what purpose did the manly virtues serve?

BATTLING POLITICAL CORRUPTION IN ALL ITS FORMS

Although Albany in the 1880s was not the old Southwest of Daniel Boone and Davy Crockett, Roosevelt was convinced that, if a man was to do good work, he would need many of the same rougher, virile virtues as the pioneer of old. The "man who goes into the actual battles of the political world must prepare himself much as he would for the struggle in any other branch of our life." If he was not to be "plundered and bullied" by corrupt politicians, he would have to stand up and fight for his rights.[28] It would take real courage, especially for a fledgling assemblyman, to face down the machines and "special interests." As TR later gleefully recounted, it was only by placing the leg of a broken chair conspicuously beside him that he was able to avert a fight with the "rough characters" on a legislative committee he was chairing.[29] In this sense, reform politics constituted something of a new "frontier."

These battles did not end when Roosevelt left the Assembly in 1884. If anything, Roosevelt, energized by his life as a ranchman, redoubled his attacks on the prevailing political culture. In two fiery magazine articles published in 1885 and 1886, Roosevelt warned against the dangers of an ignorant and lethargic citizen body that had no idea of what was going on in government.[30] Even among the more educated classes who spoke out against corruption, few understood how the system worked (how many members of his class, he wondered, knew what a caucus was?) and most had little desire to become involved in politics. In immigrant communities, things were much worse because these foreigners received their civic lessons from the local "ward heelers." Until the public conscience was aroused, machines and their bosses would continue to dominate the political process, ensuring the victory of "special interests" over the public good.

At the same time, Roosevelt was willing to grant that a political machine was not in principle bad and, even in practice, served a variety of useful social functions.[31] Not only did they provide a gathering place for party members in much the same way that gentlemen's clubs served the upper classes, but they also acted as mutual benefit associations. In poorer immigrant neighborhoods, bosses provided constituents with advice, information about social services, jobs, and financial assistance, insuring that voters would identify their interests with the fortunes of the machine. Four years later, after he was appointed to the Civil Service Commission, Roosevelt would attack the machines precisely for handing out jobs to their loyal followers. But here, he looked at the problem from the perspective of the immigrants. The hard political truth was that if a boss was known to be liberal to the poor, his corruption did not matter. Immigrants, he concluded, were "primitive people still in the clan stage of moral development," well behind even "the bourgeois stage of development" he deplored.[32]

Not only were these foreigners blind to the more obvious forms of political corruption, but being ignorant of the principles of the American republic, they brought with them unrealistic expectations about what government could do to improve their lives. In his essays, Roosevelt tried to deflate these hopes by pointing out that the services and favors they called for were not free. Ultimately it would be the immigrants themselves who wound up shouldering the burden of higher taxes, and not, as local demagogues suggested, some abstract group of taxpayers who already enjoyed more advantages than they deserved. Nevertheless, Roosevelt concluded that the problem did not lend itself to an easy solution. Men who passed their lives in "narrow and monotonous toil" could hardly be expected to understand or approve "the American doctrine of government," according to which "the state cannot ordinarily attempt to better the condition of a man or a set of men, but can merely see that no wrong is done him or them by anyone else, and that all alike have a fair chance in the struggle for life—a struggle wherein, it may as well at once be freely though sadly acknowledged, very many are bound to fail, no matter how ideally perfect any given system of government may be."[33]

If what he meant was that the newly arrived immigrants should not be deceived into thinking that government could guarantee that everyone would succeed regardless of their talent, effort, and luck, much as Benjamin Franklin (another of his heroes) had warned earlier immigrants that fowls in America did not fly about "ready roasted, crying *Come eat me!*,"[34] Roosevelt chose his words poorly. For he came off sounding less like a practical politician in the spirit of Franklin or Lincoln, and more like a Social Darwinist indifferent to the plight of the poor. It was one thing to try to get the immigrants to have realistic expectations of what government could do to make their lives better, but quite another to demand that they acquiesce to a system in which "very many" of them were "bound to fail." Privately, Roosevelt was even harsher, writing to Henry Cabot Lodge that the immigrants' failures were largely their own fault or the "mere operation of the laws of nature."[35]

Nor were these struggling newcomers likely to be impressed by his holding up as a model the "tens of thousands" of Americans who acted on the "sublime virtue of disinterested adherence to the right, even when it seems to benefit others, and others better off than they themselves are."[36] What was missing from this civics lesson was Hamilton's shrewd observation that the best way to get most men to do their duty was to make it in their interest to do so, humorously brought home in Franklin's writings, or Lincoln's insight that hope is better than despair.[37] All too often, Roosevelt's early advice to the immigrants oscillated between patrician condescension, larded with Social Darwinist nostrums, and unworkable idealism of a distinctly German cast. The "American doctrine of government" that he preached was not quite as American as he thought. Certainly, it was not the Americanism of his heroes.

IMMIGRATION AND THE LIMITS OF ASSIMILATION

Although in his histories, Roosevelt had emphasized the primacy of the old English stock in shaping a distinctive American nationality, in practical politics he accepted more readily than many of his class the most recent influx of immigrants from eastern and southern Europe, focusing his efforts on assimilating them as rapidly and thoroughly as possible. As Roosevelt explained in "True Americanism," by assimilation he meant a willingness to learn English (he would give immigrants five years to learn the language or face deportation); adapt to American culture (he deplored the hyphenated American); take pride in American history (he would have immigrants celebrate the Fourth of July instead of ethnic holidays such as St. Patrick's Day); embrace American political principles (by which he meant a strict separation of church and state that would deny public support to the mostly Catholic parochial schools); and, by the third generation, to intermarry. In turn, he firmly believed that the state must guarantee all citizens their rights, neither discriminating against nor favoring anyone on the basis of ethnic origin or religious belief. Roosevelt denounced the efforts of the American Protective Association to treat Catholics like second-class citizens; "know-nothingism, in any form," was "utterly un-American." "True Americanism" was "a question of spirit, conviction, and purpose, not of creed or birthplace."[38]

It was not that Roosevelt, whose paternal side of the family was Dutch, thought all ethnic and religious groups were equal; he clearly did not. *The Winning of the West* teemed with judgments about the ethnic (or what Roosevelt called "racial") characteristics of the settlers. Germans and French Huguenots ranked highest, while Scots-Irish Presbyterians, by far the most numerous, were faulted for their "fondness for drink" and quarrelsome disposition.[39] He was even less impressed by the first-generation Irish Catholics who served with him in the New York legislature.[40] Assessing the qualifications of Jewish immigrants from Poland and Russia to serve on the New York police force, Roosevelt observed that they were "very intelligent" but worried that "centuries of degradation and oppression" had stunted their manliness.[41] Still, even if the different European immigrant groups did not start out on the same moral, intellectual, or even physical level, Roosevelt was prepared to accept them, as long as they were resolved to put aside their old ways and become "true" Americans. Some groups would assimilate more readily because they had fewer obstacles to overcome, but he was confident that in time all the European immigrants, whether Catholic or Protestant, Christian or Jew, Irish, Italian, Slav, or Magyar, could adapt to their new American environment.[42]

In this sense, assimilation functioned as the political counterpart to Roosevelt's Lamarckianism. Although TR accepted and indeed made ample use of the Darwinian idea of natural selection or survival of the fittest when it suited him, he did not regard it as the most important explanation of evolutionary progress. As he observed in his 1895 review of Benjamin Kidd's *Social Evolution* (a work he found suggestive but "very crude"), often it was the less fit that survived, while the fittest died out or dwindled in number. If progress were the greatest where the struggle for survival was most intense, then South Italians, Polish Jews, and Irish city-dwellers would be the most advanced. But Roosevelt's review suffered from its own difficulties, since he was here making the common mistake of Social Darwinists, attributing moral and social characteristics to the idea of the fittest, rather than applying the term to those who survived and passed on their genetic makeup to their numerous progeny.

What is more, like his Harvard professor, Nathaniel Southgate Shaler, Roosevelt somehow thought that natural selection and the inheritance of acquired characteristics could coexist, ignoring the fact that Darwin's explanation rested solely on random mutations, whereas Lamarck's theory allowed for intention and choice.[43] Thus, Roosevelt moved back and forth between these two competing accounts, adjusting his theory to particular circumstances. Where the immigrants were concerned, progress occurred when the "less fit" adapted to their environment and passed these acquired characteristics along to future generations. In this way, the inheritance of acquired characteristics provided a "counterbalance to the baleful law of natural selection." In time, the less fit would become "more fit" by cultivating a "love of order, ability to fight well and breed well, [and] a capacity to subordinate the interests of the individual to the interests of the community."[44] Lacking knowledge of the science of genetics, which was still in the future, Roosevelt, observing that these desirable moral qualities had been transmitted from one generation to another, mistakenly assumed that these traits depended upon biology, rather than culture and habituation.

Still, assimilation had its limits and, as might be expected from his histories, these limits were mostly racial.[45] Like most educated men of his generation, Roosevelt had been taught that race, however loosely and even inconsistently defined, was the great organizing principle of civilization. Not only did he doubt that people of different races could be easily assimilated, but he made no effort to disguise his opinion that the white race, and in particular the English-speaking people, whose expansion he had charted over the past 300 years, stood at the top of the racial hierarchy.

In "True Americanism," Roosevelt argued that "much more drastic laws" were necessary to "keep out laborers who tend to depress the labor market, and to keep out races which do not readily assimilate with our own, and unworthy individuals of all races," especially criminals, idiots, paupers, and anarchists. Expanding on this point in a review essay of Charles Pearson's *National Life and Character* written the same year as "True Americanism"(1894), Roosevelt noted approvingly that democratic nations had instinctively practiced a healthy "race selfishness" by preserving the most temperate parts of the world in America and Australia for the white race. He praised these same democratic societies for recognizing the "race foe" and excluding the "dangerous alien" from their territories. The one exception was the Negro, but Roosevelt viewed his presence in the New World as the unfortunate legacy of a time when America was ruled by a "transoceanic aristocracy" dependent upon cheap labor. Without irony, Roosevelt observed that once the United States became a democracy, it understood more clearly what its interest required. "The whole civilization of the future owes a debt of gratitude greater than can be expressed in words to that democratic policy which has kept the temperate zones of the new and newest worlds a heritage for white people."[46]

For the most part, Roosevelt's insistence on keeping out undesirable aliens was directed against the "yellow" race, since blacks had been transported to America against their will long before independence, and the once-menacing "reds" had largely been conquered. Already in *Thomas Hart Benton* (1887), Roosevelt, in one of his many asides, had defended Chinese exclusion laws on the ground that filling the Pacific Coast with "Mongolians" would be a "calamity."[47] Now, as an appointed federal official and public intellectual reviewing the most important books of the day, he continued to insist that the presence of the "Chinaman" in the United States and Australia, that is, the temperate zones, would be "ruinous to the white race."[48]

Roosevelt's support for Chinese exclusion was based in part on a desire to protect American workers. A large influx of Chinese immigrants, willing to work for "coolie" wages would, he feared, depress wages generally. But, as his review of Pearson's *National Life and Character* made clear, Roosevelt had other reasons for doubting that the Chinese could be assimilated to American culture. Not only did they lag far behind the United States in the progress of their civilization, but most important, the racial divide was too deep. He simply could not imagine that by the third generation whites would be willing to intermarry with Asians.

Of course, Roosevelt was correct to argue that every nation had the "absolute right" to determine who could immigrate and become citizens. And he was right to insist that nations should take care to keep out all those who were undesirable, either because they were mentally or morally unfit for self-government. But there is something troubling about his insistence that the United States should actively bar members of "alien" races from immigrating and becoming American citizens.

RESPONSIBLE GOVERNMENT

At its best, Roosevelt's approach to reform during the 1880s and 1890s could be seen in an essay he published offering advice to the college graduate. It was, he thought, "always a pity" to see men, especially those with college educations, "fritter away their energies" on "pointless" schemes. Yet this was precisely what some of the most intelligent young men of his day had done. Without naming names (though Woodrow Wilson's *Congressional Government*, published in 1885, immediately springs to mind),[49] Roosevelt singled out for special criticism the recent enthusiasm for "responsible government" that called for grafting certain features of the English parliamentary system onto the American presidential model. Not only was such a proposal impractical; it was also undesirable. The English and American constitutions were "utterly incompatible," and there was no way to introduce features of the English system without first "sweeping away the United States Constitution." These reformers would have made better use of their time, he thought, if they had read *The Federalist*, which established the "ideal" for both "the student of politics and the practical politician."[50]

Turning to more recent politics, Roosevelt suggested that college students would be better advised to follow in the footsteps of Thomas Brackett Reed. A Bowdoin College graduate who came of age at the outbreak of the Civil War, Reed, like the authors of *The Federalist*, combined expertise in political science with practical experience to achieve workable reform. As Speaker of the House during the Fifty-first Congress (1889–1891), Reed was faced with an intransigent Democratic minority determined to use the filibuster and other parliamentary maneuvers to keep Republicans from getting anything done. This problem was not unique to the Fifty-first Congress; it had been growing steadily since the end of the Civil War, so that, even as the balance of power shifted back to the legislature, Congress was in danger of being reduced to an impotent debating society. It was in fact this impasse that had led some of the more academic students of the Constitution in a "curious colonialism of spirit" to look to England for guidance on how to break the stalemate in Congress.[51] Reed, however, understood that English precedent was useless in the American context and set about instead to devise a new manual of common-sense parliamentary procedures that would restore to Congress the power to legislate, as the Framers intended. "Reed's Rules" provided ample opportunity for political debate, but they also ensured that in the end, debate served the primary function of Congress, which was to make laws and have those laws reflect the will of the majority as expressed in the last congressional election. As a result, Reed quickly became Roosevelt's new manly hero. "I swear by Tom Reed. . . . Besides, I am tired of flabbiness, and I am glad to see a Republican of virility, who really does something."[52]

Alas for the cause of reform, the Republicans were thrown out of office in the next election and the Democrats proceeded to repeal the new parliamentary procedures. But their triumph was brief. Republicans, with Reed at their head, were restored to power in 1895 by the largest margin in their history as a national party. Roosevelt argued that this change in political fortune was good for the Republican Party, but even more important, it was good for the republic. "In order that a republic may exist there must be some form of representative government, and this representative government must include a legislature" capable of attending to the people's business. Congress's job was to legislate and not merely to debate, as defenders of the filibuster seemed to think. By marshalling his powers as Speaker to change the rules of procedure in the House, Thomas Brackett Reed vindicated the cause of "responsible government" in a thoroughly American way.[53]

What Roosevelt failed to appreciate, however, was that the Democrats' defense of the filibuster fit perfectly with Wilson's broader aim, which Roosevelt supported, of separating politics from administration. As R. J. Pestritto has noted, the whole point of allowing Congress to debate indefinitely was that it then would have no time "to meddle in the details of legislation," which were best left to impartial bureaucrats, trained in the new science of public administration.[54] Congress would, in some formal sense, still pass general statutes sketching out policy goals, but it would no longer "legislate" as the Framers of the Constitution intended. A new class of expert administrators attached to the executive branch or to independent agencies would write the actual "rules" that governed the country, as in fact is increasingly the case. This was the great promise of civil service reform.[55]

CIVIL SERVICE REFORM

Even as he worked with Democratic governor Grover Cleveland to enact civil service reform for New York State, Roosevelt insisted that what distinguished the two parties was the longstanding Republican commitment to this issue.[56] Since the end of the Civil War, Republicans had been in the forefront of the civil service movement, attempting to arouse public opinion against the abuses of the spoils system that had first been introduced by Andrew Jackson and perfected by his successor, Martin Van Buren. Up to that time, minor government posts had been filled using the merit principle, filtered through an unspoken tradition of deference to one's social "betters." Jackson's victory in 1828, fueled by the rise of the common man, overthrew the old order and established a new, supposedly more democratic, principle for political appointments: "to the victor belong the spoils." Now, after sixty years the spoils system had become so entrenched that many Americans had come to regard political patronage as an intrinsic element of democratic politics rather than a corruption of the founders' intentions.[57]

From the outset, Roosevelt embraced the cause of civil service reform but considered the methods of the older generation of reformers hopeless. The "timid good," as he called them, thought that their high ideals alone would turn the tide and that they could bring about their desired changes without having to enter the political arena and fight for them. Speaking before the Civil Service Reform Association in 1889, the year he was named to the federal Civil Service Commission, Roosevelt sought to distance himself from these earnest do-gooders by emphasizing that he was a "practical Republican politician," rather than a "mere theorist." Like his friend, Judge Taft, Roosevelt agreed that America needed "reformers who ate roast beef, and who were able to make their blows felt in the world."[58]

It was more than a question of approach, however. The early civil service reformers had focused chiefly on the inefficiency and waste of having politicians spend all their time filling the growing number of patronage slots with candidates who lacked the necessary job skills to the neglect of their own duties.[59] Roosevelt, too, deplored these developments, but his moral outrage was directed principally against its corrupting effects. The spoils system, he thundered, treated "all offices as fit objects wherewith to reward partisan service, as prizes to be scrambled for by the besmirched victors in a contemptible struggle for political plunder, as bribes to be parceled out among the most active and influential henchmen of the various party leaders." Sixty years later, the problem had now reached a critical stage, for no republican government could "permanently endure when its politics is corrupt and base; and the spoils system . . . produces corruption and degradation."[60]

Another vice of the spoils system was that it undermined political accountability. As the number of patronage positions increased, executive officers no longer appointed their subordinates but were forced to accept the recommendations of congressmen and influential local politicians who regarded these appointments as their own personal bailiwick. Nor was it the case that the positions were awarded to the most competent members of the victorious party—though even this, Roosevelt, a nonpartisan purist, considered "absurd." But the actual situation was much worse, for these politicians knew nothing about the applicants' qualifications as customhouse clerks or postal carriers. All too often, the jobs went to those who had rendered "adroit and unscrupulous service" to the powerful local bosses.[61] Competence and a desire to serve the public had little to do with them getting the job—or keeping it. It made no sense to turn out this army of civil servants every time the parties changed power.

The Pendleton Act of 1883 was the first serious effort to address these problems. Passed into law following the assassination of President James Garfield by a disappointed office-seeker, it initially removed about 10 percent of the federal workforce from the reach of the spoils men and, by the time Roosevelt arrived to take up his post, that number had grown to nearly a quarter. By law, these civil service positions were now to be filled strictly on the basis of merit, as determined by competitive examinations. Characteristically, Roosevelt expected that these exams would call forth an "open and manly rivalry" in which the candidate "best fitted" for the particular position would get the job.[62] Critics, however, were quick to brand the merit system elitist and aristocratic because, they insisted, the exams required knowledge of arcane matters irrelevant to the job. But Roosevelt turned the tables, arguing that it was the spoils system that was "essentially undemocratic." Although the patronage regime claimed to open political jobs to the "common man," in fact it treated these appointments as a "bribery chest" to advance the personal and political interests of a powerful few. It was "the ward boss, the district heeler, the boodle alderman, and all their base and obscure kindred," who had undermined "honest democracy" and turned it into "a corrupt and ignorant oligarchy."[63]

By contrast, the merit system championed by the reformers was "in its very essence democratic" because it opened "public service to all men, of whatever rank in life" who demonstrated practical, common-sense knowledge necessary for the performance of their jobs, and whose characters could be vouched for by three reputable citizens. In addition, it made continuance in these positions dependent solely on honest, efficient, and courteous service to the public. To a nation inured to the evils of the spoils system, Roosevelt tried to build confidence in the reforms by appealing to the authority of the founders. The merit system accorded with "the utterances and deeds of our forefathers of the days of Washington and Madison." It was, he insisted, the only one that "the founders of our own Republic regarded . . . [as] worthy of a free and high-minded nation."[64]

And in one sense he was right. In the early years of the republic, many of America's statesmen distrusted political parties and tried to remain above them.[65] As president, Washington sought out the best men for office, regardless of their political views, and attempted (unsuccessfully) to get the strong personalities in his cabinet to work together for the good of the country. But once political parties began to emerge, as they did almost immediately, both parties when they were in power tended to confine their search for the most wise and virtuous to gentlemen in their respective camps. Although the early presidents continued to pay lip service to the principle of nonpartisanship, with Jefferson famously declaring that "we are all Republicans, we are all Federalists," in practice the merit principle very quickly had to adjust itself to the realities of partisan politics.

Yet this practical accommodation seemed to be precisely what Roosevelt missed, which is ironic in view of his professed regard for *The Federalist*. For although Publius had written that the aim of every constitution should be to attract the wisest and most virtuous men to office, he also understood that men were motivated by a variety of competing interests, passions, and opinions, which would cause them to divide into political factions. There simply was no way in a free society based on consent of the governed and dedicated to the protection of individual rights that all citizens would agree on what the public good required. It was folly to rely on "enlightened statesmen" or "better motives" to adjust these differences. Men of the caliber of George Washington, who acted out of disinterested duty, were simply too rare. The only security lay in distributing political power so that each branch would have the "constitutional means and personal motives" to check the others, with a vigilant citizen body keeping watch over them all.[66]

Of especial interest here was *The Federalist*'s discussion of administration. At first glance, Publius's observation that "the true test of good government is its aptitude and tendency to produce a good administration"[67] appeared to lend authority to Roosevelt's vision of civil service reform. But drawing on the overall argument of *The Federalist*, there was a fundamental difference between Publius's position and Roosevelt's. Although Publius believed that department heads might exercise some independence in formulating policy (as in fact Hamilton did as secretary of the treasury), he did not believe—for the reasons outlined above—that politics could be taken completely out of administration, nor in a democratic republic that it should be.[68] Ultimately, federal administrators would be accountable to the chief executive, who, in turn, would be accountable to the electorate.

By contrast, Roosevelt's goal from the start was to separate the two, creating an independent civil service that would impartially administer the nation's business, applying to municipal government "the same business principles that obtain in every well-conducted private business." (So intent was he on elevating the merit principle that Roosevelt ignored the fact that even well-run companies attempted to bend government policy to their interests. And the more the bureaucracy attempted to regulate them, the more would they attempt to influence its decisions.) In his speech before the New York Assembly in support of a state civil service law, Roosevelt declared that his principal aim in supporting the legislation was "to take the civil service out of the political arena."[69] What he meant in the first instance was that the party machine should not be handing out government jobs on the basis of political favoritism, but TR was also convinced that if civil servants were chosen on the merit principle they would be able to rise above self-interest and leave their politics at the door. It was this appeal to "abstract" duty that the authors of *The Federalist* would have questioned, for they did not confuse merit with disinterestedness or professional competence with nonpartisanship. As Publius explained, the whole thrust of the Constitution was to arrange political institutions in such a way that duty and self-interest coincided.[70] Thus, however much they might have been disgusted by the corruption of the spoils system, they would have recognized that the spoilsmen had a better appreciation of the power of selfish interests than did more idealistic reformers such as Roosevelt with his "ideal of pure and decent government."[71]

Turning from theory to practice, Roosevelt enforced the provisions of the Pendleton Act with nonpartisan zeal in both the Republican administration of Benjamin Harrison and that of his Democratic successor, Grover Cleveland. Among its other provisions, the act barred political machines from raising money for their campaign chests by assessing officeholders a certain percent of their salary. Although the commission did not succeed in putting an end to political assessments altogether, Roosevelt assured those federal workers who had "the manliness to stand up and refuse to be bullied into paying an assessment" that they would not suffer, and that politicians who tried to extort money from them would be penalized.[72] Nevertheless, clamping down on this extortion produced unintended consequences, since parties had to raise money somehow. Once "political assessments" were made illegal, Republican machines found it both convenient and profitable to turn to corporate donors to finance their campaigns, cementing the relation between the Republican Party and big business, but raising new problems for Republican reformers, as Roosevelt would soon learn.[73]

In addition to enforcing the provision banning political assessments, the Civil Service Commission sought to eliminate some of the most "outrageous iniquities" of the spoils system by increasing the number of jobs classified as civil service positions. Roosevelt was particularly incensed by the extent to which the spoils system had in his own day penetrated the Indian service. It was bad enough when capable men and women were turned out of post offices or customs houses because of their political affiliations, but it was unconscionable to see this occurring on the reservations. The Indian tribes were "groping toward civilization out of the darkness of hereditary and ingrained barbarism." At this critical stage in their development, the quality of the agents was all-important. With a competent and practical man, the Indians were capable of making great strides toward civilization, but an unscrupulous agent could easily retard their progress, or ignite a useless war. Roosevelt regretted that the civil service system had no control over the appointment of the Indian agents themselves, but he was pleased that more than 700 teachers and other educational positions had been taken out of the hands of the spoils-mongers.[74] It is worth noting that Roosevelt first used the term "stewardship" to describe his work on the Civil Service Commission, which he here understood as a return to the principles of the founders.[75]

The increase in the number of classified positions also opened up opportunities for qualified blacks in public service. Up to this time, "one of the sad features of the colored problem" was that there were so few jobs available for "men of color who had raised themselves by education above the level of their fellows." After three years on the Civil Service Commission, Roosevelt could boast that fully one-fourth of the appointments in the southern states had gone to educated men and women of color, who were judged "simply and solely" on the basis of their qualifications.[76] Here perhaps is the clearest example of how Roosevelt's democratic individualism bent his racialist views in a more humane and liberal direction, though the two could never be fully reconciled.

Finally, Roosevelt was gratified by the increase in the number of white southerners appointed to civil service positions, emphasizing that the commission had scheduled additional exams throughout the region to encourage qualified candidates to apply. He was especially proud that, at a time when the Republican Party was in power, most of these appointments went to Democrats. What better demonstration of the nonpartisanship of the merit principle than to reward the minority party?

Not surprisingly, the presidents who appointed the Civil Service Commissioners were never as enthusiastic about the merit principle as the reformers, and Roosevelt's zealous enforcement almost cost him his post.[77] But it was a fact of political life that nineteenth-century presidents, Democratic and Republican, whether drawn from the reform wing or the regular organization, depended for their own political careers upon their party machines, and the machines demanded jobs for loyal supporters.[78] It was an even more important fact of political life that selfish interests could not be banished from politics, though Roosevelt's belief that politicians should be guided by disinterestedness or "abstract duty" would only become stronger over time.

Roosevelt found out the hard way how intractable these "special interests" could be when he crossed swords with John Wanamaker. As a reward for his services as campaign finance manager, President Harrison had appointed the wealthy department store owner postmaster general and named James S. Clarkson, a leading spoils politician, as his first assistant. While Wanamaker set about modernizing the post office and initiating his own civil service reforms, Clarkson distributed more than 30,000 fourth-class postmaster positions to party loyalists.[79] Outraged by these actions, the commissioner was determined to investigate, and a newly elected Democratic Congress was only too happy to oblige. By now, the spoilsmen in his own party were calling for Roosevelt's dismissal, and with no support from the White House, the young reformer was forced to cool his heels to hold on to his post. This he managed to do better than Harrison, who was turned out of office in the next election, owing partly to public disgust over the post office scandals. Returning to the White House for the second time, Grover Cleveland saw the advantage in retaining the Republican Roosevelt on the nonpartisan Civil Service Commission at least for a time, and he continued without further incident for another year. But the whole experience led TR more than once to remark, "When Dr. Johnson defined patriotism as the last refuge of the scoundrel, he was ignorant of the infinite possibilities contained in the word reform."[80]

POLICE COMMISSIONER AND THE ELECTION OF 1896

After two more years on the Civil Service Commission, Roosevelt was growing restive. Work on the commission now seemed to him a little like starting over at Harvard again after he had graduated,[81] and he cast about for a new political challenge. He seriously considered making another run for mayor of New York City in 1894, and although he decided against it, the mayoralty race focused his attention once again on the problems of city life. Reviewing Albert Shaw's book, *Municipal Government in Great Britain,* Roosevelt was struck by the tendency of the "white race" everywhere to "concentrate in great cities" at the end of the nineteenth century.[82] In the United States, this shift from rural to urban areas, coupled with a massive increase in immigration, meant that the nation must now move from "unrestricted individualism" to a mix of "individualism" and "collectivism," though the latter term must have sounded odd to American ears. Where the line between the two should be drawn was "not a matter for theory at all," but should be decided by "practical expediency." Already cities had established paid police and fire departments, which Roosevelt (wrongly) labeled "state socialism," in hopes of reassuring those who feared "further experiments" in "collectivism." He then went on to list areas where American municipal governments might usefully benefit from the British experience, including parks and playgrounds, building and sanitary regulations, water supply, and rapid transit. More controversially, and probably in response to his former mayoral opponent Henry George, he called for an investigation into the high cost of urban housing. At the same time, however, he insisted that wherever possible individuals should be left free to follow their own bent, and their rewards made proportional to effort and ability. As intellectually muddled as the review was, it did shed light on how impatiently Roosevelt grasped at ideas as he angled for his next political post.[83]

A short time later, the newly elected reform mayor William L. Strong offered him the job of police commissioner of New York City, where he was soon elected president of the four-man board. His service was, as always, colorful and energetic, with the commissioner slipping out at night undercover to expose corruption in the New York Police Department, establishing a bicycle squad, and assigning an all-Jewish police guard to an anti-Semitic gathering. Among his practical reforms, Roosevelt increased the size of the police force, hiring applicants on the basis of physical and mental abilities rather than party affiliation. It was also during this time that he made the acquaintance of Jacob Riis, whose book *How the Other Half Lives* (1890) had inspired him to work to improve the conditions of tenement life in New York City and who frequently accompanied the commissioner on his rounds.[84]

In what was undoubtedly his most unpopular decision, Roosevelt managed to antagonize the large German immigrant population by enforcing the Sunday closing laws. Saloon-keepers were furious that they could no longer bribe the police to remain open, and despite a general public sentiment in favor of honesty in government, the crackdown was highly unpopular. But Roosevelt defended his actions with an argument that echoed Lincoln's in the Lyceum Address: a law should not be enacted if it was not meant to be enforced honestly and for everyone. To tolerate bribery was to undermine respect for the law.[85] It was, however, a dilemma, for as his earlier opposition to a prohibition law made clear, he also understood that "in a community governed on the principle of popular sovereignty," it was folly to enact laws that ran so contrary to public opinion.[86]

Even as president of the police board, Roosevelt soon discovered that his powers were limited because most decisions required the unanimous consent of the board. Thus, looking back on this period in his *Autobiography*, TR concluded that his service on the commission was notable for having first planted in his mind the suspicion that the "old-school" American system of checks and balances was unworkable. Far better it would have been to have concentrated power in the hands of one or a few and devised some way of holding them accountable to the people. Roosevelt conceded that this concentration of power would not have guaranteed good government, but it would have placed responsibility squarely on the shoulders of the people, where it belonged. But by 1913, he had embraced the ideal of direct democracy, which played no part in his reform agenda in 1896. As was so often the case, Roosevelt's retrospective comments in his *Autobiography* tended to cast a more progressive glow over his early actions.

What is more, had TR reread *The Federalist* he was so enthusiastically recommending back in the 1890s (it was part of the Pigskin Library he took with him to Africa in 1909),[87] he might have realized that the stalemate on the police commission was not so much an argument against checks and balances as it was against a plural executive. In that battle, Publius was his ally. Long before Roosevelt railed against the limitations of his office as police commissioner, Publius had warned that, in trying to prevent evil, too many checks on the executive would prevent anything good from being accomplished, which was precisely Roosevelt's complaint. As Publius rightly foresaw, the tendency of a plural executive, and by extension, plural executive agencies such as the New York City Police Commission, would be to conceal faults and destroy responsibility.[88] The "old school" American political understanding, as set forth in *The Federalist*, was not only compatible with energy and responsibility, but positively encouraged it.

When the work of the commission did not absorb him, Roosevelt traveled around the country, campaigning vigorously on behalf of the national Republican ticket. As he then saw it, the stakes could not have been higher: with the notable exception of the election of 1860, the danger facing the country in 1896 was "graver than any that has menaced the country from its birth."[89] By the time he came to write his *Autobiography*, however, Roosevelt saw the matter differently and passed quickly over the election. From the standpoint of 1913, all he could say was that although he was beginning to gain some awareness of the needs of the people, he was "still ignorant of the extent to which big men of great wealth played a mischievous part in our industrial and social life."[90] But in 1896, Roosevelt saw the matter quite differently.

The choice before the public in 1896 boiled down to William Jennings Bryan, who had captured the nomination of both the Democratic and Populist parties (albeit with different vice presidential nominees), and William McKinley, along with Garret A. Hobart, on the Republican ticket. (Four years later, Roosevelt himself would be on the ticket as McKinley's running mate.) In an essay in the *Review of Reviews*, the police commissioner had great fun pointing out the differences between Bryan's two vice presidential nominees, suggesting that the Bryan campaign was incoherent. By contrast, the Republican ticket presented a united front in favor of tariff reform, hard money, a muscular foreign policy, and an independent judiciary. Roosevelt denounced attacks on the Supreme Court as "a species of atavism," in which Democrats and Populists had regressed to the ways of "their barbarous ancestors." The Supreme Court, Roosevelt reminded his readers, was intended to protect those liberties that we "have received from our forefathers in the Constitution."[91]

Although Roosevelt regularly sounded all these themes in his addresses, Bryan's electrifying "Cross of Gold" speech drove home to him "the menace of the demagogue." In a speech before the American Republican College League in Chicago, Roosevelt played to his audience by emphasizing that a Bryan victory would excite the "envy and malice" of the less able and fortunate against all those who by their own efforts and good luck had succeeded. Roosevelt emphasized that he was not claiming that college graduates were entitled to special privileges, only that they should not have their achievements held against them. This, however, was precisely what the Democrats and Populists sought to do. Bryan and his allies were not the soft demagogues of which Publius had warned, who rose to power by flattering the people and playing to their vanity, but the more malignant form that would foment class hatred for the purpose of overturning "civilization."[92] (It is worth emphasizing that Roosevelt defaulted to this politically formless term, rather than thinking in terms of regimes.) Roosevelt likened Bryan's political sympathizers, especially men like Eugene V. Debs,

Ben Tillman, and Governor John Peter Altgeld of Illinois, to the French Revolutionaries and Paris Communards.[93]

Turning to the candidate himself, Roosevelt protested against Bryan's indiscriminate attacks on "non-producers," implying that those who did not work with their hands were social parasites. Could it in fairness, he asked, be maintained that literary men such as Lowell, Emerson, and Hawthorne had "produced" nothing, or that all capitalists were evil? This was to abandon common sense and fall prey to "every European dreamer and European agitator." Americans should judge men by their character rather than the social class from which they came. As Washington and Lincoln, one a wealthy planter, the other a lawyer who rose from humble beginnings, demonstrated, good men came from all walks of life. Roosevelt urged his audience to remain true to the legacy of "orderly liberty" inherited from "our forefathers" and to resist the siren call of the demagogue.

When challenged in print by Thomas E. Watson, Bryan's running mate on the Populist ticket, Roosevelt apologized and denied that he had meant to include Watson among the agitators he denounced.[94] Nevertheless, the suspicion arises that, even as he warned of "the menace of the demagogue," Roosevelt was not entirely averse to practicing these political arts himself, particularly against a man such as Bryan, whose moralistic approach to politics so closely mirrored his own. And it is worth noting the irony that Roosevelt's defense of the courts, of "ordered liberty," and the Constitution in 1896 would be precisely the issues on which he would attack William Howard Taft in 1912 as his own position moved ever closer to Bryan's. And whereas in the election of 1896 he insisted that "the worst capitalist cannot harm laboring men as they are harmed by demagogues,"[95] in the 1912 election, the Bull Moose would fall strangely silent when it came to "the menace of the demagogue."

THE MANLY VIRTUES AND WAR

Although standing up to machine politicians and demagogues provided opportunities for a younger, more virile group of reformers to display the manly virtues Roosevelt admired, he continued to brood about the American character. The census data of 1890, declaring the frontier officially closed, did nothing to allay these anxieties. For if, as Frederick Jackson Turner argued in "The Significance of the Frontier in American History," it was the frontier that decisively shaped the democratic character of America, then the closing of the frontier posed a serious problem for the future.[96] Although Turner did not explore this issue in his famous essay, in a subsequent article he suggested ways in which the United States might continue in its dynamic growth, replicating the experience of the frontier. The "expansive energies" that had conquered the West might now be channeled by a "popular hero" into demands for a "vigorous foreign policy, for an interoceanic canal, for a revival of our power upon the seas, and for the extension of American influence to outlying islands and adjoining countries."[97] The essay was tailor-made for Roosevelt.

Early in the Cleveland administration, TR had criticized the decision to withdraw the Hawaiian annexation treaty from the Senate, and had spoken out forcefully in favor of evicting every European power from the American continent. With remarkable understatement, the author of *Thomas Hart Benton* declared himself to be "a bit of a believer in the manifest destiny doctrine."[98] In response to a territorial dispute between Britain and Venezuela over the border of neighboring British Guyana, TR affirmed the soundness of the Monroe Doctrine, decrying the "milk-and-water cosmopolitanism" of those who took the side of other countries against their own and who could speak of "patriotism" only in "inverted commas."[99]

A letter to the Harvard *Crimson*, provoked by news that faculty and students were trying to tilt American policy in favor of Britain, defended the Monroe Doctrine and recalled the college's long and honorable association with that policy.

> In its present shape it [the Monroe Doctrine] was in reality formulated by a Harvard man, afterwards President of the United States, John Quincy Adams. John Quincy Adams did much to earn the gratitude of all Americans. Not the least of his services was his positive refusal to side with the majority of the cultivated people of New England and the Northeast in the period just before the War of 1812 when those cultivated people advised the same spiritless submission to improper English demands that some of their descendants are now advising.[100]

Yet Roosevelt seems to have allowed his passion for national greatness and his political ambition to ride roughshod over the facts. For not only did the British readily agree to international arbitration to settle the dispute, but the Monroe Doctrine was never intended to apply to existing European claims in the New World. It sought only to prevent European powers from staking out new territorial claims, which was not the issue here. Nevertheless, Roosevelt's full-throated defense of the Monroe Doctrine helped set the stage for his next political move.

Once the Republicans took control of the White House in 1896, the author of *The Naval War of 1812* angled for the post of assistant secretary of the navy, which he received in April 1897. Although he was only the *assistant* secretary, Roosevelt lost no time in laying out a new vision for America along lines sketched by the influential naval strategist Alfred Thayer Mahan. When then-Captain Mahan's *The Influence of Sea Power upon History* appeared in 1890, Roosevelt had been impressed by the connection he made between naval power and national greatness, and more particularly, by his warning that the U.S. Navy was woefully unprepared for any serious European engagement.[101]

In his first public speech as secretary, delivered at the Naval War College in June 1897 (where Mahan had until recently served as president), TR chose as his theme Washington's maxim, "To be prepared for war is the most effectual means to promote peace."[102] Responding to critics who warned of an "overdevelopment of warlike spirit," Roosevelt insisted that the danger in America arose from precisely the opposite quarter. "The United States has never once in the course of its history suffered harm because of preparation for war, or because of entering into war. But we have suffered incalculable harm, again and again, from a foolish failure to prepare for war or from reluctance to fight when to fight was proper." The men who protested against the present day buildup of the navy were part of a long line of "peace at any price" advocates, beginning with those who opposed westward expansion, and continuing on to Jefferson and Madison, who refused to strengthen the nation's defenses even as they pursued a policy that would lead to the War of 1812. These men were the kindred spirits of those who did nothing at the mid-century, leaving the United States unprepared for the "grim agony" of the Civil War. Now, amidst the prosperity of the Gilded Age, visionaries preaching universal peace made common cause with weak-willed college men to sap American resolve. More worrisome still were the business types who had "made the till of their fatherland," choosing profit over the honor of their country. At present, these were still only a small minority, but if left unchallenged, America would some day learn the bitter lesson that a rich nation grown slothful and timid is "an easy prey" for those peoples who retained their fighting edge. The task of the "wise and far-seeing" statesman was to educate Americans about the need for a strong defense and to rekindle in them a fighting spirit. The United States could not afford to delay or to indulge in the vain hope that international arbitration would maintain the peace. To do so would make the country's safety depend upon "contemptuous forbearance."[103] What America needed was a "first-class fleet of first-class battleships."

In a bow to the architects of American prosperity, who were busily constructing summer "cottages" in Newport within a stone's throw of the Naval War College, Roosevelt acknowledged that "thrift, energy, and business enterprise" were necessary elements of national greatness. But, doubling down on an old theme, he insisted, "there are higher things in this life than the soft and easy enjoyment of material comfort. It is through strife, or the readiness for strife, that a nation must win greatness."[104] To be sure, the new secretary noted that it was not always necessary to *go* to war to demonstrate national greatness. Sometimes, as in the showdown with England over Venezuela, the willingness to stand up for one's rights, coupled, if necessary, with an impressive display of force, was sufficient to ensure that a nation's interests and honor were safeguarded. But, for this audience especially, the speech tended to emphasize, indeed even to glorify, "the supreme triumph of war" as the means to national greatness. Courage was not simply the first of the virtues, but almost the sum of them.[105]

The policy implications of his speech were clear. As he later explained in *The Rough Riders,* he had strongly favored American intervention in Cuba to drive the Spanish from the New World when the Democrats were in power. Now that the Republicans were back in office, it was incumbent upon him to do everything possible to bring about the end in which he so "heartily believed."[106] As early as November 1897, Roosevelt confided to naval officer William Wirt Kimball that there were two good reasons for the United States to welcome a war with Spain. First, America had both an interest and a humanitarian duty to intervene on behalf of the Cubans, and second, war with Spain would give Americans "something to think of which isn't material gain," while at the same time providing the army and navy with valuable combat experience at little risk.[107] Unlike the Civil War, this conflict would bind the nation together in a spirit of shared sacrifice and struggle in the service of lofty ideals.

After the explosion of the *Maine* in Havana harbor on February 16, 1898, Roosevelt moved aggressively to prepare the navy for war. Taking advantage of his boss's temporary absence later that month, acting secretary Roosevelt ordered Admiral George Dewey to coal up his ships and sail toward the Philippines. Roosevelt's action allowed him to take credit for Dewey's victory over the Spanish at Manila Bay within days after war was formally declared, paving the way for the American occupation of the Philippines.[108]

Naturally, the assistant secretary of the navy was keen to see action, and in the months leading up to the war, began to plot to get himself sent to the front. However valuable his services had been in building up the navy, TR confessed he would eat his heart out if he had to remain at his desk in Washington.[109] For Roosevelt and many of his generation, the Spanish-American War offered the chance of a lifetime to prove themselves on the field of glory, and in Roosevelt's case, overcome the shame of his father's having bought a substitute in the Civil War. But his biographer Henry F. Pringle went too far when he spoke of Roosevelt's "lust for war," as if he were simply bloodthirsty.[110] Roosevelt's motives were more complicated. Clearly, he romanticized war, but as his letter to Kimball suggested, humanitarian and political considerations also figured into his calculus, as did laudable personal motives, which Pringle overlooked. "It would not be honorable," Roosevelt confided to his brother-in-law, Douglas Robinson, on the eve of the war, "for a man who has consistently advocated a warlike policy not to be willing himself to bear the brunt of carrying out that policy." Since he wished to pursue a career in politics, he added, it was especially important that he be willing to practice what he preached.[111]

And practice it he did. The Rough Rider's charge up Kettle Hill won for him a national reputation as a war hero, which he then used to defend an active American presence in the world. In a speech before the Hamilton Club of Chicago, Roosevelt urged his countrymen to embrace "the strenuous life" of sacrifice and service. If Americans were to remain true to the legacy of their forefathers (or in his case redeem that legacy), they must not "shrink from danger, from hardship, or from bitter toil." Men must not shrink from righteous battle, or women from motherhood.[112] It was only through strife that a nation could achieve greatness. There was, of course, no guarantee that Americans would be victorious, but far better it was "to dare mighty things, to win glorious triumphs, even though checkered by failure, than to take rank with those poor spirits who neither enjoy much nor suffer much, because they live in the gray twilight that knows neither victory nor defeat." If Americans aimed to be a "really great people," then they "must strive in good faith to play a great part in the world." There was poetry in his appeal. Roosevelt spoke to men who were capable of "feeling that mighty lift that thrills 'stern men with empires in their brains.'"[113]

On the question of expansion, Roosevelt's thought was evolving rapidly. In his review of Charles Pearson's *National Life and Character*, published only five years earlier, Roosevelt had treated the British colonial effort dismissively, arguing that "merely political conquests," which established a small "governing caste," were "insignificant" compared with "the kind of armed settlement which causes new nations of an old stock to spring up in new countries."[114] And he predicted that in the end, the native peoples would remain largely unchanged by their encounter with "European blood," eventually overthrowing them. As for the Europeans, Roosevelt agreed with Pearson that they could not prosper for long in tropical countries. But this did not matter, since the Europeans, the British above all, had had the foresight to claim the most temperate parts of the globe for themselves and to people these areas with their own kind.

But after the American victory over Spain, Roosevelt made a quick about-face. He now judged Britain's rule in India and Egypt more favorably, first because it trained up generations of expert colonial administrators "accustomed to look at the larger and loftier side of public life,"[115] and second, because it provided even greater benefits to the Indians and Egyptians. "The expansion of England throughout the Nile valley has been an incalculable gain for civilization."[116] Imperialism, or "merely political" conquest, was clearly no longer "insignificant." This was true not only for Britain, but for every "expanding" civilization. The French had conquered Algiers, putting an end to the Barbary pirates, while Russia moved eastward to subdue the Turkoman. The time had come for America to join the ranks of the expanding powers. If it did not, Roosevelt warned, the United States would forfeit "its right to struggle for a place among the peoples that shape the destiny of mankind."[117]

The Rough Rider had no patience with those critics of the war who opposed America's imperial ambitions and took the side of the natives against their own country. He dismissed concerns about "liberty" and "the consent of the governed" as mere "cant," the foolish prattling of those unwilling to "play the part of men." Nor was he impressed by the argument that the United States had no business involving itself in other countries because it had not yet put its own house in order. That there was still work to be done at home was no reason for America to shirk her responsibilities abroad. Having acquired Spain's island possessions after the war, the United States could not simply abandon them to their fate. Puerto Rico was not large enough to become an independent nation, so the United States must govern it "wisely and well, primarily for the interest of its own people." Eventually, Cuba would have to decide for itself whether to become an independent state or "an integral portion of the mightiest of republics," though he glided over the difficulties of assimilating the Spanish-speaking island to the English-speaking American culture.[118]

The Philippines, he conceded, posed the gravest challenge. At present, her people "were utterly unfit for self-government" and showed "no signs of becoming fit" anytime soon. Those who counseled withdrawal, whether from timidity, petty economic motives, or misguided humanitarianism, merited nothing but contempt. If the United States pulled out of the Philippines, the country would slip into utter chaos until some "stronger, manlier power stepped in" to do the work Americans had been too fearful to do. "If we drove out a medieval tyranny only to make room for savage anarchy, we had better not have begun the task at all." But Roosevelt had more faith in the American character. In manfully accepting its responsibilities, the United States would demonstrate to the world that it was now capable of standing with the greatest nations.[119]

In "The Strenuous Life" and "Expansion and Peace," published later that year, Roosevelt attempted to turn the tables on his opponents by claiming that the best way for America to secure peace was not to withdraw from the world and become the "China of the western hemisphere,"[120] but to support the expansion of civilization. "Every expansion of a great civilized power means a victory for law, order, and righteousness." He recognized the paradox of this assertion: that peace could sometimes be won only through war, but righteous peace was the only kind of peace worth pursuing. Those who sought "peace at any price" or who thought that peace could be achieved by "fair dealing" alone failed to understand that barbarian powers would only yield to superior force. "It is only the warlike power of a civilized people that can give peace to the world," and once these civilized nations lost their "great fighting qualities" and became "over-peaceful," the barbarians would renew their assaults. "Such a barbarian conquest would mean endless war." It was only because northern Europe had not lost its warlike spirit that the Mediterranean coasts were not "overrun either by the Turks or by the Sudan Madhists."[121] If these barbarian forces had nothing to fear but the weak-willed southern Europeans, the entire continent would be overrun, and "endless war" would follow, as it always did when barbarians ruled. For the same reason, Roosevelt was confident that American expansion would bring peace to the Philippines.

In addition to securing peace, Roosevelt rested the case for expansion on three arguments. First, as he never tired of saying, expansion offered a route to national greatness. Here, Roosevelt reminded critics of American imperialism that both nations that expanded and those that did not ultimately declined, but the ones that expanded left "heirs and a glorious memory," while the others left neither. In antiquity, the great nation was Rome; now, the torch had passed to England, and by extension, to America: "the great expanding peoples which bequeath to future ages the great memories and material results of their achievements, and the nations which shall have sprung from their loins, England standing as the archetype and best example of all such mighty nations."[122]

Second, expansion was a necessary part of the life cycle. In foreign policy, especially, Roosevelt tended to view the state as an organism subject to certain biological imperatives. America was a young and vigorous nation, still in the growth stage of development. Its entire history up to this point had been "one of expansion," which Americans now considered "a part of the order of nature."[123] At this point, the United States had only two choices: grow or shrink. "When great nations fear to expand, shrink from expansion, it is because their greatness is coming to an end."[124] They then entered a stationary stage, which, although it might last for a while, signaled the beginning of old age, and thus of decline.[125]

And finally, picking up on Rudyard Kipling's theme in "The White Man's Burden," Roosevelt saw expansion as a boon to the savage peoples themselves. Although the United States was a newcomer to imperialism (given the opposition to American imperialism Roosevelt avoided using this word), it had so far acquitted itself well. The Rough Rider proudly noted that "never in recent times has any great nation acted with such disinterestedness as we have shown in Cuba." After freeing the island from Spanish tyranny, the United States had worked to establish free education, law and order, material prosperity, and sanitary conditions, and was by 1901 (or so it seemed) "establishing them in a free and independent commonwealth." In the Philippines, progress was slower, and Roosevelt was forced to acknowledge "occasional wrong-doing." But overall, he insisted that American rule had "incalculably benefited" the natives. "The Tagalogs have a hundredfold the freedom under us that they would have if we had abandoned the islands. We are not trying to subjugate a people; we are trying to develop them and make them a law-abiding, industrious, and educated people, and we hope ultimately a self-governing people. In short, in the work we have done we are but carrying out the true principles of our democracy."[126]

But what precisely were "the true principles of our democracy," or to put it another way, how could imperialism, or rule over others without their consent, be squared with republican self-government? This was the question that such diverse opponents of empire as Yale sociologist William Graham Sumner, Roosevelt's former professors, William James and John W. Burgess, Harvard President Charles W. Eliot, and his one-time Republican hero, Thomas Brackett Reed, had raised, and which Roosevelt, when he was not dismissing their concerns as "cant," or questioning their manliness, largely sidestepped by changing the terms of the debate. Instead of focusing on the distinctive character of the American regime or its "true principles," Roosevelt spoke more generally of the expansion of "civilization" over barbarism. Under this rubric, there were no important differences among the United States (a federal republic), Great Britain (a limited monarchy), France (then in its third republic), Wilhelmine Germany (an increasingly unstable monarchy), and tsarist Russia (an absolute monarchy).[127] All were part of the expansion of civilization, and as such, contributed to the spread of law and order, and of peace. Seen from this perspective, the distinctive American problem of reconciling imperialism with republicanism disappeared.

Roosevelt tried to get around this difficulty in another way as well, by arguing that American policy in the Philippines was no different from how the United States had acquired vast stretches of the American West. And for those opponents who invoked the principles of the Declaration, it must have given him a special pleasure to insist that there was an "exact parallel" between what Jefferson did in Louisiana and what was now going on in the Philippines. The author of the Declaration and of the "consent of the governed doctrine" did not believe he was required to ask the Indians, or even the white settlers, whether they wished to become part of the United States. The great majority of the French and Spanish inhabitants, in fact, were "bitterly opposed to the transfer." Nor did Jefferson worry when he sent in troops to prevent insurrection, or appointed a governor and other officials without consultation. American policy in the Philippines, Roosevelt declared, was no more "imperialistic" than Jefferson's policy in Louisiana.

But, in fact, the parallel was far from "exact." For although Jefferson did not immediately seek the consent of the governed, he only suspended the principle temporarily, out of necessity, and did not repudiate it. Louisiana was admitted to the Union on an equal footing in less than a decade. The "empire of liberty" that Jefferson envisioned consisted of English-speaking, largely Christian, readily assimilated "Americans," who would be self-governing within their states, with all the guarantees and protections of the federal Constitution. In the Louisiana Territory, there was no question that the Constitution followed the flag.[128]

Roosevelt, by contrast, rejected the social compact theory of the Declaration in favor of a more developmental (historicist) liberalism. In this view, peoples did not move from an "abstract" state of nature to civil society by a deliberate act of consent, but rather progressed by stages from barbarism to civilization, which was why "civilization" mattered more than the particular regime. Imperialism was morally justified because it advanced the long-term interests of the ruled, hastening their transition from barbarism to civilization. Unlike the older social compact liberalism, which regarded rule by force as illegitimate, Roosevelt's developmental liberalism permitted illiberal means for the sake of advancing supposedly liberal ends.

More important than consent, Americans had a "higher duty of promoting the civilization of mankind," which justified ruling over "alien" peoples by force.[129]

Moreover, in contrast to Louisiana, Roosevelt envisioned American rule over the Philippines extending into the indefinite future, and not only because the natives were so backward. It would also be a sign of weakness to haul down the flag where once it had flown (even if, as the Supreme Court would later rule, full constitutional protections did not follow).[130] The more accurate parallel, then, would seem to be between Roosevelt's expansionist foreign policy and his defense of Manifest Destiny in his histories, for both shifted the emphasis away from individual liberty and consent and toward expansion and national greatness. Yet even this parallel was not exact, since Manifest Destiny sought to annihilate or remove the Indian tribes and weaker races to make way for Americans, while expansion sought to rule over "alien" races indefinitely for their own good.

Roosevelt's embrace of imperialism raised a second question as well: were there any geographical limits to expansion? Unlike Hamilton, who worried about how far republican government could be extended (especially when the West supported his Democratic rivals), or Jefferson, who, even as he championed an "empire of liberty," casually remarked that the West might one day secede from the Union, Roosevelt seemed to set no limit to how far the American empire over alien peoples might extend. Although in his review of National Life and Character (1895) Roosevelt had largely agreed with Charles Pearson that the white race could not prosper for long in the tropics, this limit was climatological, not political. And even then, he held out the possibility that advances in transportation might make permanent rule possible by allowing a complete change of some "vigorous northern race" every generation. After the American victory in 1898, however, he seemed to suggest that the only limit to colonial expansion lay in the willingness of a people to embrace "the strenuous life" and to dare great things.

Finally, there was a third, more empirical question: how strong was the evidence that expansion was always accompanied by peace? Here again, Roosevelt might have heeded the lesson of The Federalist, where Publius warned that "the love of power or the desire of pre-eminence and dominion" as well as "the jealousy of power, or the desire of equality and safety" are two of the most powerful motives for war.[131] By contrast, Roosevelt seemed to take it for granted that all the "expanding civilizations," regardless of their regimes, would help to maintain peace. Yet in little more than a decade, the nations of Europe would be engulfed in a world war, fueled in part by colonial ambitions and the desire of Germany for its "place in the sun."

REFORM AND THE FOUNDERS

From the start, Roosevelt's relationship to the more national-minded founders he most admired was ambivalent. He had first entered political life to root out the corruption that had crept in with the advent of Jacksonian democracy and to restore the republican government to the high moral purpose it had stood for in the days of Washington and Lincoln. To that end, he sought to attract good men to office and to raise the tone of public life. Like Publius, he warned against demagogues who flattered the people or, worse, sought to foment class warfare. In language that recalled *The Federalist* he defended an independent judiciary as a safeguard to individual liberty. He resisted calls for government to assume responsibilities that belonged more properly to the individual, though he also believed that as social conditions changed, government should take on additional tasks that had once been left to the private sphere. He welcomed the massive influx of European immigrants, but insisted that they assimilate themselves to American culture.

In foreign policy, Roosevelt's debt to Washington was especially great. Taking as his starting point Washington's maxim that "to be prepared for war is the most effectual means to promote peace," he made the case for a strong national defense and sought to awaken his countrymen to America's growing responsibilities in the world. He emphasized the need to rely on American power rather than international arbitration, and like Publius, understood that "mere refraining from wrong-doing" would not ensure that no wrongs were done to the United States.

Yet despite his admiration for Washington and for *The Federalist*, Roosevelt departed from their principles in several important respects and these differences colored his politics right from the beginning. Consider, first, their different understandings of human nature. Whereas *The Federalist* had argued that it was unrealistic to expect men to separate their interests and passions from their political opinions, Roosevelt was much more idealistic. Somewhere along the way he had absorbed the argument that virtue must rise above self-interest. Accordingly, he exhorted his countrymen to practice the "sublime virtue of disinterested adherence to the right" and to work together in a spirit of shared sacrifice. The authors of *The Federalist*, of course, had not ruled out the possibility that the best men might act from "better motives," but they had no confidence that the majority of individuals could routinely rise to this level, and so preferred to rely on institutional arrangements backed up by elections. Roosevelt, by contrast, crucially emphasized the importance of character, which helps to explain his early impatience with the separation of powers as well as his belief that "the right sort" of civil servants would be able to rise above political considerations.

From the outset, Roosevelt was also more hostile to the commercial republic than was Hamilton. Both men had studied ancient history, though the difference in their approaches was telling. Roosevelt, who had cut his teeth on Edward Augustus Freeman, viewed the Greeks and Romans largely as a racial narrative, whereas Hamilton paid more attention to their politics.[132] America's first secretary of the treasury sought an alternative to Rome's martial virtue and found it in the commercial republic. Commerce, Hamilton believed, would open new avenues for greatness to enterprising men so that they would not be forced, as in ancient Rome, to seek it through military exploits alone. By affording ambitious individuals opportunities to realize their diverse talents, the commercial republic would win their loyalty and cement their affection.[133] Hamilton labored under no illusions that the rich were morally superior to the poor; each class had its own peculiar vices. But he did allow that the vices of the wealthy, if properly channeled, were "probably more favorable" to the well-being of the country.[134]

Nevertheless, Hamilton was careful not to push the advantages of the commercial republic too far. Unlike some of the more "visionary" anti-federalists, who argued that commercial ties rendered a stronger Union unnecessary, Hamilton dismissed the idea that the "spirit of commerce" would usher in a new era of peace and cooperation as "the deceitful dream of a golden age."[135] All that commerce had done was change the objects of war; it had not made war obsolete. Fortunately, the wealth that commerce generated would also allow America to build the defenses it would need to protect itself. As Washington's aide-de-camp in the Revolutionary War, who also served under him in the Whiskey Rebellion, Hamilton revered and respected the life of the soldier. But he did not regard military service as the sine qua non of manly virtue.[136]

Entering politics at the height of the Gilded Age, Roosevelt saw nothing of the heroism or greatness of commercial ideals, which he dismissed as "sordid" and "mean." Moreover, he doubted that the interests and motives of businessmen could be as easily channeled toward the common good as perhaps Hamilton thought. Even in ordinary times, profit and honor too often pointed in opposite directions.[137] Added to these considerations, Roosevelt had won his own name in military battle, reinforcing his high estimation of combat. (For his charge up Kettle Hill, he believed he merited the Congressional Medal of Honor and was not embarrassed to lobby for it.)[138] As his full-throated support for the Spanish-American War and "expansion" suggested, Roosevelt saw greatness primarily in military terms. The Spanish-American War offered Americans the opportunity to display their manly virtues by fighting for a "lofty ideal" that transcended material interests. At the same time, the expansion of American power would aid the spread of civilization and demonstrate the country's willingness to undertake great deeds.

Here, again, there are good reasons to doubt whether Hamilton or Washington would have seen American imperialism as it unfolded at the end of the nineteenth century as a path to national greatness. In *Federalist* No. 11, Hamilton observed that Europe had for too long "plumed" herself as the "mistress of the world," entitled by her own sense of superiority to rule over Asia, America, and Africa. It would be, Hamilton insisted, the responsibility of the United States "to vindicate the honor of the human race, and to teach that assuming brother moderation." America would demonstrate to the world that she "disdain[ed] to be the instrument of European greatness." The United States, which had thrown off the British yoke, should be the last country to try to impose it on others by force. The "empire" Hamilton envisioned in *Federalist* No. 1 was grounded on respect for natural rights and consent.[139]

Finally, although during these years Roosevelt remained faithful to the idea of limited government, he often justified his position using arguments from evolutionary biology. His policy prescriptions during this period often display a hard Darwinian edge that is missing in the original. When the founders invoked the laws of nature, they did so to ground their moral principles. Moreover, by acknowledging a "decent respect for the opinions of mankind" and submitting the facts "to a candid world," they believed that even in the midst of war, there was still time for thoughtful deliberation.

For Roosevelt, however, the laws of nature signified nothing but the Darwinian struggle for existence. And once the issue became survival, there was no time to deliberate. Necessity demanded immediate action. His Darwinianism may have been to some extent offset by his Lamarckianism, that is, his belief that individuals could cultivate and pass on to their offspring certain desirable qualities, but the "virtues" he most prized were rooted in the biological imperative to survive. Women must "breed," and men must fight. Here again, Roosevelt's emphasis on the manly virtues to the near exclusion of all other moral virtues (to say nothing of the intellectual virtues) placed a premium on willpower without much mediation by reason.

In sum, although during this period Roosevelt shared with the more national-minded founders a commitment to limited, but energetic, national government, his reasons for doing so were not theirs. Indeed, given his tendency to view politics through the lens of biological progress and historical development, he had no principled reason to resist the steady expansion of government. Much as he struggled to insist, his "American Ideals" were not those of his heroes. Already, in 1895 he thought he had detected a "pattern" in which "every race as it has grown to civilized greatness" tended to move away from laissez-faire toward a buildup of state power.[140] Moreover, he regarded the extent of this buildup to be a question of mere "expediency." How far he would carry these thoughts when he assumed executive power was now the question.

4. Introduction to Executive Power

There could be no doubt that Theodore Roosevelt possessed the temperament of an executive. He was naturally drawn to bold projects and impatient for results. Patrician though he was, Roosevelt had no interest in joining the ranks of genteel reformers who discussed plans for civic uplift from the safe remove of their parlors and clubs. He longed for the chance to command men and to hold his own in the rough-and-tumble of political life. When it came to executive power, Roosevelt thought large. His heroes were George Washington, whose fighting courage helped found the American republic, and Abraham Lincoln, whose steadfast determination preserved it.

While writing *Gouverneur Morris,* Roosevelt had worked his way through Madison's *Notes on the Constitutional Convention* and had at least some understanding of the Framers' arguments in favor of executive power. Lodge's edition of Hamilton's works, together with his biography of the treasury secretary, would only have reinforced Roosevelt's general disposition toward an energetic executive. Moreover, as he frequently observed, the best statesmen were those who, like the authors of *The Federalist,* applied their theoretical insights to practical politics (though it is not clear how carefully, or even whether, he had read Hamilton's papers on the executive). Still, Roosevelt was familiar with at least some of the Framers' theories; what he now sought was practical experience. Since 1882, he had been in and out of politics, serving in various legislative and administrative capacities, but the opportunity for decisive action had largely eluded him. Although he could point to a string of accomplishments, ranging from municipal and state reform to his work on the federal Civil Service Commission under Presidents Harrison and Cleveland, all too often he found himself frustrated by the inefficiency and stalemate that characterized legislative bodies and bureaucratic organizations.

Only once before the outbreak of the Spanish-American War had he been granted the opportunity to exercise executive responsibility of any consequence. As acting secretary of the navy for an afternoon when his boss was away he ordered Admiral Dewey to sail for the Philippines, setting the stage for the American victory at Manila Bay and laying claim to Spain's Pacific empire.[1] After war was declared, Roosevelt, who had served as an officer for three years in the New York National Guard, worked together with Colonel Leonard Wood to assemble, equip, and drill the First United States Volunteer Cavalry. The regiment, drawn principally from rugged southwesterners skilled in "wild horsemanship" and firearms quickly earned the sobriquet The Rough Riders, even though it also included a fair sampling of well-born, polo-playing college men eager to serve.

As Roosevelt related in *The Rough Riders*—his firsthand account of the regiment's exploits in Cuba, published in 1899 while he was governor—one of his first tasks was to establish military discipline among his recruits, both the "high-spirited adventurers" from the Southwest and his social equals from the East. Without question, Roosevelt had a talent for inspiring and leading his men. It was his responsibility, as lieutenant colonel, to make clear to the college men who were not officers that they would have to take orders from him and be willing to perform the ordinary dull work of a soldier as readily as they were to display their heroism.[2] More importantly, as an officer, he did not flinch from the grim business of war. So eager was he to see combat that he connived to get his regiment on board a transport ship that had been assigned to other units. And when rumor (which turned out to be false) reached him with news that Colonel Wood had been killed, he took charge of the regiment without hesitation.[3] In battle, he showed a readiness to improvise, disregarding the advice of the field manuals for commanders to remain at the rear. Heedless of physical danger, he charged to the front, leading his troops up Kettle Hill. He took special pride in having killed a Spaniard with a revolver that his brother-in-law had retrieved from the sunken battleship *Maine*.[4]

But Roosevelt displayed more than "3 a.m. courage"; he was also prepared to do what was necessary to provide for his troops and to enforce his own notions of justice. In *The Rough Riders*, Roosevelt was unsparing in his criticisms of bureaucratic ineptitude, complaining about the scarcity of food, the inanity of issuing winter uniforms to troops about to launch a summer campaign in the tropics, and poor logistics. As a volunteer officer, he did not have to worry that his criticisms would harm his career and was willing to take the lead in conveying the dissatisfaction of the regular army officers to the top brass in Washington.[5] But perhaps the most telling incident was when, acting on his own authority, he offered a volunteer who had been court-martialed, sentenced to a year's hard labor, and dishonorably discharged a second chance to redeem himself on the front. When the youth acquitted himself, Roosevelt pardoned him even though he was aware that he had "not the slightest power" to do so. Questioned later about his action, he claimed that the soldier did not know what was expected of him, and that his pardon was justified by "wartime exigencies."[6] Military necessity, whether real or imagined, would continue to supply a template for extra-legal action. The lesson he took from the war was that men who aspired to lead must sometimes, especially in times of emergency or necessity, bend the rules for the sake of righteousness.

Roosevelt's military triumphs propelled him onto a much larger stage and gave his political career fresh momentum. In the wake of the victory he did so much to bring about, the colonel emerged a national hero, with seemingly no limit to his political ambitions. Scarcely had his regiment been disbanded at Montauk Point than he was approached about running for governor of New York. Although as an assemblyman Roosevelt had been a thorn in the side of the New York Republican machine, party bosses reluctantly concluded that the Rough Rider offered the best, if not the only, path to electoral victory and backed his nomination for governor. In the last mayoral contest, independent Republicans had clashed with machine elements, dividing the party in two. Adding to Republican woes, the incumbent governor, Frank S. Black, had been plagued by scandals arising from the costs of enlarging the Erie Canal. Only by jettisoning the sitting governor and nominating a popular war hero could the Republicans hope to pull off a victory.

The New York governorship, which had twice before served as a springboard to the presidency, would prove a most congenial outlet for Roosevelt's prodigious moral energy. For the first time in his political career, he would have the chance to shape the political agenda, rather than simply respond to it. If he succeeded, Roosevelt would be well situated for a presidential run in 1904, extending what he hoped would be the era of Republican dominance inaugurated by the election of McKinley in 1896. Just as important, the governorship afforded Roosevelt the chance to begin to think about the purposes to which executive power should be put. This was not yet a constitutional theory, a reflection on the role of the executive in republican government, as much as it was a moral philosophy or theory of justice. For the time being, Roosevelt would use his office to secure a "just balance" between the claims of the rich and the poor, warning against arrogance and contempt on the one side and envy and resentment on the other.[7] As he saw it, the task of the executive was to push for reforms that would moderate the extremes and bring both sides closer to a virtuous mean: corporations would now be forced to pay their fair share of taxes, but their efforts would be amply rewarded; laborers would receive greater legal protections, but not to the extent of undermining initiative and industry. The advice was straight out of Aristotle, updated to the nineteenth century. It is worth noting that Roosevelt went so far as to cite the philosopher in one of the essays he published while governor and would reread parts of *The Politics* while in the White House.

Of course, these attempts to discover a mean would require a high degree of judgment, prudence, patience, and self-control. Will and energy, if divorced from steadiness of character, would not only compromise a "just balance," but also, as Roosevelt himself would observe in his perceptive study of *Oliver Cromwell*, threaten the very foundations of constitutional government. For Roosevelt, whose actions were always informed by his own highly developed sense of righteousness, such moral freewheeling posed a perennial danger. The temptation to elevate character and lofty ideals, while dismissing the constitutional restraints that impeded action, was great. But for the moment, these problems lay in the future. As governor, Roosevelt would manage both in his rhetoric and his policies to steer a middle course aimed at ameliorating social and economic problems, while emphasizing the limits to what republican government could rightly be expected to accomplish.

THE EXECUTIVE IN ACTION

The new governor wasted no time in getting down to business. His First Annual Message, delivered on Inauguration Day, sought to capitalize on a newfound sense of national unity in the wake of the American victory over the Spanish and a readiness to address common problems. From the vantage point of Albany, there was much that the states, exercising their police powers, could do to protect the health, safety, and morals of the people. Roosevelt began by calling for stricter enforcement of laws already on the books regulating the number of hours women and children under fourteen might work, scrutinizing sanitary conditions in stores and buildings, and improving safety on the railroads. In addition, he proposed a new law that would increase the number of factory inspectors monitoring sweatshop labor, a cause he had championed during his days in the Assembly. Recalling his visits with Jacob Riis to the Lower East Side while police commissioner, he created a Tenement House Commission to investigate living conditions among the poor.

Roosevelt also reached out to rural interests. He sought to assure farmers that the state would act to protect them from "improper competition" by making sure that the cost of transporting their produce to market was not "excessive," a preview of the battles between railroads and shippers that he would face as president. And at a time when the agricultural population was shrinking and growing numbers of urban dwellers depended on distant farmers and livestock owners, he also saw an increased role for state government in fighting disease in plants and animals as well as making sure that food was safe and truthfully packaged.

At the same time, Roosevelt sought to set limits to the reform impulse by warning against the simple-minded tendency to think that state action was the cure for all problems. Government should be enlisted to "shackle cunning," but it must be careful not to discourage industry and initiative or fall in with sentimental "soup-kitchen" philanthropy.[8] Ultimately, Americans must take responsibility for their own lives. Beyond seeing to it that all parties played by the rules, there was little that government could do. This was not the laissez-faire position he had been introduced to at Harvard, because government would have to assume responsibility for a growing number of tasks that individuals were no longer able to perform, but it was still a vision of limited government.[9]

In the aftermath of the Spanish-American War, Roosevelt took a special interest in the condition of the New York National Guard, where he had earlier risen to the rank of captain. He spoke out strongly against the practice of calling up guard units for active duty to make up the shortfall in the regular army and noted the hardship to families, especially when tours of duty were extended because the army was stretched too thin. The best policy was to increase the size of the regular army and reserve the guard for domestic duty. If, when war broke out, guardsmen wished to transfer to active duty, as the outspoken advocate of the manly virtues assumed many of them would, provision should be made for them to do so. Finally, he called for adequate funding for the "regimental hospital."[10]

There was, however, one subject on which the new governor temporized: taxation. Roosevelt made no proposals, but his observation that the present system was "in utter confusion, full of injustices and of queer analogies" served notice that some revision of the tax laws was in the offing. Within a matter of months, he delivered two separate messages to the legislature, the second in extraordinary session, convened for the express purpose of enacting a tax on franchises. In the first of these messages, Roosevelt sought to reassure business interests that he did not share the populist and socialist "outcry against corporations as such." Large industrial combinations had made their money by providing "great benefits to the country," and it would be both shortsighted and wrong to deprive them of their "ample rewards."

Nevertheless, he insisted, "there is evident injustice in the light taxation of corporations." Making every allowance that could be made for individual initiative and enterprise, the corporation was a creature of the state government and as such "should pay the State a just percentage of its earnings as a return for the full privileges it enjoys."[11] Nowhere was this truer than with the monopoly franchises awarded to corporations for public utilities and services. When, in addition, these franchises became more valuable as a result of technological innovations, corporations should return a portion of their profits to the public. Simple justice demanded, for example, that when streetcars switched over from horsepower to electric power, vastly increasing their profitability, they should assume their fair share of the tax burden. But as things stood in 1898, the franchises paid no taxes, and this was wrong.

Yet Roosevelt was in a difficult position. He had come to power without a political organization of his own and, if he wanted another term, he could not afford to antagonize the Republican machine. Before taking action, therefore, the governor signaled to Boss Thomas C. Platt that he was willing to work with the party machine in shaping the final outcome of the law. Two bills were before the legislature, the first authorizing municipalities to tax franchises as real estate, and a competing measure that would tax franchises as personal property. Roosevelt preferred the first measure because he thought that property taxes were more difficult to evade. Nevertheless, he had reservations about the provision giving localities the power to levy the tax, especially in New York City, where a corrupt Tammany Hall would determine the assessments. If, for that reason, the Republican machine preferred to tax franchises as personal property, Roosevelt would sign the opposing measure. But he meant to sign one of them. Platt, who had no love for Roosevelt and had backed his candidacy only out of necessity, objected in principle to both bills and urged the governor not to sign either.

In reply, Roosevelt set forth what would become his patented formula: government must use its power to secure a "just balance" among the different social classes and competing economic interests.[12] He warned party leaders that the complete immunity from taxation enjoyed by the franchises served only to inflame public opinion and to strengthen the most radical elements of the labor movement. If Republicans continued to look the other way and deny that there were evils that needed to be corrected, the people would turn to populists, socialists, and Bryanists, which would only intensify class conflict. A modest tax on the franchises could actually work to the Republicans' advantage by showing that the party was not in the pocket of the wealthy, but "stood squarely" for the interests of all. Accordingly, Roosevelt signed into law in the spring of 1899 a tax on franchises, treating them as real estate, but with the state rather than the localities assessing and collecting the taxes.

Defending the new law in his Second Annual Message, Roosevelt pointed out that the previous method of taxation, which excluded corporations owning public franchises, while shifting the burden onto property owners, was no longer "adequate to secure justice when applied to the conditions of our complex and highly specialized society." The point of the franchise bill was to establish "exact and equal justice," nothing more, but also nothing less. It was not intended to persecute corporations, or to deprive them of a "just return" on their investments. But property that derived its value "from the grant of a privilege by the public" must be taxed "proportionately to the value of the privilege granted." The principle that corporations assume their "full and proper share of the public burdens," Roosevelt announced, "has come to stay."[13]

In contrast to his success in enacting the bill to tax franchises, the issues surrounding the great business trusts involved "a hundred phases" that continued to bedevil him. Dealing with issues such as the relation between property owners and wage laborers, the proper role of the state toward public utilities, the correct response to "extreme poverty" at a time when "humanitarian sentiment" was growing, and many others would require "courage, caution, and sanity." Again, he held up as his model the authors of *The Federalist*, arguing that modern-day reformers would need to bring the same thoughtful engagement to the problem of the trusts as Publius had brought to the creation of the federal system.[14] Unlike the populists, who wished to smash these economic behemoths in a fruitless attempt to turn the clock back to a simpler era, Roosevelt believed that large combinations of capital were the inevitable result of industrial development. The corporations were not going to go away; nor did he want them to. Although the great fortunes made in recent years had exacerbated the conflicts between the rich and the poor, most of those fortunes had been amassed, "not by injuring mankind, but as an incident to conferring great benefits on the community." Still, this was not always the case. "Some of the wealth has been acquired, or is used, in a manner for which there is no moral justification." The question was what should be done about this.

Roosevelt himself was not sure and sought the advice of McKinley's newly appointed secretary of war, Elihu Root.[15] Reading a draft of his Second Annual Message, Root found the mention of "moral justification" dangerous, and suggested language to tone it down. For the most part, the governor heeded the secretary's advice. Quoting a "profound political and social thinker" (the Anglo-Irish historian William Lecky), Roosevelt's final draft distinguished between those actions that were morally offensive and those that inflicted actual harm or injury. Although, as was already clear from essays such as "American Ideals," Roosevelt did not especially like or admire men who, he thought, devoted their lives exclusively to making money, Root had persuaded him (at least for the time being) that it was not the role of the government to legislate how these great industrial barons spent their fortunes. In a free society, vulgar displays of wealth could only be checked by public opinion. "Any attempt to interfere by statute in moral questions of this kind, by fettering the freedom of individual action, would be injurious to a degree far greater than is the evil aimed at."[16] In contrast to what he would later argue in his New Nationalism, Roosevelt here maintained that government was justified in proposing legislation to regulate the acquisition and use of wealth only when the rights of the individual were violated and actual harm had been done.

That grave abuses sometimes existed, however, Roosevelt had no doubt. Misrepresentation or concealment of facts, unscrupulous promotion, overcapitalization, unfair competition, price gouging, and exploitation of workers he counted among the chief offenses. Although later as president Roosevelt would insist that the states were too feeble to check these abuses, as governor he believed the states, using their police powers, possessed considerable resources to deal with these problems. As a first step, he called for amending the state corporation laws to require businesses to make public more information about their operations. By shining a light on the business practices of corporations and holding them more accountable, Roosevelt sought to strike a sensible middle position that would fend off demagogues' more radical demands to smash the trusts or nationalize the corporations.[17]

Moving from the trusts to labor, TR could boast that many of the proposals he had recommended in his First Message had already been enacted and were now being adequately enforced. Once again, he sought to strike a balance between protecting vulnerable workers by limiting their hours and affording more industrious laborers the opportunity to advance through their own superior efforts. (Here too, he would later reverse himself, condemning the *Lochner* decision for striking down a New York law mandating maximum hours in bakeshops.) Although he failed in his attempt to enact a liability law, he claimed to be applying the same principle of balance in this case as well: employers should not be unreasonably burdened, but government should take steps to protect those employed in dangerous occupations, along with families shattered by injury or death.

In his First Annual Message, Roosevelt had little to say about the conservation of the state's natural resources, but by the following year he was brimming with proposals. Having consulted with Gifford Pinchot, who was then chief of the Division of Forestry for the United States, Roosevelt for the first time embraced the novel idea of scientific management, arguing that the state forests should be actively managed and made as productive as neighboring private forests. There was no sign, however, that the governor believed (as he later would) that public management could be more efficient than private ownership, or that he thought of conservation as anything more than a patchwork series of proposals to protect the state's natural resources from needless waste or destruction. To this end, Roosevelt called for tighter measures to prohibit dumping all dyes, sawdust, and wood pulp into rivers and streams and recommended a ban on articles of clothing or ornaments made out of bird feathers or skins. Songbirds, especially, should be "rigidly" protected. At the same time, the author of *Hunting Trips of a Ranchman* (1885), *Ranch Life and the Hunting Trail* (1888), and *The Wilderness Hunter* (1893) encouraged his fellow New Yorkers to take up "hardy outdoor sports, like hunting" that would strengthen manly fiber in danger of being lost in the commercial East. "Men who go into the wilderness, indeed men who take part in any field-sports with horse or rifle, receive a benefit which can hardly be given by even the most vigorous athletic games."[18] Finally, unlike Pinchot, who showed little interest in the preservation of natural resources for their own sake, Roosevelt called on the legislature to preserve the Palisades as a "splendid national monument."

GOVERNING IN PROSE: A NEW RHETORIC

Just as Roosevelt's term as governor was guided by the desire to find a "just balance" among the different social classes and competing economic interests, his essays during this period also hit a mean between his earlier aloofness from the problems of the poor and his later calls for Americans to rise above their material interests in the name of national unity and brotherhood. A decade earlier, he had looked on immigrants who turned to local ward heelers for assistance as moral primitives. These newcomers, he thought then, did not yet understand the "American doctrine of government," which held each individual largely responsible for his own life, even though in this struggle for existence, "very many were bound to fail."[19] But now, his perspective enlarged by wartime service, a wider circle of political acquaintances, and executive responsibility, Roosevelt could understand why the poor might prefer machine politicians who attempted to satisfy their needs to reformers who acted from a feeling of moral superiority (though he probably did not realize he was describing his younger self).[20] Gone from these later essays is the callous Social Darwinism that sometimes crept into his earlier writings, replaced now by a greater emphasis on "fellow feeling."

In his essay "Fellow Feeling as a Political Factor," Roosevelt celebrated the decline of geographical and religious divisions in America and urged his countrymen to look past class differences and treat each other as individuals. Throughout rural America, fellow feeling was well advanced; the task now was to hasten its spread to urban areas. As he knew from personal experience, this would not be easy because the classes were more segregated in the cities and elite opinion was solidly opposed to mingling. Nevertheless, the only way to overcome present social and economic problems was to treat people from other classes with sympathy and mutual respect. Without such sympathy, there could be no moral imagination, no solidarity of sentiment, and no effective political reform. At the same time, Roosevelt warned that fellow feeling must not be allowed to deteriorate into gross sentimentality, where largeness of heart turned into softness of head.[21]

Roosevelt also took a sensible approach toward the problem of political corruption. In "The Eighth and Ninth Commandments in Politics," the governor tackled the thorny issue of campaign contributions, speaking out against the special consideration elected officials extended to the economic interests that had contributed generously to their campaign chests. (It will be recalled that this problem became acute for the Republicans after civil service reforms outlawed the imposition of assessments on political appointments.) In response, the perennial Democratic presidential candidate, William Jennings Bryan, had proposed a law prohibiting campaign contributions by corporations. Roosevelt, however, dismissed the idea as "ridiculous," first because it could never be made effective, and second because it was designed to "deceive during the campaign the voters least capable of thought."[22] Instead, he argued for full disclosure of all contributions and urged voters to select men of good character who would pursue impartial justice, neither favoring nor punishing these business interests. As opposed to Bryan and the Democrats, Roosevelt warned that there were two great political dangers to republican government, corruption and demagogy.

"The menace of the demagogue," about which he had sounded the alarm in 1896, posed an ongoing threat.

Two other essays, also published in 1900, rounded out the essentially moderate character of his term as governor. In "Promise and Performance," and "Character and Success," Roosevelt repeated his familiar warning that there were limits to what government could reasonably be expected to accomplish, but here too subtle differences in tone set these essays apart from his earlier pronouncements. Although he continued to insist that the best government could do "little more than provide against injustice," while holding out to each individual the opportunity to "rise or fall on his own merits," the emphasis here was on success, and not, as he had argued a decade ago, on resigning oneself to failure or to the inexorable working out of the laws of nature.[23]

Moreover, having reasonable expectations with regard to government was good for the citizens themselves. For when men were "misled by over-effusiveness [sic] in promise" and gave their support to the politician who "cheerfully guarantees the immediate millennium," they lost their capacity for self-government.[24] Citizens who demanded that their leaders deliver the impossible were "not merely leaning on a broken reed, but are working for their own undoing." At the same time, politicians should never promise more than they could reasonably deliver. The best type of fellow feeling was one that strengthened "the manly fiber" by teaching citizens "thrift, energy, self-mastery, and business intelligence." The essay concluded with a quotation from Aristotle cautioning that in politics, "two principles have to be kept in view: what is possible, what is becoming: at these every man ought to aim."[25] To let the best become the enemy of the good would lead to doing nothing; on the other hand, to fail to temper what was possible with some understanding of what was fitting would lead to crude opportunism or rank self-interest.

When he was not carrying out his program of moderate reform, Roosevelt, as we have seen, traveled around the country to rally support for America's imperial ambitions. After the success of his speech before the Hamilton Club in Chicago, exhorting his countrymen to take up "the strenuous life," the governor made a swing out west in June, where he was greeted by enthusiastic crowds, urging him to run for the presidency. Sensing a new mood in the country, he followed up with "Expansion and Peace," published that December. Not content to lay out his foreign policy views in broad outline, Roosevelt then took the politically perilous step of criticizing the administration's treaty arrangements with Great Britain regarding an isthmian canal. Secretary of State John Hay had just negotiated a treaty with Great

Britain, whereby Britain would give up its rights to build and maintain a canal jointly with the United States, on condition that the canal remain un-fortified. Roosevelt objected to the provision, warning of the security risks to America in time of war, when enemy ships might use the canal to gain strategic advantage over the United States. Hay naturally resented the brash governor's intrusion into matters of state, reminding Roosevelt that the Constitution gave the treaty-making power to the president and the Senate. But Roosevelt's noisy protests ultimately bore fruit.[26] The Hay-Pauncefote Treaty between Panama and the United States, concluded during Roosevelt's first term as president, stipulated that the canal would be fortified.

THE LITERARY GOVERNOR: *OLIVER CROMWELL*
AND THE "MASTER SPIRIT"

As remarkable as it seems, not even these activities absorbed Roosevelt's prodigious energies. While governor, he had published *The Rough Riders* to great popular acclaim and then agreed to follow up for Scribner's with a "sketch" of Oliver Cromwell. Roosevelt dictated the entire manuscript during a month-long vacation at Sagamore Hill in July 1899, while Arthur Hamilton Lee, the British military attaché, who had been with the Rough Riders in Cuba, was visiting. The biography first appeared in six install-ments from January to June of 1900 and then was published in book form later that year. Despite the speed with which it was written, *Oliver Cromwell* stands out as the most psychologically penetrating of his historical studies. As in his earlier works, Roosevelt could not resist pointing out the parallels between his subject's day and his own, but he was also led to reflect more broadly on the relation between energetic leadership and republican con-stitutionalism, especially in times of social and political upheaval.

In an introduction to *Oliver Cromwell* written after Roosevelt's death, Arthur Hamilton Lee speculated that Roosevelt felt a certain affinity for the Lord Protector. Both were fighting men who loved manly sports. Both championed liberty and had to deal with the problems of reconstruction that followed in the wake of civil wars. Both took the same dismissive view of political pedants and mere theorists who only talked about good gov-ernment. Lee also hinted at a deeper bond: Roosevelt was "essentially a preacher," who "was not ashamed to invoke the Sword of the Lord and of Gideon."[27] Like Cromwell, Roosevelt fought for the right as it was given to him to see the right, but in keeping with the teachings of the Social Gospel, the battles he waged were aimed solely at eradicating earthly evils. In Lee's view, TR practiced "the highest form of Christianity," which was "good citizenship."[28]

Roosevelt too noted certain parallels between the two men and their times. He praised Cromwell's capacity to inspire his troops in the New Model Army, emphasizing that it was strong-willed, vigorous men who succeeded (much as he had in training the Rough Riders). Elsewhere, he criticized the commercial Dutch of Cromwell's day (though it could just as easily have been eastern businessmen in the Gilded Age) for thinking that the mere desire for peace could avert war and that if, despite their best efforts, war should come they could rely on their wealth and their reserve strength to prevail. Roosevelt also saw a certain similarity in their attitude toward political parties. Cromwell was not, to use one of Roosevelt's favorite words, a "doctrinaire," but rather, much like the independent Republican governor of New York, he understood that he would have to ally himself with some party, even if he did not completely agree with their ends. In this regard, he took aim at laissez-faire economists, who criticized the Navigation Acts in Cromwell's day and the system of protective tariffs in his own, arguing that what worked under one set of conditions might not work as well in another. Finally, the governor warned against modern-day puritans bent on outlawing innocent pleasures, rather than directing their energies to "the fundamentals of social morality, civic honesty, and good government." Projecting his own theory of "just balance" onto the actions of the Lord Protector, Roosevelt concluded that the task of a "master spirit" such as Cromwell was to find a *via media* between those who thought the revolution had gone too far and those who thought it had not gone far enough.[29]

As entertaining as these vignettes are, the true significance of *Oliver Cromwell* lies elsewhere. At the time he was writing it, Henry Cabot Lodge had planted the idea that Roosevelt accept the vice presidential nomination, if it were offered. Roosevelt, flush from his successful western tour, was at first open to the idea, viewing it as an honorable office that might lead to an even bigger prize.[30] As he pondered his next political move, Roosevelt used the Cromwell sketch to reflect upon the relation between energetic executive power and constitutional government, offering shrewd psychological insights that applied in equal measure to both subject and author. As such, *Oliver Cromwell* provides a baseline that can be used to chart Roosevelt's evolving views of executive power and republican constitutionalism during his presidency and afterward.

Returning to the theme of the opening chapter of *The Winning of the West*, Roosevelt argued that Cromwell's significance lay in having initiated the great 300-year movement of the English-speaking peoples onto the center of the world stage. The rise of the English-speaking people began with the overthrow of the despotic Stuart king, Charles I, proceeded to the Glorious Revolution, and thence to the New World, where it was further advanced by the American Revolution and finally the Union triumph in the Civil War. As in his earlier history, Roosevelt attributed this movement largely to "the irresistible march of events," though Cromwell was one of those "master spirits" who was able to seize the opportunities history cast before him.[31]

Nevertheless, even this mightiest of men fell short in important ways. For one thing, unlike the authors of The Federalist, Cromwell was a purely practical man. A practical man was certainly better than a merely theoretical man, but from the standpoint of statesmanship, the best was a combination of the two.[32] As a result, Cromwell was not interested in larger constitutional questions or the rule of law. "He failed to see that questions of form— that is, of law—in securing liberty might be themselves essential instead of, as they seemed to him, non-essential." All of Cromwell's practical energy was directed toward alleviating particular acts of oppression and injustice, which he tried to remedy by assuming dictatorial powers. Roosevelt was willing to grant that extreme circumstances called for extreme measures. "In great crises it may be necessary to overturn constitutions or disregard statutes," but he added, "such a remedy is always dangerous even when absolutely necessary." And when strong men made a habit of emergencies to set themselves above the constitution and the laws, it was a sure sign of "decay."[33] In the end, Cromwell's failure to appreciate the importance of constitutional forms to securing orderly liberty meant that the revolution he set in motion would be stillborn.

In Roosevelt's judgment, Cromwell's failure could be attributed to two factors. First, Cromwell and his "saints" had not reached the "stage" where they could tolerate religious differences and make the compromises necessary to establish a constitution. Although Roosevelt saw Cromwell as inaugurating a great modern movement for religious, political, and social liberty, there remained a "medieval" aspect to the struggle that eventually doomed it. There is perhaps no clearer statement of Roosevelt's position (or of his differences with the natural rights philosophy that underlay the American Constitution) than his observation that England in the seventeenth century was not yet fit to govern itself unaided. "Such fitness," he wrote, " is not a God-given natural right, but comes to a race through the slow growth of centuries, and then only to those races which possess an immense reserve fund of strength, common sense, and morality."[34] It would take several more centuries of historical development before the Puritans' sincerity, stern morality, and loftiness of aim would reach its fruition.[35]

Yet Roosevelt was not willing to lay all the blame on the slow grinding of the historical process. Character counted too, and not simply the flaws. All of Cromwell's qualities, "both good and bad, tended to render the forms and narrowly limited powers of constitutional government irksome to him."[36] Yes, Cromwell was "cursed with a love of power," a "dictatorial habit of mind," and an impatience with legal and constitutional forms, but his strength, his "intensity of conviction," and "delight" in exercising powers for what he thought were righteous ends also caused him to reject constitutional limitations on his actions. Reading these and similar passages, one must wonder whether Roosevelt could comment so perceptively because there were even deeper "affinities" in the characters of the two men. In any case, the young Roosevelt offered words of advice that he himself might usefully have heeded in 1912: "It is very essential that a man should have in him the capacity to defy his fellows if he thinks they are doing the work of the devil and not the work of the Lord, but it is even more essential for him to remember that he be most cautious about mistaking his own views for those of the Lord."[37]

Although Cromwell's character partly accounted for the failure of the English Commonwealth, the English people were also to blame, for they had not yet developed those qualities that would allow them to work out their own "destiny" by elevating men who would be their leaders, rather than their masters. Of course, a "great and patriotic leader" might have helped them along by his prudence, self-denial, and disinterestedness, but these were not qualities that the Lord Protector, who retained a certain unattractive "medieval" side, possessed. In the end, the first stirrings of the modern movement fell victim to history. Neither a "master spirit" such as Cromwell nor the English people themselves had progressed to that stage of development where they were "really capable of freedom and of doing mighty deeds in the world."[38]

Yet, paradoxically, by granting so much sway to history, Roosevelt ran the risk of thwarting the very development of liberty and self-government that he desired. For, as political philosophers as different as Kant, Tocqueville, and Nietzsche had all warned, when individuals believed themselves to be mere pawns in the historical process, they might well lose the capacity and the will to act for themselves. Yet so in thrall to historical development was Roosevelt that he assumed that human nature would continue to "evolve." Here, he confused progress in political science, which was possible, with faith in the progress of human nature. Whatever progress the English-speaking peoples had made in perfecting the art of free government from the time of Cromwell to George Washington, and it was considerable, the authors of *The Federalist* were correct in arguing that human nature was largely unchanging.

It was Roosevelt's great insight in *Oliver Cromwell* to recognize that, for freedom to flourish, executive power must be subordinated to constitutional limitations. But his historicist assumptions prevented him from recognizing that the temptations of power were just as real in his day as they had been in Cromwell's. Consequently, he failed to see that he, too, might be cursed with the same impatience with legal and constitutional forms that thwarted his "imperious" will, or display the same "fatal incapacity to acknowledge that there might be righteousness in other methods than his own." The signs were already there in *Oliver Cromwell*, where Roosevelt chafed against the "tendency in the law" toward what he called "the deification of technicalities," or the triumph of the letter of the law over the spirit. The question now was what he would do when he suddenly found himself elevated to the presidency and faced with his first emergency.[39]

5. Executive Power and Republican Government

By his own account, Roosevelt came into the White House with "no deliberately planned and far reaching scheme of social betterment" and no firm views on the place of executive power in the republican constitutional order. Foremost in his mind was the lesson of his one-term governorship: if he were to have any chance of winning renomination in 1904, he could not afford to antagonize the party bosses and their corporate backers by moving too far from the policies of the slain president. To reassure the party chieftains, Roosevelt announced that he would retain McKinley's cabinet, though Roosevelt being Roosevelt, he was bound to seek opportunities for bold, decisive action.

Within months of becoming president, Roosevelt would face his first political crisis with the anthracite coal strike of 1902. But even before this emergency, he began to develop a two-pronged strategy aimed at asserting greater federal control over the trusts. In his First Annual Message, he called for the creation of a new federal agency to gather information about all businesses operating in interstate commerce. While Congress considered his proposal to establish what would become the Bureau of Corporations, Roosevelt also attempted to resuscitate federal antitrust law by bringing suit against the Northern Securities Company under the Sherman Antitrust Act. He tackled railroad rebates and called for greater administrative control over railroad rates. From the start, Roosevelt also charted a new course on conservation, with a far more active role for the executive as steward of America's natural resources. In foreign affairs, he sounded the call to national greatness, issuing the Roosevelt Corollary to the Monroe Doctrine, laying the groundwork for the Panama Canal, and making the case for American rule over the Philippines.

After his landslide reelection, Roosevelt spent his political capital muscling through the Hepburn Act, which regulated railroad rates, and then used that victory to call for greater regulatory controls, not just over the railroads, but across the entire industrial economy. In the waning years of his presidency, he would fight a losing battle to convert the Bureau of Corporations into a full-fledged regulatory agency and wage what he would later term "bitter war" against the trusts. On other fronts, he wove his piecemeal conservation projects into a powerful conservation "movement" designed to preserve what he feared were America's dwindling resources. And finally, he continued to make the case for national greatness by sending the Great White Fleet around the world, even as he reluctantly came to see how difficult it would be for the United States to carry out his imperial ambitions in the Philippines.

To gain support for his policies, Roosevelt continued to talk about the need to strike a "just balance" between political extremes. As he had done while governor, the president attempted to elevate the character of the citizenry by warning against the dangers of envy and resentment on the one hand and contempt and arrogance on the other. Republican government must steer a "sane" middle course between violent mob rule and plutocracy. When asked in 1903 by his old Columbia Law School classmate, Nicholas Murray Butler, what he had been reading while in the White House, Roosevelt included alongside Lincoln's writings and a host of other works "parts of Aristotle's *Politics*."[1] Although Roosevelt did not specify which parts of *The Politics* he found instructive, his speeches suggest that he was particularly taken with Aristotle's advice that the republican statesman should try to shore up whichever of the two political extremes, democracy (rule by the many who were poor) or oligarchy (rule by the few who were rich) was politically weaker, while warning both sides not to succumb to their characteristic vices.

Over the course of his two terms, however, Roosevelt's understanding of balance would undergo an important change. Initially, he regarded the threat from mob violence, spurred by anarchists, socialists, and Bryanites as the more serious danger. But after his landslide reelection, and especially after 1906, TR concluded that the plutocrats now posed the greater threat and threw the whole weight of his office against them. With the forces of progressivism now ascendant, Roosevelt was convinced that it was only by waging "bitter war" against the trusts that he could steer what he thought was a "middle" course, while remaining the leader of the reform wing of his party.

Although Roosevelt found the idea of a "just balance" morally satisfying and rhetorically useful, it did not supply a constitutional basis for his use of executive power. Yet as he had made clear in his biography of Oliver Cromwell, executive power, especially in a republic, must be subordinated within a larger constitutional framework. Roosevelt had criticized the Lord

Protector for his impatience with legal and constitutional forms, his "fatal incapacity" to recognize that others might also be motivated by righteous beliefs, and his failure to develop a theory that would guide and restrain his actions. But like Cromwell, Roosevelt would perceive "emergencies" and maneuver to evade the restraints of legal and constitutional forms. And he would launch himself into transports of self-righteousness, seeing nothing but villainy in his opponents.

Unlike Cromwell, however, Roosevelt would develop a theory, two in fact, first of "inherent powers" and later of "stewardship," to try to reconcile his use of executive power with republican constitutionalism. Along the way, he would give new meaning to the word "regulate" and argue for a broad interpretation of "commerce." But in so doing, he would move further and further from the ideals of the men he claimed most to admire, Washington and Lincoln, as well as from the political theory of *The Federalist*. Instead of regulating the economy to ensure the honest and smooth functioning of free markets, Roosevelt proposed far-reaching government controls on both public utilities and the entire industrial economy, which he euphemistically called "supervision." And in carrying out his conservation measures, the president increasingly sought to circumvent the separation of powers, preferring to work with like-minded bureaucrats in the executive branch or on commissions appointed by him and appealing directly to public opinion to build support for his measures. Only in foreign policy, where the Framers (at least those he admired) intended executive power to operate most freely, would Roosevelt's view of executive power approximate that of his heroes, though, even then, his theory tended to float free from the Constitution.

THE ANTHRACITE COAL STRIKE AND THE "STEWARDSHIP" THEORY OF EXECUTIVE POWER

Although Roosevelt came into the presidency promising to give the great captains of industry their due, the anthracite coal strike provided fresh proof (if he needed any) that "strong and forceful men" were sometimes capable of great abuses. Since the spring of 1902, coal miners had been on strike in eastern Pennsylvania, demanding pay increases, shorter hours, and a change in the system for weighing coal. John Mitchell, the head of the United Mine Workers, had offered to submit the miners' demands to mediation, but the coal operators refused to recognize the union or to give in to its demands. The operators were still smarting from having been pressured by Mark Hanna on the eve of the 1900 elections to make concessions to striking miners and were determined not to give in a second time. Speaking for the mining interests, George F. Baer, President of the Philadelphia and Reading Railroad, brushed aside any suggestion that the operators sit down with John Mitchell. "The rights and interests of the laboring man will be protected and cared for—not by the labor agitators, but by the Christian men to whom God in His infinite wisdom has given the control of the property interests of this country, and upon the successful Management of which so much depends."[2] Here on public display, Roosevelt fumed, was precisely the kind of arrogance borne of wealth and power he had repeatedly condemned.

That same day, the president wrote to his attorney general, Philander C. Knox, asking, "What is the reason we cannot proceed against the coal operators as being engaged in a trust?"[3] In response, Attorney General Knox advised him that the coal operators were not combined in such a way that the antitrust laws could be used against them (and even if they were, the remedy would have to be sought in a long, drawn-out court battle). Despite Republican frustrations, Roosevelt confided to Lodge and Hanna, there was "literally nothing, so far as I have yet been able to find out, which the national government has any power to do in the matter."[4] Nor could he think of anything that Congress might do to provide any "immediate benefit."

This point requires emphasis. So accustomed are we to thinking that the federal government can always find some constitutional principle on which to act, that it comes as a surprise to learn that even Roosevelt was stymied. At the time of the coal strike no legal precedent existed for forcing owners of private property who were not legally organized as a trust and who were not operating in interstate commerce (in 1902 mining was not considered to be part of interstate commerce) to negotiate an industry-wide labor agreement with union leaders whom they refused to recognize. Roosevelt was back in "Cowboy Land."

Despite the absence of legal authority, the president nevertheless decided that he had to *do something*. In his view, the dispute did not just involve two clashing private interests; the coal strike had become "a matter of vital concern to the whole nation." There were not simply two interests involved, there was also the public interest to be considered. With so much at stake, this was no time to follow "the Buchanan principle of striving to find some constitutional principle for inaction."[5] Though he did not say it publicly, the president was acutely aware that there was also a fourth interest: the Republican Party. With fall approaching and the campaign season about to begin in earnest, Roosevelt worried that declining anthracite supplies might create a coal famine that would cost Republicans dearly in November. Henry Cabot Lodge was already warning of "a political disaster" in Massachusetts and throughout New England and pressed Roosevelt to do something, or if he had no authority to act, at least appear to be doing something.[6]

As pressure mounted, the president invited both sides to meet with him in Washington, even though he conceded that he had "no legal or constitutional duty—and therefore no legal or constitutional right—in the matter." Despite Roosevelt's best efforts to broker an agreement, the talks ended in failure. The operators refused to budge, demanding instead that Roosevelt send in federal troops to put down alleged violence in the coalfields and, following the precedent in the Pullman Strike of 1894, use the Sherman Antitrust Act to bring suit against the miners. He was also aware that the *federal* government had no power to intervene unless government property (such as the mail) was attacked or the governor of the state requested federal troops to restore order.[7] But, as he complained to Mark Hanna, the coal operators were not going to let "such a trifling detail as the United States Constitution" stand in their way.[8] What particularly irked him was their refusal to acknowledge that the public had any rights in the matter. Writing to the Republican governor of Massachusetts, Roosevelt charged that the operators were "apparently utterly ignorant of the old common-law doctrine of innkeepers, tavern owners and the like; such as the right of estovers under which a peasant could take wood that was not his if necessary for the preservation of life and health in winter weather."[9]

Yet Roosevelt was grasping at straws. His common law examples jumbled two different doctrines, neither of which remotely applied to the current crisis. Under the common law doctrine of estovers, tenants had a right to gather firewood for their own needs that belonged to the lord of the manor, but it is difficult to see how that doctrine could be extended to a right of the federal government to trench on private property in defense of a generalized public interest. As to innkeepers and coachmen (not tavern owners), it is true that the common law obliged them to lodge and carry all paying customers, lest travelers be subjected to the dangers of being stranded on the roads in medieval England, but as with estovers, this related to particular individuals in particular circumstances. Although by the time of the coal strike, the Supreme Court had recognized that certain businesses (in this case grain elevators) might be "affected with a public interest," *Munn v. Illinois* (1877) applied only to state regulation and not to the federal government. Similarly, according to constitutional precedents existing at the time (to repeat: mining was not considered interstate commerce), the dispute between coal operators and miners was entirely intra-state.[10]

Nevertheless, on these flimsy legal grounds, Roosevelt went on to develop a contingency plan for federal troops to seize and operate the mines if no solution could be reached, even though such a plan lacked any constitutional basis. The president then conveyed this information to Oswald Garrison Villard, journalist and publisher of the *New York Evening Post*.[11] News of the plan prompted J. P. Morgan to use his influence with his coal associates and, within days, they agreed to a commission. In a concession to the operators, each of the companies and their workers would present their grievances separately to the commission so that the operators did not have to recognize or deal directly with the U.M.W. All that remained was the wrangling over the members, which, much to Roosevelt's amusement, was quickly resolved to his satisfaction. Roosevelt had scored his first major victory. Not only was the coal strike ended before the cold weather and the election but, for the first time, the president of the United States had used his office to settle a dispute between property owners and workers that did not favor organized business, but dealt "squarely" with both sides.

Roosevelt was, however, acutely conscious of the precedent he was establishing by intervening in the coal strike, to say nothing of the "evil precedent" he would have set had he used federal troops to seize the mines. "Every strike," he worried, "would mean that some people will accuse me of being the cause of it by having settled this coal strike, and others will insist that I interfere to stop it, heedless of the fact that such interference or intervention of mine, as in the case of the coal strike must occur only in extreme cases."[12] He was, in short, determined not to allow his mediation to give rise to a general expectation that the president would henceforth intervene whenever there was the first sign of difficulty.[13] But given Roosevelt's penchant for bold action, coupled with the public's enthusiastic approval of his handling of the affair, the very suggestion of a crisis would prove difficult for him to resist.

Years later in his *Autobiography*, Roosevelt offered his successful intervention in the coal strike as a primary example of his "stewardship" theory of the presidency. As Roosevelt then explained it,

occasionally great national crises arise which call for immediate and vigorous action, and that in such cases it is the duty of the President to act upon the theory that he is the steward of the people, and that the proper attitude for him to take is that he is bound to assume that he has the legal right to do whatever the needs of the people demand, unless the Constitution or the laws explicitly forbid him to do it.

Under such circumstances, the president had a responsibility to act affirmatively, and "not content himself with the negative merit of keeping his talents undamaged in a napkin."[14] Looking back on his years in the White House, TR could boast, "under this interpretation of executive power I did and caused to be done many things not previously done by the President and the heads of the departments." Nevertheless, he felt it necessary to add, "I did not usurp power, but I did greatly broaden the use of executive power."[15]

As Roosevelt described it in 1913, stewardship was simply the latest iteration of the Jackson-Lincoln view of the presidency, in which the chief executive construed the powers of his office broadly and defended them from attacks by the coordinate branches. The alternative to the stewardship theory was the "narrow legalistic view" that "the President should solve every doubt in favor of inaction as against action, and that he should construe strictly and narrowly the constitutional grant of powers both to the National Government and to the President." During the coal strike, Roosevelt had attributed this position to James Buchanan, but in the *Autobiography* he also blamed his handpicked successor, William Howard Taft.[16] Roosevelt was willing to grant that some men held this view "conscientiously," though he thought their motives "misguided." But, at bottom, whether a man followed the Jackson-Lincoln or the Buchanan-Taft view boiled down to character and temperament.[17] Those who adhered to the Buchanan-Taft precedent were basically weak-willed, motivated by a "desire to avoid trouble and responsibility." By contrast, followers of the Jackson-Lincoln-and-now-Roosevelt school were men of strong and vigorous character, who did not shrink from their duty "to do efficient work for the people."[18] But try as he might to assimilate stewardship to the Jackson-Lincoln model, TR's novel theory went well beyond how Jackson, and even Lincoln, understood executive power.[19]

Indeed, at first sight, Roosevelt's identification with Andrew Jackson is puzzling, given his assessment of his presidency in *Thomas Hart Benton*. There, the young historian had criticized Jackson and his followers for blindly equating the voice of the people with the voice of God, to the detriment of individual rights. As for the policies that followed from this craven majoritarianism, Roosevelt could scarcely conceal his contempt for Jackson's ill-conceived war on the bank. Such an "assault" on the "money power" could succeed only by appealing to the ignorance and envy of the poor, which was fatal to republican self-government. In fact, Jackson himself was "an ignorant, headstrong, and straight-forward soldier" whose election was proof, if any were needed, that the majority was not always right.[20] It was, he thought then, the responsibility of the republican statesman to resist these destructive impulses.

In time, however, these very defects became strengths in Roosevelt's eyes. Like Jackson, Roosevelt too came to believe majority tyranny no longer posed a danger to republican self-government and championed efforts to give the people a more direct say in government. And again like Jackson, Roosevelt warred against the "money" power of his day, the trusts. Even then, however, Old Hickory was never a perfect model for the kind of executive power Roosevelt envisioned because his actions were mostly defensive. Jackson vigorously deployed the powers of his office to fight against nullification, stand up to the courts, and worst of all, return power to the states. A loyal unionist he was, but not a strong nationalist.

By contrast, Lincoln was and remained Roosevelt's *beau ideal.* In the first great crisis of his presidency, Roosevelt turned to Lincoln for guidance, rereading his writings and studying his actions. At critical moments during the Civil War, most notably, when he suspended habeas corpus and emancipated the slaves in the rebellious states, Lincoln had exercised powers not specifically granted to the executive by the Constitution. Roosevelt saw in these actions a model for his own unprecedented plan: like the Civil War, the coal strike was a great national emergency. If allowed to stretch on into winter, the shortage of coal would cause terrible suffering, rioting in the streets, and possibly even all-out class warfare. The president was not prepared to sit idly by and watch the crisis unfold. Nor did he wish to preside over what was sure to be electoral defeat in November. Thus, although there was nothing in the Constitution that specifically authorized him to do so, he determined to use his good offices to try to bring the coal operators and miners together. Still, although the president's efforts to broker a "Square Deal" between the coal operators and miners were novel, this was not the most controversial part of his stewardship theory.

If these negotiations failed, Roosevelt worried that the impasse might lead to a general strike that "would have meant a crisis only less serious than the civil war." Even if a general strike were averted, the cold weather alone would spell "misery and violence in acute form in our big cities." Under these circumstances, the president would send in federal troops to seize the mines and run them "as receiver for the government." After working out the details, Roosevelt then informed his attorney general and secretary of war of the plan, but to absolve them of all responsibility, made it clear that he was not seeking their advice. The decision would be his and his alone; he would act "just as if we were in a state of war." To Winthrop Murray Crane, Republican governor of Massachusetts, TR confessed that he could think of no precedent for such action "save perhaps those of General Butler at New Orleans." Nevertheless, "it was imperative to act, precedent or no precedent, and I was in readiness."[21]

Representative James E. Watson made the same point more colorfully, if perhaps anecdotally. Apprised of Roosevelt's plan, Watson is said to have asked, "what about the Constitution of the United States? What about seizing private property for public purposes without the due process of law?" In Watson's telling, Roosevelt "stopped suddenly, took hold of my shoulder and turned me about facing him and looked squarely into my eyes as he fairly shouted, 'The Constitution was made for the people, and not the people for the Constitution.'"[22] Though the irony appears lost on him, Roosevelt, like the coal operators he detested, was also not prepared to let "such a trifling detail as the United States Constitution" stand in his way (unless he was already beginning to view the Constitution as a living document, responding to the ever-changing needs of the people).

Despite Roosevelt's efforts to tie his stewardship theory back to Lincoln's actions in the Civil War, there could not be any more dramatic example of the differences between their views of presidential power. When Lincoln acted, he was engaged in an actual civil war in which the fate of the Union was immediately at stake. He had taken a constitutional oath to "take care" that the laws be faithfully executed, which required him to move decisively against the eleven seceding states that no longer recognized the authority of federal laws. What is more, he had formulated his Emancipation Proclamation as he did precisely to remain within the bounds of the Constitution, and he was careful to cite the constitutional basis, however controversial, for his action. In issuing the Emancipation Proclamation, Lincoln cited his powers as commander-in-chief in wartime and defended the measure on the ground of "indispensable necessity." Further, the proclamation applied only to those areas of the country in actual rebellion, and not to slavery everywhere. In his view, his oath of office forbade him from indulging his own abstract judgment that slavery was wrong. As he understood the oath of office, he could only act for the purpose of preserving the Constitution, and not for bringing about wholesale social changes, no matter how desirable.[23]

In the judgment of William Howard Taft, who did not hold the crimped view of executive power Roosevelt attributed to him, the difference between the two presidents was that "Mr. Lincoln always pointed out the source of the authority which in his opinion justified his acts, and there was always a strong ground for maintaining the view he took." At no time did Lincoln ever claim, "whatever authority in government was not expressly denied him he could exercise."[24] In fact, Lincoln explicitly declared that he did not believe the presidency conferred upon him "an unrestricted right to act officially" upon his own judgment and feeling about what was right. When he took measures that might otherwise have been unconstitutional, he did so because he had taken an oath of office to preserve the Constitution, which required him first to save the Union.

Taft, who at the time he published his criticism of TR's stewardship theory was Chancellor Kent Professor of Law at Yale University and who would later serve as Chief Justice of the United States, emphasized that Roosevelt was not faced with so grave an emergency as Lincoln but decided to treat the coal strike *as if* it were an impending civil war. Had his attempt to broker an agreement between the operators and the miners failed, TR, on the prearranged "invitation" of the governor of Pennsylvania, would have ordered federal troops to seize the mines and operate them until the strike was resolved. But as Taft noted, Roosevelt was not sending in troops to suppress rebellion, the only basis on which he was authorized to act, but rather to seize private property and distribute it without "any court proceeding of any kind," for the benefit of the people of other states.[25] Nevertheless, if the president gave the order, General Schofield assured him that he was prepared to "run the mines notwithstanding interference from strikers, operators, or the federal courts."[26]

What, precisely, was the constitutional or statutory warrant for such action? Both his attorney general and secretary of war had already agreed that invoking the Sherman Antitrust Act, as one overheated argument making the rounds suggested, was "an absurdity" because the coal operators were not legally organized as a trust. (And to make matters worse, Knox advised that if the Sherman Act did apply it might also have to be used against the labor union.)[27] The president's legal options were limited. In letters at the time, Roosevelt cited old common law doctrines as well as his wartime powers as commander-in-chief to justify seizing the mines. It is not clear that even he was convinced by these arguments, however.[28] Indeed, when he finally formulated it, the whole point of the stewardship theory was precisely that the president did not have to cite a specific constitutional provision or statute for his actions so long as the needs of the people required it and it was not explicitly forbidden. Nor could TR think of any precedents that might apply, except "perhaps" that of General Butler in the Civil War. It was an unfortunate, but telling, example. After the Battle of New Orleans in 1862, Benjamin Butler ruled over the city in dictatorial fashion until he was relieved of his command for excessive severity. Discussing this "precedent," Taft pointed out that Roosevelt's proposed use of the army, unlike

Butler's, was motivated by a benevolent impulse not to see people suffer; nevertheless, "no one who looks at it from the standpoint of a government of law could regard it as anything but lawless."[29]

Thus, in this first crisis, even as Roosevelt invoked the authority of Lincoln, he was less interested in vindicating Lincoln's emergency expansion of executive power to *defend* the Constitution than with overcoming the obstacles that the Constitution posed to satisfying "the needs of the nation" in an emergency. Indeed, as historian William Harbaugh observed, "within the year he was describing the episode without reference to the Constitution," claiming instead that as " the head of the nation" he "obeyed the supreme law of duty to the republic."[30] Harbaugh correctly speculated that Roosevelt was reaching for something like a doctrine of inherent power. In fact, Roosevelt briefly flirted with this idea later in his second term to justify the expansion of his regulatory regime.

INHERENT POWERS AND CONSTITUTIONAL LIMITATIONS

Speaking at the dedication of the new capitol building in Harrisburg, Pennsylvania, in the run-up to the midterm elections in 1906, Roosevelt floated for the first time his theory of inherent power. The setting provided him with the opportunity to link the doctrine back to the distinguished founder and Pennsylvania jurist, James Wilson. In Roosevelt's telling, Wilson was the first to develop "the doctrine (absolutely essential not merely to the efficiency but to the existence of this Nation), that an inherent power rested in the Nation outside of the enumerated powers conferred upon it by the Constitution, in all cases where the object involved was beyond the power of the several States and was a power ordinarily exercised by sovereign nations."[31]

What Roosevelt neglected to say was that Wilson had made his argument for inherent powers in 1785, while the United States were still under the feeble Articles of Confederation. In "Considerations on the Bank of North America," Wilson maintained that, in addition to the powers expressly delegated to Congress by the Articles, the United States also had "general rights, general powers, and general obligations" that resulted from its being a union of the whole. Citing the last lines of the Declaration of Independence, the Pennsylvania jurist then claimed that the Confederation Congress possessed the powers that all independent states enjoyed, including, in this instance, the power to charter a bank, but also "the purchase, sale, defence [*sic*], and government of new territories."[32]

Perhaps sensing that an essay written in defense of the "inherent power" of the Confederation Congress to charter a bank was not the most constitutionally compelling, Roosevelt instead cited "a remarkable letter" Wilson had written to George Washington in 1791, after the new Constitution had been ratified. But the full text of the letter does not support Roosevelt's argument. Wilson was here offering to prepare a digest of federal laws that would set forth the principles on which the Constitution was founded. At the time, he was at work on a digest of the Pennsylvania constitution, and as someone who had been involved in the framing of both the state and new federal constitutions, he considered himself superbly qualified for the assignment. Wilson assured the president that in his proposed digest "neither vacancies nor interferences will be found, between the limits of the two jurisdictions. For it is material to observe, that both jurisdictions compose, or ought to compose, only one uniform and comprehensive system of government and laws."[33] Quoting freely and interpolating from Wilson's letter, Roosevelt then added that this was precisely the present situation regarding the great corporations. "Certain judicial decisions have done just what Wilson feared; they have as a matter of fact left vacancies, left blanks between the limits of possible State jurisdiction and the limits of actual national jurisdiction."[34]

Perhaps. But, even if we accept that a personal letter is any guide to constitutional interpretation (itself a dubious assumption), was Wilson here reiterating his argument for "inherent power"? Wilson was one of the strongest nationalists at the Federal Convention and thereafter on the Supreme Court, but it is unclear whether even he would have endorsed Roosevelt's position. For one thing, the governmental framework under the Articles of Confederation was very different from that under the Constitution. Government under the Articles consisted of a unicameral legislature with very limited powers. There was nothing remotely akin to the "necessary and proper" clause of Article I, and no provision at all for "executive power."

After the states agreed to form a "more perfect Union," the case for "inherent power" (at least in domestic affairs) was radically diminished. The Constitution provided broad powers to Congress by specific delegations of Article I, Section 8, and added a doctrine of implied powers in the "necessary and proper" clause. The difference between the two doctrines, which Roosevelt appears not to have grasped, was subtle, but critical. Implied constitutional powers were inferences from the powers *enumerated* in Article I. These inferences might vary with the circumstances, affording implied powers great flexibility, but they were always tethered to specific delegated powers. This was the position of Washington, Hamilton, and Marshall regarding the power of the federal government to charter a national bank. By contrast, Roosevelt's doctrine of "inherent powers" would have allowed the government to exercise *additional* powers outside of those conferred upon it by the Constitution, whenever new circumstances such as the rise of industrial capitalism made it impossible for the older arrangements to function effectively, and the "object involved was beyond the power of the several States and was a power ordinarily exercised by sovereign nations."[35]

Moreover, to the extent that something like inherent power was retained in the Constitution, it is usually understood to operate solely in the context of Article II, and then mostly in foreign affairs. Such inherent power emphatically did not reside in the "Nation," as Roosevelt asserted.[36] In his eagerness to discover some rationale for the expanded regulatory authority he sought, Roosevelt jettisoned analytical precision. Did he mean that the people of the nation in their sovereign capacity possessed inherent power? If so, he was confusing inherent power with popular sovereignty. More likely, he meant that the federal government, as the embodiment of the nation, possessed inherent powers to act.[37] But this raised an ever larger question: what was the connection between inherent powers and the theory of an energetic, but limited, national government set forth in *The Federalist*? What became of the compact theory of government? Of federalism? Of the separation of powers? If the Nation and the State were now in some foggy sense one, and possessed of inherent power, there was no limit to what the national government might do.[38] Given the confusions in Roosevelt's theory of inherent powers, it is perhaps not surprising that he did not continue to insist upon it. And indeed, one year after Roosevelt's Harrisburg Speech, the Supreme Court in *Kansas v. Colorado* emphatically rejected the argument for inherent power.[39] For Roosevelt, the doctrine was merely a way station and a not altogether coherent one on the road to his stewardship theory of the presidency.

THE ANTITRUST APPROACH TO CONTROLLING
CORPORATE POWER

Even before the coal strike, Roosevelt was determined to strengthen the powers of the federal government over the great industrial combinations. As he had when he was governor, the president's First Annual Message called for legislation that would require the trusts to open their books to public scrutiny. But since it was unlikely that Congress would respond to his proposal to create a federal agency within a new cabinet department of commerce and labor anytime soon, the president also decided to resuscitate the Sherman Antitrust Act. Since the law was already on the books, the president could act without having to gain congressional approval.

Passed in 1890 with the support of farm associations, small businessmen, and consumer groups, the Sherman Antitrust Act sought to calm widespread fears that the growth of large-scale industry threatened the core principle of equal rights by pitting individuals in an uneven contest against the new industrial behemoths. Section One flatly prohibited "every contract, combination in the form of trust or otherwise, or conspiracy, in restraint of trade or commerce." Section Two further declared the "attempt to monopolize, or combine or conspire with any other person or persons, to monopolize any part of the trade or commerce among the several States" a felony, punishable by fine, imprisonment, or both.[40] On its face, then, the statute seemed to mandate a return to the individual entrepreneurs of Jacksonian democracy, and thus to be on a collision course with the emerging corporate economy.

Nevertheless, the legislative history of the act suggested that the picture was more complicated. For despite the unequivocal language of the bill, the principal framers of the Sherman Act understood the statute to enact the common law doctrine barring only "unreasonable" restraints of trade that operated to the detriment of the public.[41] And this in turn introduced another ambiguity: lawmakers themselves were unclear whether the public interest required the protection of individual entrepreneurs from their giant competitors (in which case the corporations should be broken up) or lower prices and more improved services for the consumer (which would argue in favor of the more efficient combinations).[42] Compounding these difficulties, the law imposed not merely civil, but criminal sanctions for its violation.

In an early test of that law in 1895, *U.S. v. E. C. Knight*, the Supreme Court interpreted "commerce" narrowly, calling into question the statute's utility in battling the trusts. Congress, it ruled, had no power to break up the giant trust because sugar refining was "manufacture," a purely local activity, and not "commerce," construed as transportation and trade subsequent to manufacture. The Sugar Trust, therefore, could only be regulated by the state in which it was incorporated or in states where it operated, and not by Congress under its power to regulate "commerce" among the states. Although the decision has been widely characterized as an effort by a laissez-faire Court out to protect big business from government regulation, a good case can be made that the Court was making a last-ditch effort to preserve a role for the states in regulating the economic activities of the trusts under their police powers.[43] But the effect of the decision, coupled with William McKinley's election the following year, was to promote an unprecedented round of corporate mergers, including the creation of American Tobacco, International Harvester, and U.S. Steel, stoking even greater social unease.

From the start, Roosevelt believed that the *Knight* case had been incorrectly decided and following Lincoln in *Dred Scott*, he was determined to see it overturned. But the creation of the Northern Securities Company in 1901, establishing a regional railroad monopoly under the control of James J. Hill, E. H. Harriman, and J. P. Morgan, provided him with a different opportunity to breathe life back into Sherman Act reinforcement. Ironically, another Supreme Court opinion, two years after *Knight*, appeared to open the way for Roosevelt to bring suit against this politically attractive target. For in *U.S. v. Trans-Missouri Freight Association* (1897), the Court interpreted the Sherman Act literally as proscribing all combinations in restraint of trade, rather than reading it in the light of common law doctrine barring only "unreasonable" restraints. Pursuant to his constitutional duty to see that the laws were faithfully executed, Roosevelt could move against Northern Securities on his own and score political points for so doing.

Consulting only with his attorney general, Philander C. Knox, and leaving the rest of his cabinet in the dark, TR stunned the financial markets by bringing suit under the Sherman Act in February 1902.[44] Nevertheless, the new president's decision to prosecute the Northern Securities Company won great favor with the public. The railroads had long been the focus of populist ire; lingering worries about rate discrimination, rebates, and the like rekindled old arguments about the railroads' undue power over the economy. Adding to these anxieties, the battle among the railway titans for control of the Northern Pacific rail line had sent its stock soaring to $1,000 a share, before tumbling and bringing the market down with it. Roosevelt could not but be offended by speculation that enriched the wealthy few at the expense of the public interest. Taking on the Northern Securities Company would bring not only economic, but more important, political and moral satisfactions.

Two years later, the Supreme Court, in a five-to-four decision, handed Roosevelt his victory, and the Northern Securities holding company was dissolved. Although the decision did nothing to overturn *Knight*, it did provide the federal government with one important tool for dealing with corporate power: antitrust prosecution under a literal reading of the Sherman Act. Roosevelt's only disappointment was that his first Supreme Court appointment, Oliver Wendell Holmes, for whom he held such high hopes, voted in the minority. Holmes's dissent led the president to remark bitterly, "I could carve out of a banana a judge with more backbone than that."[45]

However witty Roosevelt's retort, Holmes's dissent, siding with the common law reading of the statute, should not be so easily dismissed—least of all by Roosevelt, who welcomed the development of large corporations. As Holmes observed, the language of the statute was, in fact, "very sweeping," outlawing "every" combination. Taken literally, as the majority insisted on doing, it did seem to outlaw partnerships of whatever size and thus to "disintegrate society so far as it could into individual atoms." As such, it would be much more than an attempt to regulate commerce; it would actually constitute an effort "to reconstruct society," which far exceeded Congress's powers, and was never, Holmes insisted, its intent. In language that under other circumstances would have pleased Roosevelt, Holmes confessed that he could not shake the "natural feeling" that the statute aimed to strike only at those great combinations that had caused "just anxiety on the part of those who love their country more than money," even though the language of the statute stated otherwise. Moreover, the penalties the law imposed were not merely civil, but criminal, a distinction the majority conveniently chose to ignore. If the defendants had in fact broken the law, they should be punished as the Sherman Act directed. The majority could not have it both ways, finding the defendants in violation of the statute, but declining to impose criminal sanctions. Finally, Holmes argued that the railroad combination was not formed for the purpose of "excluding others from the field." The operators had joined together for the purpose of creating a more efficient railway system, which was what critics of the railroads insisted they wanted. With remarkable prescience, Holmes concluded that if one were to follow the logic of the majority's broad interpretation of "commerce," there would be "no part of the conduct of life" with which Congress might not interfere (though Roosevelt would probably not have been troubled by this). The upshot, as Holmes famously remarked, was that "great cases," meaning cases that arouse the interest of the public, "make bad law," an opinion that would later be echoed by Albro Martin in his careful study of America's railroad regulatory policy.[46] Reviewing the origins of the decline of American railroads in 1971, Martin concluded that much of the popular anger against the railroads arose from practices that had already been discontinued after the panic of 1893. Rather than continue to engage in ruinous rate wars or ill-conceived pooling arrangements, the great railway magnates, led by James J. Hill, had voluntarily joined together to integrate their operations and create a more efficient and well-managed regional rail system. Over the last decade, they had managed to impose order on the strife-ridden industry.[47] Moreover, the decision to break up the holding company was particularly odd coming from Roosevelt, since he had repeatedly claimed that business combinations were a fact of modern life and should only be prosecuted when they engaged in fraudulent or abusive practices, which was not the case here. As Roosevelt himself conceded in his *Autobiography*, the men who created the Northern Securities Company "had done so in an open and above-board fashion," following the precedent established in the *Knight* case. Yet so essential was it to establish the power of the federal government over these industrial giants that, years after the fact, Roosevelt remained convinced that it was "vital" to destroy the railroad holding company.[48]

A final irony is that, having resuscitated the Sherman Act, antitrust prosecutions were never Roosevelt's weapon of choice in reining in the trusts. Despite the popular reputation he enjoyed as a "trust-buster," after the *Northern Securities* case, TR would use the Sherman Act sparingly, bringing half the number of suits in the space of his seven-plus years in office as Taft did during his one term. After this first victory, TR would invoke the law only against "bad" combinations such as Standard Oil and the Meat Trust, which he accused of collusion, price-fixing, and other corrupt business practices. Indeed, by his second term, if not earlier, Roosevelt had come to regard the law in its present form as "useless, and even vicious" because it made no distinction between "good" and "evil" combinations, and indeed, his regulatory policy rested on this very distinction. Corporations that served the public or cooperated with the administration in correcting past abuses should not be broken up. Not all restraints on competition were "unreasonable."

In an argument reminiscent of Holmes's dissent in the *Northern Securities* case, Roosevelt would later condemn the Sherman Act as "profoundly immoral" because it forbade men from doing what they had to do, which was merge and grow in order to survive.[49] He called on Congress to amend the law to prohibit only those combinations that did actual harm to the public, through predatory pricing, capital inflation, and the like. Yet even then he thought the Sherman Act a clumsy and inefficient way of making corporations behave responsibly, since the Justice Department could only prosecute a small number of cases, and these took years to conclude. Indeed, after he succeeded in strengthening the regulatory powers of the Interstate Commerce Commission (ICC) through the Hepburn Act in 1906, he thought the railroads should be removed from antitrust law altogether. In what is perhaps the final irony, by the time the Supreme Court ordered the Standard Oil trust dissolved in 1911, Roosevelt no longer saw what good could come from dissolving the trust "into forty separate companies, all of which will still remain really under the same control."[50] But by then, Roosevelt was completely disenchanted with Taft and eager to distance himself from his policies.

In a nutshell, then, Roosevelt's first attempt at asserting federal control over these giant combinations through antitrust prosecution was riddled with difficulties and contradictions. He took on Northern Securities because it offered him the chance to breathe new life into the Sherman Act and it was a popular thing to do, even though many of the problems that had made the railroads so unpopular had been eliminated. Moreover, Roosevelt himself had been a champion of consolidation, and yet he hailed a Supreme Court decision that seemed to call all industrial combinations into question, and attacked the justice who grasped the absurdity of that position. Over the next few years, Roosevelt would retreat from antitrust policy, favoring a policy of government regulation and reserving antitrust prosecutions only for "bad" trusts. But this made Roosevelt's antitrust policy far too dependent upon his personal discretion. It also, arguably, put him at odds with the Supreme Court's ruling in *U.S. v. Trans-Missouri Freight Association*, which outlawed *all* such combinations, not simply "bad" ones, a precarious position for the chief executive charged with enforcing the country's laws.[51] Companies that cooperated with his efforts to expand regulatory control would be spared antitrust prosecution, while those that did not might find themselves hounded by the Justice Department. Thus, it was no surprise that corporations, especially those with well-established market shares, would begin to see the benefits of federal regulation, with its promise of predictability and preferential treatment, paving the way for what critics would later condemn as "crony capitalism."

THE TOILS OF RAILROAD REGULATION

Roosevelt's attempts to curb the abuses of corporate power proceeded along two distinct lines. At the same time that he invited the Supreme Court to revisit the Sherman Antitrust Act, he also pushed to increase economic regulation, starting with the railroads. The case for railroad regulation was stronger than in any other sector of the economy since the railroads were considered "natural monopolies" invested with the public interest. Although privately owned and operated, the great rail lines had been granted a certain measure of governmental authority (the right of eminent domain) and received government subsidies in the form of valuable tracts of land and below-market loans. In exchange for these privileges, the railroads were expected to provide service to all without discriminating as to rates or commodities shipped. But in the early days, fierce competition among the railways led to many abuses, followed by irate calls for government action.

At first, the task of regulating the railroads fell to the states, but in 1887 Congress passed the Interstate Commerce Act, which prohibited price-fixing, discriminatory rates, rebates (secret refunds demanded by large shippers), and preferential treatment by the railroads. Pursuant to the act, Congress established its first regulatory agency, the ICC, which was given a narrow mandate. The ICC could hold hearings, take evidence, and make a determination whether a particular railroad rate was "reasonable and just," but it had no power to set rates or to enforce its decisions, which were referred to the courts. Nevertheless, the ICC gradually began to set maximum shipping rates in cases where it found a given rate to be "unreasonable and unjust." In response, the Supreme Court whittled away the commission's authority, and granted the lower courts wide latitude to hear appeals from the commission's orders.[52] This was the background when, in 1902, Roosevelt asked Congress to amend the Interstate Commerce Act to give it more teeth.

Congress responded by passing the Elkins Act the following year. Named for West Virginia Senator and railroad supporter Stephen B. Elkins, the bill served railroad interests by making it a crime to offer or receive rebates and requiring railroads not to deviate from their published rates. Through the act, railroads hoped to escape from having to offer large shippers secret discounts that cut into their profits. Yet despite the criminal penalties, giant shippers such as Standard Oil and Armour regularly violated or circumvented the law, demanding rebates from railroads in exchange for their high volume of business, or imposing large fees for providing private tankers or refrigerated cars to transport their goods. These specialized carriers improved quality and efficiency, but smaller shippers resented what they considered the "unfair" advantages afforded larger competitors. To make matters worse, the railroads, which had high fixed costs, tried to compensate for their lost income by raising rates where they could, charging higher prices on less competitive routes and for shipping other commodities. Such "discriminatory" practices further enraged farmers and small shippers, producing a chorus of voices demanding increased government supervision of the railroads. Only the approaching presidential election slowed the momentum for further federal control. But after his landslide victory in 1904, Roosevelt returned to the issue with renewed vigor.

In his Fourth Annual Message, delivered shortly after his reelection, Roosevelt called for increasing the regulatory powers of the ICC over the railways. Railroad men, who had contributed handsomely to TR's reelection campaign, could not have been reassured to learn that the president did not "at present" favor a proposal circulating in the House to give the commission a general authority to set railroad rates.[53] Instead, Roosevelt supported a more modest measure that would give the ICC authority to determine what a "reasonable" rate should be after it had been challenged and found "unreasonable." Although the commission's decision would remain subject to judicial review, it reflected Roosevelt's preference for administrative authority over that of the courts. Rate structures, he thought, were essentially economic decisions to be made by impartial experts. (Perhaps it was part of his general lack of interest in economic questions, but at no point did he pause to wonder what "expertise" these bureaucrats possessed that would enable them to make sound economic decisions.) Still, to satisfy due process requirements, the courts could not be bypassed altogether. In this version, the ICC's ruling would go into effect immediately and obtain unless and until the courts reversed it. In the past, railroads could count on years of delay as the challenges made their way through the judicial system. Now, the burden would be shifted onto them immediately. What is more, the bill expanded the power of the ICC to include terminals, pipelines, storage facilities, and ferries. Alarmed by the House bill providing for general rate-making powers, the railroads launched a full-scale lobbying and public relations campaign to defeat the measure. Roosevelt countered with an extended campaign to enlist support for his own, more modest, version of the bill.

Speaking before the Union League Club in Philadelphia, the president reminded his audience that the club had been founded to uphold the principles of Lincoln and urged its members to take the lead in fighting for railroad regulation. (Where the former Illinois railroad lawyer would have stood on federal rate regulation is less than clear, however.) Roosevelt cast the issue of regulation in starkly moral terms: "the great highways of commerce" must be kept "open alike to all on reasonable and equitable terms." Only the government could protect both the railroads and the shippers and put the big shipper and the little shipper on an equal footing; only the government could insure that the railroads and the shippers alike were both "given justice" and "required to do justice." But the speech ended with a blunt warning that "neither this people nor any other free people" would "permanently tolerate the use of vast power conferred by vast wealth and especially wealth in its corporate form," unless that economic power was controlled by the still "higher power" of government.[54]

TR's deft use of the "bully pulpit" won him widespread public support, but it failed to sway Republican leaders in the Senate, who remained adamant that the courts retain the final authority to determine whether a given rate was "reasonable." They were concerned not only about due process, but also whether Congress could constitutionally delegate its legislative powers to an administrative agency. For in contrast to the quasi-judicial role of the ICC under its original charter, Congress was here being asked to delegate its legislative power to set railroad rates. Brushing aside these constitutional concerns, Roosevelt returned at length to the issue in his Fifth Annual Message. As a gesture of goodwill, he indicated his willingness to compromise on one point: rather than have the ICC determination go into effect immediately, as he had initially proposed in his Fourth Message, the ruling would now do so only "after a lapse of a reasonable time."

As Republican leaders in the Senate worked to thwart the bill, Roosevelt threw his weight behind a coalition of southern Democrats and Republican insurgents, who backed a more radical measure. When that alliance proved too fragile, Roosevelt swung back to the proposal endorsed by the party regulars, giving more authority to the courts. Once again demonstrating his political skills, the president leaked information about the illegal rebates Standard Oil received from the railroads just as Congress was debating the matter, rallying public opinion behind him. TR then signed off on a measure that gave the courts the final say, insisting this was what he had always wanted. Critics on the left assailed him for conceding too much, but in the public eye, the president came out a winner.[55]

In *The Rhetorical Presidency*, political scientist Jeffrey Tulis has praised Roosevelt for steering a middle path between the more restrained statecraft of the Framers, which regarded demagoguery as the great evil of popular government, and the modern rhetorical presidency, which attempts to shape public policy by appealing directly to the people. According to Tulis, Roosevelt did so with a twist, however, employing demagogic arts in pursuit of moderate aims to defeat the real demagogues on both the right and the left. In his view, Roosevelt's success lay principally in his decision to frame the argument in moral terms having broad public appeal. More than any other industry of the time, the railroads were a lightning rod for popular discontent about the growing divisions between the rich and the poor, the powerful and the powerless. Where once the railroads had promised to unite Americans, they had become the most visible symbol of everything that divided them. By linking rate regulation to larger questions about justice, equality, and fairness, Roosevelt could build general support for the principle, while leaving the details to be ironed out by Congress.[56]

Up to a point, Tulis's assessment is convincing. Roosevelt did indeed use moral arguments to rally the country behind what seemed like moderate aims. And as he had done so successfully in the past, Roosevelt warned the railroads that their opposition to all legislation would only strengthen those calling for government ownership of the railroads, something he strongly opposed. The president cast himself as the friend of the honest railroad man and honest shipper alike, and insisted, against opposition on his left, that their great talents deserved to be amply rewarded. As if to underline this last point, at a critical phase in the Senate hearings, TR infuriated insurgents within his own party by lashing out, not at the railroads, but at muckraking journalists for carrying their criticisms of businessmen too far.[57]

Nevertheless, Tulis's analysis does not accurately capture what Roosevelt was up to in defending the Hepburn Act. For one thing, Roosevelt's appeals to public opinion on railroad reform were not the exception to an otherwise more traditional understanding of the executive office, in which the president addressed his arguments to Congress rather than the public. Roosevelt was a master of using the press and the new magazines to stir up public opinion on any number of "crises" he faced in office, from the coal strike to his last great battle over conservation.[58] In this respect, the modern "rhetorical presidency," in which the president tries to circumvent Congress whenever his proposals meet with resistance and appeal directly to public opinion, begins with Roosevelt and not Woodrow Wilson.

Moreover, given Roosevelt's rejection of social compact theory and his general views of historical development, it is simply not plausible that Roosevelt was using these unconventional methods merely to preserve the Framers' Constitution under radically changed economic conditions. Roosevelt himself implied as much in his 1905 Inaugural Address where he observed that Americans of his day had "outgrown" the perils that faced "our forefathers." All that united the men of his day with "our fathers who founded and preserved this Republic," was a certain "spirit." And indeed, no sooner did Roosevelt achieve his goal with the enactment of the Hepburn bill than he began calling for additional regulatory measures over both the railroads and the entire industrial economy that would imperil even the most energetic of the Framers' visions of limited government. Like his heroes, Roosevelt summoned the nation to lofty ideals, but his ideals were no longer those of the founders.[59]

Finally, and closely related to this last point, Roosevelt no longer viewed railroad regulation as a way to remedy specific abuses or strike a "just balance" among competing economic interests. As his Fifth Annual Message, delivered in December 1905 while the Hepburn bill was still being debated, made clear, TR's moral vision now reached toward something grander.

We desire to set up a moral standard. There can be no delusion more fatal to the nation, than the delusion that the standard of profits, of business prosperity, is sufficient in judging any business or political question—from rate legislation to municipal government. Business success, whether for the individual or for the nation, is a good thing only so far as it is accompanied by and develops a high standard of conduct—honor, integrity, civic courage. The kind of business prosperity that blunts the standard of honor, that puts an inordinate value on mere wealth, that makes a man ruthless and conscienceless in trade, weak and cowardly in citizenship is not a good thing at all, but a very bad thing for the nation. This government stands for manhood first and for business only as an adjunct of manhood.[60]

In such moments, Roosevelt's rhetoric clashed with Publius's more down-to-earth observation that the principal task of modern legislation was simply to regulate competing economic interests, not transcend them. But as he would make clear in his "Man with the Muck-Rake" speech the following spring, Roosevelt no longer believed that it was sufficient for businessmen to gain their fortunes by staying within the limits of "mere law-honesty." They must now aim at "great services to the community as a whole," toward which government regulations would presumably direct them.[61] Underneath Roosevelt's talk of sanity and self-restraint was the fantastical idea that regulation could serve as an exercise in national character building, if not moral transformation.

It was, therefore, inevitable that Roosevelt would come to regard rate regulation as only the "first step" toward a more thoroughgoing control of the railroads, which he promptly did in his next Annual Message.[62] By 1908, Roosevelt was calling on Congress to grant additional powers to the ICC to set "any rate and practice on their own initiative," as well as to make decisions about schedules, routes, and equipment.[63] The commission should also be given control over railway finance, including the issuance of stocks and bonds, to make sure that the railroads plowed their profits back into improving the lines, rather than merely enriching their owners.[64] Although Roosevelt continued to present his proposals as a sensible middle way between "law-defying wealth" and "vindictive and dreadful radicalism," the regulatory regime he envisioned was morphing into something more prophetic, something that would, as he suggested in his Inaugural Address, speak to "the things of the soul."[65] And indeed, in one of his special messages to Congress in 1908, Roosevelt would insist that the movement in which he was engaged was never "purely economic. It has a large economic side, but it is fundamentally an ethical movement," which aimed at the "moral regeneration of business."[66] There could be no more striking contrast with the sober realism of *The Federalist* than Roosevelt's earnest longing for a moral regeneration, through government regulation no less, that would redirect the passions and interests of its citizens toward "lofty ideals."

In this sense, John Milton Cooper, Jr., is closer to the mark when he concludes that Roosevelt's "greatest failure as president lay in his attempt to get people to avoid class politics and rise above material concerns."[67] It is not that modern democracies are incapable of transcending their selfish interests ("the things of the body," in Roosevelt's language), but they usually do so only in emergencies and, when the crisis has passed, they return to business as usual. Roosevelt's mistake was to assume that regulation could effect a transformation of human nature, moving men and women beyond selfish individualism and uniting them across class lines. No wonder he refused until the very end to give up on Lamarckianism. But as the authors of *The Federalist* understood, only a few individuals were capable of genuine disinterestedness, and it was prudent not to rely solely upon them. The idea that an entire nation could be so completely changed Hamilton would rightly have dismissed as merely another "deceitful dream of a golden age."[68]

The opposite side of Roosevelt's moral approach to railroad regulation was his casual indifference to economics. Although Roosevelt's moral rhetoric appealed to both an irate public and small shippers incensed about rate discrimination and favoritism, from the standpoint of a free economy many of these decisions made little sense. There were good market reasons why rates were higher in cities and towns where there was no competition, and why large shippers were able to negotiate more favorable rates. Nor was it necessarily "unfair" that the shippers who provided private refrigerated or tanker cars to transport their products received special consideration from the railroads.[69] Justice, for Roosevelt, was one thing; supply and demand another.

In *Enterprise Denied*, his seminal study of railroad regulation, Albro Martin concluded that even though Roosevelt cast himself as a "crusader," he was far "too intelligent" to be classed with more run-of-the-mill demagogues. Compared to the opinions circulating among college professors, editors of influential magazines, and reform-minded souls, Roosevelt's positions on regulation were certainly "more scientific," and "far-seeing." TR went out of his way to emphasize that he was not hostile to the railroads, and, in his later messages, was even willing to allow the railways to raise rates, so long as the profits were used to make capital improvements, and the rate increases did not take place in election years.[70]

But at the same time, Roosevelt, like most of the "informed opinion" of his day, never questioned whether "government controls over the important policies of a basic industry, such as railroad transportation," would work. Caught up in the spirit of progress and reform, Roosevelt and those around him displayed a touching faith in the capacity of disinterested experts to resolve complex and technical economic questions regarding rates, schedules, and equipment.[71] He shared their excitement that the newly emerging fields of social science would equip selfless administrators to make the right decisions. These opinion setters had abandoned the idea that markets could generally do a better and more efficient job of sorting out these complex, economic questions. Instead, Martin asserted, they gave themselves over to the "exhilarating notion that men who lacked the experience, the economic power, and the enlightened self-interest of the leaders of big business could nevertheless establish the patterns by which such great aggregations of property fitted into the nation's economy."[72] Nor did it occur to them that "efficiency" was not what big government does best, that regulatory agencies could be captured by "special interests," or that they might make bone-headed decisions. Roosevelt, who had launched his career battling government corruption, and who had firsthand experience with how inept the bureaucrats in Washington were at supplying the troops in Cuba, somehow never doubted that this new class of government experts, who shared his lofty ideals, would promote the public interest.

If Martin's tone was caustic, it was because he convincingly documented how regulation helped to destroy the railroads in America, first, by focusing on problems and conditions that no longer existed (what he calls "archaic progressivism"), and second, by assuming that these problems could be resolved by disinterested bureaucrats acting in the public interest. Instead, within a decade after Roosevelt left the presidency, the ICC was captured by private interests hostile to the railroads and denied the rate increases that were necessary to make capital improvements in their lines. Seeing no opportunity for profit, investors turned to the unregulated trucking industry, which flourished at the railroads' expense. Martin is careful not to blame Roosevelt for these developments, which took place after he left office. But since Roosevelt so forcefully articulated the assumption that administrators would act as just and wise adjudicators of the nation's complex economic questions and viewed regulation as an exercise in moral regeneration, he cannot be altogether exonerated.[73]

THE BUREAU OF CORPORATIONS AND
THE NEW REGULATORY ORDER

Beyond gaining greater control over the railroads, Roosevelt was determined to extend the regulatory powers of the federal government to all
corporations operating in interstate commerce. Despite his pledge to continue McKinley's policies, less than three months after his inauguration
Roosevelt asked Congress to establish a new administrative agency within
the executive branch that would gather information about corporate business practices, which the president could then, at his discretion, make public. As when he was governor, Roosevelt was convinced (in some vague
Kantian sense) that the mere threat of publicity would be sufficient—or
at least make a good start—at controlling corporate abuses. Accordingly,
he sought to reassure business leaders that the proposed agency posed no
threat to honest corporations. Indeed, just as consolidation and combination had introduced greater cooperation among the trusts, so too would
the proposed agency usher in a new era of cooperation between business
and government.[74]

To justify the legislation and to blunt the objection that any such government agency would infringe upon property rights or the liberty of contract,
the president argued that

> when men receive from government the privilege of doing business
> under corporate form, which frees them from individual responsibility,
> and enables them to call into their enterprises the capital of the public,
> they shall do so upon absolutely truthful representations as to the
> value of the property in which the capital is to be invested. . . . Great
> corporations exist only because they are created and safeguarded by our
> institutions; and it is therefore our right and our duty to see that they
> work in harmony with these institutions.[75]

Though the professors who taught him political economy might have protested, at a general level, there was nothing objectionable about his argument
that government should intervene to ensure that the corporations served
the broader public purposes for which they were intended. The authors of
The Federalist had envisioned precisely such a role when they observed that
the regulation of competing economic interests formed "the principal task
of modern legislation."[76] The immediate question Roosevelt had to answer
was why the *federal* government, rather than the states, should regulate the
trusts. The more long-range question was whether Roosevelt's evolving un-

derstanding of "regulation" could be squared with that of even the most nationalistic of the Framers.

In tackling this first question, Roosevelt acknowledged that when the Constitution was adopted it was generally agreed that the states would exercise this responsibility. The states, after all, had chartered the corporations, and the states were equipped with police powers to regulate, "so far as was then necessary, the comparatively insignificant and strictly localized corporate bodies of the day." But political and industrial conditions had changed "in ways that no human wisdom could foretell." In the early years of the republic, states had chartered corporations for narrow purposes invested with a public interest but, by the middle of the nineteenth century, they had begun to enact general corporation laws that fostered the growth of a national economy. At present, corporations continued to be chartered in particular states, but their operations now crossed state lines, and often they did little business in the state in which they were incorporated. Moreover, states, for their own economic reasons, had few incentives to supervise the actions of these companies. If the regulations in one state became too burdensome, businesses would simply incorporate somewhere else, as Standard Oil did when it moved from Ohio to New Jersey. Whatever the formal powers of the states, for all practical purposes, it was now "impossible to get the adequate regulations through State action."[77]

Accordingly, Roosevelt asked Congress in his First Annual Message and, after it failed to act, again the following year, to authorize additional powers so the federal government could supervise corporations involved in interstate commerce. The measure, he thought, could be justified under Congress's power to regulate commerce among the states. If, however, in view of the recent Supreme Court ruling in *Knight* that interpreted "commerce" narrowly, the lawmakers did not believe such a law was constitutional, then they should draw up an amendment to the Constitution. Just as businesses had evolved from individual proprietorships to giant combinations, so too, Roosevelt thought, must the Constitution adapt to meet these new economic realities.

Roosevelt was not content simply to appeal to Congress, but tapping the rhetorical possibilities of his office, embarked on a speaking tour to drum up popular support for his proposal. Addressing a crowd of 20,000 in Providence, Rhode Island, Roosevelt once again sought to strike a mean between two vicious extremes. Although condemning corporate "evils," he took pains not to inflame more than necessary popular animosity against wealthy industrialists. As he would many times, TR concluded his speech with a special plea to the middle and working classes not to allow themselves to be swept up in a "spirit of sullen resentment" when they saw those around them who were no more deserving doing so much better. Combining Old Testament language with the argument of Aristotle's *Politics*, he warned Americans not to let envy and hatred so poison their natures that they wound up, as in the days of Jeshurun, destroying the sources of their own prosperity.[78] In such moments, Roosevelt acted the part of the republican statesman, attempting to elevate the character of the citizens by moderating their destructive passions.

Despite Roosevelt's efforts to build support for the new agency, Congress was still reluctant to act on his proposal. For one thing, the measure was not popular with the business interests that supported the Republican Party. Judge Elbert Gary, chairman of U.S. Steel, was clearly in the minority at the time when he testified, "I would be very glad if we had someplace where we could go, to a responsible governmental authority and say to them, 'Here are our facts and figures, here is our property, here our cost of production; now you tell us what we have the right to do and what prices we have the right to charge.'"[79] Most corporate heads worried that being forced to disclose information about their business practices would put them at a competitive disadvantage, or worse, expose them to criminal sanctions. As it turned out, their fear that information supplied to government bureaucrats might be used against them in criminal prosecutions was not groundless, as both the meat packers and the Standard Oil trust would soon discover. Nor were they wrong to suspect that Roosevelt's modest first step was just the beginning of what would turn out to be his most far-reaching attempt at regulatory control.

Congress was not merely protecting the interests of the business classes, however; it was also defending its own turf. As the authors of *The Federalist* had foreseen, the separation of powers not only helped to limit government, but just as important, it gave to each branch the necessary power and motivation to defend themselves against encroachments from other branches. Lawmakers saw all too clearly that the bill Roosevelt favored would shift power away from the legislature and the courts to the executive branch and its new administrative apparatus. Congress had already ceded power over the railroads to the ICC; now Roosevelt was proposing a new bureau that would operate across the entire industrial sector, and whose commissioner would report directly to the president.

In this contest between the executive and the legislative branches, Roosevelt possessed considerable weapons of his own, both formal and informal. At a critical moment in the congressional debate, TR leaked word that John D. Rockefeller, Sr., the personification of a "bad" trust, had sent telegrams to six U.S. senators expressing his opposition to the bill. The story turned out to be false, but it solidified public opinion in favor of the proposal, and in February 1903 Congress agreed to establish the new agency. Under its charter, the Bureau of Corporations was limited to collecting data about corporate business practices, which the head of the bureau would turn over directly to the president. He, in turn, would use his broad discretionary powers to decide whether to make the bureau's findings public as well as recommend further regulatory measures to Congress.

As Roosevelt had explained, the underlying assumption for creating the bureau was that the threat of exposing a corporation's business practices would deter corporate abuses. But from its first investigation of the meatpacking industry, the conflicting demands on the bureau revealed the weaknesses of this assumption.[80] On the one hand, the bureau was charged with gathering information that the president might use to propose additional legislation, and if it was to enlist the cooperation of the corporations, its reports had to be measured and impartial. On the other hand, if the threat of publicity were to be effective in controlling misbehavior, the reports would need to satisfy a public hungry for sensational details. Here in preview was the dilemma that Roosevelt would face as a modern "rhetorical president."

In contrast to *The Federalist*, which opened and closed with a warning about demagogues and which defended the design of the executive precisely because it enabled the president to stand up to the momentary whims of the people, Roosevelt actively sought to arouse the public to the need for more regulation. To allay any fears that he might be practicing what *The Federalist* derisively called "the popular arts," Roosevelt warned his audiences against envy and resentment. Nevertheless, in attempting to influence both Congress and the public, Roosevelt would learn the hard way that the rhetorical devices he adopted to persuade one group often backfired with the other. In its investigation of the meatpacking industry, the bureau aimed its report at lawmakers and wound up antagonizing the public with its dry analysis. The bureau would err in the opposite direction in its investigation of Standard Oil, abandoning any pretense of objectivity in order to arouse public opinion. Only once, when he disclosed information gathered by the bureau about illegal rebates to Standard Oil at a critical moment in the debate over railroad regulation, would Roosevelt succeed with both Congress and the public. The modern "rhetorical presidency" TR helped to forge was a chariot harnessed to two horses that even the most skillful executive would find difficult to drive.

On top of these political problems, the bureau ran into legal difficulties as well. Before his reelection, Roosevelt had side-stepped the question of whether the new agency would turn over information it had obtained from the meat packers regarding the recent rise in the cost of beef to the Justice Department, which was conducting its own criminal probe of the Beef Trust. As Roosevelt initially envisioned the bureau, its purpose was to gather information to aid the president in proposing new legislation and which he could make public if he so chose. He said nothing about the bureau assisting the Justice Department in its criminal investigations and seemed unaware of the legal problems this would raise. But after the election, Roosevelt interpreted his landslide victory as a mandate to crack down on the trusts. Accordingly, he instructed his commissioner of corporations to deliver the bureau's findings to government prosecutors, in effect, turning the Bureau of Corporations into an arm of the Justice Department and provoking a successful legal challenge from the meat packers.[81]

Brought face-to-face with the limits of publicity as a tool to control corporate misbehavior, Roosevelt concluded that the powers of the bureau needed to be significantly expanded. Up to this point, the agency had investigated particular industries, but it had no "affirmative" regulatory powers, being limited by its charter to gathering information. Beginning in 1907, however, and coinciding with his ramped-up attacks on antitrust prosecutions as a tool for reining in corporate power, Roosevelt endorsed legislation that would transform the bureau into a full-fledged regulatory agency. As he explained in his Seventh Annual Message, the agency he had in mind should be empowered to deal with "all manner of abuses," including predatory pricing and overcapitalization, and not simply Sherman Act violations of restraint of trade. To that end, he called for a federal incorporation or licensing law that, as it proceeded through the legislative process, would have allowed the bureau to grant or revoke the license at its discretion. It would further have empowered the agency to bring suit against corporations under the Sherman Act and to bar from interstate commerce any corporation that had its license revoked. Although the licensing provision would be, strictly speaking, voluntary, in practice, corporations operating in interstate commerce would have had little choice but to register, and once in the system, regulation would be open-ended and ongoing. In keeping with Roosevelt's growing criticism of the courts, the proposed legislation made scant provision for judicial review.[82] TR continued to push these proposals until he left office, in his last year sending ever more insistent messages to Congress, imploring them to act. In a Special Message to Congress of January 31, 1908, Roosevelt repeated his call for a federal licensing power and, in addition, asked Congress to outlaw short selling and cornering the market, which he considered morally no better than gambling. But Congress was in no mood to accommodate him, and the bureau, even without these enhanced powers, was plagued by problems of Roosevelt's own making, problems that went to the heart of his conception of executive power and his capacious understanding of "regulation."

As business historian Arthur M. Johnson pointed out in his essay on the Bureau of Corporations, there were "serious shortcomings" with the way the agency was conceived, since it granted wide discretionary power to the president and made the bureau subservient to Roosevelt's will. "The resulting invitation to make arbitrary distinctions between 'good' and 'bad' corporations was too patently inconsistent with sound public policy to be institutionalized."[83] And in fact this was exactly what Roosevelt did when he allowed J. P. Morgan's U.S. Steel Corporation to acquire Tennessee Coal and Iron in flagrant disregard of the Sherman Act he was pledged to enforce. Even before he articulated his "stewardship" theory, Roosevelt was convinced that as president he was uniquely positioned to articulate the needs of the nation and to take whatever actions were required to advance that end. Discretion, fortified by righteous conviction, was essential to his understanding of executive power.

Roosevelt's proposed changes only magnified the problems. Analyzing the particulars of the 1908 Hepburn bill that would have expanded the powers of the bureau, Martin J. Sklar concluded that Roosevelt's mistake was to model the bureau on the extensive regulatory powers granted to the ICC, ignoring the difference between the railroads, which were common carriers invested with a public interest and therefore subject to greater government regulation regarding rates, capitalization, investment, and the like, and the larger industrial sector of the economy. This did not mean that there should be no regulation of these corporations, only that the model should not be the extensive powers granted to the ICC. Yet the bill Roosevelt favored would have granted the executive complete control over "the business operations in general and investment decisions in particular, of corporate enterprise, backed up by the power of summary dissolution of delinquent corporations." Along with the ICC, the bill would have made the Bureau of Corporations "the arbiter of contracts and arrangements that determined not only corporate structure and capital formation, but also either directly or indirectly, prices of goods and services." Had the legislation been enacted, the bureau would then have become "a vast centralized planning and administering agency," extending its sway over all of the industrial economy and paving the way for "state-directed corporate capitalism."[84] In terms of its organization and its reach, the proposed Bureau of

Corporations would have been a far grander enterprise of control than the Federal Trade Commission that replaced it in 1914.

Put another way, Roosevelt's understanding of the role of the Bureau of Corporations went well beyond what the Framers understood by "regulation." In his highly suggestive essay, John Adams Wettergreen pointed out that the Constitution itself distinguishes between "regulate" and "govern." The former is a limited power, which aims at making capitalism function smoothly according to its own economic rules. Against advocates of laissez-faire, Wettergreen maintained that the market could not spontaneously reconcile all private and competing interests; the task of government was to mark off the boundaries of what constituted legitimate business activity.[85] But as the Framers understood it, the scope of regulation was limited to preserving a free economy. This was what Publius meant in *Federalist* No. 10, when he observed that "the regulation of these various and interfering interests forms the principal task of modern legislation."[86]

By contrast, "govern" refers to the "distinctive power of the sovereign" to command, and it is telling that the Constitution employs the term only in connection with the armed forces and the District of Columbia. If the executive-administrative agencies were to possess the power to *govern* the economy and make all its rules, commerce would no longer be free—or prosperous.[87] To put it another way, if the government were to run the economy the way that the ICC ran the railroads (or worse, the way Defense Department budgets for the military), the economy would no longer be the great engine of wealth production. And yet, this was precisely what Roosevelt, by the end of his second term, was proposing: government would now be commanding the economy, with businesses reduced to agents of the state.[88] Paradoxically, the "cooperative" relationship Roosevelt envisioned between government and business rested on continuous executive control. No wonder, then, that the Hepburn bill died in the Senate Judiciary Committee, which scored it as "a most serious departure from the fundamental principles of our Government, and [which] would do violence to what we conceive to be due process of law."[89]

THE CONSERVATION MOVEMENT AND
THE GROWTH OF NATIONAL POWER

The conservation movement brought together many of the most important strands of Roosevelt's evolving theory of executive power. It was the area where his stewardship theory first took legal shape, and which he would later offer as one of its prime exhibits. In creating the National Forest Service, increasing the number of national parks, establishing national monuments, and setting aside wildlife and bird refuges on public lands, Roosevelt cast himself as America's steward, conscripting biblical imagery to describe the responsibilities of the president for the health of the earth (and much else). At a time when more Americans were clustering in cities, these spaces would offer spiritual refreshment as well as opportunities to strengthen the manly virtues. Moreover, conservation, with its myriad projects to reclaim arid public lands, provided an energetic executive like TR with additional opportunities to undertake (in the language of *Federalist* No. 72) "extensive and arduous enterprises for the public benefit."[90] Only the federal government, and to be more precise only the disinterested experts within the executive branch, could coordinate and carry off these vast engineering projects that Roosevelt would later maintain nearly rivaled in scope the construction of the Panama Canal.

Nevertheless, the popularity of these projects, especially the national parks—the most visible and enduring symbol of Roosevelt's conservation program—should not obscure the more controversial ideas that informed them. For the conservation movement was an offspring of the larger progressive impulse and shared many of its preoccupations: a fear that America's natural resources had been squandered by selfish private interests and would soon run out; a desire to shift policymaking away from Congress and into new bureaucratic agencies that could articulate and execute national goals; and finally, a wish to redefine property rights and therewith the individual's relation to government. Like progressivism itself, conservation offered an open-ended agenda capable of indefinite expansion.[91]

The conservation movement is very much the story of a partnership between TR and Gifford Pinchot. Pinchot, a wealthy easterner and Yale graduate, whose family fortune derived from lumbering (!) and land speculation, had been encouraged by his father to study scientific forestry in Switzerland, France, and Germany. Like others of his generation who studied in Europe, he came away convinced that state-directed management practices were superior to the waste and inefficiency of private ownership in America. Zealous in the promotion of his newfound ideals, he warned that if the United States continued on its present course there would not be sufficient supplies of timber for homes, furniture, heating, and railroad ties. To prevent this looming "timber famine," government must assert greater control over the national forest reserves. It could no longer simply lock them away for some future emergency, but must actively manage them for the public good.[92]

Roosevelt and Pinchot, who had previously consulted about forest policy while Roosevelt was governor, were united in their desire to change American forestry practices, and their success in doing so laid the foundation for the worldwide conservation movement they helped to launch in 1907. Indeed, writing to Pinchot at the end of his presidency, Roosevelt spoke of "a peculiar intimacy" between them based on having "worked on the same causes" and having "dreamed the same dreams." Later, TR would go even further, calling Pinchot the "moving and directing spirit" in most of his administration's conservation efforts, as well as "counselor and assistant on most of the other work connected with the internal affairs of the country." Among all of the men who served their country during his presidency, Roosevelt concluded, Gifford Pinchot, "on the whole, stood first."[93]

The bond between the two men was not only intimate; it was also immediate. At the president's request, Pinchot, who at the time was chief of the Division of Forestry for the United States, prepared the statement on "Forest Conservation" for Roosevelt's First Annual Message and worked tirelessly during his first term to have control of the forest reserves (then housed in the Land Office of Department of the Interior) moved to the Division of Forestry in the Department of Agriculture.[94] In furtherance of this end, Roosevelt also appointed Pinchot to two early presidential commissions, both of which, with Pinchot's persistent lobbying, recommended the transfer. Nevertheless, Congress remained cool to the proposal. Only after Roosevelt's landslide reelection did it pass the Transfer Act in 1905, giving Pinchot control of the national forest reserves, complete with its own independent revenue stream for five years. Now the real work of conservation would begin.

Once in control of the national forest reserves, Pinchot floated the idea of imposing fees for grazing and waterpower rights, an idea that Roosevelt later described as part of his "stewardship" theory.[95] In his *Autobiography*, TR credited the legal officer of the Forest Service, George Woodruff, with developing this idea. As the former president explained, since many of the existing laws were clearly insufficient to protect the nation's resources, and Congress was too beholden to "special interests" to amend them, it became necessary to "supplement" these existing laws with "executive Action" in the public interest. From now on, whoever used public lands for private profit would have to reimburse the public; "the rights of the public to the natural resources outweigh private rights,—and must be given its first consideration." As stewards of the nation's resources, the Forest Service would now impose grazing and water-power fees, regulate the rights of the railroads and other corporations to develop their lands in the reserves, and withdraw valuable coal and mineral lands if the government could not obtain adequate compensation. In further elaboration, he wrote, "I acted on the theory that the President could at any time in his discretion withdraw from entry any of the public lands in the United States and reserve the same for forestry, for water-power sites, for irrigation, and other public purposes."[96]

Whether deliberately or not, Roosevelt leaves the reader with the impression that his administration was acting without any prior authorization from Congress, guided only by the principle that they could do anything the public good required, so long as it was not explicitly forbidden by the Constitution or the laws. And he further suggests that in twice upholding the administration's actions, the Supreme Court validated his stewardship theory of presidential power. But this is not accurate. While he was president, Roosevelt was not simply acting on his "theory," but executing the law. For Congress had in fact authorized the secretary of agriculture to make rules and regulations to achieve the objects pertaining to the occupancy, use, and preservation of the national forest reserves. The question before the Court in *U.S. v. Grimaud* (1911) was whether Congress had unconstitutionally delegated its legislative power in conferring these capacities on the secretary. The Court declared that it had not.[97] Although Congress was barred from delegating legislative power, it could delegate administrative authority because it would be impracticable for Congress to try to make rules and regulations for such varying conditions. Roosevelt's discussion blurred the difference between his conception of the executive as the steward of the nation's resources, executing the laws of the land, and his more grandiose constitutional theory, according to which the president could take any action that the needs of the nation required so long as it was not explicitly prohibited by the Constitution or the laws.

Elsewhere in his *Autobiography*, Roosevelt made similarly misleading claims about his establishment of the first bird reservation at Pelican Island. In this case, Florida ornithologists had advised the president that if he did not act swiftly and declare the island a bird preserve, the Department of the Interior might be forced to open it up for settlement, destroying the pelicans' breeding ground. In what has now become Roosevelt's legendary response, the president asked his attorney general, "Is there any law that will prevent me from declaring Pelican Island a Federal Bird Reservation?" When told no, he replied, "Very well, then I so declare it," and cited no authorizing legislation.[98] But again, Roosevelt's action was not nearly as untethered from the Constitution as he implied.

As far back as 1890, the office of the attorney general had thoroughly studied Supreme Court opinions and historical precedents regarding the legal authority of the president to reserve federal lands. Although in this case there was "no specific statutory authority," the courts had long recognized "the right of the executive to place such lands in reservation, as the exigencies of the public may require . . . either by proclamation or executive order."[99] No wonder then that "no one ventured to test its legality by lawsuit."[100] Roosevelt's establishment of bird reserves on federal lands may have been a novel use of executive power, but it was not quite the presidential fiat of legend.[101]

Moreover, there were real limitations to what a president could accomplish by executive order alone. Without congressional appropriations, the sanctuaries received no federal funds and were forced to rely on private contributions and volunteers, or to piggyback on other federal reclamation projects, the aims of which did not always mesh with those of the bird preserves. The problem became acute at the end of his presidency when Roosevelt moved aggressively, creating twenty-five refuges on February 25, 1909, one week before he left office. Although Roosevelt would later boast that between March 14, 1903, and March 4, 1909, he established by executive order fifty-one bird reservations in seventeen states and territories, including Puerto Rico, Hawaii, and Alaska, nearly a third of these would later be withdrawn or have their refuge status revoked.[102]

Among Roosevelt's earliest successes were water conservation and the reclamation of western public lands. Having worked as a rancher in the Badlands, TR had firsthand experience of the difficulties of eking out a livelihood in the arid West.[103] Both state governments and private companies had earlier attempted irrigation projects, but their efforts had come to naught. Roosevelt, who had won the Republican nomination for governor of New York in part because of scandals surrounding the state-financed Erie Canal, knew firsthand the defects and limitations of state governments. Only the national government, he thought, could undertake the vast engineering efforts necessary to make these parched lands attractive to settlers, and only the executive could carry out such projects efficiently.

Acting on Roosevelt's recommendation, Congress moved swiftly to pass the Newlands Reclamation Act of 1902. The new law authorized the federal government to construct dams and carry out irrigation projects throughout the West, funded by the sale of public lands. If all went according to plan (which it did not), the project would be self-funding, saving taxpayers in the East and Midwest, who opposed the measure, from having to foot the bill.[104] The act also vested authority for selecting the location of these sites in the secretary of the interior and handed over the administration of the law to the newly created Reclamation Service, which, with its own income stream, was freed from dependence on annual congressional appropriations. In effect, the new law shifted power away from Congress toward scientific experts who presumably were better positioned to determine which projects best served the public interest, and perhaps they were. (There may not be a completely satisfactory solution, especially once the scope of government projects was expanded.) But as with economic regulation, Roosevelt assumed that the placement of these reclamation projects was a purely technical decision; it did not occur to him that these bureaucrats would themselves be choosing among competing interests and creating clear winners and losers.[105] Seen from the perspective of the administrative state, the Newlands Act established a pattern for executive-legislative relations. But it was not one that Congress, increasingly shut out of conservation decisions, would rush to embrace again.[106] Indeed, when the same Senator Newlands proposed a law modeled on the Reclamation Act to carry out the recommendations of the Inland Waterways Commission in 1907, it went nowhere.

Yet Roosevelt was not content simply to work with sympathetic members of Congress to achieve his conservation goals. He also established a series of presidential commissions, often without congressional authorization, to cut through the red tape in formulating policy. It was in these commissions that the heavy lifting was done, with Gifford Pinchot playing a critical role on each of them. Early in Roosevelt's second term, the Commission on Departmental Methods, or Keep Commission, as it was called after its chairman, Assistant Secretary of the Treasury Charles Keep, recommended a major overhaul of the executive departments, with the Forest Service (headed by Pinchot) held up as a model of organizational efficiency.[107] The hand of Gifford Pinchot could also be detected in its ambitious recommendation to consolidate the four divisions within the Interior Department into one, accountable directly to the secretary. That the new secretary of the interior was Roosevelt's first head of the Bureau of Corporations and conservation ally, James Garfield, was clearly an important consideration in the commission's recommendation.[108] By this time, however, Congress had grown increasingly wary of Roosevelt's reliance on commissions and refused even to appropriate the $25,000 to pay for its work. Undaunted, Roosevelt implemented the commission's recommendations by executive order, further infuriating lawmakers.

Up to this point, Roosevelt's approach to resource management had largely been piecemeal: forests, irrigation, the open range, and other matters had each been treated as distinct and separate problems. But beginning in 1907, TR began to emphasize the totality of the conservation movement and the need for a more comprehensive government plan to preserve America's supposedly dwindling resources. Prompted once again by Pinchot and W. J. McGee, head of the U.S. Geological Service and another conservation ally, the president appointed the Inland Waterways Commission to come up with a plan for reviving the nation's declining water transportation system and to coordinate these measures with the railways.

The scope of TR's ambition was breathtaking. Addressing the Deep Waterway Convention in Memphis, Tennessee, the president made it clear that he favored a multiuse approach that focused not just on navigation (the constitutional source of federal power over waterways), but also irrigation, water purity, flood prevention, and waterpower. The aim was to treat each waterway, starting with the Mississippi, and then extending to the Columbia and other great river systems, as comprehensive units rather than bundles of local interests. Again, Roosevelt assumed he could take the politics out of these decisions by turning them over to a bureau of scientific experts. Not only was this unrealistic, but the scientists themselves had no monopoly on wisdom. Some of their recommendations, such as draining the swamps at the mouth of the Mississippi, which Roosevelt endorsed, turned out to be serious environmental mistakes.

Caught up in the spirit of the burgeoning conservation movement, Roosevelt saw the work of the commission as extending even beyond the nation's waterways. Accordingly, he charged it to consider "the orderly development and conservation, not alone of the waters, but also of the soil, the forests, the mines, and all the other natural resources of our country."[109] In making its recommendations, the commission was greatly assisted by the work of the Bureau of Corporations, whose present head, Herbert Knox Smith, was conveniently doing double service as a member of the Inland Waterways Commission. In that capacity, Roosevelt later singled out Smith's contribution in helping the commission to understand the critical relation of water transportation to rail rates and terminal access, bolstering the case for greater railroad "supervision" as part of an integrated national transportation policy.[110]

Senator Francis G. Newlands, vice-chairman of the commission and member of the Senate Committee on Interstate Commerce, also did double duty.[111] The author of the 1902 Reclamation Act helpfully drew up a bill, granting the new executive agency the broadest administrative discretion since his earlier measure. Under the proposed plan, Congress would set up a $50 million fund, which the commission could tap at its own discretion for projects it alone would determine.[112] Not surprisingly, the bill encountered serious opposition both in Congress, which did not relish handing over broad powers to the commission, as well as from the Army Corps of Engineers, which opposed a multiuse approach. Not even Roosevelt's highly publicized steamboat trip down the Mississippi to drum up support could save the measure; it died quietly in committee.

It was not just the sweeping provisions of the bill that sank it. Congress was still smarting from what John Milton Cooper, Jr. has called Roosevelt's "most arrogant display of presidential power."[113] In February 1907, Congress, in full cry against Roosevelt's removal of millions of acres of forestlands in the West, had attached a rider to the annual appropriations bill for the Agriculture Department stripping the president of his power to create more reserves in six western states. Working feverishly, Pinchot and his staff drew up a plan for TR to establish twenty-one new reserves, totaling 16 million more acres, days before he signed the appropriations bill. Although technically legal, the creation of these "midnight reserves" brazenly evaded Congress's intention, which Roosevelt later justified by invoking his "stewardship" theory. This was the background when the Congress not only shelved the Newlands Act, but also refused even to appropriate money to fund the Inland Waterways Commission.

The showdown between the two elected branches served only to reinforce Roosevelt's opinion that Congress, tethered to local interests, was incapable of providing for the national welfare. Abandoning all pretense of balance, the president warned that if "the reactionaries" in Congress refused to act, he would find a way around them. For the first time in American history, TR summoned the nation's governors, along with prominent environmental organizations, the Inland Waterways Commission, and sympathetic representatives from both the legislative and judicial branches to a conference at the White House in May 1908 to discuss "the weightiest problem now before the nation," the conservation of its natural resources.[114] If Congress would not go along with his plans, he would simply bypass it.

In his opening address, Roosevelt warned that Americans stood in danger of rapidly exhausting the natural resources upon which their greatness as a nation depended. For some time now, the president had been warning about the danger of a "timber famine" if the present rate of forest destruction was allowed to continue. Yet despite the vast increase in the forest reserves, the problem had only gotten worse. More than half the nation's supply of timber was now gone. Moreover, "many experts" predicted that "the end of coal and iron is in sight," and that the "enormous stores of mineral oil and gas are largely gone." It was, the president warned, "ominously evident that these resources are in the course of rapid exhaustion," presumably because they had fallen into private hands where they would be wasted.[115]

Faced with this perceived national emergency, Roosevelt called for a comprehensive federal plan to develop and, where possible, renew the nation's resources for future generations. Some resources, such as minerals and fossil fuels, were nonrenewable. These must be used wisely, which meant that, wherever possible, they should remain under federal control until they were depleted. But at least Roosevelt and his fellow conservationists believed that they should be used, and not simply locked away. Other resources, such as forests, waterways, and soil should be developed in such a way that they were renewed and improved for future generations. Overall, the conference reflected the conservationists' conviction that the resources of the nation could be managed most efficiently for the public good by the federal government, and more precisely, by independent agencies within the executive. The conference concluded with a call for the creation of state and federal commissions to mobilize support for the conservation movement. Later, in his *Autobiography*, Roosevelt would praise the Governors' Conference for the "effectiveness and rapidity" with which it acted to meet the growing crisis. Short of war, it was "doubtful" whether "any idea of like importance" had succeeded in so capturing the imagination of the country.[116]

Hoping to capitalize on the momentum from the Governors' Conference, Roosevelt established the National Conservation Commission one month later—again by executive order, and without consulting Congress. The president further infuriated lawmakers by folding the Inland Waterways Commission that they had refused to fund into this new and larger commission and naming as chair Gifford Pinchot. By the end of his term, Congress and the president were at loggerheads, with Congress attempting to prevent Roosevelt from establishing any more commissions without their specific authorization. As almost his last official act, he notified Congress that he would not have signed the bill if he thought the provision had any constitutional merit, and that, having signed it, he would have refused to obey it had he remained in office.

In the meantime, he pushed forward with the National Conservation Commission. Its task was to compile a complete inventory of the nation's resources from departments and government agencies that could then be used as a basis for comprehensive national planning.[117] As Roosevelt later observed, the work of the Bureau of Corporations, under Herbert Knox Smith, proved invaluable to the commission (of which he was a member) and to the conservation movement in general. The bureau's investigation of standing timber in the United States had revealed a dangerous shift toward private ownership. "Forty years ago three-fourths of the standing timber in the United States was publicly owned, while at the date of the report four-fifths of the timber in the country was in private hands." What was worse, Roosevelt complained, private ownership was now concentrated "to such an amazing extent that about two hundred holders owned nearly one-half of all privately owned timber in the United States; and of this the three greatest holders, the Southern Pacific Railway, the Northern Pacific Railway, and the Weyerhaeuser Timber Company, held over ten percent."[118]

Although Roosevelt adduced no evidence of wrongdoing, the mere fact of private ownership was now suspect, and a 10 percent market share divided three ways was sufficient to raise the alarm of "private monopolies" that had to be brought to heel. Nowhere does he acknowledge that private companies might be led by considerations of self-interest to manage these resources wisely. Commenting on the bureau's investigation of the timber industry, and its important contribution to the Conservation Commission, Roosevelt quoted Smith approvingly:

> It was important, indeed, to know the facts so that we could take proper action toward saving the timber still left to the public. But of far more importance was the light that this history (and the history of our other resources) throws on the basic attitude of, tradition, and governmental beliefs of the American people. *The whole standpoint of the people toward the proper aim of government, toward the relation of property to the citizen, and the relation of property to the government, were brought out first by this conservation work.*[119]

Indeed it was. By emphasizing the threat of future "famines," the conservation movement provided Roosevelt with the "emergency" he needed to move the nation away from its now outmoded commitment to individual rights, private property, and limited government, and to do so without obviously raising the specter of class warfare.[120] From the standpoint of progressivism, that was conservation's great promise, and it continues so today.

"STEWARDSHIP" IN FOREIGN AFFAIRS

Roosevelt's presidency coincided with the emergence of the United States as a rising power on the world stage, a development that Roosevelt was determined to exploit to the fullest. In the words of *Federalist* No. 51, the president possessed not only the "constitutional means," but also the "personal motives" to do so. As he cheerfully confessed toward the end of his term, he was temperamentally disposed to establish precedents for a strong executive wherever he could.[121] Yet TR's obvious delight in exercising these powers to the fullest should not be taken to mean that he was interested simply in power. Roosevelt sought and used power to advance the "lofty ideal" of national greatness—in both domestic and foreign affairs. As he remarked on more than one occasion, all nations in the end must decline; the only question was whether when they were at the height of their powers they had accomplished mighty deeds that lived on in memory.

In TR's view, the foundation of American greatness in foreign affairs lay in military and especially naval preparedness as the best guarantor of peace, a preference for the exercise of national power over international arbitration where vital national interests or honor were concerned, a vigorous assertion (actually a reinterpretation) of the Monroe Doctrine, and (at least until the end of his presidency) American rule over the Philippines for the foreseeable future. Unlike some of his progressive allies, who focused their attention primarily on the amelioration of social and industrial conditions at home, Roosevelt believed that a vigorous domestic policy went hand in hand with a more active role in foreign affairs.[122] Both for him were essential elements of national greatness.

As in domestic policy, Roosevelt summed up his assertive use of executive power in foreign affairs under the heading of "stewardship." In his *Autobiography*, TR would offer his resolution of the crisis in Santo Domingo, his acquisition of the Panama Canal, and his decision to send the Great White Fleet around the world as examples of his "stewardship" in international affairs. His discussion of the Philippines, though brief, provided an important corrective to his earlier, full-throated embrace of American imperialism.

It is less than clear, however, that Roosevelt needed to resort to his "stewardship" theory to justify his actions in international affairs. From the beginning of American constitutional development, there were interpreters, notably Hamilton in the "Pacificus" papers, whose conception of executive power in *external* matters was sufficiently broad to support all that TR undertook without resorting to his extra-constitutional justification. Nevertheless, however Roosevelt explained his assertive foreign policy, the precedents he established would pave the way for bold presidential action in external affairs in the future.

As president, Roosevelt was determined to reinstate the Monroe Doctrine as the cornerstone of American policy in the region. As far back as *The Federalist*, Hamilton had argued that one of the advantages of union was precisely that it would allow the United States to play an "ascendant" role in the New World. More than a quarter of a century later, Hamilton's vision inched closer to reality when President James Monroe announced that the United States would regard future "territorial aggrandizement" by non-American powers anywhere in the Americas as an act of aggression.[123]

In its original formulation, the Monroe Doctrine did not preclude other countries from entering into financial agreements with Latin American nations, or enforcing them by "the usual methods" if they failed to honor their agreements.[124] Thus, when Great Britain and Germany blockaded Venezuela for nonpayment of debts in 1902, Roosevelt did not object. Delinquent nations needed to be "spanked."[125] But when TR began to fear that the Kaiser harbored territorial ambitions toward Venezuela, he quietly informed his majesty that the United States was prepared to use force if Germany did not immediately agree to international arbitration. Although Roosevelt did not believe that the United States should rely primarily upon arbitration to settle disputes, he recognized that it could sometimes be a useful tool where vital national interests were not at stake, and arbitration was backed up by a willingness to use force as a last resort. The successful resolution of the conflict at The Hague was an early victory for his policy of speaking softly but carrying a big stick.[126]

When, however, a new financial crisis erupted in the Dominican Republic, Roosevelt concluded it was no longer enough to keep the European creditor nations from territorial aggrandizement. The United States would also have to prevent them from gaining more subtle forms of financial control. He therefore instructed his secretary of war, Elihu Root, to announce what would become known as the Roosevelt Corollary to the Monroe Doctrine: "If a nation shows that it knows how to act with decency in industrial and political matters, if it keeps order and pays its obligations, then it need fear no interference from the United States. Brutal wrongdoing, or an impotence which results in a general loosening of the ties of civilized society, may finally require intervention by some civilized nation, and in the Western Hemisphere the United States cannot ignore this duty."[127] As the dominant power in the region, the United States would now do what it would not allow the Europeans to do: intervene in the domestic politics of other American nations in order to maintain stability and order, and keep non-Europeans out.

At the same time, Roosevelt hoped that the situation in the Dominican Republic might stabilize itself so that the United States would not have to get involved at all. Amid charges of imperialism, he insisted that he had about as much desire to annex the Dominican Republic as "a gorged boa-constrictor might have to swallow a porcupine wrong-end-to."[128] But as the situation continued to deteriorate, and several European powers prepared to seize control of those seaports with customs-houses, Roosevelt entered into an agreement with the Dominican government to have the United States take over the collection of customs revenues in order to satisfy the claims of foreign creditors.

In his Fifth Annual Message to Congress, Roosevelt requested speedy approval of the protocol by the Senate. Instead, he met with stiff resistance from Democrats and certain members of his own party, who joined together to deny him the requisite two-thirds majority.[129] Faced with this impasse, TR carried out the protocol by executive order for two years with the informal support of the leaders of both parties and turned a deaf ear to critics' charges of usurpation.

Later in the *Autobiography*, Roosevelt translated his actions into the language of "stewardship" as applied to foreign affairs. "The Constitution did not explicitly give me power to bring about the necessary agreement with Santo Domingo. But the Constitution did not forbid my doing what I did. I put the agreement into effect, and I continued its execution for two years before the Senate acted; and I would have continued it until the end of my term, if necessary, without any action from Congress." Nevertheless, Roosevelt conceded there were limits to this informal arrangement: "it was far preferable that there should be action by Congress, so that we might be proceeding under a treaty that was the law of the land and not merely be a direction of the Chief Executive which would lapse when that particular executive left office."[130]

Panama raised a different question. Here the Senate had consented to the treaty that the administration had negotiated with Colombia to construct a canal across the Panamanian isthmus. But when the Colombian Congress unanimously rejected the agreement, Roosevelt concluded that the United States had only two options: either Panama must rise up and declare its independence from Colombia, or if Panama failed to act, American forces should "at once occupy the Isthmus anyhow, and proceed to dig the canal."[131] In the event, the Panamanians did rebel, and within days the United States entered into a treaty with the newly independent nation to build the canal on essentially the same terms as it had offered to Colombia.[132]

Although the decision was immensely popular with the American public, it aroused the ire of anti-imperialist intellectuals, who condemned it as a violation of both the Constitution and international law.[133] As he had done with the Philippines, Roosevelt retorted that the Panama Canal could be considered unconstitutional "only if Jefferson's action in acquiring Louisiana be also treated as unconstitutional."[134] But compared with the Philippines, Roosevelt was on firmer ground here. With the exception of the ten-mile Canal Zone, the United States did not actually take over Panama, and even there, Roosevelt took steps to allay Panamanian fears that the United States would interfere with their business interests or diminish their prestige as an independent nation.[135] Nevertheless, critics continued to condemn Roosevelt's actions in Panama as both an abuse of executive power and a blatant act of American imperialism. As in the coal strike, however, his opponents would have had a stronger case had Panama not revolted and TR had sent in American troops anyway.

Roosevelt took the same broad view of executive powers when it came to the construction of the canal. After he left office, he conceded that if he had followed precedent, he should have allowed Congress to set policy for the construction of the canal. But Congress insisted on operating by a commission, and unlike the conservation commissions TR appointed, could never agree on a plan of action. Roosevelt would later recall that he had "tried faithfully to get good work out of the commission and found it quite impossible; for a many-headed commission is an extremely poor executive instrument." Accordingly, when Congress refused to appoint a head, he issued an executive order enlarging the powers of the chairman so that he achieved virtually the same result.[136] In 1918, four years after the canal was completed, Roosevelt could remark with only a little exaggeration, "I deemed it better not to have a half century of debate prior to starting in on the canal; I thought that instead of debating for half a century before building the canal it would be better to build the canal first and debate me for a half-century afterward."[137] The construction of the Panama Canal was an extraordinary feat of civil engineering; it was, in his view, another of those "arduous enterprises," that redounded to American greatness and could be brought to timely completion only by vigorous executive action.

Nevertheless, Roosevelt could justly be censured for his treatment of the Colombians.[138] His Third Annual Message to Congress publicly denounced the leaders of that once-friendly nation for standing in the way of what TR regarded as his duty not only to Americans, but also to the Panamanians and indeed to all mankind. "This great enterprise of building the interoceanic canal cannot be held up to gratify the whims, or out of respect to the governmental impotence, or to the even more sinister and evil peculiarities, of people who, though they dwell afar off, yet, against the wish of the actual dwellers of the Isthmus, assert an unreal supremacy over the territory."[139]

Roosevelt was right about the importance of the canal, but he was certainly not speaking softly. Nor did his views moderate with the passage of time. In 1915, he dredged up all his old arguments, made more intense by partisan rancor, to oppose Woodrow Wilson's conciliatory overtures toward Colombia, and it was not until after Roosevelt's death that the United States finally negotiated a treaty of reparation.[140]

Although the Roosevelt Corollary provoked charges of imperialism and executive overreach in Latin America, the one place where TR most clearly did pursue a policy of imperialism, even if he refused to call it that, was in the Philippines. Roosevelt's First Annual Message praised the "masterful" American race for its "disinterested zeal" in ruling over an "alien people," while emphasizing the enormity of the task. The Philippine people were starting from a point far behind where "our ancestors" had been more than thirty generations ago. If Roosevelt had any worry, it was that the United States was moving too rapidly in granting the natives local self-government.[141]

As president, Roosevelt tended in his public addresses to shift the focus away from America's civilizing mission and more toward the slow but steady progress of the Philippines toward self-government, but privately he remained skeptical. "In dealing with the Philippines," he confided to Rudyard Kipling in 1904, "I have first the jack fools who seriously think that any group of pirates and head-hunters needs nothing but independence in order that it may be turned forthwith into a dark-hued New England town-meeting."[142] Nevertheless, events domestic and foreign were driving home to him how difficult it would be for the United States to persist in its imperial ambitions. There was, he belatedly recognized, a difference between what the British monarchy could do and what the American republic could do.[143]

On the home front, he had come to see how foreign policy could be held hostage to electoral politics. For two years, Democrats and members of his own party in the Senate had blocked the treaty with the Dominican Republic, and then accused the president of usurping power. He had also failed to get Americans to take an interest in events in Venezuela or Cuba, even though the Monroe Doctrine had long been the cornerstone of American policy in the region. In the Philippines, it was clear that a prolonged period of American rule would require a steady supply of first-rate administrators, ready to act with "lofty and disinterested efficiency." But with the inevitable shifts back and forth between the two parties, such leadership was far from assured, especially since Democrats were calling for immediate independence and withdrawal. Nor could he count on the patience of the American people to persevere in carrying out this "onerous duty."[144] Thus, he reluctantly concluded that the United States had little choice but to hasten the move toward self-government and scheduled the first legislative elections for the spring of 1907. In his final State of the Union Address, he praised the meeting of the Philippine legislature as a development "absolutely new in Asia" and ventured that independence might come "within a generation."[145]

The rising power of Japan also contributed to Roosevelt's reassessment of the long-range prospects for American imperialism in the Philippines. Roosevelt's offer to mediate an end to the Russo-Japanese War further affirmed the importance of the United States on the world stage and won for him the Nobel Peace Prize in 1906. But the Japanese came away from Portsmouth feeling slighted, and relations further deteriorated as anti-Japanese sentiment mounted on the West Coast. With talk of war brewing in Japan, Roosevelt now had to consider the possibility that, in the absence of fortifications or a strong naval presence, the Philippines had become America's "heel of Achilles."[146]

Accordingly, Roosevelt continued his two-pronged strategy of treating Japan with the respect due a rising nation while simultaneously building up the navy. From its fifth-ranked position at the start of his administration, the U.S. Navy moved into second place, behind only Great Britain by the time he left office. As the situation with Japan grew more tense, Roosevelt decided to send the navy on a cruise around the world. At the time, neither the British nor the Germans thought that any navy could successfully sail around the world, which made it all the more important for the United States to make the test. As Roosevelt confided to his secretary of state, Elihu Root, "it was absolutely necessary for us to try in time of peace to see just what we could do in the way of putting a big battle fleet in the Pacific, and not make the experiment in time of war."[147] The voyage, Roosevelt hoped, would have a salutary effect on public opinion, but its principal purpose was to impress upon the Japanese the strength and determination of the United States to defend its overseas possessions.

In the *Autobiography*, Roosevelt boasted that he made the decision "without consulting the Cabinet, precisely as I took Panama without consulting the Cabinet." The remark about Panama was unfortunate, but Roosevelt was otherwise on solid ground. "A council of war never fights, and in a crisis the duty of a leader is to lead and not to take refuge behind the generally timid wisdom of a multitude of councilors." Although Roosevelt did not keep his secretary of state in the dark, he was under no constitutional obligation to consult with his cabinet before acting. As Hamilton explained in *The Federalist*, energy in the executive required freedom of action.[148]

Where Roosevelt did get into trouble was with Congress, which complained that it had not been consulted. Members from the eastern states especially objected to leaving the Atlantic seaboard defenseless as the fleet sailed across the Pacific. In a testy exchange, Eugene Hale (R-Maine), chairman of the Senate Committee on Naval Affairs, informed the president that the fleet "should not and could not go because Congress would refuse to appropriate the money." But Roosevelt shot back that he "had enough money to take the fleet around to the Pacific anyhow, that the fleet would certainly go, and that if Congress did not choose to appropriate enough money to get the fleet back, why, then it would stay in the Pacific."[149] He got his money; the world got his message. The Japanese extended an invitation to the fleet to visit its ports, and shortly thereafter, the two countries agreed, among other things, to maintain the status quo in the Pacific and to respect each other's territorial possessions. It was, Roosevelt later wrote, his single most important contribution to peace.[150]

Roosevelt's two terms were marked by an assertive use of executive power to advance his ideal of national greatness. But what, if anything, did his "stewardship" theory add to the conduct of foreign affairs—other than to detach executive power from the Constitution? There was a better way. Had Roosevelt reviewed the papers on the executive in *The Federalist*, and even more important, read the "Pacificus" papers, he would have discovered constitutional arguments for the energetic use of executive power in foreign affairs. Indeed, Hamilton considered these essays so important that he wished to have them included in later editions of the *Federalist*.[151] There is, however, no evidence that Roosevelt ever seriously considered them. Even Henry Cabot Lodge, whose 1886 biography of Hamilton Roosevelt did read, made only one fleeting reference to the papers, and never addressed their arguments.[152]

Writing as "Pacificus," Hamilton argued that the language of the Constitution suggested important differences in the way the Framers understood legislative and executive power. In Article I, only those powers "herein granted" were "vested" in Congress, whereas Article II stated without qualification that "the executive power" was "vested" in the president.[153] Although the Constitution went on to enumerate specific powers entrusted to the president, including commander-in-chief of the armed forces, the unqualified term "executive power," especially when compared with the more carefully delineated language of Article I, suggested that the Framers wished to give, or at least were not averse to granting, the president wide powers to act for the public good in foreign affairs. Indeed, with foreign affairs foremost in his mind, Hamilton specifically rejected the idea that the president was limited to those powers enumerated in Article II.

In his expansive reading, enumerated powers were merely specific in-stances of a general executive power, which was limited only by its "confor-mity to other parts [of] the constitution and to the principles of free gov-ernment." Even then, Hamilton argued that the constitutional limitations on executive power in foreign affairs, i.e., that only Congress had the power to declare war, and that treaties must be ratified by a two-thirds vote of the Senate, should be read narrowly in order to leave the executive the maxi-mum flexibility of action. Indeed, the president might even take steps that could commit the nation to war, in effect giving the executive a share in the war power with Congress, though in this instance the president was doing precisely the opposite, keeping the country out of war (hence Hamilton's choice of a pseudonym).[154]

By allowing for the exercise of broad presidential power, Hamilton went a long way toward reconciling the thorny issue of executive prerogative with republican government. In the *Second Treatise*, John Locke had ar-gued that, because the laws could not always provide for every contingency, the executive must be equipped with a prerogative power to act for the public good in the absence of law, and sometimes even against it. Locke's defense of the prerogative offered one means of dealing with the unfore-seen difficulties that inevitably arise in political life, but it did so by plac-ing the executive outside the constitution, which was particularly troubling in a republic.[155] By contrast, Hamilton sought to "constitutionalize" the prerogative by construing executive power broadly, especially in foreign affairs, subject only to the qualifications and exceptions contained within the charter and "the principles of free government."[156]

The qualifying phrase, "principles of free government," suggests an im-portant distinction between the energetic, but limited, role Hamilton envi-sioned for government in domestic policy, and Roosevelt's more expansive theory, to which we shall return at the end of the chapter. But in foreign policy, the two were, more often than not, in accord. An energetic execu-tive was necessary precisely in times of emergency, such as during the cri-sis in Santo Domingo or the rebellion in Panama, when decisions needed to be made swiftly, and the nation had to speak with one voice. He was also necessary for undertaking "extensive and arduous enterprises," such as constructing the Panama Canal, or building up the navy, which required "considerable time to mature and perfect."[157] These undertakings, aimed at the "public benefit," could best be carried out under the firm direction of one man, ultimately responsible to the people under the limitations set forth in the Constitution.

Of course, the Constitution does not insist on such a broad interpretation of executive power, and Hamilton's fellow collaborator on *The Federalist*, James Madison, disputed his defense of broad executive power in both foreign and domestic affairs. The genius of the Constitution is precisely that it leaves to each president to determine how much or how little he will make of the office, though in so doing, it guarantees that the political branches especially will permanently struggle against each other. That struggle would become acute during the last two years of Roosevelt's presidency.

THE BALANCE TIPS

Like Oliver Cromwell, Theodore Roosevelt was a statesman of puritan sensibilities, determined to use his high office to fight for the right as he saw it. He brought with him to the White House a theory of justice, derived in no small part from Aristotle, and translated into the vernacular of the "Square Deal." As yet he had no constitutional theory and relied principally on his own moral compass. If he could strike a mean between the extremes of mob rule and plutocracy, steer a course between the envy and resentment of the poor and the arrogance and contempt of the wealthy, while introducing sensible reforms, he might then avert the class warfare that had doomed earlier republics. After his landslide reelection, Roosevelt returned to these themes, preaching, "This government is not and never shall be government by plutocracy. This government is not and never shall be government by a mob." To Aristotle's sober counsels, he now added those of Edmund Burke, warning that men who would govern themselves must first "put moral chains on their own appetites." If they failed to do so, then some "controlling power" would have to check their "will and appetite" from "without."[158] Writing to two English friends near the end of his presidency, Roosevelt again insisted that he had tried to steer a "sane" middle course between "the Scylla of mob rule and the Charybdis of subjection to plutocracy."[159] But as Roosevelt lashed out against the courts, railed against Congress, and seethed at the "rottenness" of economic life, it became more and more difficult to view him as the voice of sensible moderation. So it is worth asking: how could a president who came into office reading Aristotle and quoting Burke wind up so "unbalanced" by the end of his term?

The Burke quotation may provide a clue. For Roosevelt found it difficult to restrain his own moral indignation (indeed, reveled in his indignation) and, therefore, needed some "controlling power" that would impose restraints on his "will."[160] As long as he needed the support of the Old Guard for renomination, he was compelled to seek reasonable compromises that positioned him near the political center. But after his landslide victory in 1904, TR no longer felt the same pressure to accommodate the conservative wing of his party, especially since he had announced on election night that he would not seek another term. Moreover, during his first term, Roosevelt only had to navigate between Republican regulars who sided with the trusts and the Bryanite wing of the Democratic Party. Given this political constellation, Roosevelt could plausibly put himself forward as the voice of the sensible middle. The Elkins Act prohibited rebates on railroad rates, the one reform on which both shippers (at least small shippers) and the railroads could agree. The Bureau of Corporations started out with a limited mandate to gather information in formulating new legislation and to deter corporate abuses with the threat of adverse publicity.

For a time even after his reelection, Roosevelt managed to find common ground between the two wings of his party. The Hepburn Act, though arguably laying the foundation for the administrative state, was modest in its original reach and managed to satisfy the Old Guard on some points. The Transfer Act seemed a sensible move that placed the forests under the supervision of the foresters, bringing desirable efficiencies to the management of the nation's resources. The problem was that each of these acts paved the way for new measures, which rapidly escalated after the 1906 midterm elections. For in truth, the progressive movement with which Roosevelt increasingly identified did not seek merely to enact specific reforms, but rather to lay the foundation for limitless future changes by leaders who discerned the evolving needs of the nation.

Although Republicans were able to hold on to their majority in 1906, Democrats cut into their numbers. Even more important, insurgents within Roosevelt's own party gained ground, putting pressure on him from within. Sizing up the results, the president concluded he had no choice but to try to hold the "left center together."[161] To the extent that there was a turning point in Roosevelt's presidency, this was it. His Sixth Annual Message, delivered a month after the election, made clear that the Hepburn Act was just the beginning of government "supervision" over the railroads, and that much more must be done, not only to establish effective control over the railroads, but indeed, over all corporations engaged in interstate commerce. To that end, he now proposed legislation to convert the Bureau of Corporations into a full-fledged regulatory agency, with sweeping powers over the entire industrial economy. Despite his misgivings over the Sherman Act, he launched a new round of antitrust prosecutions and, reversing the position he had taken as governor, called for a ban on campaign contributions by corporations. He ramped up the rhetoric against the wealthy, coming out in favor of a graduated inheritance tax and a progressive income tax. Drawing on the success of the forest movement, he threw the full weight of his office behind the conservation movement to impose greater federal controls over all natural resources, broadly defined. Convinced that Congress could no longer legislate in the public interest, he tried wherever possible to work around it, by taking his campaign directly to the people and appointing commissions responsible to him alone. Wherever possible, he fought to shift power away from Congress and into the unelected bureaucratic agencies that were staffed with high-minded experts armed with the new tools of social science.

More surprisingly, he turned on the courts. Whereas throughout his early political career Roosevelt had defended an independent judiciary as indispensable to liberty, he now attacked it for refusing to go along with his ever more intrusive understanding of "regulation" and his sweeping view of interstate commerce. In the wake of the 1905 *Lochner* decision, the former law student pointedly advised judges to be more attentive to the "reasonable demands of those they served," apparently convinced (as he was when he criticized Holmes for his opinion in the *Northern Securities* case) that there were no compelling constitutional arguments for opinions that did not coincide with his views. And by his Eighth Annual Message, he effectively eliminated the line between making the law and judging it, arguing that judicial decisions all boiled down to a matter of social philosophy. To insure "the peaceful progress of our people during the twentieth century we shall owe most to those judges who hold to a twentieth-century economic and social philosophy and not to a long-outgrown philosophy, which was itself the product of primitive economic conditions."[162] The idea that all thought was determined by economic conditions would have been instantly familiar to Marxists, but TR instead cited Burke.

Even as Roosevelt increasingly came to view politics as an ideological struggle between "reactionaries" or "ultra-conservatives" and progressives, he continued to insist on the need for balance. But his understanding of balance had changed. In the past, he had worried more about the dangers from mob violence, but now, pulled leftward by insurgents in his own party and infuriated by corporate resistance to his policies, Roosevelt came to regard the plutocrats as the greater menace. As he explained to Arthur Lee,

Again and again in my political career I have had to make head against mob spirit, against the tendency of the poor, ignorant, and turbulent people who feel a rancorous jealousy and hatred of those who are better off. But during the last few years it has been the wealthy corruptionists [*sic*] of enormous fortune, and of enormous influence thru their agents of the press, pulpit, colleges and public life, with whom I have had to wage bitter war.

A few days later, Roosevelt repeated the Scylla and Charybdis trope to Trevelyan, declaring that he had spent "the last six years" of his presidency fighting against the "upgrowth in this country of the least attractive and most sordid of all aristocracies," the money power, a danger he had once denied could ever grow up in America.[163]

In the *Politics*, Aristotle had argued that the best practical regime was a polity, which combined elements of democracy and oligarchy. Polity was not a mathematical mean between the two extremes, but depending upon the circumstances, might fall closer to democracy or oligarchy. The philosopher's advice to statesmen was to shore up whichever side was weaker. Thus, from an Aristotelian perspective, it was odd that at the very moment when the left was gaining strength, Roosevelt doubled down on the plutocrats and threw his weight behind the "poor, ignorant, and turbulent people," backing their goals, though not their methods. By this point, however, Roosevelt had given himself over to the progressive cause and could no longer plausibly claim to be "disinterested." His theory of justice had shifted, and "balance" was now little more than a rhetorical ploy, a useful tool for attacking not only "malefactors of great wealth," but "swollen fortunes" that were of "no benefit to perpetuate."[164]

In so doing, Roosevelt had to admit that he might actually have accelerated, even exacerbated, the financial panic in October 1907, but he considered his actions necessary to bring the corporations to heel. He also conceded that his attacks on the trusts had often placed him on the side of the demagogues he despised, though he had, a bit too conveniently, satisfied himself that he was not acting "from any unworthy motives."[165] Yet the accusation clearly bothered him, and well it might have, given Hamilton's warnings against the demagogue in *Federalist* No. 1, which could be traced back to Aristotle's *Politics*. Right up to the end of his presidency, he continued to insist that he had not been "actuated by any selfish motives, by motives of self-interest," and denied that his opposition to plutocracy was "due to the usual demagog's [*sic*] desire to pander to the mob, or to the no more dangerous, but even more sinister, desire to secure self-advancement under the cloak of championship of popular rights."[166]

This new idea of "balance," understood as waging "bitter war" against the trusts, "not in any demagogic way but with the sincere effort to stand for a government by the people and for the people," complemented his discovery of "inherent power," which allowed the federal government, acting on behalf of the nation, to exercise powers beyond those enumerated in the Constitution wherever the object exceeded the power of the states and was "a power ordinarily exercised by sovereign nations." No wonder Roosevelt concluded that more power "inheres" in the presidency than in "any other office in any great republic or constitutional monarchy in modern times." But he was confident that as long as men with lofty ideals occupied the office—men who obeyed the "moral law" of "efficient and disinterested service"—the traditional two-term limit was sufficient to guard against the abuses of "inherent power."[167]

In practice, Roosevelt was more restrained than his theory, but even his practice was a far cry from the principles of Washington and Lincoln, whose views of executive power could, in important respects, be traced back to Hamilton. There is no doubt that in both *The Federalist* and the "Pacificus" papers Hamilton defended a broad interpretation of executive (and, indeed, of legislative) power, but there were significant differences between the two. For one thing, although Hamilton, like TR, believed that executive power was limited by the specific prohibitions in the Constitution and by legislation, he also argued that the executive was constrained by "the principles of free government." Although nowhere did Hamilton explain precisely what he meant by that phrase, he gave ample indication that these principles were rooted in the protection of natural rights, including the right to property, and that they rested on the consent of the governed. For whatever differences divided the Framers on points of government, these were the first principles on which they all agreed. It is true that Hamilton was not an advocate of laissez-faire economics, but this should not be construed to mean that he was a statist. He favored government support for infant manufactures, but this was to promote economic diversity and private enterprise in the newly developing nation. Government intervention was intended to serve as a temporary spur to individual efforts, not a permanent bridle on them. Nothing in Hamilton's writings suggests that he would have backed the establishment of administrative agencies, staffed by bureaucrats largely insulated from the political process and equipped with broad discretionary powers over the economy.[168] Granting the ICC the power to set railroad rates and schedules, make a physical valuation of the railroads to determine their capital needs, and supervise the issuance of railroad bonds and securities would have exceeded Hamilton's understanding of what free government should do. Even more objectionable would be an agency like the expanded Bureau of Corporations, which would have extended the executive's regulatory reach over the entire industrial economy, influencing corporate structure and capital formation, as well as prices for goods and services. For Hamilton, the role of the republican statesman in shaping economic outcomes was far more limited, and remained subject to classical liberal ends. Moreover, Hamilton would have found TR's confidence in disinterested bureaucratic expertise unrealistic.[169]

Just how far Roosevelt had drifted from Hamilton's principles during the course of his presidency became clear from two essays he published within weeks of leaving the White House. The essays, published in *The Outlook*, a Social Gospel journal edited by Lyman Abbott, set forth where Roosevelt and his supporters could and could not work with socialists. By socialism, TR understood the Marxist version, which advocated class warfare and violent revolution, as well as the abolition of private property and of the state, all of which the president denounced. He also rejected the Marxist principle of justice, according to which each should receive according to his needs, arguing that it would reward the vicious and the lazy. But he was more than willing to work with others who called themselves socialists and worked to bring about far-reaching reforms. Some of these "socialists," he thought, were really just "advanced" liberals, and others, although utopian visionaries, supported practical reforms that were worth considering. He urged his followers not to be put off by the label. In place of the older liberal principle of justice, according to which each individual received according to his merit, Roosevelt would reward each according to his "service to the community." In some instances, this service would require "large accumulations of capital," but other forms of "service" required no capital at all. Presumably, wise and just administrators would sort this out, guided by the Social Gospel principle that each man was in a very real sense his brother's keeper. But however superficially attractive the maxim, "What is mine I will in good measure make thine also," the use of executive power for this end was clearly incompatible with Hamilton's understanding of "the principles of free government."[170]

Finally, as already noted, Hamilton believed that executive power operated most fully in foreign affairs. To the extent that he foresaw a need for the president to act energetically in domestic policy, it was to meet a sudden emergency. Although Hamilton thought that the president needed to have the power to respond to such crises, he did not envision using the emergency as a pretext for permanently reshaping and enlarging the powers of the national government. At the time of the coal strike, TR, too, recognized that the exercise of extraordinary power in time of emergency created a dangerous precedent. But for a man of Roosevelt's temperament, the temptation proved too great. As the conservation movement gained momentum, he used the threat of an impending timber famine, which never materialized, and warned of likely shortages in coal and iron, oil and gas, to expand government control over America's natural resources. But this was not all. For the conservation movement would help to launch a wholesale reconsideration of the relationship of the individual to the state, especially where property rights were concerned. Thwarted in these efforts by Congress, and bowing to his self-imposed term limit, Roosevelt would return to these issues with renewed vigor in the years after he left the presidency.

6. Progressive Crusader

Theodore Roosevelt was only fifty when he left the White House, younger than the vast majority of American presidents when they entered the office. As such, he perfectly illustrated the dangers foreseen by *The Federalist* in setting term limits on the executive. What would become of such ambitious men, Hamilton wondered, when, after occupying "the seat of the supreme magistracy" and wielding the highest executive power, their term of office abruptly came to an end and they were forced to return to private life, "wandering among the people like discontented ghosts and sighing for a place which they were destined never more to possess?"[1]

At first, Roosevelt seemed to accept his retirement with equanimity. As he confessed to the British historian George Otto Trevelyan, had he not been constrained by the two-term precedent established by Washington, he would indeed have liked to have run again and kept his "hands on the levers of this mighty machine." That the machine had grown much mightier during his term in office was, ironically, one of Roosevelt's principal arguments for not seeking another term. Having done all that he could to enlarge the powers of the presidency, the only real safeguard against abuse was to step down from office. If the people ever came to regard a strong leader as indispensable, this might indeed pose a danger to free institutions. However, "I don't think that any harm comes from the concentration of power in one man's hands, provided the holder does not keep it for more than a limited time, and then returns to the people from whom he sprang." Accordingly, Roosevelt concluded, "When I am thru with the Presidency, I am thru with it, definitely and once and for all."[2]

Of course, he was not, and partly for the reason that Hamilton anticipated. Although hunting wild animals in Africa might take his mind off politics temporarily, it would not do so for long. Even on safari, news of William Howard Taft's more controversial decisions—signing the Payne-Aldrich tariff, replacing James Garfield with Richard Achilles Ballinger at the Department of the Interior, and firing Gifford Pinchot from the Forest Service—had reached him, triggering fears that his successor might not be up to the task of carrying on his legacy. A letter to Lodge, written in March

1910 from the Upper Nile, reflecting on why Pinchot had provoked Taft to fire him, sounds very much like a thinly veiled account of Roosevelt's own motivations. Pinchot, he wrote, "loved to spend his whole strength, with lavish indifference to any effect upon himself, in battling for a high ideal; and not to keep him thus employed rendered it possible that his great energy would expend itself in fighting the men who seemed to him not to be going far enough forward."[3]

Even more than Pinchot, TR had entered the political fray to battle for high ideals, *American Ideals*, as he titled one of his early publications, *Realizable Ideals*, as he would later call another. Some of these ideals—devotion to duty, national greatness, and love of country—remained constant, but others, notably his understanding of liberty and justice, "evolved" over time. His six-week European speaking tour following the safari provided him with the opportunity to set forth his latest version of these ideals and to test them against what he saw there. He had stopped in Europe to be celebrated, but he used the visit to observe and learn. Wherever he went, he sought out social reformers and gathered information about the workings of the European welfare states. Somewhere along the way, he read Herbert Croly, whose *Promise of American Life* provided a firmer theoretical argument for his progressive vision.

Returning to the United States in June 1910, Roosevelt found the Taft administration too much allied with the conservative wing of the Republican Party for his comfort and insurgents eager to solicit his help. In the midterm elections that fall, the former president would throw his prodigious energy into charting a New Nationalism for the Republican Party, and, like Pinchot, would oppose all who resisted the forward movement, including the sitting president. This mix of energy, ambition, and idealism allied with righteous indignation would propel the "discontented ghost" back to the very center of the national political stage and keep him there for another decade.

EUROPEAN TOUR

Before leaving office, Roosevelt had accepted an invitation to deliver the prestigious Romanes lecture at Oxford University. Other invitations, notably from the Sorbonne and the University of Berlin, quickly followed. While still in the White House, Roosevelt completed the three speeches during the winter of 1909.[4] It is not surprising, therefore, that the addresses, each in their own way, circled back to the principal domestic concerns of his late presidential years: the importance of character, the relation between rights and duties, human rights and property rights, and the need for a stronger federal government to address social problems. A fourth, his Nobel Peace Prize acceptance speech, delivered in Christiania (now Oslo), was composed while on safari in Africa and offered specific proposals designed to secure peace.[5] In addition, he gave a number of impromptu addresses, the most revealing of which was his speech before the Cambridge Union. In an otherwise jocular evening, Roosevelt reminded his audience that there was always "an element of chance" to human greatness. Without a war or domestic crisis, no man could hope to become a great general or great statesman. Had Lincoln lived in peaceful times, he would never have been remembered today. What Roosevelt did not say (but surely understood) was that he himself had been president in peaceful times, had in fact won the Nobel Peace Prize for mediating an end to the Russo-Japanese War, and was still aching for the chance to do great deeds.[6] His travels through Europe would help him set a course for his return to politics.

Making his way up the African continent in March 1910, TR offered a full-throated defense of British imperialism at Khartoum and Cairo before delivering the first of his European addresses on April 23 at the Sorbonne. Speaking as the private citizen of one great republic to those of another, Roosevelt invited his audience to reflect on what "Citizenship in a Republic" required in the present age. To listeners perhaps not well acquainted with American history, the former president began by sketching the "primitive" qualities that had been necessary to tame the New World. The "hard materialism of the frontier days" had accentuated all those "vices and virtues, energy and ruthlessness, all the good qualities and all the defects of an intense individualism, self-reliant, self-centered, far more conscious of its rights than its duties, and blind to its own shortcomings."[7] But this stage was now over, replaced by the "hard materialism of industrialism." Citizens of both great republics could no longer afford to focus selfishly on their rights, but must begin to pay more attention to the duties they owed the state.

Roosevelt then turned to a theme he had long been preaching: in countries that meant to govern themselves, young men, especially well-born, educated young men, must be willing to enter into the political fray. "It is not the critic who counts; not the man who points out how the strong man stumbles, or where the doer of deeds could have done them better. The credit belongs to the man who is actually in the arena, whose face is marred by dust and sweat and blood; who strives valiantly; who errs and comes up short again and again." Roosevelt expressed only scorn for those "tepid souls" who knew "nothing of the great and generous emotion, of the high pride, the stern belief, the lofty enthusiasm, of the men who quell the storm and ride the thunder."[8] Anyone hearing these words might well wonder how long the life of quiet retirement the Rough Rider claimed to welcome would satisfy him.

Beyond urging college men to become involved in politics, Roosevelt emphasized the importance of cultivating the more commonplace virtues. But then the former president announced, "Even more important than the ability to work, even more important than the ability to fight at need, is it to remember that the chief blessings for any nation is that it shall leave its seed to inherit the land." At a time when the birthrate was dramatically declining in France, the former president and father of six admonished his young listeners that if their generation chose to engage in "willful sterility," whether from a desire for ease or out of fear of pain, risk, and effort, republican government could not survive. "If we of the great republics, if we, the free people who claim to have emancipated ourselves from the thralldom of wrong and error, bring down on our heads the curse that comes upon the willfully barren, then it will be an idle waste of breath to prattle of our achievements, to boast of all we have done."[9] The first duty of the citizen, Roosevelt preached, was to bear "many healthy children" and then to provide for them. "Race suicide," as Roosevelt elsewhere called it, was not a new worry.[10] What was new was that Roosevelt was here raising the delicate matter with the citizens of the French republic, warning them that nations whose populations were declining could not hope to remain great.

But, as he signaled at the outset, the core of his address centered on the relationship between rights, especially property rights, and the kind of character necessary to republican citizenship. With the spectacular fortunes of his own country clearly in mind, Roosevelt urged his audience not to admire individuals simply because they were rich. It was not the mere possession of money that mattered, but how it was earned and used. If a rich man provided no "corresponding benefit to the nation as a whole," or even if he remained idle, declining to place his talents and wealth in the service of a greater cause, then far from admiring him, his fellows should make him feel that he is an "unworthy citizen of the community."[11]

What precisely Roosevelt meant was unclear, however, because he did not explain what he meant by a "benefit to the nation" or elaborate on how the wealthy should be made to feel "unworthy." Were they to be subjected to the scorn and disapproval of their fellow citizens (as he had argued while governor), or did he have in mind stronger measures? The one new paragraph that he inserted into his prepared remarks on the morning of the lecture (apparently the result of his discussion of vested interests with French intellectuals the evening before)[12] did little to clear up the matter. Although he asserted that human rights and property rights usually went together and must both be safeguarded, he also thought that when there was a "real conflict" between the two, property rights must give way to human rights.

Above all, Roosevelt advised, in thinking about these problems, the first duty of the citizen was to avoid being doctrinaire. "We can just as little afford to follow the doctrinaires of extreme individualism as the doctrinaires of extreme socialism."[13] The one triumphed by "greed and cunning," the other preached class warfare and violent revolution. The former president candidly admitted, however, that he saw "great advantage" to certain socialist principles, which would doubtless color what he might consider a "real conflict" between human rights and property rights, or conversely, a "benefit to the nation."[14]

At the same time, Roosevelt was quick to distance himself from more radical demands for equality of condition, holding up as the model Lincoln's interpretation of equality in the Declaration of Independence. When Jefferson wrote that all men were created equal, Lincoln argued, he did not mean that they were equal in every respect, but rather that they were "equal in certain inalienable rights, among which are life, liberty, and the pursuit of happiness." What made Roosevelt's argument confusing, however, was that earlier in his talk he had criticized "pioneer" Americans for their too great insistence on rights, and now he was quoting Lincoln approvingly on the centrality of these very rights.[15] Was Lincoln's reference to the inalienable rights of the Declaration a throwback to a more individualistic, selfish era or a valuable roadblock against an all-encroaching equality of condition?[16]

Moreover, after seeming to agree with Lincoln about the importance of these inalienable rights, Roosevelt then went on to suggest that these rights be subordinated to the principle of "duty," understood as "service" to the nation. Perhaps the former president thought that he was simply splitting the difference, finding a mean between equal rights and the democratic socialism to which he was increasingly drawn, but then he was mistaken. If, in a "real conflict" with human rights, property rights were to be circumscribed, the limiting principle would have to be supplied by liberal political philosophy, and not by socialism, however "moderate." It would have to begin by acknowledging, with Lincoln and the founders, that individuals are by nature entitled to the fruits of their labor. Any restrictions on property would then have to be for the sake of enlarging individual freedom and opportunity and not to provide equality of opportunity to render service to the state.[17] It is worth noting that, although TR would continue to associate himself with the principles and policies of Lincoln—indeed, he would cite him with even greater frequency in the Bull Moose years—he would never again mention Lincoln's insistence that all men and women were equal in their inalienable rights.

In the second of the three speeches he had prepared while still in the White House, this time in Germany, Roosevelt took an entirely different tack, focusing, for obvious reasons, not on the common needs of republics, but on racial stock and culture. Addressing the audience at the University of Berlin, which was celebrating its centennial, the former president began by observing that not only was there a large amount of German blood flowing through America's veins, but also that "much of the thought that shapes our minds" was German. Because the United States had no graduate institutions of its own until very recently, generations of Americans had been trained in German universities, cementing the bond between the two nations. His speech, entitled "The World Movement," made no mention of Lincoln or the Declaration, but was instead suffused with the spirit of German philosophy. At the University of Berlin, where Hegel had once lectured, Roosevelt traced the movement of history from one stage of civilization to another up until 400 years ago, when, with the invention of printing and the discovery of America, the movement toward a truly world civilization began.

His audience was probably unaware that Roosevelt had already covered this great pageant from a different angle in the opening chapter of *The Winning of the West*, where he had recounted the rise of the *English*-speaking peoples, first in their struggle with France for control of the New World, and then as they spread into Australia, New Zealand, and India. Here, Roosevelt diplomatically avoided any mention of Anglo-American dominance. Instead, he emphasized the rise and spread of a modern European civilization that was taking root around the world, binding nations together more closely than ever before as ideas circulated freely from country to country. In his speech, Roosevelt did not view this development as a way to export American ideals, but rather as an opportunity for the United States to catch up with what other nations were doing. "When in America we study labor problems and attempt to deal with subjects such as life insurance for wageworkers, we turn to see what you do here in Germany, and we also turn to see what the far-off commonwealth of New Zealand is doing."[18]

Comparing the present stage of historical development with earlier civilizations, Roosevelt wondered whether the "constantly accelerating velocity" of the world movement might cause it to spin out of control and crash. All previous civilizations had declined, and Roosevelt once again worried that softness would "eat like acid" into the virile, fighting virtues, corroding manly fiber. In raising this issue, one could hear the echoes of his argument, more than a decade earlier with Brooks Adams, who had asserted that as civilization advanced, economic man tended to supplant the more emotional and artistic types that flourished in earlier civilizations, leading inexorably to decay and decline.[19] Roosevelt, who himself had no love for "economic man," rejected this "gloomy" philosophy of history then, and now in Berlin, insisted that no law of decline determined the fate of modern Europe. The future would depend on the willingness to do "mighty deeds" and the character to see them through.

As in Paris, Roosevelt emphasized the need to cultivate the all-important homely, everyday virtues. Men must be willing to work, to be good husbands and fathers, and of course to keep up their "fighting edge"; women must be good housewives and the mothers of "many healthy children." But there was also a need for intellectual leadership to lift the spirit and focus religious sensibilities on the needs of the soul in this world. It was here, in "that power of organization, that power of working in common for a common end," that the German people had distinguished themselves "in such signal fashion during the last half century."[20]

That Germany during this period had imposed a top-down "state socialism" under its Iron Chancellor, Otto von Bismarck, and that it lacked anything resembling the culture of local liberty and regard for individual rights that Americans had long considered vital to republican self-government, did not trouble Roosevelt. As his Sorbonne speech suggested, it was precisely this "pioneer" mentality that he sought to overcome. Although there were clearly aspects of German life that he did not admire, the rise of the administrative state, staffed by expert civil servants, made a deep impression upon him. Indeed, if the men of the future continued on this path, the former president allowed himself to "dream" that the world movement might lift civilization "to a higher and more permanent plane of well-being than was ever attained by any preceding civilization." Roosevelt's peroration is worth quoting in full because it offers further evidence of how far he had moved from the principles of the Americans he claimed most to admire:

> It is no impossible dream to build up a civilization in which morality, ethical development, and a true feeling of brotherhood shall alike be divorced from false sentimentality, from the *rancorous and evil passions* which, curiously enough, so often accompany *sentimental attachment to the rights of man*; in which a high material development in the things of

the body shall be achieved *without subordination of the things of the soul*; in which there shall be a genuine desire for peace and justice without loss of those virile qualities without which no love of peace or justice shall avail in any race; in which the fullest development of scientific research, the great distinguishing feature of our present civilization, shall yet not imply a belief that intellect can ever take the place of character—for from the standpoint of the nation as of the individual, it is character that is the one vital possession.[21]

Making every possible allowance for Roosevelt's good manners, his desire to speak to the Germans on their own terms, to ring all the changes on Hegelian idealism, the "dream" is difficult to reconcile with the political principles of his heroes. Here, the inalienable rights of the Declaration are reduced to "sentimental attachments," all too frequently accompanied by not merely selfish passions, but ones that are rancorous and *evil*. In so speaking, TR gave no indication that these rights had any moral character, i.e., that they imposed reciprocal obligations to respect the rights of others, or that they were linked not only to self-interest, but also to the moral sense, as Lincoln insisted. Instead, morality, brotherhood, and ethical development were juxtaposed to the natural rights tradition, which, he suggested, was grounded on man's low, selfish nature, and reached no higher than the merely material.

Equally striking was that Roosevelt, who routinely railed against sentimental philanthropists and utopian speculators, seemed here to have joined hands with them. In his "dream" the usual tensions that beset political life all but disappeared. Once peoples reached this higher plane of well-being, the desire for peace and justice would flourish, but with no loss to the virile virtues. Perhaps, as his former professor William James suggested, manly men would discover new ways to test themselves, imitating the discipline and sacrifice that military combat had previously called forth, only now in peaceful projects that function as the "moral equivalent of war." Indeed, as Wilfred M. McClay has observed, the search for a moral equivalent of war "has informed most Progressive efforts to build a comprehensively organized and morally purposeful nation." From TR's day to the present, war imagery, as in the war on poverty or the war on drugs, has frequently been employed to advance the cause of social reform.[22]

But however much this dream would live on in the hearts of progressives, for Roosevelt it was nothing more than a momentary idyll. Indeed, accepting the Nobel Peace Prize in Christiania a week earlier, the former president had not indulged in any gauzy hopes about the future, but laid out a series of practical proposals, all the while insisting that righteousness, not peace, must be the highest goal.[23] And later, after the Great War broke out, Roosevelt, breaking with his pacifist supporters, would urge his countrymen to wage war against Germany for the sake of righteousness.[24] Here in Berlin in 1910, however, Roosevelt allowed himself to "dream" of the day when peace and justice walked hand in hand.

If the guiding spirit of his Berlin talk was German philosophy, Roosevelt once again switched gears as he traveled to Oxford to deliver the Romanes Lecture, the longest and most intellectually ambitious of his speeches.[25] The title of his address, "Biological Analogies in History," nodded to the great English evolutionary biologists, Charles Darwin (whom Roosevelt singled out by name in his address) and Thomas Huxley (who had delivered the Romanes lecture in 1893). Roosevelt, who was both an amateur historian and scientist, began by observing that although there was no exact parallel between the birth, growth, and death of species and that of human societies, there were nevertheless "analogies" both "strange" and "striking" between the two.[26]

Nevertheless, he was careful to note that there was still much that scientists could not explain. Expert opinion was, for example, divided over the relative weight of natural selection, mutation, and the inheritance of acquired characteristics in explaining the evolution of species. If the "biological analogies" held up, caution was called for in explaining how complex societies developed and declined.[27] Although he did not venture his opinion here, Roosevelt was inclined to give more weight to the inheritance of acquired characteristics. "Biological Analogies in History" thus afforded him a fresh angle from which to drive home the importance of character for national survival and greatness, since he thought (mistakenly) that the virtues he admired could be biologically transmitted from one generation to another.

The former president readily acknowledged that it was not always possible to explain how species became extinct or why nations declined, but he thought he did know what went wrong in Holland, and the lessons for Britain and America were clear. Once a great commercial power, the Dutch were ruined by "decentralization," which robbed the central government of all "efficiency," and "short-sighted materialism," which proved "fatal." The Dutch grew very wealthy, and mistakenly came to believe that they could hire others to fight for them on land, while at the same time refusing to keep up their navy. They thus learned the hard way that "to be opulent and unarmed is to secure ease in the present at the almost certain cost of disaster in the future." Although Holland did not disappear from the family of nations, she was swept from a "commanding position" into "an eddy, aside from the sweep of the mighty current of world life."[28]

The fall of Rome provided another cautionary tale: free peoples could escape being mastered only by being able to master themselves. What was required, above all, was "a high and stern sense of duty, of moral obligation," followed by "self-knowledge and self-mastery." To remain free, citizens would have to forswear the debilitating love of luxury and the taste for "vapid and frivolous excitement." In modern times, the most "ominous sign" of "self-indulgence and love of ease" was the "diminution of the birth-rate" throughout the civilized world.[29]

As he had done in Berlin, Roosevelt was willing to draw lessons from the past to warn about decline in the present, but he saw no point in making predictions about the future. Similarly, he was loath to push the biological analogies too far, so that what at first appeared as "strange" and "striking," now seemed to be "true in only the roughest and most general way."[30] Indeed, as he neared his conclusion, Roosevelt dropped the analogies altogether and focused instead on the problems that faced the two English-speaking nations both abroad and at home. The former president had already touched on the subject of rule over alien peoples in his impromptu remarks in Christiania, where he defended American actions in Latin America and the Philippines, though understandably he gave no hint of his growing reservations regarding American imperialism in the Philippines.[31]

In his Khartoum, Cairo, and Guildhall addresses, Roosevelt had forcefully defended British policy in Africa and had gone so far as to criticize the foreign office for seeming to hesitate in the wake of the assassination of Britain's Egyptian viceroy. If the British meant to remain in Africa, and Roosevelt left no doubt that they should, they could not be cowed into granting self-government to those who thought it meant "crime, violence, and extortion, corruption from within, lawlessness among themselves and towards others."[32] Now, in the Romanes Lecture, he once again dismissed the objections of "Little Englanders" and "forcible-feeble imperialists."[33] In the end, it came down to a question of character: truly great civilizations distinguished themselves by their manly virtues and their ability to stand up to aggression. Those that risked greatly lived on in memory, while the more timid nations simply faded away without a trace. Despite the protests of anti-imperialists, neither Britain nor America had so far "yielded to the craven fear of being great."[34]

On the domestic front, Roosevelt informed his audience that the United States was "trying on a scale hitherto unexampled to work out the problems of government for, of, and by the people." Repeating lines from his Berlin address, he preached a "spirit of broad humanity; of brotherly kindness; of acceptance of responsibility, one for each and each for all," while again eschewing sentimentality and weakness. But in contrast to his German remarks, which made no mention of rights, or the lecture in Paris, which subordinated rights to duty, and spoke vaguely about "service" to the State, Roosevelt here insisted that "true liberty" consisted in protecting the rights of others, especially the rights of minorities. Justice, he thought, required that each be rewarded according to his merit. At the same time, however, Roosevelt condemned "doctrinaire theories of vested rights or freedom of contract." Seeking to find some middle ground, he insisted he wanted to protect "individual rights—including property rights" while doing everything realistically possible to better social conditions. Beyond serving notice that property rights would now have to give way to "human rights," it was difficult to fathom where his comments might lead. Toward the end of the Romanes lecture, TR attempted to distinguish himself from his British hosts by insisting that he was a "radical democrat," but his vague remarks on social policy gave no indication of how true his self-description would turn out to be.[35]

During his six-week tour of the European capitals, the former president not only met with monarchs and heads of state but also sought out government officials and social reformers to get a closer look at what the Europeans were doing. Accompanied by S. S. McClure and Lawrence F. Abbott (son of *The Outlook* editor, Lyman Abbott), Roosevelt met with the German minister of state and public works to discuss government aid to the elderly and impoverished. Under Bismarck, Germany had pioneered the welfare state, introducing health insurance as early as 1883, and accident, old age, and disability programs by 1889. In Denmark, he sought to learn more about government assistance to the aged, which, following Germany's example, had been established in 1891. In England, he talked with Liberal party leaders, Henry Herbert Asquith, David Lloyd George, and Sir Edward Grey. England had already introduced workers' compensation laws and old age pensions, and would in 1911 pass the National Insurance Act, providing for health and unemployment insurance.[36]

Seen from the perspective of these European states and the world movement for which they stood, America must have appeared backward indeed. It was one thing to write, before he had actually been there, that the United States looked to Germany for guidance on labor policy; it was quite another to observe these programs firsthand. Nor was it only the problems of urban life that interested him. Following up on the report of his last presidential

Commission on Country Life, he examined cooperative farming in Denmark, and stopped in at the Museum of Country Life in Budapest. Back on his native soil, he would confess himself "rather ashamed" that there was nothing like this museum in America.[37] Even Hungary was more advanced than the United States.

Nevertheless, Roosevelt noted a few troubling developments. In a long and insightful letter to Trevelyan recounting his European visit, Roosevelt confided he was "puzzled" to discover in Denmark that "the very great growth of what I should call the wise and democratic use of the powers of the State toward helping raise the individual standard of social and economic well-being had not made the people more contented."[38] He was also "saddened" to see that in Sweden socialists thought they could overcome class hatred by preaching population control, which for Roosevelt amounted to "race suicide."[39] But these were exceptions to his overall positive assessment of what intelligent government action might do. At a time when European nations were experimenting with the welfare state and socialist parties were making gains across the continent, Roosevelt believed he had glimpsed the future. Having thus gauged the actual "force and direction of the social movement" in Europe, TR began to think seriously about how, apart from the Socialist Party, which was inextricably linked with violence, class warfare, and the abolition of private property, a form of social democracy more advanced than anything he had proposed as president could be brought to America.[40]

THE CROLY CONNECTION

In November 1909, while Roosevelt was off on safari, Herbert Croly published *The Promise of American Life,* which offered both an argument and a blueprint for the kind of reconstruction the former president had in mind. Among the many early reviews, the book had received a brief, favorable notice in *The Outlook,* where Roosevelt, even in Africa, remained on the masthead as a contributing editor. Not surprisingly, the anonymous review singled out for special mention the chapter dealing with American reformers, of whom Roosevelt was the most prominent.[41] Then in April 1910, at Croly's urging, his friend Learned Hand sent Roosevelt a copy of the book, commending its "neo-Hamiltonian" approach and linking its political ideas with those of the former president. By coincidence, Henry Cabot Lodge also wrote to TR that April to recommend the book (though his assessment was more measured), and Roosevelt responded that he had "at once" ordered the book from Macmillans of London. Exactly when, over the course of the next few months, Roosevelt read *The Promise of American Life* is not clear, but on July 31, the former president wrote to the author: "I do not know when I have read a book which I felt profited me as much as your book on American life. There are a few points on which I do not agree with you, yet even as to these my disagreement is on minor matters; indeed chiefly on questions of emphasis." Roosevelt then expressed the wish that he were better able to get his advice to the American people in "practical shape according to the principles you set forth."[42] The forty-one-year-old Harvard College dropout must have been ecstatic to read that the former president promised to use his ideas "freely" in speeches he was preparing to make and to receive an invitation to visit the former president in his office at *The Outlook*.[43] That fall, campaigning in the midterm elections, Roosevelt would summon the country to a New Nationalism, borrowing the phrase that Croly had used to describe TR's approach to reform while president.

It is not difficult to understand Roosevelt's favorable impression of the book. Croly's narrative largely tracked his own, blaming Jefferson and his followers for most of the country's ills and praising Hamilton for his far-sighted nationalism and broad construction of federal powers.[44] Hamilton could be faulted for his distrust of democracy, but the Virginian's suspicion of national power, combined with his attachment to equal rights, encouraged excessive individualism, mediocrity, and drift. The promise of American life, Croly argued, surely meant something more than the equal right of individuals to pursue their private, selfish goals, taking for granted that everything would automatically work out for the public good. If the promise meant anything, it had to be a conscious ideal, freely adopted, of progressive improvement in the economic and moral condition of the nation as a whole, and not simply an agglomeration of self-interested parts. For this promise to be fulfilled, Americans would need to rethink their political tradition, and, while this reassessment would not leave either side intact, it would necessarily do "more harm" to the Jeffersonian side of the tradition.[45]

However much Roosevelt agreed with Croly's interpretation of the Federalists and the Republicans, it was most likely the chapter on "Reform and the Reformers" that commanded his attention. Croly's treatment of "Theodore Roosevelt as Reformer" was a masterpiece of flattery. Of all the present-day reformers, Croly cooed, Roosevelt was the best because he alone had grasped the significance of the national idea. Like Hamilton, TR stood for the ideal of constructive national power, but Roosevelt was "Hamiltonian with a difference." His was a New Nationalism that for the first time married the principle of vigorous national action to democracy. As president, Roosevelt had put his New Nationalism into action, first, by giving to "men of special ability, training, and eminence a better opportunity to serve the public," and second, by restoring the Republican Party to the high moral purpose it had pursued under Lincoln.[46]

Still, not even Croly's "hero" was immune to criticism. Roosevelt's vaunted "Square Deal" was nothing more than an updated version of the Jeffersonian principle of "equal rights for all, special privileges for none" that denied to American democracy any more constructive purpose than eliminating unfair privileges. It was not enough to enforce the rules of the game; the rules themselves had to be changed. Government must no longer serve as an impartial umpire seeking a "just balance" but should discriminate "constructively" in favor of its friends. Even so, Roosevelt built better than he knew or than he cared to admit; his program was both "more novel and more radical" in two respects: first, it implied a view of democracy that departed from the Jeffersonian principle of equal rights, and second, despite his insistence in playing by the rules, Roosevelt's policies seemed to point toward a revision of those very rules.

However, since "candid and consistent thinking" was not Roosevelt's strong suit, Croly doubted that Roosevelt understood the full implications of his actions. Despite his constant call for balance, the "prophet of the Strenuous Life" had allowed his will to dominate his intellect, destroying his own internal balance by his "sheer exuberance of moral energy." Roosevelt was more than a manly man; he was Thor, "wielding with power and effect a sledge-hammer in the cause of national righteousness."[47] Although the hammer blows were instinctively well aimed, they cried out for a superintending intelligence that would give direction to his mighty efforts.

This would be Croly's contribution. He would show the former president what he had so far only intuitively grasped: the embrace of the national idea must necessarily lead, not simply to the reform, but the "reconstruction" of republican government in America. What the country needed was "in truth equivalent to a new Declaration of Independence" that would resolve the fundamental tension between equality and liberty at the heart of the old republic and enable Americans "to organize their political, economic and social life in the service of a comprehensive, a lofty, and a far-reaching democratic purpose." Thus liberated, Americans would no longer regard their Constitution with "superstitious awe"; they could reclaim their sovereignty and free the American spirit from its legal "bondage."[48]

Then again, Croly averred, perhaps no elected politician could trumpet such a bald repudiation of America's foundational principles. Like the phi-

CHAPTER SIX

losopher who escaped from the cave in Plato's *Republic*, a "man in public life who told them that their 'noble national theory' was ambiguous and distracting, and that many of their popular catch-words were false and exercised a mischievous influence on public affairs, would do so at his own personal risk and cost." Only after the program had been successfully implemented could there be "plain speaking," and even then, the task would probably fall to men such as Croly who had little to gain or lose politically by their "apparent heresies."[49]

Despite these vaulting claims on Croly's part, most historians have been skeptical of his actual influence on the former president, rightly pointing out that Roosevelt himself had championed most of the positions Croly espoused before his book was published. If anything, they insist, Roosevelt's influence on Croly was much stronger than the other way around. It was by observing Roosevelt in action as president that Croly formed his program for national action.[50] However, it may well be that historians have focused too much on practical policy questions, such as federal "supervision" of all corporations involved in interstate commerce, progressive inheritance taxes, labor legislation, and the like, where Roosevelt did indeed take the lead, and not enough on political philosophy. As his letter to Croly suggested, the former president wanted to talk to Croly about how practically to present his program according to the *principles* Croly had laid out; he was not looking for specific policy recommendations. Croly's greatest contribution was to confirm Roosevelt in his social democratic views, deepen the arguments in their favor, and embolden him to press forward with his agenda.[51] Especially after his European tour, Roosevelt was looking for arguments that would help him persuade his countrymen to adopt reforms that would move the United States closer to the European welfare state, adapted to American conditions. From this perspective, Croly's principal contribution was to lay bare the inadequacies of the Declaration's commitment to "equal rights," with its implicit safeguards for private property, and to argue that the Constitution should not be allowed to interfere with the sovereignty of the people to determine their collective destiny.

In "Reconstruction; Its Conditions and Purposes," the chapter immediately following his discussion of Roosevelt as reformer and the most important of the book, Croly employed a series of metaphors to illuminate the defects of "equal rights." He began with a horticultural image: Americans took for granted that the "divergent demands of the individual and social interest" could be reconciled by "grafting the principle of equality onto the thrifty tree of individual rights, and the ripe fruit thereof can be gathered merely by shaking the tree."[52] As Croly had already made clear in earlier portions of his book, he rejected Americans' "childlike confidence" that the "social interest" could be addressed adequately by allowing each individual to pursue his or her own selfish interest. The promise of American life could only be fulfilled by "a large measure of individual subordination and self-denial."[53] But Americans' faith that everything would turn out well without having to make any sacrifices was only half of the problem. Packed into the metaphor was the suggestion that individual rights had their origins in an earlier aristocratic era, where they were the privilege of a few.[54] The Declaration then sought to extend these rights to everyone, but the "graft" between aristocracy and democracy had produced an odd hybrid, full of "dangerous ambiguities and self-contradictions."[55]

To illustrate these ambiguities, Croly switched to a second metaphor, arguing that Americans viewed equal rights in terms of a footrace in which everyone started from the same point, and then finished up unequally owing to their differing abilities. But this popular conception overlooked the extent to which private property affected the outcome. How much did success depend upon individual effort, and how much was it determined by the structural conditions within which the race was conducted? Was private property one of the rights to be protected, or was it part of the problem? Depending upon their political dispositions, patriotic Americans saw the race in strikingly different ways. Croly left no doubt where he stood:

> Americans who talk in this way seem wholly blind to the fact that under a legal system which holds private property sacred there may be equal rights, but there cannot possibly be any equal opportunities for exercising these rights. The chance which the individual has to compete with his fellows and take a prize in the race is vitally affected by material conditions over which he has no control. It is as if a competitor in a Marathon cross country race were denied proper nourishment or proper training, and was obliged to toe the mark against rivals who had every benefit of food and discipline. Under such conditions he is not as badly off as if he were entirely excluded from the race. With the aid of exceptional strength and intelligence he may overcome the odds against him and win out. But it would be absurd to claim, because all the rivals toe the same mark, that a man's victory or defeat depended entirely upon his own efforts. Those who have enjoyed the benefit of wealth and thorough education start with an advantage which can be overcome only by very exceptional men,—men so exceptional, in fact, that the average competitor without such benefits feels himself disqualified from the contest.[56]

Although the principle of equal rights sought to bind Americans together, in fact, Croly argued, it did just the opposite by pitting individuals against each other and holding them responsible for outcomes that largely depended on larger social and economic forces over which they had no control. To fulfill the promise of American life, individual property rights would have to give way to "the interest of the community as a whole" and to a more equitable distribution of wealth. Private property would remain "in some form," but its nature and influence would have to be radically transformed.[57] But to do this, Americans would first need to reclaim their sovereignty as a people. If popular sovereignty meant anything, it most assuredly included the right of the people to determine their destiny as a nation, removing constitutional protections for property rights that Croly believed made no sense under present social and economic conditions.

Still, although the footrace analogy illustrated some of the ambiguities to which the idea of equal rights gave rise, it did not explain why Americans had frequently failed to elect the best men to office or why they resisted giving them more power. At this point, Croly introduced a third metaphor, likening equal rights to a marriage that produced "unnatural children." Most of the progeny took after the equality side of the family tree, mediocre in talents and distrustful of those who succeeded. Unable to see beyond their "own barren and insipid purposes," they resisted giving greater power to those who excelled, clinging to the delusion that the national interest could be advanced without government intervention. Meanwhile, those exceptional individuals who exercised their liberty "inevitably conquered," and then used their victories to perpetuate themselves at the top of the economic and political order. In short, the "marriage" of equality and rights tended to produce two types of Americans: "average" democrats and the entrenched plutocrats, "whose nature it is to devour one or the other of their parents."[58] To escape these "murderous" consequences, Croly urged Americans to subordinate both liberty and equality to "human brotherhood," which promised to reconcile these warring principles on a higher moral plane.[59]

Although Croly had begun by criticizing the "graft" of equality onto the tree of liberty, the reconstruction he proposed was not without its own "dangerous ambiguities and self-contradictions." At times, he suggested that his project was to subordinate equality and liberty to brotherhood. At other times, he spoke of grafting socialism onto individualism, and then subordinating both of these principles to nationalism.[60] How Croly thought these doctrines could be made to cohere was left largely unexplained, except for the suggestion that a democratic nation could not rest satisfied with human nature as it was, but must bend its efforts toward changing and improving it. "In the complete democracy a man must in some way be made to serve the nation in the very act of contributing to his own individual fulfillment. Not until his personal action is dictated by disinterested motives can there be any harmony between private and public interests."[61] Presumably, the "men of special ability, training, and eminence" Roosevelt had recruited to government service would craft incentives to move this project along, fulfilling the age-old wish, so powerfully expressed in Plato's *Republic,* of overcoming the tension between the interests of the individual and the interests of the community.

About one thing Croly was surely right, however. No one who warred as ferociously against the core principle of equal rights, attacked so frontally the right of private property, and showed as much contempt for ordinary citizens could hope to succeed in American politics. Even in his wildest moments, TR had never thought to blame the idea of equal rights for the ills of the country; nor did he regard "average" Americans as a stumbling block to his progressive goals. The principal culprits were those "doctrinaires" on the right (both plutocrats and judges), who recognized no limits on the right to property, and their counterparts on the left, who preached class warfare and violent revolution. Nevertheless, Roosevelt had opened the door, first in his socialism essays, and then in his Sorbonne and Berlin addresses, by observing, however vaguely, that there were some socialist principles he found attractive and by calling for the subordination of rights to duties. Croly's attack on equal rights would reinforce these inchoate ideas at just the moment TR was about to launch a new phase of his political career.

NEW NATIONALISM

One month after the former president wrote to Croly praising *The Promise of American Life,* the Colonel, as he now preferred to be called, embarked on a western speaking tour aimed at drumming up support for Republican candidates in the upcoming midterm elections.[62] Taft's support in that region, where the Republican insurgency was strongest, had fallen off precipitously, and Roosevelt took upon himself the thankless task of trying to help western progressives without alienating the conservatives within his party.[63] Although he failed in this immediate object, historian John Milton Cooper, Jr. considers these speeches "the most extended, reflective exposition of his domestic political thought," and his "best political testament." George E. Mowry offered praise of a different kind, calling Roosevelt's Osawatomie address "the most radical speech ever given by an ex-president" of the United States, a view seconded recently by Kathleen Dalton.[64] Unconstrained by the demands of practical politics, the former president felt free to speak his mind, and did.

The tour began in Denver, where the Colonel, addressing the Democratic-controlled Colorado legislature, launched into an attack on the courts for creating a neutral "borderland" in which neither the states nor the federal government had power to act. Unlike their counterparts in the legislative and executive branches, the judiciary had not kept pace with industrial development during the last forty years. It was "ruinous" for the courts to stand in the way of social legislation (as they had in the *Knight* and *Lochner* decisions) because what they were really doing was "arbitrarily and irresponsibly" blocking the "people's rights." Then, echoing Croly's insistence that the people should reclaim the right to determine their own destiny, Roosevelt declared, "the people, through their several legislatures, national and state, have complete power of control in all areas that affect the public interest." The Colonel did not explain what precisely he meant by this: was he working to get the *Lochner* decision overruled, as Lincoln tried to do with *Dred Scott* and he himself attempted with *Knight*? Or was he suggesting that the people, acting through their elected representatives, had the power to override unpopular decisions themselves?[65] Eventually, he would clarify his position, but his response would further divide the Republican Party. The role of the courts in the constitutional order would turn out to be one of the major issues in the 1912 election.[66]

From Denver, Roosevelt traveled east to Osawatomie, Kansas, where he delivered the most famous of his campaign addresses, "The New Nationalism." Speaking in the place where John Brown and his sons had killed five pro-slavery men in 1856 and now a locus of Republican insurgency, Roosevelt sought to apply the "spirit" of Lincoln to the problems facing the present day, ignoring the fact that Lincoln had never appealed to anything as airy as the "spirit" of the Declaration or the Constitution, but insisted on the *letter,* repeatedly quoting both the documents and seeking guidance from the intentions of the Framers.

As TR framed it, New Nationalism strove to complete, if not actually transcend, the work that the slain president had begun by placing the national interest above sectional or personal advantage. Accordingly, Roosevelt was critical of local attempts to deal with national problems, and "impatient" with the obstacles thrown up by the "overdivision" of government powers that impeded "efficient" national action. For the first time, Roosevelt here cast the executive as the "steward" of national well being, though the label itself added nothing to his capacious understanding of the office while president. As in Denver, he demanded that the judiciary place human welfare above property rights, and that legislatures be more responsive to the will of the people. Special interests, he thundered, must be "driven out of politics."

To inoculate himself against charges of being too radical, Roosevelt began with a series of quotations from Lincoln. The first, from a speech to Germans in Cincinnati shortly before his inauguration, declared that men had a duty not only to improve their own lives, but also "to assist in ameliorating mankind."[67] Lincoln's spontaneous remarks could hardly be said to constitute a major policy statement, but they did serve Roosevelt's general purpose in emphasizing duties rather than rights (and rather abstract duties at that). The second, from Lincoln's Reply to a Committee from the Workingmen's Association of New York in 1864, was more substantial. "Labor is prior to, and independent of capital. Capital is only the fruit of labor, and could never have existed if labor had not first existed. Labor is the superior of capital, and deserves much the higher consideration." Roosevelt then added a second quotation from the same speech: "Capital has its rights, which are as worthy of protection as any other rights. . . . Nor should this lead to a war upon the owners of property. Property is the fruit of labor; . . . property is desirable; it is a positive good in the world." This in turn was followed by a third, "thoroughly Lincolnlike sentence: — 'Let not him who is houseless pull down the house of another, but let him work diligently, and build one for himself, thus by example assuring that his own shall be safe from violence when built.'"[68] Because Roosevelt would quote these lines about labor and capital repeatedly during the next decade, attempting to enlist Lincoln in the progressive cause, it is worth trying to understand what the sixteenth president meant.

In this speech (and elsewhere), Lincoln sought to refute the argument, first popularized by southern slaveholders, and then taken up by some northern industrialists, that capital was the source of all labor; that is, that no one, either slave or free, would labor unless there was first someone to buy or hire him. The only question was whether hired labor or slavery was more efficient. As Lincoln had explained in his First Annual Message, portions of which he quoted directly in his address to the New York workingmen, proponents of this view further assumed that free men were forever destined to remain in that dependent condition, and that it was good for civilization that they should.[69] Lincoln did not dispute the obvious fact that there was a connection between capital and labor (some men did work because others had hired them), but he did deny that capital was the source of *all* labor. If anything, the relation was the reverse: in a free and democratic society, capital was the *fruit* of labor, and not its source. On this point, TR agreed with Lincoln: capital "could never have existed if labor had not first existed." If given the opportunity, free men would willingly labor because they hoped to profit and improve their life situation.

The relationship between labor and capital in turn was linked to Lincoln's understanding of the right to property. Once again, Lincoln followed the founders (and Locke) in arguing that the right to property was grounded in the right of every human being to his or her own body, and consequently, to the fruits of his or her own labor.[70] This was a natural right that existed prior to the establishment of government, and in fact was one of the principal objects for which government was established. Although more individuals had labored for themselves in Lincoln's day than at the time of the New Nationalism speech, Lincoln's point was that no one, of necessity, was ever bound to remain a laborer for life. In fact, the general rule in America was that many individuals had started life working for someone else (including some of the wealthiest men in Roosevelt's day). Through thrift and hard work they had reached the position where they had not only become independent, but were also able to hire others, sometimes many others, to work for them.[71] Indeed, Lincoln seemed to go out of his way to emphasize to the New York workingmen this message of hope: "That some should be rich shows that others may become rich, and hence is just encouragement to industry and enterprise."[72] Tellingly, Roosevelt omitted these lines from his own speech. Although Roosevelt concluded with Lincoln's exhortation to build one's own house rather than tear down the house of another, he did not share Lincoln's faith that individual talent and effort when protected by law were generally sufficient to produce just rewards and to give hope to those who had not yet prospered. To put it another way, Lincoln still believed in the justice of the footrace, and Roosevelt no longer did.

Reminding his audience that he had always stood for the "Square Deal," TR spelled out what Croly had argued was only implicit in Roosevelt's program while president: "I mean not merely that I stand for fair play under the present rules of the game, but that I stand for having those rules changed so as to work for a more substantial equality of opportunity and of reward for equally good service." The problem with the present rules was that some men "possess more than they have earned" while others "have earned more than they possess."[73] Only government, acting on behalf of the citizens of the United States and against the "sinister" special interests, could remedy this "unfair money getting" by formulating "new conceptions of the relations of property to human welfare."[74] Under this new dispensation (Croly's "constructive discrimination"), it was "not even enough that it [property] should have been gained without doing damage to the community. We should *permit* it to be gained only so long as the gaining represents benefit to the community."[75] In contrast to Lincoln's belief in the natural right of men and women to the fruits of their labor, Roosevelt planted the axiom that government, and not the individual, was the source, and therefore the determinant, of all property rights. The conclusion thus seems inescapable that, although TR found Lincoln useful in warding off accusations that his views on property were too radical, Roosevelt's New Nationalism was philosophically more indebted to Herbert Croly than to Abraham Lincoln.

Nor was it only the acquisition of wealth that needed to be "supervised," but also its use. In what could only be described as a caricature of the classical liberal view, Roosevelt asserted that the man who "wrongly holds that every human right is secondary to his profit, must now give way to the advocate of human welfare, who rightly maintains that every man holds his property subject to the general right of the community to regulate its use to whatever degree the public welfare may require it."[76] Here then was the answer to the question posed by the Sorbonne address. In Paris, Roosevelt had asserted that citizens should not admire those whose fortunes were of no "benefit to the nation," but he had not spelled out what he meant. The New Nationalism resolved this ambiguity by making it clear that both the acquisition and use of property could now be regulated to whatever degree the public welfare required.

In this new republic, the object of government was not to secure individual rights, but to ensure that wealth somehow benefited the nation. Accordingly, the negative rule that the property not "damage" the community was no longer sufficient. A new, higher threshold would now have to be met: only those fortunes that were "honorably obtained and well used" for the good of the nation would be permitted. And what principally "benefited" the nation was a significant redistribution of the wealth. Even fortunes that rendered "service" to one's fellows were suspect if they were "overpaid."[77] Roosevelt was surely correct when he observed that New Nationalism implied "a policy of far more active governmental interference with social and economic conditions in this country than we have yet had."[78]

To that end, he repeated the major policy recommendations he had fought for yet failed to enact during his second term as president. Railroads should not (at least at this point) be publicly owned, but they should be thoroughly regulated. To satisfy western insurgents, he again called for a physical evaluation of all railroad property.[79] The Hepburn Act, and now the Mann-Elkins Act of 1910, had made a start in regulating the railroads and setting rates, but "we must go yet further." The powers of the ICC should be "largely increased." How far he did not say. Combinations that controlled the "necessities of life" should also be thoroughly regulated; in fact, all businesses operating in interstate commerce should be completely "supervised" by something like an enhanced Bureau of Corporations. Franchises should only be granted for a limited period of time. Congress should establish an "expert tariff commission" that would act, not on behalf of special interests, but for the nation as a whole. "Swollen" fortunes should be subject both to a graduated income tax and a graduated inheritance tax. Defense spending should be increased; conservation efforts redoubled.

Not only should "the use of wealth in the public interest" be regulated, but also "the terms and conditions of labor." This was not primarily to expand the opportunity for each individual to develop his talents for his own purposes, but "to give him a chance where he will reach a place in which he will make the greatest contribution to the public welfare."[80] Workmen's compensation, laws regulating labor conditions for women and children, and improved education were cast in terms of making good *citizens*. At the moment, Roosevelt was not prepared to go as far as the La Follette insurgents, who favored measures that would involve the people directly in the policymaking process. He did, however, endorse the direct primary, weakening the stranglehold that parties exercised in the nominating process, a decision that would prove fateful in the 1912 campaign. Even still, he failed to anticipate that his top-heavy regulatory policies might leave him vulnerable to Woodrow Wilson's charge of fostering a debilitating paternalism that actually undermined self-government.[81]

Although New Nationalism proved popular with western progressives, reaction in the East was far more critical, and Roosevelt was forced to adopt a new rhetorical strategy. In a speech to Republican regulars in Syracuse on September 17, TR insisted that "the New Nationalism really means nothing but an application to new conditions of certain old and fundamental moralities." His western speeches chiefly repeated proposals he had made while president, developing them only "very slightly," and principally by drawing on the ideas of Abraham Lincoln.

Nearly half of the Syracuse speech attempted to show that there was nothing radical about his criticism of recent court decisions. Had not Lincoln assailed the Supreme Court's decision in *Dred Scott*? Was there anything extreme about agreeing with the dissenting justices' opinions in both *Knight* and *Lochner*? Even President Taft, while serving as a U.S. circuit judge, had recognized the importance of "intelligent scrutiny and candid criticism" of decisions rendered by men who enjoyed life tenure.[82] Had he taken such an approach in Denver, Roosevelt was convinced that his remarks would not have caused nearly the stir that they had. Privately, he conceded that it was "a blunder of some gravity" not to have included in Denver the historical precedents for his criticism of the courts.[83]

More important in reassuring eastern Republicans was the essay "The Progressives, Past and Present," which appeared in the September 4 issue of *The Outlook*. After reading it, Lodge expressed relief at his friend's "carefully guarded" comments, venturing the guess that reports of the revolutionary character of the Osawatomie speech had been exaggerated by the Kansas insurgents for their own purposes.[84] And indeed, the overall tone of the article was more temperate, especially in its efforts to reassure the captains of industry that New Nationalism would provide incentives and opportunities for them to excel. But beneath the more conciliatory rhetoric, the message remained the same, and *pace* Lodge, in several crucial respects was made clearer and stronger.

In Syracuse, Roosevelt had attempted to walk back the radicalism of New Nationalism by arguing that it was nothing more than the application of old moralities to new conditions. But the question never turned on the old *moralities*; it was whether the old *political principles*, "the principles of the fathers," as Roosevelt here called them, still applied. And in *The Outlook* essay, he stated more than once that they did not. To go back to the political theories of a century ago would "accomplish nothing whatever," for these were the very theories that had given rise to corporate power and vast private fortunes. The old theories of government were designed for sparsely populated eighteenth century agricultural conditions, where perhaps "their benefits outweighed their disadvantages," but such theories were "hopeless" under the present industrial conditions. This was no reflection on the wisdom of the fathers; it was merely an acknowledgment that social and economic conditions had changed. The answers to today's problems could not be found by looking backward, only forward.[85]

Despite Croly's criticisms of the "Square Deal," Roosevelt continued to insist on "equal rights for all, and special privileges for none." But the slogan was now reinterpreted in the light of Croly's analysis. To realize this "ideal" today, equal rights must be construed very differently from the way they were a century ago. Rather than leave it to each individual to make what he could of himself, running the risk that unrestricted liberty would wipe out "even approximate equality," or conversely, that a too-rigid equality would annihilate "every shred of liberty," government must now step in to "make men, as nearly as they can be made, both free and equal, the freedom and equality necessarily resting on a basis of justice and brotherhood."

In concrete terms, justice and brotherhood required that government take "constructive" action to address the problems arising from the right to private property. As at Osawatomie, the new and more stringent test that property rights had to meet in New Nationalism remained the same. It was not enough that the fortune should have been gained without damaging the community; "we should permit it to be gained and kept so long as the gaining and the keeping represent benefit to the community." But Roosevelt then added a new condition: "the fortune must not only be honorably obtained and well used"; it was "also essential that it should not represent a necessary incident of widespread, even though partial, economic privation." What he seemed to be saying was that larger, more efficient businesses should not be allowed to destroy smaller, less competitive operations, despite the costs, both economic and political, in propping them up. And indeed, in a Labor Day speech in 1917, Roosevelt would make this suggestion explicit and then go on to support additional taxes on the excess profits of larger and more efficient businesses to level the playing field.[86]

Roosevelt only compounded the problem when he then insisted that government ensure that all individuals receive "a just share of the good things to which they are legitimately entitled." Of course, in a general sense, he was right. As Publius remarked in *Federalist* No. 51, "justice is the end of government." But what did TR mean by a "just share," and what were the "good things" to which all individuals were "legitimately entitled"? How far was he willing to go to declare success?[87] Three times he declared that the rules of the game would need to be changed to bring about a "more substantial measure of equality in both moral and physical well-being." What concretely he meant was that it was no longer sufficient that government supply the *conditions* of justice — the rule of law and protection of private rights and property. Now government itself must become the *means* by which "social justice," understood as a "substantial" redistribution of wealth, would be attained. It was difficult to see what the more conservative Lodge found reassuring in this essay.

Despite his heroic efforts, Roosevelt's attempts to unite the party and secure a Republican victory in the midterm elections ended in failure. Several prominent candidates he had stumped for were swept out of office, and Republicans lost control of the House. Although they retained their majority in the Senate, Democrats and insurgents had the numbers to forge an anti-Taft majority there.[88] Meanwhile, in New Jersey, Democrats succeeded in electing Princeton University president Woodrow Wilson governor of the state.

Addressing the Chamber of Commerce in New Haven, Connecticut, one month after the election, Roosevelt cast himself as a "radical," who "most earnestly" wanted to see his "radical programme" carried out by "conservatives." Such an approach, he assured them, would be gradual and experimental, testing the results at every step to make sure that they really did advance the forward movement. The task of sober, responsible businessmen was to see that these "far-reaching" social and industrial reforms were accomplished in a "sane" and "moderate" way. In making his case, TR urged his listeners to rise above their own selfish material interests by working to promote the rights of the laboring man.

Dilating on another of Croly's themes, he appealed to their disinterestedness, arguing that precisely because they would not personally benefit from improving the plight of the workers, they were ideally poised to take up the lead. "I don't wish to see a movement for the betterment of conditions of labor tainted with the selfishness inevitably accompanying a movement where those who are benefited are the only ones that take the lead in it." Workers, he thought, had little choice but to consider their own selfish interests, but businessmen enjoyed the luxury of being able to rise above their material concerns. They therefore had an obligation both to their country and to their moral principles to do so. Acting out of disinterestedness would remove the "taint of selfishness" from their actions, demonstrating that businessmen did not view material prosperity as an end in itself, which Roosevelt dismissed as a "sordid type of life." Instead, he appealed to the higher principle of brotherhood, reminding them that they were their brothers' keepers, duty bound to offer "disinterested labor, effort, and leadership."[89]

Croly's criticism of equal rights as a footrace also found its way into Roosevelt's speech to the chamber. Once again, the Colonel was not content simply to have each runner compete in the race, running at his own speed, but insisted that the rules of the game needed to be changed to afford, "as far as humanly possible," the opportunity for each individual to compete on a level playing field. But in contrast to his argument in "The Progressives, Past and Present," where he maintained that the political principles of the founders no longer applied under current economic and social conditions, TR insisted that he was upholding the intention of the Framers, which he here interpreted as treating each man on his worth as a man, neither helped by privileges he had not earned, nor hindered by those he did not possess. In one sense, he was correct: in rejecting monarchy and titles of nobility, the Framers *had* "set their faces like flint" against hereditary privilege. But Roosevelt was surely misleading when he suggested that he was faithful to

their intentions. As he understood perfectly well, the Framers believed that
the rule of law and the protection of private rights would be sufficient to
produce a free and just society. The whole point of New Nationalism was
that these guarantees were no longer enough. Justice, or more accurately
social justice, required the government actively to intervene to bring about
a greater degree of economic equality.

Aside from this rhetorical sleight of hand, there was also the question of
tone. Granting that he was focusing on the particular temptations and vices
to which businessmen were prone (just as he did when he addressed audiences of laborers),[90] it is difficult to understand how Roosevelt thought he
could persuade the members of the chamber of commerce when he could
scarcely disguise his disdain for their way of life. How would this crowd of
largely self-made businessmen have reacted to Roosevelt, a son of inherited
wealth, as he lectured them to avoid "sordid content and self-satisfaction"
and preached the rewards of disinterestedness and a "higher life" of ren-
dering service to others? Not only were Roosevelt's true feelings too close
to the surface, but his rhetoric suggested that he was uncertain whether to
appeal to their fear that if they did not support him the movement would
be taken over by radicals, or to their pride in being able to rise above their
material interests and fall in with the forward movement.

Lastly, there was also something mildly amusing about a self-proclaimed
radical attempting to instruct conservatives about what it meant to be a
conservative, just as there was when Roosevelt dropped the name of Edmund Burke into his presidential messages, hoping to cloak his progressive
proposals in conservative garb. Having cast the debate in terms of progress
and reaction, TR sought to close off all but one avenue for conservatives:
their job was to temper, but never to obstruct the inevitable forward movement.[91] Roosevelt was unwilling to grant that there may have been a principled and not simply "reactionary" alternative to his progressive vision.
To put it another way, he did not believe that the principles of the Framers
could be adapted to the conditions facing the country at the beginning of
the twentieth century. Only a wholesale reconstruction of the American
republic, "conservatively" implemented, to be sure, could align the United
States with the "world movement" he had glimpsed in Europe.

NEW NATIONALISM AND POPULAR RULE

In the wake of bruising defeats in the 1910 midterm elections, insurgents,
led by Wisconsin Senator Robert M. La Follette, formed the National Pro-

gressive Republican League to rally progressives for a primary challenge to Taft. Although Roosevelt had declined to endorse Taft for reelection, he also kept his distance from the league. Under La Follette's leadership, the league had endorsed direct democratic reforms that put it at odds with New Nationalism. Whereas Roosevelt's plan sought to expand the regulatory powers of the national government to deal with the social problems created by industrial capitalism, the league came out squarely behind reforms that would return power to the people. Its Declaration of Principles called for popular election of senators; direct primaries for elective officials; direct election of delegates to national nominating conventions, with the opportunity for delegates to express their choice for president and vice president; amendments to the state constitutions providing for the initiative, referendum, and recall; and a corrupt practices act.

Despite these differences, Roosevelt took it upon himself to introduce readers of *The Outlook* to "Progressive Nationalism," emphasizing points of agreement with his speeches in Denver and Osawatomie and soft-pedaling its direct democracy elements.[92] But he was clearly searching for some way to bring the eastern and western progressives together. A follow-up essay, "Nationalism and Popular Rule," attempted just this. Roosevelt began by praising *The Promise of American Life,* calling it "the most profound and illuminating study of our national conditions which has appeared in many years." But instead of emphasizing Croly's (and his) reliance on a greatly expanded national government to carry out the will of the people, he now warned that unless the United States succeeded in establishing a government "of, by, and for the people," its national existence "both historically and in world interest" would lose "most of its point." By assimilating Croly to the Gettysburg Address, Roosevelt attempted to bridge the gap between New Nationalism and direct democracy, and then for good measure, align it by way of Lincoln with the world movement.

After this deft opening, Roosevelt then moved on to consider recent progressive demands for popular government, declaring that "most Western Progressives, and many Eastern Progressives (including the present writer), will assent to these five propositions, at least in principle." Although conceding that on most of the points there was room for honest differences of opinion, Roosevelt provisionally endorsed four of the five principles. Without going into the merits of the argument for the direct election of senators, he instead pointed out that the Framers' intentions regarding the election of the president had been quietly reversed, providing further evidence for the progressive position that the Constitution must "evolve" to keep pace with the times.

The biggest stumbling block for eastern progressives was the proposition calling for the initiative, the referendum, and the recall. Ideally, TR still believed that if legislatures were composed of high-minded men who represented the needs of the people rather than the special interests, there would be no need for such reforms. And, of course, the people already possessed a remedy: they could vote corrupt representatives out of office. That citizens had not always roused themselves to do so should temper the insurgents' hopes for the initiative, referendum, and the recall. Roosevelt was especially concerned that too-frequent reliance upon these devices would undermine the deliberative function of representative assemblies, drawing citizens into the "minutiae of legislation" where they had no expertise or holding the public hostage to frivolous ballot measures. He exhorted supporters to keep in mind that these devices were only means to good government and not ends in themselves. Yet having voiced his reservations, TR reminded opponents that the reason the referendum and initiative had been proposed was because representative bodies had frequently failed in their duty to represent the people. New England progressives especially had no reason to object to direct democracy in the West when their own region had perfected the "much more radical" town meeting. By the end of the year, he was privately signaling that, whatever the defects of direct democracy, he could support such measures.[93]

Conspicuously missing from this discussion, however, was any mention of the courts. By his own admission, Roosevelt had "blundered" in attacking the courts so frontally in Denver, and he was careful not to make that mistake again. In a series of editorials in *The Outlook* on "Nationalism and the Judiciary," Roosevelt focused on the question of constitutional interpretation, drawing on historical examples and citing judicial opinions and legal scholars to cloak his arguments with authority. He rejected the idea that the Constitution embodied timeless principles, which it was the task of the courts to apply, arguing instead for an evolutionary or historicist approach: "the courts must grow and change in opinion, just as other bodies of national expression grow, and the nation itself grows."[94] In particular, he attacked the "doctrinaire theory of eighteenth century individualism," best summed up in "right to absolute liberty of contract," which he thought ultimately contradicted itself, using the principle of liberty to "enslave" wage earners.

Not surprisingly, the jurists and statesmen he most admired seemed to be progressives *avant la lettre*. He agreed completely with one Judge Alfred Spring of New York, who praised John Marshall because he made the Constitution "march" to the tune of progress "by vesting power in simple, terse sentences, adaptable to circumstances as they come along." In turn, Marshall was merely channeling the "spirit" of Hamilton, whom TR singled out as the least demagogic of public men. He was, therefore, to be trusted when he observed that "a government ought to contain in itself every power requisite to the full accomplishment of the objects committed to its care, and to the complete execution of the trusts for which it is responsible, free from every other control but a regard to the public good *and to the sense of the people*."[95] Roosevelt himself added the emphasis, but wittingly or not, he completely distorted Hamilton's meaning.

The argument was taken from *Federalist* No. 31, where Hamilton was defending the general power of the national government over taxation to fulfill its specific responsibilities for the national defense and to secure the public peace. These were "the objects committed to its care," not thorough government control of the economy. As anyone familiar with his argument in *Federalist* No. 78 would recognize, Hamilton was emphatically not making the case that the courts ought to respond to *"the sense of the people"* to redistribute wealth. If anything, Hamilton, much like the younger Roosevelt, believed that the duty of the courts was to safeguard the Constitution and individual rights, including property rights, from an overbearing majority and their all-too-responsive representatives.

Although deploring the "substantive due process" interpretations that had led the Court to elevate the "liberty of contract," Roosevelt was not altogether opposed to the idea of "substantive due process" himself. For what else could his statement that he was not for "merely legal justice," but for "ethical justice, moral justice," or at other times, "social justice," mean? If justice was not to be found in the written law, established precedents, the intentions of the Framers, or in the first principles underlying the law, then where was it? As a progressive, TR was now convinced that justice unfolded historically, though there was nothing mysterious about its meaning. All that the ethical judge needed was a "modern type of mind," one that showed sympathy for the plight of the average workingman rather than allegiance to formal legal principles, established precedents, or what he regarded as the obsolete political principles of the eighteenth century.[96]

Here and elsewhere, Roosevelt was open to a number of approaches to constitutional interpretation: judicial deference to the political branches, pragmatism, and sociological jurisprudence, as long as they delivered the desired results. Precedents, he thought, citing Dean George Kirchway of the Columbia Law School, should not be regarded as necessarily binding, but treated as "signposts" for judicial consideration. The courts were not interpreters of "obscure oracles handed down from a remote antiquity," but rather "interpreters of the popular sense of morality and right and the popular sense of justice."[97] In short, Roosevelt was making a case for what would later be known as "the living Constitution." But rather than appeal directly to the people to amend the Constitution, TR argued that the Courts, drawing on the advice of experts, could quietly and more efficiently bring the Constitution up to date. This, he insisted, was what the American people demanded, and citing Croly, he warned that the failure of the courts to respond would erode popular confidence in their national government.

Only in the last of these editorials did Roosevelt broach the ticklish subject of judicial recall. What should be done if the courts continued to ignore "true human justice," as Professor Roscoe Pound put it, if they persisted in arguing from first principles of reason and logic to the detriment of "the human factor"? Roosevelt took note of proposals circulating in the states to recall federal judges, or to limit their term of office, but he rejected them both because he thought they would undermine the dignity and usefulness of the federal judiciary. He did not, however, altogether rule out the removal of federal judges along the lines laid down in the New York and Massachusetts constitutions. In these "conservative" states, judges could be removed on address by a sufficient majority of both houses of the legislature, in effect making removal more akin to impeachment than to recall. If there were objections even to this method, then the only alternative was to keep up the pressure through vigorous criticism.[98]

However much Roosevelt disagreed with certain Supreme Court decisions, notably *Knight* and *Lochner,* it was the state courts that drew most of his ire. Although the states possessed "police powers" that permitted them to enact legislation to protect the health, safety, and morals of their citizens, in a few high-profile cases the courts had invalidated these laws. As a young assemblyman in New York, Roosevelt had fought successfully to enact a law regulating tenement factories, only to see the New York Court of Appeals strike it down. More recently, that same court had declared it unconstitutional to fix the closing hours of work for women laborers and had struck down workmen's compensation laws on the ground that they violated "liberty of contract." But, as Howard Gilman has shown, state courts were nowhere near as hostile to social legislation as Roosevelt suggested; nor was the case against *Lochner* as simple and straightforward as he made it out to be.[99]

In an impassioned speech that October on "The Conservation of Womanhood and Childhood," and again in an editorial in *The Outlook,* "Judges and Progress," in January 1912, Roosevelt came out squarely in favor of the recall of unpopular state court decisions. TR now regarded as "self-evident" the right of the people to determine for themselves whether they wished to see these policies adopted, rather than surrender their power to the courts. In his view, the courts had imposed an "outworn philosophy" on the people, "usurping" the power of the people to set their own course. Citing not only the usual cast of jurists, legal scholars, and now social workers (who provided the facts for the new sociological jurisprudence), Roosevelt also invoked international legal standards, observing that such measures had already been enacted by "nearly all civilized countries in Europe, by Australia, by New Zealand, by the Transvaal, by the principal provinces of the Dominion of Canada, and, in a partial form at least, by one or more of the South American Republics." If these civilized nations had decreed such laws just and desirable, then American constitutionalism must give way to the world movement.[100]

To that end, TR "earnestly" recommended that the next New York State Constitutional Convention and "any or all other States where it may be found necessary" include provisions that "will enable the people to decide for themselves, by popular ballot after due deliberation, finally and without appeal, what the law of the land shall be in cases such as those I have mentioned where the courts of the State have refused to allow the people to establish justice and equity." To assure ample time for deliberation, he thought that no vote should take place within six months of a court ruling. The decision of the people would then be final, unless the Supreme Court weighed in on the matter. Roosevelt's speech before the Ohio Constitutional Convention the following February would simply enlarge and extend what he had been saying to select audiences for months.

In both his New York address and essay in *The Outlook*, Roosevelt was also careful to point out that he was not advocating the "recall" of individual judges, but only of their misguided decisions. And even then, he emphasized that this was a second-best solution. Better it would be if judges deferred to legislatures in the first place, rather than impose their own views on the populace. Nor was he seeking to apply the principle of recall to all court decisions. Suits affecting private individuals, or cases between man and man, should be decided without recourse to popular opinion and "with inflexible regard to the eternal principles of justice." Recall of judicial opinions applied only to those great questions of public policy, which the people had never surrendered to the courts or to anyone else, and must be allowed to decide for themselves. How they would distinguish between the "eternal principles of justice" informing their private suits and the great public law questions where justice and equity clearly "evolved" was not a question Roosevelt addressed.[101] Nor was it clear what recourse the people might have from decisions made by independent administrators who, if the former president had anything to do with it, would increasingly be making policy.

It was not that Roosevelt had failed to consider the relation between the bureaucracy and the people, but rather that he tended to view it as unproblematic. Although free government meant that the people ruled themselves, they also welcomed "leadership and advice." Citizens, he averred, would be "content to let experts do the expert business" to which they were assigned, "without fussy interference," so long as they carried out the general aims of the people and did not try to substitute their own. Like Croly, Roosevelt did not consider that these "disinterested" experts might turn out to have interests of their own, or that they might carry out their mission in a high-handed rather than high-minded manner.[102]

If, by the end of 1911, Roosevelt had come to accept the direct democratic reforms favored by western insurgents, he remained steadfast in his belief that the best way to bring the corporations to heel was through regulation. Two recent developments, he thought, had strengthened the case for increased government "supervision" of the economy. First, the Supreme Court had revisited its interpretation of the Sherman Act in its Standard Oil and Tobacco Trust opinions, handed down that spring. In what was arguably a reversal of its 1897 decision in *United States v. Trans-Missouri Freight Association*, the Court now held that the Sherman Act prohibited only unreasonable combinations in restraint of trade. Insurgents, who favored vigorous antitrust prosecutions to smash big business, were infuriated by the decisions, but Roosevelt sensed a political opportunity. A scaled-back Sherman Act meant there was a greater need for government to regulate all other businesses operating in interstate commerce to make sure that they served the public interest.[103]

Second, although Taft continued to support TR's proposed regulatory policies, he had also shown an increased appetite for trust-busting, which proved popular with the public.[104] The final straw came when the president announced, on Roosevelt's birthday no less, that he was initiating an antitrust suit against U.S. Steel for its acquisition of the Tennessee Coal and Iron Company. Roosevelt had personally approved the merger during the financial panic of 1907, assuring J. P. Morgan that the acquisition would not run afoul of the government's antitrust enforcement. Taft's action prompted Roosevelt to lash out in an editorial in *The Outlook*, defending both his decision and his overall regulatory policy.

In "The Trusts, the People, and the Square Deal," Roosevelt once again called for the establishment of a regulatory agency armed with powers comparable to those of the ICC, including the power "in extreme cases" to set prices on goods produced by monopolies, "as rates on railroads are now controlled." Ultimately, he thought that some administrative agency of the national government would have to be given "complete power over the organization and capitalization of all business concerns in inter-State commerce," including labor questions. He brushed aside charges that such far-reaching government control would eventuate in socialism by arguing that his "conservative" policies would in fact defuse growing support for socialism.[105] The only sensible alternative to socialist demands for the na-tionalization of ownership was thoroughgoing government control, not in-discriminate antitrust enforcement. Faced with a choice between criminal antitrust prosecution, as U.S. Steel now was, or administrative regulation, Morgan and his interests saw even more clearly the advantages to "cooper-ating" with the government and rallied behind the Colonel. How he would bring together corporate leaders and insurgents who demanded direct de-mocracy and trust-busting remained to be seen.

THE MAN IN THE ARENA

To some extent, Roosevelt was playing defense with the insurgents. Wis-consin Senator Robert La Follette had already announced his candidacy in June 1911 and won the support of prominent progressives, including the Pinchots. But after a disastrous speaking engagement in early February, La Follette's campaign collapsed, clearing the path for Roosevelt. Appearing before the Ohio Constitutional Convention on February 21, the Colonel unofficially declared his candidacy with manly bravado: "My hat is in the ring and I am stripped to the buff."[106] Roosevelt clearly relished the op-portunity to introduce his platform to the public in Taft's home state, and especially at the Ohio Constitutional Convention. In contrast to the state legislatures, which were all too often dominated by machine politicians, delegates to constitutional conventions were widely believed to be more disinterested than the "special interests" that had corrupted the political process.[107]

Once again, Roosevelt tried to cloak his new understanding of property rights in the mantle of Lincoln, repeating the sixteenth president's state-ments on labor and capital to support his view that property rights were merely provisional and had to be justified by their benefit to the public.[108] As radical as this notion was, however, it paled by comparison with the stir caused by Roosevelt's endorsement of the initiative, referendum, and especially, judicial recall. To his critics, Roosevelt's public support for direct democracy seemed nothing less than a rejection of constitutional government. Roosevelt, by contrast, saw it as a *restoration* of constitutionalism, though there was good reason to doubt whether the constitution he wished to "restore" was that of the Framers.

In *The Federalist*, Publius had ruled out direct democracy in favor of representative democracy. Indeed, so central was representation that Publius had made that principle the very definition of republican government. Representation, Madison had argued in *Federalist* No. 10, would create a space between the people and their government, filtering out the destructive passions and selfish motives that might prevail when the people conducted public affairs themselves. By encouraging deliberation and compromise, representation would not simply serve as a substitute for pure democracy, but would actually improve upon it by safeguarding against majority faction or tyranny. In *Federalist* No. 39, he had gone even further, arguing that representation did not even require direct elections. Later, discussing the distinctive virtues of the Senate, Publius maintained that what distinguished the American republic from its classical models was precisely the "exclusion of the people in their collective capacity from any share" in the operation of government. As a last resort, the authors of *The Federalist* relied on the courts to provide additional security for private rights.

Earlier in his political career, Roosevelt himself had staunchly defended the old constitutional order. But he was now convinced that party bosses had distorted the Framers' intention, serving large corporate interests and manipulating the votes of newly arrived immigrants instead of fostering the public good. Although the Framers had not anticipated the development of the party system, the authors of *The Federalist* would probably not have been surprised by Roosevelt's indictment of state legislatures. As Madison observed, most representatives were nothing more than "advocates and parties to the causes which they determine." This in fact was one reason why he had defended the *large* republic; by extending the sphere, he hoped to ensure that a better quality of citizen would be elected and that by representing more interests, he would be beholden to no one interest in particular. How to ensure that the state legislatures reflected the will of the people, rather than those of the special interests, was the immediate question before Roosevelt. There was also a more general question: what was the place of these reforms in the constitutional order? Or more precisely, what was the constitutional order in which these mechanisms would operate?

Roosevelt's remarks in support of the initiative and the referendum suggested that he was not entirely clear in his own mind. At times, he seemed to view them as a way to correct the defects that had crept into the Framers' Constitution. Here and elsewhere, he was careful to insist that he was not recommending that these devices be adopted everywhere, but only where the legislature had manifestly thwarted the people's will. Far from destroying representative government, these mechanisms would help to insure that it functioned properly—in the public interest. Direct democracy was not a substitute for representation, as some of his critics charged, but a way to hold it accountable.[109] Indeed, there was a case to be made for these reforms, provided that they did help to restore the Framers' Constitution.

Responding to his critics, TR declared himself an emphatic "believer in constitutionalism," opposed only to the "false constitutionalism" and "false statesmanship" that attempted to "trick" the people out of their rightful power, much as Aristotle in the *Politics* had warned oligarchs against devices meant to deceive the people. His rhetoric was meant to reassure, but the Colonel's discussion of the ends of government, the purpose for which constitutions are ultimately established, suggested that his constitutionalism had wandered far from that of the Framers. The aim of good government, he insisted in words that closely tracked *The Promise of American Life*, was "to secure by genuine popular rule a high average of moral and material well-being among our citizens" by redistributing wealth more justly.[110] Popular rule would promote the "efficiency" of the individual, removing the obstacles that prevented him from working toward "a higher and better and fuller life" for himself and the nation as a whole. There should be, Roosevelt advised the Ohio delegates, nothing that would block the power of the people from doing what they thought was necessary to promote the "general welfare."[111] This clause, along with "We the people" and an overbroad reading of the power to "regulate" interstate "commerce," would become the rallying cry of progressives from Roosevelt's day to the present, providing the constitutional fig leaf for the transformation of the old order. Roosevelt and his critics were talking past one another: each in his own way was committed to "constitutionalism," but they meant very different things.

The issue was joined most forcefully when Roosevelt came out in support of judicial recall. The Colonel was particularly outraged that in his home state of New York the Court of Appeals had declared unconstitutional several reform measures, seemingly ignoring the state's responsibilities for the health, safety, and morals of its citizens. As more recent scholarly studies have shown, however, such decisions were actually quite rare. Moreover, judges who struck down social legislation during this period were not doing so because they wished to impose their own laissez-faire philosophy on others, but because they believed that the police powers of the state were only legitimate insofar as they protected everyone and did not discriminate either in favor of or against any one class. This was precisely what Roosevelt, instructed by Croly, now sought to challenge. Legislation *ought* to discriminate in favor of working men and women so that they could more efficiently serve the nation.[112]

Citing "one of the ablest jurists in the United States" (who nevertheless remained nameless), Roosevelt lashed out against the courts for disregarding "the aroused moral sentiment of the community" and overstepping their legitimate powers by making the law, rather than simply judging it.[113] He paid lip service to the need for an independent judiciary that would stand up to "popular clamor," but the thrust of his argument was that judges could not take refuge in "mere legal formalism" devoid of sympathy for and understanding of popular needs. Compounding the problem, he thought, was that when the courts declared a law unconstitutional they effectively left the people with no political remedy other than the cumbersome process of amending their constitution. In addition to supporting judicial recall, then, Roosevelt also recommended that the Ohio delegates make it easier to amend their constitutions so that the will of the people might more easily prevail.

Considering the two alternatives, Roosevelt believed that recall was preferable to constitutional amendments that would strip the courts of their power to review social reform legislation and narrow the scope of due process. The amendment process took too long, was too cumbersome, and, as the history of the Fourteenth Amendment illustrated all too clearly, could be misinterpreted by the judiciary. Because recall involved only one court decision, the people could execute their will swiftly, without fear that it would be misconstrued later. Judicial recall would help the people to appreciate the progressive virtue of efficiency. By circumventing the forms, Roosevelt would produce "better results," and more quickly.[114]

Although Roosevelt was also willing to support the recall of particular judges on grounds of corruption or for adhering to an "outworn" judicial philosophy, most of his attention continued to be focused on the recall of particular decisions. The "Charter of Democracy" and subsequent speeches laid out the "machinery" in more detail. If a sizable portion of the population opposed a ruling, they ought to be able to petition to bring it before the voters in a subsequent election. To ensure adequate deliberation, Roosevelt was now willing to extend the waiting period from the six months he had initially proposed to two years. If, after that time the voters upheld the recall, the decision would be final unless reversed by the Supreme Court.[115]

Roosevelt brushed aside worries that the people might disagree, or even that they might quickly reverse themselves. Had not the courts, even the Supreme Court, done precisely the same things?

Addressing the Ohio Constitutional Convention, Roosevelt could pass over the thorny question of whether he would apply judicial recall to the *federal* courts. But the logic of his position—that the people should rule absolutely—suggested that there was no principled reason that recall could not be extended to the federal judiciary, up to and including the Supreme Court. In a private letter to Henry Stimson shortly before the convention, Roosevelt conceded as much. Though personally upright, Justices Peckham, Fuller, and Brewer were "menaces to the welfare of the Nation, who ought not to have been left there a day." Moreover, because he regarded Lincoln's attacks on *Dred Scott* as practically a recall and thought that there should have been some way short of impeachment to remove Chief Justice Taney from the bench, limiting recall to the state courts was simply a prudential decision designed to placate conservatives. To be sure, Roosevelt continued to insist that he had no sympathy with "sweeping general attacks" upon the federal judiciary, but he clearly had even less sympathy with the refusal of these courts to uphold social justice. After Columbus, he was even more emphatic, writing to Croly that eventually the people would take control of interpreting the Constitution "even in national matters."[116]

Just at the moment that he was announcing his candidacy, Roosevelt's public endorsement of judicial recall—even though restricted to the state courts—set off a torrent of criticism, pushing him back onto the defensive and undoing much of the work he had done to woo more conservative Republicans to his cause. Assessing his move, George Mowry called it "an egregious mistake," sincerely felt, but "disastrous."[117] For the rest of the primary season, Roosevelt would be forced to defend judicial recall, drawing attention away from other more popular elements of his program. Judicial recall would cost him the support of Elihu Root and Henry Cabot Lodge,[118] both of whom had endorsed his New Nationalism, and virtually guarantee that he would lose the Republican nomination. For Roosevelt, however, the courts were central to the political reconstruction he envisioned, and not to have taken them on would have rendered his program of social and industrial reform toothless.

Taft, a former federal judge, was also quick to pounce on Roosevelt's proposal, branding it an attack on "well ordered liberty" and the constitutional order. As John Milton Cooper, Jr., has rightly observed, the upcoming election would keep these issues in the fore, raising questions of such moment that they "verged on political philosophy." Indeed, as political scientist Sidney Milkis has argued, in a real sense, "the most important exchange in the constitutional debate" would not be between Roosevelt and Wilson, but between "TR and Taft," the self-proclaimed constitutionalist in the race.[119]

Forced to defend judicial recall, Roosevelt went on in subsequent speeches to challenge Taft's assertion that the will of the people needed to be hemmed in by constitutional restraints. Citing "that keen and profound thinker," James Bryce, Roosevelt dismissed Tocqueville's observation that the principal danger to republican government was majority tyranny.[120] But the idea was not some exotic French import, to be refuted by invoking a British authority, however illustrious. It was rather the animating argument of *The Federalist*. Madison had famously warned in *Federalist* No. 10 against the dangers of majority faction animated by a passion or interest adverse to the rights of others or to the public good, and disputes over the amounts and kinds of property ranked high on his list of likely dangers. Hamilton, too, had worried about majority faction, though his fears took a somewhat different form. In both the opening and closing essays of *The Federalist*, Hamilton had raised the specter of the demagogue who incited the people to unjust action by posing as a friend of liberty, an argument Roosevelt himself had made against Bryan in the election of 1896 and against Jackson's war on the bank in *Thomas Hart Benton*. Only a complex constitution could place sufficient obstacles in the way of majority faction while at the same time allowing the majority to rule. It was a mark of their political wisdom that the people had recognized their fallibilities and sought to restrain them.

Roosevelt now rejected this argument, insisting that with the rise of industrial capitalism the real danger arose from minority tyranny, that is, from the bosses and special interests. Fears of majority tyranny were not only mistaken, they also betrayed an unwarranted distrust, and even "dread," of the American people.[121] In contrast to Taft and his "reactionary" supporters, TR looked to the kindly Lincoln, who, he thought, trusted in the people completely. But this was a sentimental and misleading portrait. Although Lincoln tried to win men over by persuasion and understanding, urged sympathy with human foibles, and displayed a noble magnanimity, his view of human nature was rooted in a classical liberal and Christian appreciation of human fallibilities. When he affirmed his commitment to government "of the people, by the people, and for the people" he was not suggesting that direct democracy should now replace the constitutional checks the people had freely imposed on their will.

To be more precise, when Lincoln announced in his First Inaugural that the people and not the Court were ultimately sovereign, he was not proposing that they recall the *Dred Scott* decision. Instead, he sought to work within the constitutional framework to overturn the decision. As chief executive, he vowed to enforce the law, but he also worked to arouse public opinion, which would determine the 1860 election and permit a change in the Court's composition, all in accord with Article III. In the end, the decision was reversed, but it took the Civil War and two constitutional amendments. *Dred Scott* was not "recalled."

DIRECT DEMOCRACY AND CHARACTER

Even as TR embraced the right of the people to rule absolutely, he was careful to insist that this right entailed a corresponding increase in responsibilities. Americans could not hope to throw off their constitutional restraints without first cultivating a strong sense of duty and self-control. Genuine self-government demanded that the individual first govern himself; he must learn to master his appetites and follow the dictates of conscience rather than self-interest. What America needed was a genuine moral awakening, one that would marry progressivism with the teaching of the Social Gospel so that citizens would come to "think of rights as developed in duty rather than only of their individual rights."[122] Although Roosevelt continued to summon Americans to the old virtues of self-control, sacrifice, courage, and personal responsibility, these virtues would now be pressed into the service of the state and its highest mission, helping citizens to see that they were truly their brothers' keepers.

Like most men and women of his class, Roosevelt had been raised in a devout Christian home, where bible reading and church attendance were woven into the fabric of family life. But the combined effect of Darwin and Hegel had been to shift the traditional Christian concern with salvation in the afterlife to the here and now. Roosevelt captured this move perfectly when he observed in *Oliver Cromwell* that in the United States all of the major faiths were learning "the grandest of all lessons, that they can best serve their God by serving their fellow men, not by wrangling among themselves, but by a generous rivalry in working for righteousness and against evil."[123] From henceforth on, religion would focus on the duties individuals owed to each other as they worked to bring about a more "ethical state" here on earth.

This new moral awakening must perforce begin with the family. No nation could hope to achieve greatness or ascend to a higher plane of civilization unless its home life was sound. "The home, based on the love of one man for one woman and the performance in common of their duty to their children, is the finest product of Christianity and civilization."[124] Accordingly, this father of six once again took aim at the "coldness," the "selfishness," the "love of ease," and "shrinking from risk" that led "cheap and shallow" men and women to put off marrying and bearing children, preferably many children. "Willful sterility is as much a crime against the race in the case of the one child or two-child marriage as in the case where there are no children." America needed a radical shift in public opinion that would "shame" those "small souls" who neglected their fundamental duty to preserve the race for the sake of "cheap self-indulgence and vapid excitement."[125] Roosevelt took every opportunity to do just that, calling such Americans unpatriotic and warning that if they did not accept their duty to have children, he for one would "not mourn" their eventual extinction because they would thus have proven that they were "not fit to cumber the ground."[126] Still, reversing the population decline would take more than a shift in public opinion: the state itself would have to assume a larger role in encouraging family formation. In the future, unmarried men might well be asked to pay a "far higher share of taxation," and it was right that they should.[127]

A Victorian through and through, Roosevelt preached sexual purity and "moral cleanliness." He warned that sexual experimentation and a general loosening of morals were signs of social decay and advised men and women to marry early. He practiced what he preached. Roosevelt himself had married right after college, and after the death of his first wife, the young widower and father of Alice had married his childhood sweetheart and sired five more "healthy children." While president, TR used his bully pulpit to reinforce this message. He called for a constitutional amendment giving the national government the power to regulate marriage and divorce, arguing that nothing was "so vitally essential to the welfare of the nation" as the "home life of the average citizen."[128] Rising divorce rates, he warned his audience at the Pacific Theological Seminary, were a sure sign that something was "rotten" in American society. So, too, was the "cuckoo" style of parenting that shifted the important work of raising children from the family onto the schools.[129] However much education might reinforce the moral lessons of the home, it could never replace them.

The first duty of the average man was to be a good husband and father, supporting his family financially and tempering discipline with love. At the same time, Roosevelt, addressing an audience of Protestant seminarians, was keen to dispel the misconception that being a decent man meant being weak. A healthy society could not afford to be divided between "nice, well-behaved, well-meaning little men with receding chins and small feet," and "robust efficient creatures who don't mean well at all." He urged ordinary Americans to stand up manfully for righteousness, by refusing to have their souls corrupted by wealth. At the same time, he urged them not to rest satisfied with "mere law honesty," which observed the letter of the law while violating its spirit.[130] If, however, a man shirked his responsibilities as husband and father, the state should actively interfere and force him to do his duty.

Although there was work for the husband and father in the home, by far the larger share of the responsibility fell to the wife and mother. For the average woman, the home was the sphere in which she could best exercise her distinctive responsibilities to care for her husband and family and to raise many healthy children. Roosevelt saw marriage as a partnership in which husband and wife were "on a full equality of right," united in "the strongest sense of duty," but in which the tasks and duties were "on many points necessarily different."[131] No mother ever had an easy time, but Roosevelt asked, "what mother would barter her experience of joy and sorrow in exchange for a life of cold selfishness, which insists upon perpetual amusement and the avoidance of care, and which often finds its fit dwelling-place in some flat designed to furnish with the least possible expenditure of effort the maximum of comfort and luxury, but in which there is literally no place for children?"[132]

Accordingly, the former president continued to press for legislation and social policies that would strengthen the family. Mothers and children should not be permitted to work in any way that interfered with their duties in the home. "The ruin of motherhood and childhood by the merciless exploitation of the labor of women and children is a crime of capital importance." At the same time, widowed mothers with children and women whose husbands had deserted them must be provided for. Drawing on the recommendations of the First White House Conference on the Care of Dependent Children, delivered in the waning months of his presidency, TR now came out in favor of mothers' pensions.[133] In cases of desertion, however, he emphasized that *the care must not be given in such way as to encourage the man to shirk his duties.* So-called reformers who, out of "sentimentality or false humanity," envisioned the state assuming primary responsibility for the family were "working for the corruption and dissolution of the entire social fabric."[134] Unlike these utopian reformers, Roosevelt was confident that he could use government to reinforce and even improve the character of its citizens, while taking care that the primary responsibility remained with the family and the individuals themselves.

Roosevelt, who would assemble what Kathleen Dalton has called his Female Brain Trust during his Bull Moose Campaign and continue to draw on them for policy proposals,[135] acknowledged that some talented women might pursue fulfilling careers outside the home, but he considered them exceptions. There were "certain old truths" that would be true as long as the world endured, and which "no amount of progress" could alter.[136] Where women were concerned, nature trumped history. "Those who suppose that the granting of the vote is going to effect radical and fundamental changes in the facts of biology, the development of instinct and its significance in human action, are fools of the very blindest kind."[137] Citing a variety of authorities, TR confidently—though mistakenly—predicted that the average ideal woman of the future would look very much like the ideal woman of his day. It was, therefore, "unfortunate" that certain leaders of the suffrage movement tried to advance their cause with public protests and "vicious" attacks on middle-class morality. *"The last way in which to secure the rights of women is to abrogate the duties of men."* He was equally impatient with those "fools" who "prattle[d]" about the need for women to pursue careers to escape "economic dependence." Marriage established a "healthy economic interdependence" between husband and wife; efforts to achieve "economic independence" based on "a false identity of economic function" spelled ruin. For good measure, Roosevelt added that any husband who treated his wife as an "economic dependent" in marriage needed "severe handling by society or the State."[138]

Consequently, throughout the primary season TR remained at best a "tepid" supporter of woman suffrage.[139] He believed that women themselves should be the only ones to decide whether, in light of their family responsibilities, they wanted the right to vote. In his view, women's suffrage was "unimportant" compared with the duties that all good citizens, men and women, must undertake. The duty of a mother was to raise her children to lives of service and to teach them that their happiness consisted in doing their duty.[140] A mother did her children no good, and indeed much harm, if out of misplaced tender-heartedness, she allowed them to grow up lazy and self-centered. She herself was to set an example of duty and love that would reach well beyond the home. In her willingness to accept a life of self-sacrifice, woman as wife and mother became the moral template for the new model citizen. For all his insistence on the manly virtues, Roosevelt's progressivism, at least in domestic politics, had a distinctly feminized side.[141]

THE CONSERVATION OF HUMAN RESOURCES

Increasingly, Roosevelt came to view efforts to strengthen the family as part of the larger conservation movement he had helped to launch. Convinced that Taft had betrayed his program, TR now tried to reclaim conservation as a campaign issue. In his New Nationalism swing across the West, Roosevelt had given two speeches addressed specifically to conservation issues, and at Osawatomie declared it "a great moral issue" that involved "the patriotic duty of insuring the safety and continuance of the nation." During his second term as president, Roosevelt had gradually expanded the reach of the movement geographically to include North America and then the world. Now he hinted at a different kind of expansion, one that would encompass human as well as natural resources. "Let me add that the health and vitality of our people are at least as well worth conserving as their forests, waters, lands, and minerals, and in this work the national government must bear a most important part."[142]

The fire at the Triangle Shirtwaist Factory in March 1911, which claimed the lives of 146 garment workers, provided him with the opportunity to drive home this point. Speaking in Manhattan that fall under the joint auspices of the Civic League and the Child Welfare League, Roosevelt began by observing that it was a crime against our children for this generation to waste its natural resources. But it was a still greater crime if we handed that heritage over to "an impoverished and debilitated" younger generation.[143] He called for the establishment of a Children's Bureau within the Department of Commerce and Labor that would gather information on the condition of working children and compile existing state legislation that might act as a spur to other states. These reforms would depend, however, upon an aroused public opinion demanding the enactment of such laws. Experts alone could accomplish nothing without the active backing of the public.

Roosevelt applauded the establishment of a state factory commission, appointed in the wake of the Triangle disaster to investigate safety and conditions in large manufacturing plants, but he was even more concerned about what went on in New York's tenement-house factories, which fell outside the commission's purview. "A home workshop is neither a home nor a factory." To call the home a "factory annex" was "an invasion of the home which should not be tolerated. The home workshop is a factory without a closing hour." For the conservation of the family, it must be outlawed.[144] On the same grounds, he also called for laws restricting the number of hours that women and children could work as well as the end of the continuous seven-day workweek. Without such protections, "what kind of government, what kind of social conditions will you have from an electorate where the grown men and women have spent their childhood in such fashion?"[145] Character and conservation now converged.

As his campaign began in earnest, Roosevelt also sought to cast business regulation as a conservation measure. An editorial in *The Outlook* entitled "The Conservation of Business—Shall We Strangle or Control It?" barely concealed Roosevelt's frustration with fickle corporations that, in the wake of the Standard Oil and Tobacco Trust court decisions, now decided that Taft's antitrust policies were preferable to Roosevelt's regulatory regime. He sought to bring the corporations back to their senses by arguing that

> just as we aim at the conservation of our physical resources, and at the conservation of the manhood, womanhood, and childhood of the people, so we must aim at the conservation, that is, at the wise control and development, of business upon the existence of which the prosperity of the whole people so largely depends. In business we must conserve ideas, conserve efficiency, conserve "up to date" methods, just as we conserve our forests, our streams, our natural resources.[146]

Only TR's regulatory policies could "conserve" those large corporations upon which the prosperity and progress of the nation ultimately depended. It was a testimony to the power of the conservation movement and the grip it held on the popular imagination that Roosevelt even attempted to couch the argument in these terms. In hindsight, however, this was only the beginning, and a modest one at that. Over the next century, the conservation movement and its contemporary offspring would continue to extend their reach over the economy, providing the rationale for ever-increasing regulatory powers.[147]

Rural life naturally provided a fertile field for conservation efforts. Until Roosevelt's presidency, the national government had largely confined itself to dispensing advice, through the Department of Agriculture, on soil conservation. But during his last year in office, Roosevelt, concerned about the steady migration from farm to city and the declining quality of rural life, established the Commission on Country Life. Through its fact-gathering mission, the Commission on Country Life had determined that farmers were not enjoying their fair share of the nation's progress and prosperity. Part of the problem was that farms were not as productive as they could be, but middlemen were also eating into the farmer's profits, keeping his returns low, while at the same time increasing costs to the consumer. Convinced that in this area, too, Taft had failed to provide leadership, TR returned in the campaign to the problems of country life, folding them into the larger conservation movement and its newfound interest in human resources.

With the European trip still fresh in his mind, Roosevelt recommended that Americans look to see what the most progressive European nations had done to improve the quality of rural life in their countries. Beyond that, he suggested using the churches as counterparts to the urban social service organizations to bring people together and organize them into co-ops. Although churches would continue to carry out their spiritual mission, Roosevelt largely viewed them as service agencies working for the "practical betterment of mankind."[148] Education, too, might be tailored to the needs of rural youth. If properly organized, farmers could be counted on to insist that the resources of the nation be shared with the people as a whole and not simply given to the privileged classes to exploit for their own benefit. With the right leadership, farmers could become a powerful political bloc, providing valuable support for the progressive movement.[149]

THE ROAD TO ARMAGEDDON

Since his return to the political stage in 1910, Roosevelt had made several different attempts to seize the leadership of the progressive wing of his party. But after his speech to the Ohio Constitutional Convention, the Colonel increasingly sensed that the Republican Party could no longer serve as a vehicle for his progressive agenda. To make matters worse, his opponents were also claiming to be progressives, proving that they had not "the faint-est conception" of what the term really meant. He would set the record straight, and in so doing, set the stage for a new kind of party realignment, one that would not simply reshuffle the deck, but effectively put an end to both the local, interest-based Democratic and Republican parties. Under his progressive leadership, the country could now rise above these low ma-terial concerns.

Given his emphasis on character, it was not surprising that TR began by contrasting the personal qualities of progressives and their opponents. The fundamental difference, "as old as civilized history," was between those in-dividuals who stood for "the forward movement," for "the uplift and bet-terment of mankind," for trust in the people and those men whose "narrow vision" and "small sympathy" closed their hearts to "the wrongs of others." Every man who fought "fearlessly and effectively" against special privilege and for social justice was entitled to call himself a progressive. Roosevelt repeated his view that progressivism was not principally a question of support for the "machinery" of direct democracy, which depended upon the particular circumstances. At the same time, failure to support these reforms where they were necessary marked one as a "reactionary." Here, Roosevelt singled out Taft's opposition to the direct primary, disputing his charge that it would promote "impulsive action" on the part of the people. Deliberate action was the desideratum, but even "impulsive action" by the people was preferable to the corrupt state conventions that had nominated Taft. In the end, the question of who was a progressive circled back to the issue of character: men of "vision" and "action" who fought for justice and fair play were entitled to use the term; those who resisted were branded as reactionaries. There were no legitimate differences of principle at stake, simply a contest between right and wrong, forward and backward.[150] If parties could be realigned on this basis, there would effectively be only one party, for who would want to be on the side of backward and wrong?[151]

Despite Roosevelt's strong showing in the Republican primaries, it was likely that the Republican Convention would nominate Taft. Speaking to his supporters at the Convention on the eve of the Republican nomination, Roosevelt was filled with righteous indignation at the national committee's decision not to seat many of the delegates pledged to him. Looking back over the course of the campaign, he regretted that so few captains of industry and corporation lawyers had joined his cause. These were men for whom life had been easy and who might have greatly strengthened the progressive movement by offering their disinterested support. The only explanation Roosevelt could offer for why they declined to do so was "class consciousness." In his eyes, they acted out of an "unmanly fear" of all change and a desire to "live softly," oblivious to the cares and toils of ordinary people. At some level, he conceded that many of them were respectable and worthy, but they lacked "all intensity of conviction," preferring to remain on "the plane of low ideals." They wanted things to go on as they were, even though the things they possessed were not "rightly theirs," and social unrest was rising. "Our opponents, the men of reaction, ask us to stand still. But we could not stand still if we would; we must either go forward or backward."[152]

To lend moral weight to his argument, Roosevelt again turned to the majestic words of Lincoln. The contest in which he was now engaged was the same one that had given birth to the Republican Party. "It is the eternal struggle between two principles—right and wrong—throughout the world. ... The one is the common right of humanity, the other the divine right of kings. It is the same principle in whatever shape it develops itself. It is the same spirit that says: 'You toil and work and earn bread, and I will eat it.'

No matter in what shape it comes . . . it is the same tyrannical principle." In his view, there was no difference between slaveholders or tyrannical kings and wealthy businessmen—all of them were parasites, living off the labor of others. What Roosevelt failed to see was that the injustices against which he was fighting were simply not of the same magnitude as those Lincoln battled.

For one thing, industrial workers, many of them first-generation immigrants, surely labored under harsh conditions, but they were not, in Marx's terminology, "wage slaves" tethered to their jobs. Life in America held more promise—if not for them, then certainly for their children—than they could hope for in their old countries, and most of them knew it. For another, the businessmen he attacked *did* work. Many, as Lincoln observed, had started out modestly and risen to success. Consequently, Roosevelt's attempt to cast his opponents as reactionaries allied with the forces of tyranny was not a winning rhetorical strategy.[153] Since Lincoln was his ideal, he might have heeded the lesson of his Temperance Address, which warned reformers not to preach in "thundering tones of anathema and denunciation." Instead, ignoring even his own advice in *Oliver Cromwell,* he concluded his speech with the rallying cry, "we stand at Armageddon and we battle for the Lord," apparently convinced that his views and those of the Lord were the same.[154]

Denied the nomination of the Republican Party, the Colonel decided to bolt—even though it was unlikely that he could win the presidency as a third-party candidate. Since he had launched his political career in 1884 by declaring his loyalty to the Republican Party even though dissatisfied with its choice, the question is why did he bolt in 1912?[155] Of course, ambition had something to do with it, though it was not the vulgar sort that desired merely power. Roosevelt's soul was moved by considerations of honor and greatness, his own and that of his country—both real and imagined. Especially since his European tour, he had sensed that America was part of a larger "world movement," pointing toward loftier ideals and new arrangements of power. He had, as Jane Addams observed in her speech seconding him as the Progressive Party candidate for president, "caught the significance of the modern movement." Starting in the 1880s with Germany, the nations of Europe, each in their own way, had moved toward the creation of welfare states. If, TR warned, the United States did not take "sane" steps to catch up, the only alternative would be violent revolution and class warfare.[156] The increasing appeal of the Socialist Party, committed to the overthrow of the capitalist system, added urgency to his message. Neither of the two major parties offered a way forward; they were nothing but "husks." In

TR's mind, the Progressive Party offered the only sensible alternative to un-fettered capitalism on the one hand and scientific socialism on the other.

Having broken with the conservatives in the Republican Party, Roosevelt now threw his lot in completely with his Social Gospel and Progressive base. The third way he proposed would not be simply welfare capitalism, but some form of democratic socialism. If the state did not actually own the means of production, it would heavily regulate them, and impose pro-gressive taxes to pay for social welfare programs. He would try to co-opt softer socialist support by incorporating many of the party's policy propos-als shorn of their class warfare rhetoric, while reassuring Americans that socialism came in many forms and that not all of them were evil. In fact, he considered the socialism of many of his followers nothing more than an advanced form of liberalism.[157] Roosevelt and his following of Social Gospelers and political activists, sporting their red bandanas, would help America to catch up with the forward movement and complete the great work of national reconstruction. If he succeeded, he would help to usher in a new republic; if he failed, at least he would fail nobly. It was a "duty" that had to be undertaken, and no one else, he was convinced, could do it.

Duty was not the only reason he bolted. TR challenged the Republican establishment because he believed he had been done an injustice, and for a man like Roosevelt, it was unthinkable not to fight back. He had, after all, won the vast majority of delegates selected in state primaries. If the people had been allowed to vote in Republican primaries throughout the United States, the Colonel did not doubt that he would have been their over-whelming favorite. But instead, the national committee, with Elihu Root as temporary chair, had rejected many of the delegates pledged to him. Under the circumstances, Roosevelt believed that he had no alternative but to fight for what was right. When duty and self-righteousness coincided, Roosevelt was bound to answer the call.

BULL MOOSE

By the time the Progressive Convention met in August, Roosevelt knew who all three of his opponents would be and tailored his "Confession of Faith" partly in response to them. The big upset was that the Democrats had chosen former Princeton political science professor and one term Gov-ernor of New Jersey, Woodrow Wilson, allowing the Democrats to claim that they, too, embraced the forward movement. TR therefore stressed that he himself had not become a progressive by reading about it in the library or studying in his "closet," but by long experience in political life. Against the perennial Socialist candidate, Eugene V. Debs, the Colonel cast himself as the "sensible" radical alternative. Unlike Debs, he did not wish to abolish private property or discourage entrepreneurial risk taking altogether. Instead of emphasizing class conflict, he appealed to the ethical precepts of the Social Gospel, reminding Americans that they were indeed their brothers' keepers. As he had earlier written, this precept did not require individuals to ignore their interests entirely, but it did enjoin them to act on the principle that "What is mine I will in good measure make thine also."[158]

The Progressive Party platform would establish a new "contract with the people," ensuring that government served their needs, rather than the interests of corrupt party machines. Most of the proposals in the "Confession of Faith" were not new: direct democratic reforms, enhanced regulatory measures, redoubled conservation efforts, and increased calls for social justice.[159] Regarding the latter, the task of the "industrial statesman" was first to encourage prosperity and then to see that it was distributed fairly. Casting the issue in terms of conservation, he called for measures to prevent "human waste." The federal government should collect from businesses statistics about the number of deaths, injuries, and occupational diseases and then establish minimum health and safety standards. Convinced that minimum wages were a necessity, he supported impartial commissions to establish them. Even though there was no explicit constitutional warrant, he had reason to hope that forward-thinking judges would discover some way to uphold these measures. Workers, he added, should be paid a "living wage," one that would allow the wage earner to care for his family, save for old age, and still have enough left over for education and recreation. Night labor for women and children should be ended and the seven-day workweek abolished. In those industries where continuous operation was required, he urged three shifts of eight hours each, rather than two of twelve hours. Recognizing the importance of the women's reform network in the Progressive Party, he moved from a previously "tepid" defense of women's suffrage to a full-throated endorsement.

In addition to these social justice reforms, Roosevelt now for the first time came out in favor of measures that would provide workers with social *security* by offering insurance against sickness, unemployment, and old age. Unlike workers' compensation, these conditions had not previously been considered "liabilities" because they occurred "naturally" and no blame attached to them.[160] It was, however, "abnormal" to expect workers to shoulder these costs alone; the burden should be shared by industries, employers, wage earners, and "perhaps the people at large."[161] The German welfare state could serve as a model, with the caveat that any such system be "adapted to our different life and habits of thought."[162]

Roosevelt also singled out Germany's successful policy of promoting "cooperation" between business and government. Only by conforming to "the world movement" could America hope to compete successfully in international trade. Citing the work of Charles Van Hise, president of the University of Wisconsin, Roosevelt praised his efforts at making the state a laboratory for social and industrial experiments. Van Hise's advocacy of "concentration, co-operation and control" offered another way for TR to advance his own views of the proper relation between business and government. Concentration would permit economies of scale, while cooperation among smaller businesses would eliminate the "waste" that resulted from unfettered competition. Granting these first two factors, control by regulatory agencies was essential to ensure "fair competition, elimination of unfair practices, conservation of our natural resources, fair wages, good social conditions, and reasonable prices."[163] The progressive plan would loosely follow the German model, with the state and business working "cooperatively" to promote the general welfare.

In another striking example of how localities might serve as laboratories for social experimentation, Roosevelt suggested that Alaska might make a good test case for efficient federal intervention. Precisely because the territory was so undeveloped, it offered the best possible conditions for trying out progressive remedies that would be "difficult to apply in old settled communities without preliminary experiment."[164] To that end, he recommended that railways and telegraph lines be publicly constructed, owned, and operated. Government leases should favor immediate development of natural resources, with threats of forfeiture and taxes to discourage speculation. Roosevelt's idea of experimentation was limited to discovering which progressive programs were most effective.

For the third time in his speech, TR lavished praise upon Germany, this time for the "efficiency and wisdom" of its tariff policy. Roosevelt had no doubt that a protective tariff was necessary and desirable; he categorically rejected Britain's policy of free trade. But in America, where Congress established the tariff schedules, the rates tended to favor the interests of business. Instead, the United States should follow the German example, and establish a permanent commission of nonpartisan experts that would "scientifically" determine what the tariff should be, taking into account the interests of the consumer and the wage earner rather than those of the business classes. Although Roosevelt acknowledged that the Constitution clearly gave the legislature the power to impose tariffs, he thought that, for the good of the nation, Congress should cede this power to an independent commission.

At the same time, the Colonel denied that the tariff was in any significant way responsible for the high cost of living, which he acknowledged to be a problem. To provide relief to the consumer, he recommended instead a system of price controls, progressive taxes on "swollen fortunes," and taxes on land held for speculation, all the while trying to reassure the captains of industry that he did not wish to discourage entrepreneurial initiative. But Roosevelt's strong suit had never been economics. From his failed ranching venture in the Badlands, he had never shown much interest in the business side of things and seemed to have only the vaguest notion of how companies prospered. As he reportedly confessed to one associate, "It tires me to talk to rich men. You expect a man of millions, the head of a great industry, to be a man worth hearing, but as a rule they don't know anything outside of their own businesses." This was not something that "an intelligent person wants to know."[165] For him, the burning questions were never economic, but always moral; his was a crusade for the "eternal principles of righteousness," unfolding historically and sung to the tune of "Onward, Christian Soldiers."

Even before the Progressive Convention met in Chicago, the Colonel had to grapple with a political question that should have been more embarrassing to his "crusade for righteousness" than it turned out to be: Should the party convention include black delegates from the South? Roosevelt was still smarting from the decision of black Republicans to stick with Taft back in June. Had they sent delegates to the Convention who supported him, TR was convinced he could have won the Republican nomination. But they were men of "low character," patronage appointments from rotten boroughs in states where there was no real Republican Party, who had been bought off by offers of jobs and cash. In a letter to Julian La Rose Harris, son of Joel Chandler Harris, author of the *Uncle Remus* stories, Roosevelt attempted to justify the decision of the credentials committee to exclude black delegates from Alabama, Florida, Georgia, and Mississippi to the Progressive Convention and to seat rival slates of white men instead.

Drawing on the themes of New Nationalism, Roosevelt argued that the Progressive Party sought to rise above sectional and racial politics and speak for the nation as a whole. For forty-five years, the Republican Party in the South had been "predominantly and overwhelmingly negro," and that effort had failed spectacularly. If the Progressives were to have any chance of becoming a real party in the South, they would have to do so by attracting whites. TR assured Harris that these were white men who would "set their faces sternly against lynch law and mob violence," oppose abuses such as peonage, fight to see that funds were "equitably divided between white and black schools," and "help the colored man to become a self supporting and useful member of the community." Rather than seeking help from out-siders, which succeeded only in antagonizing their white neighbors, blacks should learn to work with the whites that lived near them. Such good white men could advance the black cause better than blacks themselves could do. It was a strange argument for one who had so recently championed the cause of direct democracy and the right of the people to rule themselves. But, Roosevelt insisted, these were the hard facts of the matter, and Pro-gressives committed to advancing social and industrial justice had best ac-cept them. Besides, the Progressive Convention would include many more black delegates from northern and border states than the Republican Con-vention, which had drawn its black delegates from what was essentially a "ghost" party in the South.

Within weeks of the convention, TR repeated the arguments he had made to Harris in an essay in *The Outlook*. What Roosevelt failed to acknowledge was how paradoxical, if not contradictory, his position was, for only by play-ing sectional politics could the Progressive Party hope to become a national party, and only by pursuing a "Lily White" policy in the South could it claim to be taking the moral high ground.[166] Perhaps there were no satisfactory alternatives for a third-party attempting to make inroads in the Democratic-controlled South in 1912, but the Colonel's attempts to rationalize his position only made a bad situation worse. In the event, the party won only six states nationwide, losing all of the Old Confederacy and even the border states. The high-minded southern whites in whom Roosevelt reposed so much confi-dence apparently could not bring themselves to support the man who had entertained Booker T. Washington in the White House and called Lincoln his hero. (They voted for the Virginia-born Woodrow Wilson, who was one of their own.) It goes without saying that the "Lily White" strategy also alien-ated many blacks, who had good reason to believe that Roosevelt's elevation of duty over rights would come at a high price for them.[167]

Although the debate between Taft and Roosevelt raised profound ques-tions about the nature of republican constitutionalism, Taft's decision as sitting president to stand above the political fray meant that, once the cam-paign began in earnest that fall, the contest would quickly become a battle between TR's New Nationalism and Wilson's New Freedom. As interesting as this debate was, at bottom, both men agreed that the old constitutional order, committed to protecting individual rights against majority tyranny, must give way to new political arrangements that bowed to the popular will. From this perspective, their principal disagreement, over whether large industrial combinations should be regulated or broken up, was a family quarrel about the direction of progressivism unhinged from the Constitution of the Framers.[168] Their differences over the tariff would also prove inconsequential once the Sixteenth Amendment, which they both supported, was ratified. Nor, ultimately, were their views of individual economic self-interest in promoting the public good that far apart.[169] It is true that Roosevelt often urged men to put aside their economic interests for the good of the nation, but in contrast to his presidential years, he increasingly came to believe, with Croly, that government should actively discriminate in favor of its "friends," enacting legislation in their interests. For what else were his calls for social justice, his program of social insurance, his insistence that the wealth of the nation be more fairly distributed and its risks more equitably shared but efforts to advance the interests of the laboring classes? Particularly in his Bull Moose years, Roosevelt's entreaties to rise above the low plane of material interests were largely aimed at the better-off members of society, who he thought could afford the luxury of disinterestedness and who were duty bound to act as their brothers' keepers. His disdain for vulgar materialism and fear of violent class conflict should not be confused with a desire simply to transcend all material interests. It was only by satisfying the just demands of the people for a more equitable distribution of wealth that the nation could rise to a higher spiritual and ethical plane.

That said, there is no doubt that Roosevelt regarded the differences between the two candidates as significant. He took every opportunity to criticize Wilson's program, at times painting his opponent as a mere academic and late convert to the progressive cause.[170] As Lewis Gould has noted, because there were no formal debates in 1912, the candidates had to rely on newspaper accounts, often incomplete, to find out what their opponents were saying. In one memorable exchange, TR, campaigning in California, seized on newspaper reports of a speech Wilson had delivered in New York to question whether Wilson was a progressive at all. Wilson, who favored antitrust prosecutions over top-heavy regulation, had been criticizing Roosevelt's proposal to establish an Interstate Industrial Commission (another name for the Bureau of Corporations). The New Jersey governor then concluded his argument with the observation that "the history of liberty is a history of the limitation of governmental power, not the increase of it." Roosevelt knew only what he read in the paper, which omitted the context of the remark.[171] He jumped on the statement, branding it "a bit of outworn academic doctrine" that had long been abandoned by those with "experience of actual life." He then went on to accuse Wilson of advocating a doctrine of laissez-faire, which, if not simply empty "professorial rhetoric," placed him at odds with every piece of progressive legislation to advance the cause of social justice.

Roosevelt further insisted that it was only in absolute monarchies and aristocracies that liberty was secured by limiting government power, but those days were long gone. In modern democracies, real liberty was secured precisely by the extension of government power, acting on behalf of the "real popular need" to restrain "colossal" business combinations and prevent "the chaotic scramble of selfish interests." Any attempt to restrain government under present conditions would result in nothing less than the "enslavement of the people by the great corporations who can only be held in check by the extension of governmental power."[172]

Elsewhere, Roosevelt struck out at "the old flintlock muzzle-loaded doctrine of states' rights," attempting—quite wrongly—to paint Wilson as a Jeffersonian Democrat.[173] Wilson, however, countered effectively, charging that the Progressives were promoting an unhealthy alliance between big business and government and, by relying so heavily on bureaucratic experts, undermining the capacity of the people to govern themselves. Wilson had a point: Having championed the expansion of federal regulatory power as the best way to rein in the trusts, what would prevent government from developing a too-cozy relationship with the corporations they sought to regulate? And how would the rise of a new bureaucratic class empower citizens to exercise the virtues Roosevelt hoped to encourage?

In large measure, Roosevelt fell back on character, repeating his oft-stated view that public servants must be men of lofty ideals and strong moral fiber. Such men could be expected to render disinterested "service" and not be captured by the business interests they were supposed to control. In addition, Roosevelt now made explicit what he had previously only implied: the president, too, should be subject to recall. Although the Progressive platform said nothing about such a plan, Roosevelt declared that he personally had no objection to it. Drawing on his experience as president, TR claimed that he could do nothing without the backing of the people. Popular favor, he seemed to be saying, was the source of his power, because if he lost that support, he "ceased to have power." Unless "in fair open fighting on the stump" he could bring the people around to his way of thinking, he would prefer to step down from the presidency. Although Roosevelt's statement seemed to conflate recall and resignation (much as he had confused the recall of judicial decisions and *Dred Scott*), it marked another step in his drive to remove the distance that the Constitution placed between the people and their elected leaders. In Roosevelt's mind, the people, rather than the Constitution, were the real source of presidential power. Moreover, by making the executive more dependent upon public opinion, Roosevelt hoped to counter Wilson's charge that government by experts was too paternalistic. Ultimately, it would be the people who were calling the shots; presidents would have to be more responsive to public opinion throughout their tenure in office and not just at election time.[174]

Roosevelt's remarks may have blunted Wilson's immediate criticism that freemen needed no guardians, but recall was not without its own difficulties. If recall were to be more than notional, it would require a constitutional amendment. Beyond this hurdle, recall risked reversing the relation between the leader and the led, making the president too dependent upon the vagaries of public opinion and stoking the demagogic impulses that the Framers had sought to contain. Perhaps it was nothing more than a throwaway line, uttered in the spur of the moment, but nothing Roosevelt said later in the campaign suggests that he disavowed it.[175]

As the election approached, Roosevelt privately conceded that he expected Wilson to win. Nevertheless, he sought publicly to cast his Progressive Party run in heroic terms. In the aftermath of his attempted assassination, he could claim that the cause of "liberty and righteousness" was worth dying for. Addressing a rally at Madison Square Garden, Roosevelt, in words that harkened back to the poet James Russell Lowell, spoke of how perhaps once in a generation there comes a moment for the people to play a great part in the "age-long warfare for human rights." Twice before Americans had been summoned to great tasks. Although the challenges facing the nation in 1912 might not be as great as those that faced Washington or Lincoln, if left unattended they could spell "wide-spread disaster." America could not afford to allow "an unchecked and utterly selfish individualistic materialism" to run riot. Knowing what the problems were at the moment and facing up to them was "nine-tenths of wisdom." Unlike many of his campaign addresses, which skewered his opponents, the speech took the moral high ground, concentrating on what the Progressives were for. Mowry judged it "his greatest speech of the campaign and one of the finest of his whole political career."[176] But when the cheering was over, his party carried only six states. If it was any consolation, the Republicans carried only three.

PROGRESSIVES IN THE WILDERNESS

In the aftermath of Wilson's decisive electoral victory, TR continued to focus on the need for party realignment in hopes that the Progressives would now capture forward-looking members from both parties. Democrats, he charged, were far too wedded to states' rights and limited government ever to be a truly national and progressive party, while Republicans had betrayed the lofty ideals of the Grand Old Party by elevating property rights over human rights and denying the people's choice at their convention. Far from carrying on the principles of Lincoln, Republicans had become the spiritual heirs of the men who had warred against him. In breaking away from the Republicans, the Progressives were doing just what Lincoln had done in 1854 when he parted company with the Whigs. In 1913, it was the Progressives who were the rightful "heirs of Abraham Lincoln."[177]

Addressing a Lincoln Day banquet shortly after the election, Roosevelt quoted from the Republican Party Platform of 1854 to explain why the Progressives had formed a new party.[178] But as was so often the case when Roosevelt invoked Lincoln, he omitted the crucial sections of the Republican Party platform promising to restore "the government to the true principles of the Constitution," and to return it to its "first principles." The reason the Republican Party was founded was to rededicate the country to the principles of the Declaration and to revive what Lincoln elsewhere called "The Old Policy of the Fathers" regarding the treatment of slavery under the Constitution. Far from being a "radical," allied with the "forward movement," as TR alleged, Lincoln was, to use Roosevelt's terminology, a "reactionary," who sought to return the country to the principles of the founders. Although he by no means ruled out the possibility of progress, Lincoln never viewed the Republican Party of his day as a "manifestation of the eternal forces of human growth" that pointed only forward.[179] But between Lincoln's day and Roosevelt's, evolutionary biology and historicism seemed to make a return to "first principles" not only impossible, but also undesirable.

Having rallied the faithful, Roosevelt then largely absented himself from active politics, busying himself with his *Autobiography* and a seven-month exploration of the Amazon that nearly cost him his life. Returning to America in May 1914, Roosevelt found the political world much altered. Contrary to his expectations, Woodrow Wilson had succeeded in enacting significant economic reforms, beginning with tariff reduction accompanied by a progressive income tax and the Federal Reserve Act that stole much of the Progressives' thunder. Two more reforms, the establishment of the Federal Trade Commission, which replaced TR's Bureau of Corporations, and the Clayton Anti-Trust Act, would be signed into law that fall right before the midterm elections. As the party in power, Democrats also benefited politically from the ratification of the Sixteenth and Seventeenth Amendments to the Constitution in 1913, allowing for a federal income tax and the direct election of U.S. senators.

In foreign affairs, the outbreak of World War I that summer exacerbated tensions between TR and his Progressive Party base. At first, Roosevelt seemed willing to support the administration's position of neutrality, observing that "when giants are engaged in a death wrestle, as they reel to and fro they are certain to trample on whoever gets in the way of either of the huge, straining combatants, *unless it is dangerous to do so.*"[180] Within a month he reversed himself, however, denouncing the German violation of Belgian neutrality and calling for an increase in military preparedness. Nevertheless, Roosevelt did not wish to harm Progressives' chances at the polls by sounding too warlike, and so muted his criticism of Wilson. But after their poor showing in the midterms, the Colonel felt free to take off the gloves.

With his fledgling party in retreat, Roosevelt welcomed the appearance of new books that fall by Herbert Croly and Walter Lippmann, making the progressive case. Reviewing *Progressive Democracy* and *Drift and Mastery* in *The Outlook*, he singled out for special praise Croly's critique of "government by litigation" and Lippmann's attack on the antitrust provisions of the New Freedom.[181] Both men were now editors of the newly established *New Republic*, which Roosevelt had every reason to believe would support his brand of national progressivism, though two years later, with the Progressive Party in tatters and the alliance between Croly and TR fractured, the editors would endorse Wilson.

Back in the fall of 1912, the Colonel had capped off his campaign by observing that once in every generation there comes a moment of great historic significance. Unfortunately for Roosevelt, it was not 1912 but 1914 that was shaping up to be such a moment. As he had observed in his impromptu remarks before the Cambridge Union, so much of greatness depended upon chance. Without a serious crisis or war while he was president, Roosevelt lacked the opportunity to display the full range of his talents. Now, with a world war raging, a college professor was sitting in the White House, while Roosevelt was "marooned" in a rapidly crumbling third party.[182]

Although Roosevelt continued to present himself as the face of "sane radicalism," historians have largely concluded that once the war broke out, the Colonel turned his attention toward military matters and lost interest in social reform.[183] Beyond question, there was something in Roosevelt's soul that thrilled to the call of battle. As he wrote in *America and the World War*, in words that recalled Henry V's St. Crispin's Day speech, "The storm that is raging in Europe is terrible and evil; but it is also grand and noble.

Untried men who live at ease will do well to remember that there is a certain sublimity even in Milton's defeated archangel, but none whatsoever in the spirits who kept neutral, who remained at peace, and dared neither side with hell or with heaven."[184] Compared with actual combat, the domestic Armageddon seemed to have lost much of its luster, and Roosevelt drifted back toward the Republicans.

Lending credence to the historians' charges was Roosevelt's treatment of the Progressive Party in 1916. For some time, Roosevelt had been quietly maneuvering to become the fusion candidate of both the Republican and Progressive Parties, stressing military preparedness and soft-pedaling social reform. Failing to win the Republican nomination, he declined to run on the Progressive ticket, delivering the death-blow to the party he had summoned into existence only four years earlier. That he suggested the Progressives nominate Henry Cabot Lodge instead only added insult to injury, since Lodge had refused to support Roosevelt in 1912 and opposed key progressive reforms.

But Roosevelt's turn to international affairs and military preparedness is only part of the story. For as the country moved closer to war, the Colonel not only began to speak out again on issues of social reform, but moved even farther to the left.[185] Unlike his erstwhile pacifist allies, Roosevelt viewed the impending war as an opportunity to press for even more radical reforms that would allow Americans to "reshape" their "whole civilization in accordance with the law of service."[186] Just as he had welcomed the Spanish-American War as a way to get his countrymen to rise above their vulgar materialism, Roosevelt saw in this larger conflict the prospect of an even greater moral reformation that would come through shared sacrifice and duty, and he returned again to these themes with renewed vigor.[187] Inevitably, war would lead to an increase and centralization of power, which he hoped would usher in a new era of social and industrial justice after peace was restored. Returning soldiers, men "high of soul," who sacrificed everything for "a great ideal," would demand as much, and the nation owed it to "the men who pa[id] with their bodies for their souls' desire."[188] In a series of essays, collected and published in *The Foes of Our Own Household* (1917) and *The Great Adventure* (1918), as well as other articles that the socialist *Metropolitan* declined to publish in his lifetime,[189] Roosevelt sketched out his vision for a progressive, postwar future. What was striking was that even as the United States entered into war with Germany, Roosevelt continued to profess admiration for its ideals and to pattern American reforms on the German model, singling out for special praise their military and industrial efficiency.

Writing to the Prussian-born Harvard Professor Hugo von Munsterberg in 1916, Roosevelt sought to reassure him that "true Americanism" was in fact compatible with a respect for German ideals. As he explained,

> I do not for one moment believe that the Americanism of today should be a mere submission to the ideals of the period of the Declaration of Independence. Such action would not only be to stand still, but to go back. American democracy, of course, must mean an opportunity for everyone to contribute his own ideas to the working out of the future. But I will go further than you have done. I have actively fought in favor of grafting on our social life, no less than our industrial life, many of the German ideals.

Although Roosevelt then went on to offer the innocuous example of German clubs that admitted women before their American counterparts, he insisted, and not wrongly, that he had "tried to graft German ideals and habits a dozen times, for every English ideal or habit, on American life."[190]

In his *Autobiography*, Roosevelt spelled out what he meant, restating the rights to life, liberty, and the pursuit of happiness in the Declaration so that the "graft" of German principles was unmistakable: "the rights of the worker to a living wage, to reasonable hours of labor, to decent working and living conditions, to freedom of thought and speech and industrial representation,—in short to a measure of industrial democracy."[191] Roosevelt's evolving ideals shifted the focus toward equality and economic redistribution, enforced by a powerful state, and away from the equal rights of each to life, liberty, and the pursuit of happiness, which was the distinctive "American ideal."

With Germany as the model, Roosevelt envisioned the state as a "partner" promoting cooperation in labor-business relations. It would oversee wages, making sure that workers were well paid. Managers, he conceded, could earn more, but not "fantastically" more.[192] Bureaucrats, presumed to know more about the businesses than the people who owned and managed them, would decide. The costs of war also gave Roosevelt another reason to push for progressive taxes on inheritance and "a heavily—a very heavily—graduated" tax on "excess" war profits. Out of fairness to smaller companies that might not be as competitive as larger, more efficient businesses, the "very" heavy taxes on the "excess" profits of larger combinations would subsidize their smaller competitors.[193]

Roosevelt also envisioned the government playing a direct role in disputes between labor and capital. Drawing on his experience in mediating the coal strike of 1902, TR argued that where the national interest was involved, government must be empowered to intervene directly on behalf of the public, investigating labor conditions and gathering information on safety conditions, minimum wages, maximum hours, and so on. Once it had compiled its data, the federal government would then issue a decree telling businesses what they must do. Although workers would not be required to return to work under these conditions, if the employers or "capitalists" complied with the decree, the government would ensure that there was no violence or "lawless interference" against their operations. If, however, they refused to comply, "the government itself would take hold and run the business until the orders were carried out."[194] On what constitutional authority he did not say. Although Roosevelt rejected the idea that his proposal was biased against business, elsewhere he insisted that questions of industrial justice be examined principally *"from the workers' standpoint."*[195] The rules of the game had clearly changed. If Roosevelt had anything to do with it, government would now actively discriminate in favor of its friends.

Beyond this, as part of his effort to turn "tool users" into "tool owners," TR now argued that managers, salaried experts, and wage-earners all be given a "property interest" in their "common" business, with laborers, where possible, granted some share in the profits.[196] In addition, wage-laborers should share in management and guidance. Roosevelt was willing to grant that until workers had acquired sufficient knowledge, control should be limited to the "conditions of daily work" and not extended to the business side of management. He did not, however, rule out managerial decisions at some future date, with laborers appointed to corporate boards.[197]

Improbably, Roosevelt sought to trace these policies back to Lincoln, arguing that his ideal was "a cooperative system in which each man labored and each man was to some extent an owner of the capital necessary for work." Of course, Lincoln was describing a "primitive individualism" that had now "vanished," but Roosevelt was confident that had he lived in the age of industrial capitalism he would have supported "some adaptation of cooperative ownership and management" so that workers might enjoy greater equality. What Roosevelt ignored, however, was that Lincoln championed equality of opportunity, by which he meant giving each a fair chance in the "race of life." Roosevelt, however, was now more interested in addressing what he considered the unjust inequality of results by changing the rules of the game.[198] It is doubtful that even the "spirit" of Lincoln's principles could be stretched to mean the opposite of his words. Despite his best efforts to enlist Lincoln in his cause, Roosevelt's policies more closely resembled those of Bismarck, who, even as he condemned Marxist socialism, quietly put in place key elements of the German welfare state.[199]

Finally, Roosevelt came out in favor of permanent employment, arguing that job security would reduce economic conflict even as companies introduced labor-saving machinery.[200] What he failed to see, but with the benefit of hindsight has now become clear, was that the European welfare state, with its granite protections for workers and generous social benefits, was a recipe for economic sclerosis, freezing in place a statist model of labor-capital relations that was not only expensive and inefficient, but also would undermine the very innovation and initiative he claimed to want to encourage.

As the battle over woman suffrage came to a head, Roosevelt borrowed still another idea from Germany, linking the right to vote with compulsory military and industrial service for both men and women. If men refused to serve, or women raised sons who shirked their duty, they should not be allowed to vote. By assigning all young men to "hard unskilled labor," TR hoped to promote intermingling among the classes while insuring that no one would have to devote a lifetime to these tedious tasks. Women, of course, would serve in different occupations, perhaps as day-care providers for the children of mothers who worked in factories.

In addition, he came out in favor of six months' mandatory training in military camps, though in this one instance he hastened to add that they should be modeled more on the Swiss than the militaristic Prussians, whose "grim efficiency" he nevertheless continued to admire. Every "sound-thinking democrat" must recognize that democracy could not succeed unless it demonstrated "the same efficiency that is shown by autocracy." It thus behooved Americans to study German military efficiency, which was the fount of all her many excellences. "The solidarity and power of collective action, the trained ability to work hard for an end which is far off in the future, the combination of intelligent forethought with efficient and strenuous action—all these together have given her [Germany] her extraordinary industrial pre-eminence; and all of these have been based upon her military efficiency."[201] Needless to say, Roosevelt had no patience with conscientious objectors. There was "no place" for them in the republic he sought to reconstruct; they should be "expelled."[202]

Unlike his calls for greater supervision and control of the industrial economy, Roosevelt believed that farmers could best improve their lives by forming cooperatives modeled primarily on those he had seen in Denmark and Holland. Nevertheless, he did not rule out government intervention altogether. The state should actively work to end tenant farming, either by making capital more easily available through credit unions or else buying up land and selling it to farmers as New Zealand had done. Experimentation was the watchword. In addition, he supported progressive taxation

to break up the great landed estates, especially those bought on speculation, and considered a plan to provide returning soldiers with farms of their
own, to be paid for by a tax on undeveloped land. He singled out for special
praise the Sandhills Farm Life School in North Carolina, which combined
practical agricultural instruction with uniformed military training for boys,
uniting mutual self-protection with community action.[203]

As the war in Europe devoured its young, Roosevelt turned his attention
once again to the questions of population growth and birth control. Unlike the more assertive eugenicists, he was not principally concerned with
preventing the "worthless and poverty-stricken" from having more children. Except in a small number of cases, there was little (but apparently not
nothing) the state could do to limit "the production of the unfit." What
most worried him was that college graduates, and especially the graduates
of women's colleges, the very people of "better stocks" who should be having large families, were "beguiled" by birth control. Once again, he hoped
that an aroused public opinion, coupled with the right tax policies, might
reverse this precipitous decline. "The one child family as an average ideal
of course spells death" both to the broader civilization and to the welfare
state that depended on growing numbers of workers to support its entitlements. Although a supporter of liberal immigration policies—at least from
Europe—Roosevelt did not view immigration as a solution to the decline of
the native population. "I do not want to see us Americans forced to import
our babies from abroad."[204] Accordingly, in addition to penalizing childless
couples and families with only one or two children, he now proposed that
the salaries of public officials markedly discriminate "in favor of the man
or woman with a family of *over* three children" in both income and inheritance, and where possible other taxes. As far as he was concerned, "only the
father and mother of over three children have done their full duty to the
state."[205] In place of the Constitution, with its protection of the individual
rights, TR substituted "the law of civilization," based on service to the nation.

Anticipating the return of American soldiers, Roosevelt once more im-
plored his countrymen to embrace the cause of social justice. His last essay, "The Problems of Peace—Part II," published in the *Metropolitan* one
month after his death on January 6, 1919, continued to hold up Germany
as the model for American progress, with government assuming greater
control over the economy and leading the nation to a higher plane of spiritual satisfaction and brotherhood. It was his final testimony—and so ended
the extraordinary life of Theodore Roosevelt, who began his political career praising *The Federalist* and died lamenting that Americans had not yet
caught up with the Germans.

Epilogue:
The "Heirs" of
Theodore Roosevelt

Attempting to rally the faithful at a Lincoln Day Banquet not long after his electoral defeat, Roosevelt insisted, unpersuasively, that the progressives were the only true heirs of Abraham Lincoln. Now, as the nation approaches the centennial of the Bull Moose campaign, it seems right to close by considering—in a more detached way—who the "heirs of Theodore Roosevelt" are today. As befits the man who preached the importance of breeding large and healthy families, Roosevelt's "heirs" are numerous and varied, his legacy substantial. For although TR's Progressive Party lasted only four short years, the changes wrought by the progressive *movement* he spearheaded have permanently altered the shape of American political life, in ways predictable and unpredictable that are still playing themselves out.

To begin with, there are the constitutional changes. Despite Roosevelt's complaint that the amendment process took too long and was too cumbersome, the fact is that the progressive era added more amendments to the Constitution than at any other time since the ratification of the Bill of Rights, and Roosevelt heartily endorsed them all (except for prohibition, which he supported only as a wartime measure). Then there are the institutional innovations TR championed, including an increase in federal regulatory agencies, changes to the party system, a more progressive reading of the Constitution, and the introduction of direct democratic reforms, all of which gradually took root. Added to these was his unofficial call for a new Declaration of Independence that would help to redefine rights and establish a new relationship of the citizen to government. Perhaps most important, given the primacy he attached to "the things of the soul," are the changes to the American character that a century of progressive reforms has gradually brought about.

Assessing Roosevelt's legacy and weighing the claims of his many "heirs" is no easy task, however, because Roosevelt tended to say different things at different times to different audiences. Often, he claimed to be the "sane radical," the "conservative progressive," who championed common-sense reforms as the only realistic alternative to violent socialist upheavals. But beginning after the 1906 midterm elections and especially after 1910, he became more and more the progressive crusader, rallying political activists and Social Gospelers in support of programs that pointed toward some kind of democratic socialism. He still talked the language of the "Square Deal," but he no longer saw government as an impartial umpire. Following Croly's lead, he now believed that government should not simply enforce the rules of the game; rather, it must actively take the side of its friends, redistributing wealth in the name of social justice.

Further complicating the question of who are his "heirs" is that for much of his political career, Roosevelt was not a progressive at all, but a well-meaning Republican reformer who made his reputation battling the New York political machines and powerful bosses, insisting that the big moneyed interests play by the rules and pay their share of the taxes. He went to Washington in the 1890s to end the abuses of the spoils system. At the time, he viewed civil service reform as a way to restore the republic of the Framers, attracting men of upright character to public service, rather than an attempt to lay the foundation for the modern administrative state. Although as a New York assemblyman he had championed modest social reforms, he later judged his early efforts inadequate because he had not yet been awakened to the demands of social justice.

Still heeding the lessons of *The Federalist*, the young Roosevelt warned against the dangers of the demagogue and defended the independence of the courts as the best security for individual rights, though even then he failed to appreciate the power of self-interest in political affairs. Above all, he was in the 1880s and 1890s a triumphant nationalist, whose histories celebrated the expansion of American power at home, while working actively to increase its influence abroad. Too often he viewed this power in terms that were foreign to the founders he most admired, so steeped was he in the paradigms of Darwinian evolution and German historicism. But these more theoretical differences between Roosevelt and the founders have often eluded his "heirs," who approved of the results, and therefore did not inquire too closely into the reasoning behind them. Apart from academic historians, few of those who claim his mantle today give much evidence of having studied his writings.

Not surprisingly, the Republican reformer side of Roosevelt's legacy continues to appeal to GOP mavericks, and in recent times no one more than Arizona Senator John McCain. In his 2000 bid for the Republican nomination against George W. Bush, McCain cast himself as a Republican in the TR mold. In a manner reminiscent of the Rough Rider, McCain lashed out against "special interests" in politics, defended campaign finance laws, and sought to renew in Americans, and especially the young, a sense of patriotism, duty, and honor. Although McCain failed to win the Republican nomination in 2000, Roosevelt continued to exercise a subtle influence at the Bush White House. On the advice of his top political adviser, Karl Rove, a longtime Roosevelt fan, President George W. Bush read *Theodore Rex*, Edmund Morris's study of Roosevelt's presidency, in which the parallels were not difficult to spot. Both Roosevelt and Bush were scions of the eastern establishment who remade themselves in the West. Both stood up for the right as they saw it, and neither ran away from conflict. Whether deliberately or not, there was more than an echo of Roosevelt when, a week after September 11, the president declared that he wanted Osama bin Laden, "dead or alive" (though ironically it was Bush's progressive successor, President Barack Obama, who actually delivered on the demand).[1] For wartime presidents especially, the attraction of the Rough Rider has proved irresistible. With wars raging in Iraq and Afghanistan in 2008, John McCain once again channeled the spirit of TR. As the nominee of the GOP that year, McCain, a former naval officer and prisoner of war, urged Americans to put "country first." Unfortunately, much like Roosevelt, the Arizona senator and decorated war hero had little interest in economic questions as such, which proved disastrous for him as the stock market crashed in the months before the election.

In the more rarefied atmosphere of political journals, think-tanks, and the editorial pages of the *New York Times*, a group of "big government" or "national greatness" conservatives and neo-conservatives (the labels are porous) has also kept the Roosevelt flame burning. In a series of essays in *The Weekly Standard*, beginning in 1997 and continuing through the run-up to the 2000 election, and again in an op-ed piece in 2008 in the *New York Times*, journalist David Brooks cast TR as a "conservative reformer" who was willing to expand government power to ensure order and stability in a time of economic transformation.[2] Brooks seems to have taken Roosevelt at his word that, after decades of congressional dominance, he was simply reasserting executive power as other strong presidents had done before him.

Part of Roosevelt's success, Brooks suggested, could be attributed to his energetic personality and confident fighting spirit. He believed in the "strenuous life" and did not "shrink" or "flinch" from practicing it. But as befits our more sensitive age, Brooks shies away from discussing Roosevelt's "masculine style of leadership" for fear of ridicule. It is left then to Harvard professor Harvey C. Mansfield to admire (but not too much) Roosevelt's defense of the manly virtues.[3] Instead, Brooks focused on Roosevelt's "governing philosophy," which promised both labor and capital a "Square Deal," while meting out stern justice to capitalist wrongdoing and labor violence alike. TR, he argued, succeeded in striking a "balance" between individual initiative and collective responsibility. Certainly, looking back on his presidency from the vantage point of today's federal government with its bounding proliferation of regulatory agencies, Roosevelt's domestic achievements, culminating in the passage of the Hepburn Act, hardly seem radical. But it must be remembered that during his last two years in office, Roosevelt moved farther to the left, ramping up his rhetoric against the "malefactors of great wealth" and proposing significant increases in regulatory power, his triumph in enacting railroad regulation paving the way for ever more "supervision." That none of these later initiatives succeeded has allowed more conservative "heirs" like Brooks to focus on Roosevelt's actual accomplishments rather than his more radical failed proposals and incendiary speeches.

According to Brooks, another aspect of Roosevelt's "governing philosophy" was his use of executive power to promote "national greatness." As a mighty industrial America entered the twentieth century, Roosevelt sought to elevate the public taste, hiring sculptor Augustus Saint-Gaudens to design new coinage that would rival that of the ancients and consulting with professional architects on the design of public buildings. TR strove to make all Americans feel proud of their heritage and eager to preserve it, though Brooks says nothing about Roosevelt's full-throated defense of Manifest Destiny and colonial expansion. Instead, he is keen to make sure that the Republican Roosevelt is given his due as a conservationist. He rightly praises TR for his farsightedness in expanding America's national parks and establishing wildlife preserves, ensuring that the country's natural treasures would remain unspoiled for future generations. In contrast to today's environmentalists, he emphasizes that Roosevelt wanted to see America's natural resources *developed* in a responsible manner, rather than simply placed off limits. Yet in making conservation a cornerstone of national greatness, Brooks ignores the ways in which Roosevelt exploited the fear of resource "famines" to increase executive power. He also overlooks the challenge to property rights and limited government that the growing conservation "movement" posed.

Above all, for "national greatness conservatives," and especially "neoconservatives," Roosevelt's greatest achievement was his willingness to use executive power to stand up for both the national interest and national honor in foreign affairs. Throughout his long career, Roosevelt was unwavering in his support of military preparedness, especially a strong navy, as the best means of ensuring peace. By adopting Washington's maxim, and through shrewd diplomacy, Roosevelt did in fact manage to keep the peace throughout his presidency. At the same time, neo-conservatives applaud Roosevelt's determination in building the Panama Canal and his audacity in sending the Great White Fleet around the world. Under Roosevelt's energetic leadership, the United States became a great player on the world stage, mediating an end to the Russo-Japanese War and acting as global policeman to ensure peace and stability in the Americas and the Philippines. Taking a leaf out of Roosevelt's book, neo-conservatives argue that a nation demonstrates its greatness by doing great deeds, even if they do not endorse his "stewardship" theory of executive power.[4]

For good reason, these conservative "heirs" of Theodore Roosevelt tend to pass quickly over the postpresidential years where, at least until World War I broke out, his New Nationalism focused on redefining property rights and moving the country toward a European-style social democracy. (Indeed, Brooks seems to think that TR can be enlisted in the cause of reforming Medicare and Social Security, when in fact he initially proposed these policies.) As Timothy Noah rightly observed of the 2008 presidential campaign, "McCain can call Obama a socialist, or he can call Teddy Roosevelt his hero. He can't do both."[5]

Yet once Roosevelt turned his attention back to foreign affairs, his neo-conservative "heirs" do have a further claim on his legacy. For one thing, despite his general endorsement of arbitration in his Nobel Prize speech, Roosevelt criticized both Taft and Wilson for their willingness to enter into arbitration treaties that endangered vital matters of national interest and national honor. In his view, arbitration was a useful tool in resolving international disputes, but a limited one. From Roosevelt's perspective, the nation-state represented the triumph of civilization, an achievement that he was unwilling to barter away in the name of airy internationalism or sentimental philanthropy. For another, although he endorsed the idea of a league of peace, he insisted that any new international organization consist only of *civilized* countries, and that it have the force to back up its decisions. (It is not difficult to imagine what invectives the Bull Moose would hurl at the present United Nations.)

Moreover, as the United States inched closer to war, Roosevelt returned with greater urgency to a problem he had first addressed in the 1880s: immigration and hyphenated-Americanism, which today marches under the banner of multiculturalism. With hostilities raging in Europe, he had even less tolerance for naturalized Americans who claimed dual allegiance to the countries of their birth. TR was not talking about dual *citizenship*, which for him would have been inconceivable, but the tendency of immigrants to hang on to their native languages, holidays, dress, and so on even after they had become naturalized citizens. "We must be Americans and nothing else," he insisted. Ultimately what was at stake was whether the United States would continue as one nation or dissolve into a "huge polyglot boarding-house and counting house, in which dollar-hunters of twenty different nationalities scramble for gain, while each really pays his soul-allegiance to some foreign power."[6] At a time when Prime Minister David Cameron of Great Britain, former president Nicolas Sarkozy of France, and German Chancellor Angela Merkel have proclaimed that multiculturalism has "utterly" failed, Roosevelt's insistence upon assimilation, assailed in some circles as arrogant and intolerant, begins to seem prescient. And finally, Roosevelt's patriotism and love of country, his bitter disappointment at being denied the opportunity to raise a regiment to fight in France, and his pride in having all four of his sons serve valiantly in World War I (with Quentin making the ultimate sacrifice), although by no means the exclusive preserve of Roosevelt's more conservative "heirs," seem particularly to stir their souls.

Still, to turn Roosevelt into a "big government" or "national greatness" conservative in the tradition of Washington, Hamilton, Clay, and Lincoln, is to misread both these statesmen and TR himself. For one thing, it is to disregard the important ways in which Roosevelt's policies were at odds with those of the statesmen he claimed to admire. However energetic the Washington, Hamilton, Jackson, Lincoln model, it was still too limited for Roosevelt, whose stewardship theory moved him farther away from the constraints of the Constitution. It also passes over his relentless efforts during his second term (and certainly afterward) to extend the regulatory reach of government over the industrial economy and to bring about a redistribution of wealth. In his escalating attacks on Congress and the courts, Roosevelt was not simply trying to adapt the principles of the Framers to dramatically altered social and economic conditions, but rather to help the country evolve beyond them. By his own admission, he was not interested in promoting equality of opportunity, but in changing the rules of the game to ensure social justice. To assert that Roosevelt belongs to the tradition of "energetic but limited" government as Brooks does is simply mistaken. Moreover, it also ignores the *trajectory* of his thought, which is away from the republicanism of the founders and toward European social democracy, where rights are the gift of the state. As TR happily confessed, he became more radical with age, not less.

Thus, it is not surprising that some liberals and social democrats (these terms, too, are porous) also claim to be the "heirs" of Theodore Roosevelt. At the popular level, *Time* magazine devoted an entire issue in the summer of 2006 to assessing TR's legacy, with most of the contributors drawn from the left.[7] And although John McCain may be the most prominent of today's politicians to associate himself with TR, the Bull Moose has had his share of admirers on the Democratic side of the aisle, including his distant relation, FDR, who closely tracked TR's career path to the White House. More recently, former president Bill Clinton, tutored by TR aficionado E. J. Dionne, saw him as a model for the exercise of energetic national power in solving America's problems, while former House Minority leader Richard Gephardt praised him for his progressive vision. And in the midst of the debate over health care reform, press secretary Robert Gibbs let it be known that President Obama was reading Edmund Morris's *The Rise of Theodore Roosevelt*, while his supporters urged him to act more like the Rough Rider and take on the health insurance companies. After the Patient Protection and Affordable Care Act of 2010 squeaked through Congress, Democrats, led by the president, praised TR for having first championed national health insurance a hundred years ago. And as he geared up for his re-election campaign, Obama chanelled the spirit of TR, promoting his economic message at Osawatamie, Kansas, where Roosevelt launched his New Nationalism program in 1910.

Beyond these Democratic politicians, the academic contributors to *Time*'s Roosevelt issue, especially Patricia O'Toole and Kathleen Dalton, have recently published well-regarded studies that examine TR's postpresidential efforts to advance progressive social reforms. Both take at face value Roosevelt's insistence that he was trying to steer a "sane" middle course between untrammeled capitalism and violent socialist revolution. But, like most of the standard works of the period, this formula obscures just how far to the left Roosevelt wanted to move the country.[8] It is true that he was no friend of Marxism or "scientific socialism," with its class warfare and violent revolution. Nor did he find its internationalism appealing; the withering away of the state was never part of his goal. And in contrast to prominent socialists of his day, Roosevelt did not support state ownership of the means of production, or advocate the abolition of private property. But, as Timothy Noah rightly senses, this does not mean he did not become some kind of socialist, even if he was coy about this in public.

For the most part, Roosevelt's rhetorical strategy was to insist that he was no Marxist, and then to argue that other nonviolent, democratic socialist policies were really nothing more than an advanced form of liberalism with whom well-meaning "social reformers" ought "cordially" to cooperate.[9] It was a brilliant strategy, as six-time Socialist candidate for the presidency, Norman Thomas, would confirm when he observed, "The American people will never knowingly adopt Socialism. But under the name of 'liberalism' they will adopt every fragment of the Socialist program, until one day America will be a Socialist nation, without knowing how it happened." For good rhetorical reasons, the left continues to this day to blur the line between liberalism (or when that term falls into disrepute, progressivism) and socialism.[10]

Yet without being clear on the distinctions between the two, it is not possible to assess Roosevelt's legacy or to appreciate the principled differences that divide his "heirs." Liberalism, as the founders recognized and Lincoln affirmed, begins by acknowledging the natural right of each individual to the fruits of his or her labor. This need not always dictate a policy of strict laissez-faire—at one time or another, Hamilton and later the Whigs and then the Republicans under Lincoln backed the creation of a national bank, federal support for infant manufactures, public improvements, a protective tariff, the Homestead Act, and the establishment of land grant colleges. But these programs were in the service of liberal ends: promoting equality of opportunity and the right of individuals to advance as far as their talents and luck could carry them. By contrast, the form of democratic socialism (or advanced radical liberalism) TR later advocated started from the premise that the right to property depended upon the service or benefit that this property provides to the community as a whole, with "service" largely understood in terms of promoting greater equality. Private property would still exist, since this provided the spur to economic activity. As Roosevelt frequently emphasized, there must first *be* prosperity before it can be redistributed. But, and this is the crucial point, the "right" to property is now something that is "granted" to individuals by the state.

This new "governing philosophy" (to use David Brooks's term) in turn requires a new progressive social contract. Unlike the Declaration of Independence, which assumes that individuals enter into a compact with each other to form a government that will secure their inalienable rights, the contract Roosevelt envisions is between the people and their government.[11] Government is no longer simply the guarantor of the *conditions* under which individuals freely exercise their rights, it now becomes the *source* of their rights. In exchange for granting the state increased powers to regulate industry and redistribute wealth, citizens are now "entitled" to new rights to decent living and working conditions as well as to health, unemployment, and old age insurance. Far from threatening the liberty of citizens, a powerful national government is essential to the provision of these rights.

This is where the Framers' Constitution falls short since, in seeking to protect individual rights, it limits the scope of government powers. Accordingly, Roosevelt's progressive "heirs" tend to approve of his stewardship theory of executive power, at least when it is directed toward advancing social justice. Given their commitment to greater economic equality, they continue to support progressive taxation and would favor a return to more steeply progressive levels, if not quite those that prevailed from 1945 up until the 1960s, when the top marginal income tax rate reached a staggering 92 percent. They also have no quarrel with the "living Constitution," since this is the way that progressive judges and lawyers keep pace with the times. Nevertheless, because progressivism is a *forward* movement, parts of Roosevelt's progressive program seem old-fashioned now, and others downright misguided. As John Dewey shrewdly observed in his obituary of Roosevelt, the Colonel had the good fortune to die before progressivism moved beyond his moralizing and pronounced him a "reactionary," which in some quarters it promptly did.[12]

Indeed, one of the most striking developments of the 1920s was how quickly modern liberals (as they called themselves) abandoned Roosevelt's emphasis on service to the state, with its concomitant subordination of rights to duties. After the carnage of World War I, Roosevelt's watchword to "spend and be spent," to be broken and then cast aside so long as righteousness prevailed, understandably lost much of its appeal. TR did not live to see the rise of Italian fascism, which found favor for a time at Herbert Croly's *New Republic*.[13] Whether Mussolini's early national socialism would also have been attractive to Roosevelt is difficult to say since, by 1916, when *The New Republic* endorsed Woodrow Wilson, he and Croly had parted company. On the basis of his own comments, Roosevelt's subordination of rights to duty, along with his idealization of the state, owed more to German political theory and practice. After the war, Germany, too, fell into disfavor, and modern liberals, led by John Dewey, turned to homegrown American pragmatism and a return to the primacy of rights, albeit the novel economic rights that TR had championed as part of a new social contract.

Also unappealing (if not simply "reactionary") to the contemporary left was the overwhelmingly Protestant character of the progressive movement, saturated with its hymn-singing moral revivalism. To the new waves of Catholic and Jewish immigrants who poured into the country seeking material advancement, the old progressive coalition, with its disdain for "sordid" materialism and talk of higher spiritual ideals seemed nothing more than a desiccated form of liberal Protestantism—and, as such, irrelevant to the needs and desires of newly arrived working-class Americans. Instead of dedicating themselves to "the things of the soul," modern liberals descended to earth, where they rediscovered the world of clashing economic and social interests.

For good reason, contemporary feminists also dismiss most of Roosevelt's pronouncements on women and family life as "reactionary," a throwback to the Victorian era. Historian Kathleen Dalton attempts to provide some balance by emphasizing the coterie of talented women that TR gathered around him during the 1912 campaign. In her view, feminists have not given Roosevelt sufficient credit for advancing the causes of woman suffrage, women in the professions, and women in reform politics through his recognition of "the female capacity for 'statesmanship.'"[14] This makes it all the more regrettable, she argues, that Roosevelt gets no credit for the passage of the Nineteenth Amendment, which he heartily supported in 1912, or that he is remembered principally for his views on "race suicide," patriarchy, and the manly virtues. But there is no escaping the fact that Roosevelt's fulminations against the "cold selfishness" and "vapid self-indulgence" of women, especially college-educated women who refused to perform their service to the nation by bearing "many healthy children," went right at the heart of his view of sound family life. Not surprisingly, TR can claim few "heirs" in the feminist camp.

Finally, as Dewey predicted, modern-day liberals are also likely to dismiss as reactionary Roosevelt's identification of progressivism with the civilizing mission of imperialism,[15] and to equate his insistence on military preparedness with militarism rather than peacekeeping. Even in his own day, progressivism was beginning to splinter between the Colonel and his Republican allies, who urged a buildup of military efforts, and his more pacifist supporters, who opposed any steps that might draw the United States into the Great War. Despite the possibilities for social transformation that wartime mobilization held out, and indeed helped to advance, today's liberals, chastened by two world wars, a protracted Cold War, and a series of costly local conflicts, have favored diplomatic efforts, multinationalism, and military cutbacks. Since Vietnam, they have warned against the dangers of an "imperial presidency," with virtually unchecked powers in foreign affairs.[16] And although often critical of the separation of powers as an impediment to progressive "efficiency," they have looked to the Congress and the courts to restrain executive initiatives abroad. At a time when resources are scarce, they prefer to channel the nation's substance into domestic social programs.

Moreover, when thinking about the "heirs" of Theodore Roosevelt, it is not enough simply to trace certain family resemblances in today's politics back to their original source. For Roosevelt's attempt to transform American politics produced unintended consequences, resulting in what Croly in another context called "unnatural children," who threaten to devour their patrimony. To begin with, take Roosevelt's signature concern with character, both the "hum-drum" virtues of everyday life as well as those that are necessary to preserve republican self-government. In arguing for the establishment of government-administered welfare programs, TR tried to walk a fine line between assisting worthy families in need—usually widows with dependent children or wives whose husbands had deserted them—while insisting that the primary responsibility for the well-being of the family lay with the individual, and more particularly, the husband. But already in his day, more militant progressives, more attuned to the "modern movement" than Roosevelt himself, were arguing that government must assume a larger responsibility for the material needs of the family. In time, welfare was extended to all needy people, regardless of their behavior, thus undermining precisely those virtues that Roosevelt sought to promote and contributing to the collapse of the family among the poor. Moreover, far from promoting the fulfillment of higher spiritual needs, the provision of material support tended to reinforce the "sordid materialism" that Roosevelt hoped that a more equitable society would overcome.[17] Nor did these measures miraculously bridge social divisions or foster the quasi-religious brotherhood that was supposed to replace what had become for him the more suspect ties of enlightened self-interest and attenuated social affections in the old republic.

Even more important, it is by no means only the character of the poor that has been undermined by the rise of the welfare state. As the social insurance programs that Roosevelt championed were eventually put in place, first Social Security in the 1930s, and then Medicare in the 1960s, all Americans, regardless of need, become eligible for monthly social security checks as well as health and now prescription drug benefits when they reach sixty-five (or thereabouts). Over the next two decades, an estimated 80 million baby boomers will become entitled to receive these benefits. Ironically, Roosevelt defended these social insurance programs by arguing that they would help to foster self-reliant and independent citizens, but the effect of the welfare state has been to make a growing number of Americans dependent upon government for some kind of financial assistance.[18] And this will only increase if changes in health insurance do begin to take effect in 2014. At the same time, the decline in the birthrate, which Roosevelt warned about a century ago when the average family was considerably larger, and now coupled with extended life expectancy, raises serious doubts about the economic viability of the welfare state.

Roosevelt's efforts to drive the "special interests" out of politics by outlawing corporate campaign contributions and supporting direct primaries also turned out to have unintended consequences. Although direct primaries do allow ordinary citizens a greater say in selecting political candidates, they have also increased the costs of campaigns and elections. This, in turn, has made candidates even more dependent on wealthy financial backers, as Roosevelt himself was on George W. Perkins, an associate of J. P. Morgan's, in 1912. Moreover, as government has increased its "supervision" over the economy, it has guaranteed that the "special interests" affected by these new regulations would try even harder to influence the outcome of elections. In our own day, "special interests" are no longer confined to big business or private trusts but also extend to organized labor, and especially public sector labor unions, as well as entrenched voting blocs such as "the poor," minorities, farmers, students, and the elderly.

Thus, in another ironic twist, David Brooks and William Kristol have dusted off the popular image of TR as a "trustbuster," urging reformers to take aim at these new classes of "special interests" and "public trusts" that thwart genuine popular rule. In the wake of the Republican landslide of 2010, Republican governors, led by Scott Walker of Wisconsin, have done just that, scaling back the benefits afforded to public sector unions. And in one more move Roosevelt could never have anticipated, conservatives in those states that enacted direct democratic reforms have used those very mechanisms to challenge and in some cases reverse progressive policies. Beginning with Proposition 13 in 1978, Californians have led the way, using ballot initiatives and referenda to impose caps on property taxes and to force reconsideration of controversial social legislation, including bilingual education, affirmative action, and same-sex marriage. Recent ballot initiatives in San Jose and San Diego have targeted public sector union benefits. Citizens of the Golden State have also resorted to judicial recall, refusing to reconfirm Rose Bird, chief justice of the Supreme Court of California, for her opposition to the death penalty. More recently, Iowans have voted to recall all three state Supreme Court judges who voted in favor of same-sex marriage, while Maine repealed a similar law by referendum, using progressive reforms to undo progressive policies. Adding to progressive woes, their higher profile effort to recall Wisconsin's governor Scot Walker failed spectacularly.

Moreover, the rise of the administrative state has also led to unintended consequences. Like so many progressive reformers, Roosevelt believed that an expanding federal bureaucracy would attract disinterested civil servants who, unhampered by the clumsy separation of powers or federalism, would bring a new level of expertise and efficiency to government. But as government grew in power, the stakes for a panoply of "special interests" also increased, as each group jockeyed for supremacy, not in productivity or innovation, but in obtaining regulatory advantages over their competitors. Roosevelt failed to anticipate the reasons why such bureaucracies so often turned out to be neither disinterested nor effective. Far from remaining above the fray, the agencies of the administrative state have frequently developed cozy clientele relationships with the interests they seek to regulate. Furthermore, the operations of the administrative state, spread across multiple agencies, are almost always inefficient, and sometimes inept, making them targets of public discontent, and reinforcing Americans' longstanding ambivalence, if not outright hostility, toward much of the regulatory regime. And finally, in treating citizens as children who must be ruled for their own good, bureaucracies increasingly threaten to turn a self-governing republic into the "nanny state."

Given Roosevelt's evolutionary and historicist approach to politics, his tacit rejection of his predecessors' natural rights republicanism, and his embrace of progressive ideals, it is tempting to conclude that he does not belong up there on Mount Rushmore with Washington, Jefferson, and Lincoln. But that would be too harsh an assessment, even for a critic of his thought. For with or without the gigantic face, Roosevelt will remain permanently etched in the American imagination. Why? Consider first his fighting spirit and his love of country. By the strength of his example, he sought to impart these qualities to his fellow Americans, and to teach them that "mere" life, or even "comfortable" life, could never be the highest goal. As Americans continue to send their sons and daughters to fight and die in far-off lands, who cannot be moved by Roosevelt's words to his son Archie on the death of Quentin in World War I: "he died as the heroes of old died; as brave and fearless men must die when a great cause calls. If our country did not contain such men it would not be our country"?[19] Whenever the United States is at war or in mortal peril, Roosevelt's words will touch a deep chord in the American soul.

Closely related is Roosevelt's appreciation of national greatness. Although he failed to give commercial greatness its due, and sometimes gloried too much in conquest, Roosevelt summoned his countrymen to dare greatly and attempt mighty deeds. This is good for democracies especially, where the temptations of materialism loom large. He also sought to attract better men to public life, and to elevate the character of ordinary citizens. He never wavered in his efforts to create a distinctive American nationality, in which all citizens could take pride. Lastly, he sought to preserve for future generations America's natural resources and to protect its national treasures from careless development and destruction.

The United States that Roosevelt led was also far more powerful and unified than that of his Rushmore companions, and he sought to use that power to maintain stability and order in the world, not because he was infatuated with power simply, as is sometimes argued, but because it was the responsibility of a country that aimed at greatness. Here, he remained faithful to George Washington (as well as Hamilton), arguing that military preparedness was the best means of securing peace. But, like Abraham Lincoln, neither did he "shrink" or "flinch" from war, seeing in its call to sacrifice an opportunity for nobility and greatness. In this last, he stands in sharp contrast to progressives today who call for cuts to the defense budget, and fatalistically accept (if not welcome) American decline, fearing no ill consequences for peace or freedom as the United States plays a smaller role on the world stage.

It is in his domestic policies that Roosevelt proves most untrustworthy. Although America faced profound social challenges at the turn of the nineteenth century, the top-down bureaucratic control Roosevelt envisioned to address these problems had the potential to make matters far worse. Already in 1840, Alexis de Tocqueville had warned about the "kind of despotism democratic nations have to fear," foreseeing precisely the sorts of dangers that progressive policies would bring. He predicted that democracies would attack those "forms"—constitutional, legal, and institutional—that stood between them and their immediate wishes. He also foresaw the assault on individual rights in the name of collective rights, and warned against the rise of a paternalistic bureaucracy that treated citizens as children, sapping them of the will to govern themselves. All this was predicated on Tocqueville's insight that, as a rule, democratic societies tend to love equality more than liberty. As a progressive, Roosevelt dismissed Tocqueville's warnings about the tyranny of the majority; he had nothing to say about the more subtle dangers Tocqueville saw arising in the very European societies Roosevelt would later admire and look to as models.[20]

Today, with the benefit of hindsight and a fuller understanding of Roosevelt's political thought, we can better appreciate how his ideas pointed America in the direction of all these dangers. But as the monument atop Mount Rushmore attests, Roosevelt is not our only guide. By returning to the political principles of the founders (suitably adapted to modern political and economic conditions), Americans may find their way back to an energetic, but limited, national government that is the ground of true republican greatness. Thus restored, the United States could once again lead the way at home and abroad, rather than vainly attempting to catch up with a "world movement," that, 100 years after TR's Bull Moose run, teeters on the edge of moral and financial collapse. Looking up at Mount Rushmore, it is clear, in the words of the psalmist, that Americans have been blessed with a "goodly heritage." We are not the heirs of Theodore Roosevelt alone.

Notes

INTRODUCTION

1. Gilbert C. Fite, *Mount Rushmore* (Norman: University of Oklahoma Press, 1971), 47; for a critical view of the entire project, Albert Boime, "Patriarchy Fixed in Stone: Gutzon Borglum's 'Mount Rushmore,'" *American Art* 5, no. 1/2 (Winter-Spring, 1991): 142–167.

2. TR to H. Pritchett, December 26, 1904, cited in Daniel Ruddy, ed., *Theodore Roosevelt's History of the United States* (New York: Smithsonian Books, 2010), 182.

3. Richard Hofstadter, *The American Political Tradition and the Men Who Made It* (New York: Vintage Books, 1955 [first ed. 1948]), 206–237, at 229. To this repulsive brew, Hofstadter mixed in a dollop of social psychology, suggesting an "authoritarian" personality.

4. TR's reputation also suffered after the publication of Henry F. Pringle's withering biography in 1931. After the publication of Roosevelt's *Letters*, Pringle revised and abridged the original. Henry F. Pringle, *Theodore Roosevelt*, rev. ed. (New York: Harcourt, Brace, 1955); *The Letters of Theodore Roosevelt*, 8 vols., ed. Elting E. Morison et al. (Cambridge, Mass.: Harvard University Press, 1951–1954).

5. Morison, *Letters*, 5: xiii–xxiv.

6. John Morton Blum, *The Republican Roosevelt* (New York: Atheneum, 1974 [orig. pub. Harvard University Press, 1954]), 106–107, 160, x. Blum may have been following the lead of Hofstadter, whose essay on TR in *The American Political Tradition* was titled "The Conservative as Progressive."

7. George E. Mowry, *Theodore Roosevelt and the Progressive Movement* (Madison: University of Wisconsin Press, 1948); *The Era of Theodore Roosevelt* (New York: Harper and Brothers, 1958).

8. David M. Kennedy, ed., *Progressivism: The Critical Issues* (Boston: Little, Brown, 1971), xiii–xiv.

9. Kathleen Dalton, *Theodore Roosevelt: A Strenuous Life* (New York: Alfred A. Knopf, 2002); Martin J. Sklar, *The Corporate Reconstructing of American Capitalism: 1890–1916* (Cambridge, U.K.: Cambridge University Press, 1988); John Milton Cooper, Jr., *The Warrior and the Priest: Woodrow Wilson and Theodore Roosevelt* (Cambridge, Mass.: Belknap Press of Harvard University Press, 1983).

10. Most of the criticisms of academic historians have come from libertarian legal scholars and economists. Richard Epstein, *How Progressives Rewrote the Constitution* (Washington, D.C.: Cato Institute, 2007); Thomas Sowell, *Intellectuals and Society* (New York: Basic Books, 2009).

11. Stephen Skowronek, *The Politics Presidents Make: Leadership from John Ad-*

ams to George Bush (Cambridge, Mass.: Belknap Press of Harvard University Press, 1993); *Building a New American State: The Expansion of National Administrative Capacities 1877–1920* (Cambridge, U.K.: Cambridge University Press, 1982); Sidney M. Milkis, *Theodore Roosevelt, the Progressive Party, and the Transformation of American Democracy* (Lawrence: University Press of Kansas, 2009).

12. Eldon J. Eisenach, *The Lost Promise of Progressivism* (Lawrence: University Press of Kansas, 1994); James T. Kloppenberg, *Uncertain Victory: Social Democracy and Progressivism in European and American Thought, 1870–1920* (New York: Oxford University Press, 1986).

13. James W. Ceaser, *Nature and History in American Political Development* (Cambridge, Mass.: Harvard University Press, 2006).

14. Daniel D. Stid, *The President as Statesman: Woodrow Wilson and the Constitution* (Lawrence: University Press of Kansas, 1998); Ronald J. Pestritto, *Woodrow Wilson and the Roots of Modern Liberalism* (Lanham, Md.: Rowman & Littlefield, 2005).

15. To be sure, a few older books exploring the "mind" or "worlds" of Roosevelt are still in print, the work of historians or men of letters with no serious interest in political philosophy. In recent years, only Joshua David Hawley and Paul M. Rego have examined Roosevelt's political thought. Joshua David Hawley, *Theodore Roosevelt: Preacher of Righteousness* (New Haven, Conn.: Yale University Press, 2008); Paul M. Rego, *American Ideal: Theodore Roosevelt's Search for American Individualism* (Lanham, Md.: Rowman & Littlefield, 2008).

16. Jim Powell, *Bully Boy: The Truth about Theodore Roosevelt's Legacy* (New York: Crown Forum, 2006).

17. Jeffrey K. Tulis, *The Rhetorical Presidency* (Princeton, N.J.: Princeton University Press, 1987); Skowronek, *Politics Presidents Make,* sees Roosevelt as an "orthodox innovator," who follows in the tradition of Jackson/Lincoln; in emphasizing Roosevelt's individualism, Rego, too, identifies many continuities.

18. Pestritto, *Woodrow Wilson,* 45–61.

1. THE EDUCATION OF THEODORE ROOSEVELT

1. Linda P. Gross and Theresa R. Snyder, *Philadelphia's 1876 Centennial Exhibition* (Charleston, S.C.: Arcadia Publishing, 2005), 29; Robert W. Rydell, *All the World's a Fair: Visions of Empire at American International Expositions, 1876 to 1916* (Chicago: University of Chicago Press, 1984), 22; also, Russell Weigley, Nicholas Wainwright, and Edwin Wolf, eds., *Philadelphia: A 300-Year History* (New York: W. W. Norton, 1982), 465–470.

2. United States Centennial Celebration and the Declaration of Rights, Philadelphia, Pennsylvania, July 4, 1876, at http://www.sscnet.ucla.edu/history/dubois/classes/995/98F/doc35.html (accessed March 2, 2011).

3. Rydell, *All the World's a Fair,* 28. See also Douglass's scathing Fourth of July speech, delivered in 1852, and his moving Oration in Memory of Abraham Lincoln,

delivered only a month before the Centennial opened on May 10. For a discussion of how the desire for national unity overrode considerations of racial justice, see David Blight, *Race and Reunion: The Civil War in American Memory* (Cambridge, Mass.: Belknap Press of Harvard University Press, 2001).

4. It does not detract from the nobility of the Declaration's principles that its author reverted to racial stereotyping in the *Notes on Virginia*. See Jean M. Yarbrough, *The Essential Jefferson* (Cambridge, Mass.: Hackett Publishing, 2006), 205.

5. Rydell, *All the World's a Fair*, 21–26. Rydell's argument that the worlds' fairs served to reinforce racial stereotypes and promote imperialism is greatly exaggerated, but his discussion of the 1876 Exposition does provide evidence of the "scientific" racial thinking that was much in vogue at the time. For an illuminating discussion of race and racialism, see James W. Ceaser, *Reconstructing America: The Symbol of America in Modern Thought* (New Haven, Conn.: Yale University Press, 1997), 153–158.

6. Rydell, *All the World's a Fair*, 24–25.

7. Theodore Roosevelt, *An Autobiography* (New York: Da Capo Press, 1985 [orig. pub. Macmillan, 1913]), 29.

8. Ibid., 24.

9. Ibid., 55.

10. Joshua David Hawley, *Theodore Roosevelt: Preacher of Righteousness* (New Haven, Conn.: Yale University Press, 2008), 27. As Hawley notes, Theodore was more interested in sketching the different lower species from which each of his siblings had evolved. The sketches are reproduced in *The Letters of Theodore Roosevelt*, 8 vols., ed. Elting E. Morison et al. (Cambridge, Mass.: Harvard University Press, 1951–1954), 1: 12. Disappointingly, Carleton Putnam, who studied Roosevelt's early life in the greatest detail, provides no information about Theodore's early acquaintance with Darwin. Carleton Putnam, *Theodore Roosevelt: Volume One: The Formative Years, 1858–1886* (New York: Charles Scribner's Sons, 1958).

11. Abraham Lincoln to H. L. Pierce and Others, April 6, 1859, in *Abraham Lincoln: His Speeches and Writings*, ed. Roy P. Basler (Cambridge, Mass.: Da Capo Press [orig. pub. Cleveland: World Publishing, 1946]), 489.

12. Although Spencer used the term "survival of the fittest," to his "everlasting disappointment" he had failed to grasp the principle of natural selection. In seeking to explain the process by which evolution occurred, Spencer remained wedded to Lamarckian adaptation.

13. Herbert Spencer, *Social Statics*, abridged and revised by the author (New York: D. Appleton, 1896), 372.

14. Ibid., 374.

15. Ibid., 380.

16. Ibid., 323–324. On the tendency of democracies to emphasize great impersonal forces, rather than the actions of individual men, see Alexis de Tocqueville, *Democracy in America,* trans. Harvey Mansfield and Delba Winthrop (Chicago: University of Chicago Press, 2000), 469.

17. Spencer, *Social Statics*, 324.

18. Unlike Spencer, Sumner did try to apply the Darwinian principle of natural selection to the workings of society.

19. J. Laurence Laughlin, "Roosevelt at Harvard," *American Review of Reviews*, October 1924, 391–398, at 396. Of all the reminiscences of TR's Harvard days, Laughlin's is the most perceptive. On TR and the Finance Club, see Donald Wilhelm, "The Undergraduate Roosevelt," *Colliers*, October 12, 1912, 11–24. On the basis of these contemporary accounts, it would appear that Robert C. Bannister is mistaken when he asserts that Sumner spoke on the topic of Socialism. William Graham Sumner, *On Liberty, Society, and Politics: The Essential Essays of William Graham Sumner*, ed. Robert C. Bannister (Indianapolis: Liberty Fund, 1992), 159.

20. William Graham Sumner, *The Forgotten Man and Other Essays*, ed. Albert Galloway Keller (New Haven, Conn.: Yale University Press, 1919), 503. Keller dates the paper from 1878. For a general discussion, see Mike Hawkins, *Social Darwinism in European and American Political Thought, 1860–1945* (Cambridge, U.K.: Cambridge University Press, 1997), and cf. Richard Hofstadter, *Social Darwinism in American Thought* (Boston: Beacon Press, 1955).

21. Donald Wilhelm, *Theodore Roosevelt as an Undergraduate* (Boston: John W. Luce, 1910), 15.

22. Sumner, "Socialism," in Bannister, *Essential Essays*, 159–182.

23. Ibid.

24. Ibid.

25. Sumner, "The Forgotten Man," in Bannister, *Essential Essays*, 201–222.

26. Sumner, *"Laissez-Faire,"* in *Essential Essays*, 231.

27. Sumner, "The State as an 'Ethical Person,'" in *Essential Essays*, 234–236.

28. Foreword to "Lynch-Law," in *The Challenge of Facts*, ed. Edward Galloway Keller (New Haven, Conn.: Yale University Press, 1914), 383.

29. Sumner, *"Laissez-Faire,"* in Bannister, *Essential Essays*, 227–233. Not long after the establishment of the Interstate Commerce Commission, Sumner warned in this 1896 essay that especially when a great many interests were involved, as in transportation, there was no way that human intelligence could "comprehend and adjust" them all.

30. Roosevelt, *Autobiography*, 27.

31. TR to John Burgess, April 12, 1906, Manuscript Division, Library of Congress. See also the almost identical letter of October 27, 1906, included in John W. Burgess, *Reminiscences of an American Scholar: The Beginnings of Columbia University* (New York: Columbia University Press, 1934), 369–370. Also, Eldon Eisenach, *The Lost Promise of Progressivism* (Lawrence: University Press of Kansas, 1994), 31–38.

32. In addition to those Americans who went abroad for graduate study and returned with newfound admiration for Hegel, a group of homegrown intellectuals, led by William Torrey Harris and Henry Conrad Brokmeyer, established the St. Louis Philosophical and Literary Society to disseminate Hegel's ideas.

33. Wilfred M. McClay, *The Masterless: Self and Society in Modern America* (Chapel Hill: University of North Carolina Press, 1994), 134–135.

34. Walt Whitman, *Notebooks and Unpublished Prose Manuscripts*, 30 vols., ed. Edward F. Grier (New York: New York University Press, 1984), 6: 2001.

35. G. W. F. Hegel, *Introduction to the Philosophy of History*, trans. Leo Rauch (Cambridge, Mass.: Hackett Publishing, 1988), 43.

36. Ibid., 49.

37. G. W. F. Hegel, *Hegel's Philosophy of Right*, trans. T. M. Knox (New York: Oxford University Press, 1967 [reprinted 1975]), para. 324, p. 210.

38. Ibid., 42.

39. Pierre Hassner, "Georg W. F. Hegel," *The History of Political Philosophy*, 2nd ed., ed. Leo Strauss and Joseph Cropsey (Chicago: Rand McNally, 1972), 686–714, at 694.

40. To be clear, Hegel does not seek to abolish religious freedom or still less to establish a theocratic state: *Philosophy of Right*, para. 270, and Paul Franco, *Hegel's Philosophy of Freedom* (New Haven, Conn.: Yale University Press, 1999), 300–301.

41. Hegel, *Philosophy of History*, 46, 51.

42. For a fuller discussion, see Franco, *Hegel's Philosophy of Freedom*, ch. 8.

43. Hegel, *Philosophy of Right*, para. 272, p. 175.

44. From the *Lesser Logic*, as cited in Steven B. Smith, *Hegel's Critique of Liberalism: Rights in Context* (Chicago: University of Chicago Press, 1989), 154.

45. Franco, *Hegel's Philosophy of Freedom*, 339–340. According to Franco, there is nothing else like this in all of Hegel's *oeuvre*, and the logic of the dialectic makes it doubtful that Hegel thought America—either North or South—could introduce anything new. Also, G. A. Kelly, "Hegel's America," *Philosophy and Public Affairs* 2, no. 1 (Autumn 1972): 3–36.

46. Hegel, *Philosophy of History*, 86–88.

47. Ibid., 89–90.

48. Laughlin, "Roosevelt at Harvard," 392.

49. Ibid. James Russell Lowell, for one, feared that too many would make their selections based on the ease or difficulty of the course.

50. Eliot's reforms extended even to prospective students. When Roosevelt applied to Harvard, he had a choice between two different entrance exams, each of which covered sixteen subjects and extended over three days. The first focused more heavily on the older classical curriculum, while the second was weighted more toward mathematics and science. Theodore, whose preparation for college had been unusual, would opt for the latter. Nevertheless, even the more modern course of examinations required a working knowledge of Greek and Latin (two subjects in which Theodore judged himself lagging), and all applicants were required to have a basic command of either French or German as well as demonstrate competence in English composition. Wilhelm, *Theodore Roosevelt as an Undergraduate*, 27; Roosevelt, *Autobiography*, 23.

51. Morison, *Letters*, 1: 25. According to the editor, the honor grade for electives was 70, but freshmen had no electives.

52. Roosevelt, *Autobiography*, 23.

53. Ibid., 14–21; *Theodore Roosevelt's Diaries of Boyhood and Youth* (New York: Charles Scribner's Sons, 1928), 337–351, 353–365.

54. In his *Autobiography*, Roosevelt was critical of the "not always intelligent copying of what was done in the great German universities," suggesting that Eliot's efforts to introduce greater rigor had led him to the opposite extreme and made a fetish of minutiae, 26.

55. This was a lesson Theodore took to heart. As Donald Wilhelm later observed, as president, TR used fewer words of classic origin in his public messages than Lincoln did, and sometimes chose "several Saxon words where one Latinized one would suffice." Wilhelm, *Theodore Roosevelt as an Undergraduate*, 43–44.

56. Forensics topics in 1880, Roosevelt's senior year, included: "Did Seneca's moral character accord with his philosophy?" "Ought the study of the Greek and Latin languages to be regarded as essential to a liberal education?" and "Is there any good reason to doubt whether Shakespeare wrote the principal plays that bear his name?" Each was accompanied by an extensive literature review. *Harvard University Bulletin* of Harvard University Library at http://books.google.com/books?id= FoM73jjodGIC&pg=PA156&dq=senior+forensics,+harvard,+1880&hl=en&ei= l2mWTem3J46woQGUlfXkCw&sa=X&oi=book_result&ct=result&resnum=5&sqi =2&ved=0CE8Q6AEwBA#v=onepage&q&f=false (accessed February 2, 2011).

57. Richard Welling, "My Classmate Theodore Roosevelt," *American Legion Monthly*, January 1929, 9–11, at 10. But Wilhelm recounts that Hill embarrassed his garrulous student by asking him "what he thought of undergraduates prematurely falling in love," 33. Roosevelt received a 65 in senior Forensics, which was an improvement over his 60 in junior Forensics. Nevertheless, Professor Hill was the only instructor Roosevelt mentioned by name in his *Autobiography*, 24.

58. Roosevelt, *Autobiography*, 24. As is apparent from this citation, he did not fully absorb all the rules of punctuation set forth in Hill's textbook.

59. Although Roosevelt goes on to observe that he did not "personally grow up to this particular subject until a good many years later," he gives no evidence of having understood its import. See also the discussion of Plutarch's treatment of Caius Gracchus as the "'greatest' of Roman demagogues" in James W. Ceaser, *Designing a Polity: America's Constitution in Theory and Practice* (Lanham, Md.: Rowman & Littlefield, 2011), 79.

60. Wilhelm remarks that the course was "not a very comprehensive one requiring attendance at two lectures a week during one-half of the college year," *Theodore Roosevelt as an Undergraduate*, 28.

61. The Harvard catalog incorrectly listed the title of Freeman's book; it was *Outlines of History*, not *Outlines of General History*.

62. Edward Augustus Freeman, *Outlines of History* (New York: Holt & Williams, 1872), 6–7. Since this was a student textbook, Freeman simply asserted this point and

did not try to show the "scientific" basis for his argument, which rested on researches in comparative philology and comparative mythology. For a critical discussion, see Edward Norman Saveth, "Race and Nationalism in American Historiography: The Late Nineteenth Century," *Political Science Quarterly* 54, no. 3 (September 1939): 421–441, at 425–426.

63. And like Adams Sherman Hill, Freeman would go out of his way to use words of Teutonic origin.

64. Saveth, "Race and Nationalism," 424–425.

65. Freeman had very little to say about the Roman Republic and even less about its political institutions, even though these seemed indistinguishable from the old Teutonic constitution. (As for Roosevelt's more immediate purposes, Freeman's two sentences on the Gracchi would not have provided much help, *Outline of History*, 72.)

66. Freeman, *Outlines of History*, 107–108, 164.

67. And indeed, one of Roosevelt's classmates, Albert Bushnell Hart, went on to become one of the leading proponents of this view, insisting that the Teutonic origin of American institutions should be "sharply defined in the minds of the students at Harvard." Henry Cabot Lodge, the young Harvard historian who would later become one of Roosevelt's closest friends, discovered the roots of Puritan institutions in the Teutonic tribes that had brought their ancient constitution from the German forests, in Saveth, "Race and Nationalism," 430, 424.

68. Alexander Charles Ewald, *The Crown and Its Advisers* (Edinburgh and London: William Blackwood & Sons, 1870) at http://books.google.com/books?id=6zsYAAA AYAAJ&printsec=frontcover&dq=ewald,+the+crown+and+its&source=bl&ots= cpkEzWZNmO&sig=zcF15hNfUWxPkN1rK-oRrnqnhns&hl=en&ei=3zaaTaebGM-WOsmWoaUH&sa=X&oi=book_result&ct=result&resnum=1&sqi=2&ved= oCBQQ6AEwAA#v=onepage&q&f=false (accessed February 1, 2011).

69. Henry Flanders, *An Exposition of the Constitution of the United States*, 2nd ed. rev. (Philadelphia: Claxton, Remsen, and Haffelfinger, 1874), p. 3. Flanders also hoped the book might be useful for members of the bar. At http://books .google.com/books?id=c9HuN84CFkUC&printsec=frontcover&dq=henry+ flanders,+an+exposition+of+the+constitution+of+the+us,+1874&source=bl&o ts=iAWTawxd6B&sig=xT9dEPKo2AqJ6Ele6Nyv5DznmFE&hl=en&ei=BYqaTb W-HY2Ttwf9oJi8Bw&sa=X&oi=book_result&ct=result&resnum=1&sqi=2&ved= oCBcQ6AEwAA#v=onepage&q&f=false (accessed January 25, 2011).

70. Edward S. Corwin, *The Constitution and What It Means Today*, 14th ed. (Princeton, N.J.: Princeton University Press, 1978). First published in 1920, the volume is now in its fourteenth edition.

71. Flanders, *Exposition of the Constitution*, 54.

72. Ibid., 65.

73. Ibid., 134.

74. *Federalist* No. 37, 195, emphasis added. Alexander Hamilton, James Madison, and John Jay, *The Federalist Papers*, ed. Clinton Rossiter, with an Introduction and Notes by Charles R. Kesler (New York: A Mentor Book, 1999).

75. For an extended discussion, see Harvey C. Mansfield, Jr., *Taming the Prince: The Ambivalence of Modern Executive Power* (Baltimore: Johns Hopkins University Press, 1989 [paperback edition, 1993]), especially Chapter 10. Indeed, Mansfield argues persuasively that the genius of the American Constitution lies precisely in the Framers' success at "republicanizing" a strong executive.

76. Perhaps Dunbar was attempting to introduce a comparative dimension, though Laughlin in his edited and abridged volume of Mill's work in 1884 supplied numerous American examples to make the work more accessible to his readers.

77. TR to Martha Bulloch Roosevelt, October 8, 1878, in Morison, *Letters,* 1: 33–34. In the letter he explained that the work did not come easily and that he had to work "nearly as hard on Saturday as on any other day—that is, seven or eight hours."

78. In 1884, Laughlin produced his own edited and abridged version of the work, designed to make the work more accessible for American readers. The English philosopher and noted conservative Roger Scruton has called Mill's *Principles of Political Economy* a "concealed socialist tract" that masqueraded as an exposition of Adam Smith, "Thoroughly Modern Mill," *Wall Street Journal,* May 19, 2006, A10. Laughlin prided himself on assigning arguments with opposing points of view.

79. James Geddes, cited in Putnam, *Formative Years,* 140.

80. Laughlin, "Roosevelt at Harvard," 397.

81. On Colonel Higginson's love of outdoor life and optimistic spirit, see "Authors at Home: Colonel Thomas Wentworth Higginson in Cambridge," *New York Times,* January 21, 1899, at http://query.nytimes.com/mem/archive-free/pdf?res=F2 0612FF355D11738DDDA80A94D9405B8985F0D3 (accessed February 15, 2011).

82. Wilhelm, *Theodore Roosevelt as an Undergraduate,* 30.

83. Laughlin, "Roosevelt at Harvard," 397.

84. Indeed, Laughlin reported that in later life TR greeted him cordially and announced, "There's the fellow that taught me Political Economy," adding that it was "the best course I had at the university." Ibid., 397–398. But cf. Roosevelt's comments on Richard Ely. Ely, a progressive economist who was graduated from Columbia College and received his Ph.D. from Heidelberg, taught at Johns Hopkins and later the University of Wisconsin. Of Ely, Roosevelt would later remark, "He first introduced me to radicalism in economics and then made me sane in my radicalism." Richard T. Ely, *The Ground under Our Feet: An Autobiography* (New York: Macmillan, 1938), 278–279.

85. Wilhelm reports that Shaler delighted in repeating the story of how a bag of lobsters Roosevelt was transporting on a Boston street car had gotten loose and crawled off in all directions. Apparently, Roosevelt asked so many questions in class that he had to be reminded that Shaler was "running this course," Wilhelm, *Theodore Roosevelt as an Undergraduate,* 13, 35.

86. Based on Shaler's textbook for the class, *The First Book of Geology* (Boston: Ginn, Heath, 1885), Shaler blunted Darwin's argument by speaking of the Creator, as well as entertaining the possibility that human beings evolved through both natural selection and the inheritance of acquired characteristics, 195, 201.

87. Edmund Morris, *The Rise of Theodore Roosevelt* (New York: Ballantine Books, 1979), 110.

88. Welling, "My Classmate Theodore Roosevelt," 67; Wilhelm, *Theodore Roosevelt as an Undergraduate*, 39.

89. Putnam, *Formative Years*, n. 79, 146–147, 238.

90. Morris, *Rise of TR*, 769, n. 77.

91. Putnam, *Formative Years*, 131; Welling, "My Classmate Theodore Roosevelt," 11, cites the "cursed indifference" captured by class poet, George Pellew.

92. Wilhelm, *Theodore Roosevelt as an Undergraduate*, 16–18, 28.

93. Ibid., 18.

94. "The Practicability of Equalizing Men and Women before the Law," Commencement Day Dissertation, June 1880, Harvard College Archives. Perhaps because it is called a dissertation, the essay has been widely but erroneously characterized as TR's senior thesis, most notably by Morris, *Rise of TR*, 128. The entire essay is only eight handwritten pages. Roosevelt was graduated magna cum laude and elected to Phi Beta Kappa, but he chose not to take the examination for honors in natural science and, therefore, received only honorable mention.

95. See Thomas Jefferson to Henri Gregoire, February 25, 1809, in Yarbrough, *Essential Jefferson*, 205.

96. All quotations in this section are from Roosevelt's Commencement Day Dissertation. Underlining in original. Harvard College Archives. It is worth noting, however, that the Census figures for 1870 report 5 women lawyers. In 1880, there were 75 and in 1900, the number had grown to 1,010. Cited in Robert B. Charles, "Legal Education in the Late Nineteenth Century, through the Eyes of Theodore Roosevelt," *American Journal of Legal History* 37, no. 3 (July 1993): 233–272, n. 9, 234.

97. Wilhelm notes that "he did not deliver the 'dissertation' to which he was entitled at commencement," though he offers no explanation, *Theodore Roosevelt as an Undergraduate*, 25. Putnam makes no mention of the commencement "dissertation," *Formative Years*, 196–197.

98. In fact, he would title one of his talks "The Need of a Navy," January 1898, in *Gunston's Magazine*, at http://www.theodore-roosevelt.com/treditorials.html (accessed July 20, 2011). The file name is qunti.

99. Roosevelt, *Autobiography*, 25. Although Harvard offered prizes for elocution and oral reading, Roosevelt did not compete for them, Wilhelm, *Theodore Roosevelt as an Undergraduate*, 24–25. For a list of the prizes and their recipients, see the Harvard catalogs. Morris recounts William Roscoe Thayer's recollection of Theodore's first awkward attempts at public speaking at the annual dinner of the Harvard *Crimson* in February 1879, Morris, *Rise of TR*, 109.

100. In 1893, Thayer had famously argued that judges should exercise judicial self-restraint and not strike down progressive legislation.

101. Roosevelt, *Autobiography*, 55, 212–220.

102. I rely heavily in this paragraph on Charles, "Legal Education," esp. 244,

255–256; also Robert B. Charles, Drafts on Theodore Roosevelt's legal education, 1990–1992, Theodore Roosevelt Collection, Houghton Library, Harvard University (Roosevelt R331.C38L), and Putnam, *Formative Years,* 219–220.

103. Burgess, *Reminiscences,* 213, emphasis added.

104. Charles, "Legal Education," 248–250.

105. Perhaps because Burgess's courses were "optional," Roosevelt did not see any need to pass them on to Walter Trimble, TR's Harvard roommate and Columbia Law School associate, as he did the others when he decided to drop out of law school. See especially Robert B. Charles, "Theodore Roosevelt, the Lawyer," in *Theodore Roosevelt: Many-Sided American,* ed. Natalie A. Naylor, Douglas Brinkley, and John Allen Gable (Interlaken, N.Y.: Heart of the Lakes Publishing, 1992), 121–139, at 123.

106. Burgess, *Reminiscences,* 212–213, 373–374.

107. Burgess, *Reminiscences,* 29, also 69, 197, 315, 371. And see the discussion of Burgess in McClay, *Masterless,* 136–149; also, William Henry Berge, "The Impulse for Expansion: John W. Burgess, Alfred Thayer Mahan, Theodore Roosevelt, Josiah Strong and the Development of a Rationale" (Ph.D. diss.,Vanderbilt University, 1969).

108. Burgess, *Reminiscences,* 96.

109. How his admiration for German power fit together with his battlefield oath to avoid bloodshed and seek compromise was left unresolved. Cf. Hegel, who in the *Philosophy of Right* had argued that war brings to the fore the ethical dimension of the state, para. 324, p. 210.

110. Burgess, *Reminiscences,* 121–132. Also Juergen Herbst, *The German Historical School in American Scholarship: A Study in the Transfer of Culture* (Ithaca: Cornell University Press, 1965), 110–113, 169–170.

111. See especially Burgess's essay, "The American University: When Shall It Be? Where Shall It Be? What Shall It Be?" 1884, and republished as Appendix 1 in *Reminiscences,* 349–368.

112. Julius Goebel, Jr., *A History of the School of Law: Columbia University* (New York: Columbia University Press, 1955), 419, n. 101.

113. Burgess, *Reminiscences,* 197, 207. By the time Roosevelt entered the Law School in the fall of 1880, however, Burgess was frustrated that he had not achieved his goal of putting the science of jurisprudence on a par with private law and had persuaded the Columbia Trustees to approve his plan to establish a graduate School of Political Science.

114. Ibid., 86–87. Out of 500 students enrolled in the Law School, about 50 took his classes. Goebel, *A History of Columbia Law School,* suggests that he may have "deliberately discouraged attendance by a continuous process of elimination," 421, n. 140.

115. Goebel's *History of Columbia Law School* offers the most complete picture of the courses Burgess was developing, as well as the trustees' minutes in approving them. Moreover, in an essay written in 1883, Burgess set forth his view of the

responsibility of a university professor. He must present *"his own view"* of history "derived from the most original sources attainable," "The Methods of Historical Study and Research in Columbia College," in *Methods of Teaching History*, ed. G. Stanley Hall (Boston: D. C. Heath, 1883), 215–221, at 218, emphasis in original.

116. John W. Burgess, *Political Science and Comparative Constitutional Law*, 2 vols. (Boston: Ginn and Company, 1890–1891), 1: vi (hereafter cited as *PSCCL*). Also Burgess, "Methods of Historical Study," 220.

117. Stefan Collini, Donald Winch, John Burrow, *That Noble Science of Politics* (Cambridge, U.K.: Cambridge University Press, 1983), 219.

118. H. W. Brands, *T.R.: The Last Romantic* (New York: Basic Books, 1997) speculates that TR would surely have noticed this methodological difference, 111. But for a discussion of the implicit teleology of evolution, see Gertrude Himmelfarb, *Darwin and the Darwinian Revolution* (Garden City, N.Y.: Doubleday Anchor Books, 1959), ch. 19.

119. Burgess's treatment of the state aimed to bring German idealism down to earth by harnessing it to the "objective realities" of history, political science, and practical politics. As a political "scientist," Burgess left it to the speculative philosophers to consider the "idea" of the "perfect and complete" state, while he focused on its historical development. Nevertheless, he candidly admitted that his "scientific" analysis was informed by his idealistic view of what the state must eventually become. Burgess, *PSCCL*, 1: 47–48; Burgess, *Reminiscences*, 254.

120. Burgess, *PSCCL*, 1: 67.

121. Ibid., 1: 33; also Saveth, "Race and Nationalism," 435, 439.

122. Burgess, *PSCCL*, 1: 40–48; Burgess, *Reminiscences*, 397.

123. Burgess, *PSCCL*, 1: 44–45. And see his pleas for a more complete reconciliation between the North and the South in *Reminiscences*, 289.

124. Burgess, *PSCCL*, 1: 45. Years later, in the run-up to World War I, Burgess was accused of favoring German imperialism. In his *Reminiscences*, he defended himself by arguing that what he had in mind especially was British imperialism, 254–255, though this account is not altogether accurate.

125. Burgess, *PSCCL*, 1: 46–47, emphasis added.

126. Ibid., 1: 52.

127. And see Burgess's response to his critics, who accused him of wishing to erect another Leviathan, in *Reminiscences*, 249–250.

128. So little disposed was the modern state to trample on liberty that, as a practical matter, "the state can do no wrong." Burgess, *PSCCL*, 1: 57.

129. Ibid., 2: 5–9.

130. TR recorded in his law notebook the same lesson from Professor Dwight: "In U.S. supreme power is in the people; and some of it is parceled out to Congress, some to the states, and the residuary remains with the people, in the shape of the constitution," cited in Brands, *Last Romantic*, 111.

131. Burgess, *PSCCL*, 1: 88, 176, and "The American Commonwealth: Changes in Its Relation to the Nation," *Political Science Quarterly* 1 (March 1886): 17.

132. Burgess, *PSCCL*, 1: 177; Burgess, *Reminiscences*, 251–252.

133. Burgess, *PSCCL*, 1: 176; Burgess, *Reminiscences*, 250–251.

134. Burgess, *PSCCL*, 1: 67.

135. Ibid., 1: 185, 151.

136. Burgess, *Reminiscences*, 289–305.

137. Cf. the more widespread association of positive liberty with the public, and negative liberty with the private popularized by Isaiah Berlin.

138. In this reading, the final clause of the amendment granting Congress the power of enforcement was the most important.

139. Burgess, *PSCCL*, 1: 174–179, 87–89.

140. Ibid., 1: 85. In Burgess's view, Hegel's only defect was that he tried to reach this final end without first attaining the earlier two ends, i.e., first balancing security and liberty, and then perfecting the national genius.

141. JWB to TR, November 8, 1901; TR to JWB, November 9, 1901. Manuscript Division, Library of Congress.

142. TR to Arthur Hamilton Lee, April 8, 1907, in Morison, *Letters*, 5: 644–645. Consider, however, that the letter was written after Burgess delivered his Inaugural Lecture in Berlin in 1906, where he suggested that the Monroe Doctrine had outlived its usefulness.

143. Saveth suggestively points to the Teutonic roots of laissez-faire but misses altogether the Hegelian dimension of Burgess's thought, "Race and Nationalism," 440.

144. Burgess, *PSCCL*, 1: 228, 237, 240.

145. Given the improbable marriage of Hegel and Teutonic liberty, understood as laissez-faire individualism, Burgess could at best be described as an "ambivalent consolidator" (McClay, *Masterless*, 147) or at worst a foreigner in his own land.

146. Sumner, "The Conquest of the United States by Spain" (1898) in Bannister, *Essential Essays*, 272–297.

147. Other prominent opponents of the war and of American imperialism included William James, Charles Eliot Norton, and Charles William Eliot, all of Harvard, as well as Mark Twain, Jane Addams, Samuel Gompers, and Carl Schurz.

148. See Burgess's account of his publisher canceling his book contract in *Reminiscences*, 255–257.

149. Ibid., 215–217.

150. Although he opposed American imperialism, he had nothing against the spread of German power. Cf. Burgess, *Reminiscences*, 254–255.

151. JWB to TR, November 2, 1906; November 8, 1906; December 29, 1906; TR to JWB, November 27, 1906; November 28, 1906, Manuscript Division, Library of Congress.

152. Cf. TR to Arthur Hamilton Lee, April 8, 1907, where Roosevelt questioned Burgess's "tact and judgment." He was "an interesting fellow, but very crochety" and "a political opponent." Roosevelt then added that he knew that Burgess had "always been violently against me on the Monroe Doctrine." The editors point out

that in the same speech he also expressed the opinion that the tariff was rapidly becoming "obsolete." Morison, *Letters*, 5: 644–645.

2. HISTORY LESSONS: ROOSEVELT'S AMERICA

1. Theodore Roosevelt, *An Autobiography* (New York: Da Capo Press, 1985 [orig. pub. Macmillan, 1913]), 24.

2. Theodore Roosevelt, *The Naval War of 1812*, in *The Works of Theodore Roosevelt*, 20 vols., ed. Herman Hagedorn (New York: Charles Scribner's Sons, 1924), 6: xxiv (hereafter cited as *Works*).

3. *Works*, 6: xxxvi.

4. *Works*, 6: 373.

5. Theodore Roosevelt, *Gouverneur Morris*, in *Works*, 7: 461.

6. *Naval War*, in *Works*, 6: 373.

7. *Works*, 6: 10, 373–374.

8. *Works*, 6: 373.

9. *Works*, 6: 114.

10. "The Influence of Sea Power upon History," October 1890, in *Works*, 12: 264–272, at 271.

11. *Naval War*, in *Works*, 6: 114.

12. *Works*, 6: xxvii.

13. "History as Literature," Presidential Address to the American Historical Association, December 27, 1912, in *Works*, 12: 3–24.

14. *Naval War*, in *Works*, 6: 224.

15. *Works*, 6: 23–24 n. 2.

16. *Works*, 6: 23–24, 367–368. On this point, consider the response of Alexis de Tocqueville to Arthur de Gobineau, November 17, 1853, in *"The European Revolution" and Correspondence with Gobineau*, ed. John Lukas (Garden City, N.Y.: Anchor Doubleday Books, 1959), 228–229.

17. TR to HCL, June 7, 1886, in *Selections from the Correspondence of Theodore Roosevelt and Henry Cabot Lodge 1884–1918*, 2 vols. (New York: Charles Scribner's Sons, 1925), 1: 41–42.

18. TR to HCL, August 10, 1886, in *Selections from the Correspondence*, 1: 44–45. But cf. Edmund Morris, who in *The Rise of Theodore Roosevelt* (New York: Ballantine Books, 1979) regards *Benton* as "a testament to his [Roosevelt's] developing political philosophy and theory of statesmanship," 333.

19. TR to HCL, March 27, 1886, in *Selections from the Correspondence*, 1: 38.

20. *Thomas Hart Benton*, in *Works*, 7: 5 (hereafter cited as *THB*).

21. *Works*, 6: 14–16.

22. "Shall we not fill the Wilderness with white Savages, and will they not become more formidable to us than the tawny ones who now inhabit it?" John Jay to Thomas Jefferson, December 14, 1786, cited in Ralph Lerner, "Reds and Whites:

Rights and Wrongs," in *The Thinking Revolutionary: Principle and Practice in the New Republic* (Ithaca: Cornell University Press, 1987), 139–173, at 150.

23. *THB*, in *Works*, 7: 10, 27, 13, 26; but cf. Morris, who calls his defense of Manifest Destiny "inspired," *Rise of TR*, 333.

24. *THB*, in *Works*, 7: 37–39.

25. *Works*, 7: 111–112. Benton showed "by actual statistics that up to 1840 we had paid to the Indians eighty-five millions of dollars for land purchases, which was over five times as much as the United States gave the great Napoleon for Louisiana; and about three times as much as we paid France, Spain, and Mexico together for the purchase of Louisiana, Florida, and California, while the amount of land received in return would not equal any one of these purchases, and was but a fractional part of Louisiana or California. We paid the Cherokees for their territory exactly as much as we paid the French, at the height of their power, for Louisiana; while as to the Creek and Choctaw nations, we paid each more for their lands than we paid for Louisiana and Florida combined."

26. *Works*, 7: 38, but cf. 13. It is not clear why, if the Indians had no title to the land, taking it from them could be unjust.

27. John W. Burgess, *Reminiscences of an American Scholar: The Beginnings of Columbia University* (New York: Columbia University Press, 1934), 45–47.

28. *THB*, in *Works*, 7: 37–39.

29. See especially his long footnote discussing the works of George W. Manypenny and Helen Hunt Jackson in *The Winning of the West* in *Works*, 8: 81–82.

30. John Marshall, *The Life of George Washington*, ed. Robert Faulkner and Paul Carrese (Indianapolis: Liberty Fund, 2000), 332, 358.

31. Alexis de Tocqueville, *Democracy in America*, trans. Harvey Mansfield and Delba Winthrop (Chicago: University of Chicago Press, 2000), explanatory footnote, 320.

32. Lerner, "Reds and Whites," 156. The quotations from Marshall, 147.

33. *THB*, in *Works*, 7: 114.

34. Cf. Alexis de Tocqueville, "Conversation with Mr. Sam Houston, on Indians, December 21, 1831," in *The Tocqueville Reader: A Life in Letters and Politics*, ed. Olivier Zunz and Alan S. Kahan (Oxford, U.K.: Blackwell Publishing, 2002), 59–62.

35. *THB*, in *Works*, 7: 115–116.

36. *Works*, 7: 172.

37. *Works*, 7: 173. Roosevelt's remarks are wide of the mark. The Monroe Doctrine did not question established colonies, but was aimed at future plantations.

38. *Works*, 7: 170–172.

39. *Works*, 7: 112, 28.

40. *Works*, 7: 223.

41. *Works*, 7: 103.

42. *Works*, 7: 54.

43. *Works*, 7: 108.

44. *Works*, 7: 44, 144.

45. *Works*, 7: 55–56.

46. *Works*, 7: 26, 102–103.

47. *Works*, 7: 40.

48. *Works*, 7: 48.

49. *Works*, 7: 75–76.

50. Indeed, he did not see that it was not even a real majority of the whole people that he deified, but only a portion of the population, consisting of white males of a certain age and meeting certain other qualifications, ibid., 156.

51. *Works*, 7: 48, 79–80, 157, 181.

52. *Works*, 7: 155, 83.

53. *Works*, 7: 166.

54. *Works*, 7: 33.

55. *Gouverneur Morris*, in *Works*, 7: 468–469 (hereafter cited as *GM*).

56. *Works*, 7: 328, though this apparently stood him in good stead in France. Unlike Jefferson, Morris was a shrewd judge of character and not prone to sweeping generalizations, 351.

57. Morris, *Rise of TR*, 379; John Allen Gable, "Introduction: Theodore Roosevelt as Historian and Man of Letters," in *Gouverneur Morris* (Oyster Bay, N.Y.: Bicentennial Edition published by the Theodore Roosevelt Association, 1975), ix–x. See also the references to Madison's "Debates" in *GM*, in *Works*, 7: 336, also, 330–331.

58. *GM*, in *Works*, 7: 326. This is one of the very few times that Roosevelt took a positive view of "abstract right."

59. *Works*, 7: 328–330.

60. *Works*, 7: 335–336. John Adams made a similar proposal, for which Jefferson took him to task, raising many of the same objections as TR. For a discussion of the TJ-JA positions, see Jean M. Yarbrough, "Politics and Friendship in the Adams-Jefferson Correspondence," in *Friends and Citizens: Essays in Honor of Wilson Carey McWilliams*, ed. Peter Dennis Barthory and Nancy L. Schwartz (Lanham, Md.: Rowman & Littlefield, 2001), 67–79.

61. *GM*, in *Works*, 7: 341–343.

62. By the time he published *Oliver Cromwell* in 1900, however, he had grown critical of the "tendency in the law toward the deification of technicalities, the substitution of the letter for the spirit, a tendency which can only be offset by a bench, and indeed, a bar, possessing both courage and spirit," *Oliver Cromwell*, in *Works*, 10: 299.

63. *GM*, in *Works*, 7: 337–338. Not surprisingly, after the election of 1800, Morris backed Adams's appointment of the midnight judges, arguing that they would serve as "anchors" in the republican storm. But TR objected, principally because the Federalists treated this as an opportunity to reward their friends and adherents, 450.

64. Ironically, at the same time that Roosevelt was singing Morris's praises for creating a presidential system of government, Woodrow Wilson was arguing that America needed to evolve into a parliamentary democracy, where power was ex-

288   NOTES TO PAGES 67–73

ercised not by the president but by a cabinet drawn from the majority party in Congress.

65. On only one point did his warnings come true, and then only in part. Morris feared that the West would ally with the South, forcing America into a war with some European power for their mutual benefit and at the expense of the Northeast. In 1787, the most obvious candidate looked to be Spain, which at that time controlled the Mississippi Valley. But with the retrocession of the Louisiana territory to France and its subsequent sale to the United States that danger passed. It arose again only a few years later, however, when America, led by the "House of Virginia," was drawn into a war with Britain it was ill prepared to wage, and which cost the Northeast dearly.

66. TR to HCL, February 15, 1887, in *Selections from the Correspondence*, 1: 51; also TR to Jonas S. Van Duzer, January 15, 1888, in *The Letters of Theodore Roosevelt*, 8 vols., ed. Elting E. Morison et al. (Cambridge, Mass.: Harvard University Press, 1954), 1: 135–136.

67. "History as Literature," in *Works*, 12: 3–24, at 5. Also Gable, "Roosevelt as Historian and Man of Letters," 12–13.

68. TR to Francis Parkman, April 23, 1888, in Morison, *Letters*, 1: 139–140.

69. TR to Francis Parkman, July 13, 1889, in Morison, *Letters*, 1: 172–173; "Francis Parkman's Histories," November 24, 1892, in *Works*, 12: 246–253, at 250–251.

70. "Francis Parkman's Histories," in *Works*, 12: 250.

71. Morris, *Rise of TR*, 462, where Morris praises TR's "erudition" and "breadth of his mind."

72. *The Winning of the West*, in *Works*, 8: 5 (hereafter cited as *WW*).

73. *WW*, in *Works*, 8: 7.

74. TR to Francis Parkman, April 23, 1888, in Morison, *Letters*, 1: 140.

75. John Milton Cooper, Jr., "Introduction," in Theodore Roosevelt, *The Winning of the West* (Lincoln: University of Nebraska Press, 1995), 1: vii–xxii, at xii.

76. *WW*, in *Works*, 8: 197, 208–209.

77. *WW*, in *Works*, 8: 22; *Works*, 9: 468.

78. For a discussion of the differences and similarities between Turner and Roosevelt, see Cooper, "Introduction," xiv–xvii.

79. *WW*, in *Works*, 9: 180–183.

80. As Roosevelt wrote to Parkman, the first chapter of *THB* provided an outline for *WW*, TR to Francis Parkman, April 23, 1888, in Morison, *Letters*, 1: 140.

81. *WW*, in *Works*, 8: 73.

82. *WW*, in *Works*, 8: 26.

83. In this respect, the claims of the states differed little from those of the Indians. Adopting an essentially Lockean view of property, Roosevelt argued that "the man who puts the soil to use must of right dispossess the man who does not," *WW*, in *Works*, 8: 73.

84. Congress's only mistake was to sell large parcels of land to private companies, rather than divide it into smaller plots to be sold directly to homesteaders. This error was rectified only later.

85. *WW*, in *Works,* 9: 211, 230.

86. *WW*, in *Works,* 9: 200, 219.

87. See the introduction to the later volumes by his publisher, George Haven Putnam, "Roosevelt, Historian and Statesman," in *Works,* 9: ix–xix.

88. For a list of the sources Roosevelt consulted, see "Preface," in *Works,* 8: xxxix–xliv.

89. Thomas G. Dyer, *Theodore Roosevelt and the Idea of Race* (Baton Rouge: Louisiana State University Press, 1980), esp. chs. 2–3.

90. *WW*, in *Works,* 9: 155, 44; *Works,* 8: 407; *Works* 9: 155.

91. *WW*, in *Works,* 9: 274–286.

92. Still, in a long footnote reviewing the treatment of the Indians, Roosevelt argued that the United States should now "break up the great Indian reservations, disregard their tribal governments, allot the land in severalty (with, however, only a limited power of alienation), and treat the Indians as we do other citizens," in short, as individuals, *WW*, in *Works,* 8: 80.

93. "Influence of Sea Power upon History," in *Works,* 12: 264–272.

94. *WW*, in *Works,* 9: 97–98.

95. *WW*, in *Works,* 9: 279, 285, 276.

96. *WW*, in *Works,* 9: 57. Emphasis added.

97. *WW*, in *Works,* 9: 58. And see also the chapter "The State of Franklin, 1784–1788," 139–176.

98. Alexander Hamilton, James Madison, and John Jay, *The Federalist Papers,* ed. Clinton Rossiter, with an Introduction and Notes by Charles R. Kesler (New York: A Mentor Book, 1999), *Federalist* No. 49, 282–283; Thomas Jefferson to James Madison, September 6, 1789, Thomas Jefferson to Samuel Kercheval, July 12, 1816, Thomas Jefferson to Major John Cartwright, June 5, 1824, in Jean M. Yarbrough, *The Essential Jefferson* (Cambridge, Mass.: Hackett Publishing, 2006), 176–180, 239–245, 260–266.

99. Abraham Lincoln to H. L. Pierce and Others, April 6, 1859; "The Perpetuation of Our Political Institutions: Address before the Young Men's Lyceum of Springfield, Illinois," January 27, 1838; Address at Cooper Institute, February 27, 1860, in *Abraham Lincoln: His Speeches and Writings,* ed. Roy P. Basler (Cambridge, Mass.: Da Capo Press [orig. pub. Cleveland: World Publishing, 1946]), 488–489, 76–85, 517–536.

100. Wilfred M. McClay, "The Founding of Nations," *First Things,* no. 161 (March 2006): 33–39, at 34; McClay's metaphors are more apt than Woodrow Wilson's dichotomy between the Framers' so-called Newtonian model and the Darwinian one he favored.

101. *WW*, in *Works,* 8: 411.

102. *WW*, in *Works,* 9: 44.

103. Without any sense of irony, Roosevelt accused the Indians of having no understanding of right other than the right of the strongest. *WW*, in *Works,* 8: 69–70.

104. One major exception is Roosevelt's rather Lockean argument that the right

to property is based on use, *WW*, in *Works*, 8: 70–71. By using the land only to hunt, the Indians do not make proper use of it and thus have no right to it. But within the broader context of nature understood as the survival of the fittest, his argument more closely resembles that of William Graham Sumner than it does that of the founders.

105. *WW*, in *Works*, 9: 155–156, 103–104; *Works*, 8: 68.

106. *WW*, in *Works*, 8: 5, though Roosevelt granted that for the frontiersmen, a more apt comparison was to the Hebrew Prophets, 391.

107. To repeat, adherence to natural right does not mean inflexibility, or a one-size-fits-all morality. Natural right can be qualified by necessity, and it permits a prudent adaptation to circumstances, but neither should it be confused with making history the standard for moral action. Consider also Roosevelt's distinction between "abstract morality," which would consider the frontiersmen "free booters," and "applied ethics," which takes into consideration "the greatness of the race and the well-being of civilized mankind," *WW*, in *Works*, 9: 155, and compare with Basler, *Abraham Lincoln*, 302–304.

108. *WW*, in *Works*, 8: 18; in *Works*, 9: 24.

109. *WW*, in *Works*, 8: 86.

110. Dyer, *TR and Race*, 66.

111. *WW*, in *Works*, 8: 150–152.

112. *WW*, in *Works*, 8: 552.

113. And in 1900, Henry Cabot Lodge would maintain that in establishing their local town governments, the Puritans unconsciously drew on the Jutes, Angles, and Saxons.

114. Tocqueville, in his correspondence with Arthur de Gobineau, makes precisely this point, contrasting the "exaggerated and somewhat childish trust" of the men of the eighteenth century in their power to shape their own destiny, which, for all its failings, produced "great things," with "the great sickness" of his own age that saw men as subject to forces over which they had no control. Tocqueville to Gobineau, December 20, 1853, in *Correspondence with Gobineau*, 231–233.

115. Richard Boyd, "Tocqueville's Algeria," *Society* (September/October 2001): 65–70, at 69.

116. James W. Ceaser, *Nature and History in American Political Development* (Cambridge, Mass.: Harvard University Press, 2006).

117. *WW*, in *Works* 9: 13–14; in *Works*, 8: 552. Only rarely does Roosevelt criticize their constitutional proposals, as when he dismissed a provision in the Franklin constitution that would have barred all lawyers from holding office as "one of the darling plans of the ordinary sincere rural demagogue of the day," 9: 150.

118. *WW*, in *Works*, 9: 99.

119. *WW*, in *Works*, 8: 45.

120. *WW*, in *Works*, 9: 181.

121. Cf. Tocqueville, *Democracy in America*, 325, n. 29.

3. REPUBLICAN REFORMER

1. The best discussion of the academic progressives is Eldon Eisenach, *The Lost Promise of Progressivism* (Lawrence: University Press of Kansas, 1994), 31–40. By focusing on these early academics, who had mostly studied in Germany, Eisenach shows that progressivism had begun to take root at some of the newer universities by the middle of the 1880s. On occasion, Roosevelt too described his brand of republicanism as "progressive," but this was mostly to distinguish himself from the machine politicians he opposed. See, for example, "Speech before the Young Republican Club of Brooklyn, N.Y.," October 17, 1885, in *The Works of Theodore Roosevelt*, 20 vols., ed. Herman Hagedorn (New York: Charles Scribner's Sons, 1924), 14: 58–67, at 58 (hereafter cited as *Works*).

2. Theodore Roosevelt, *An Autobiography* (New York: Da Capo Press, 1985 [orig. pub. Macmillan, 1913]), 57, 62–63.

3. "Address before the Liberal Club," Buffalo, N.Y., September 10, 1895, in *Works*, 14: 192–206; also, "The College Graduate and Public Life," August 1890, in *Works*, 13: 36–46, at 42.

4. "Address before the Liberal Club," in *Works*, 14: 192–206, at 199–200.

5. The law, which even Roosevelt conceded was badly drawn up, was struck down by the Court of Appeals the following year. The court's decision, however, would later figure prominently in his attack on the judiciary.

6. "The Mayor's Power of Removal," March 12, 1884, in *Works*, 14: 33–36, at 33.

7. Although Henry Cabot Lodge had replaced Henry Adams as lecturer in American history at Harvard during Roosevelt's student years, TR did not take any courses with Lodge and did not meet him until later. In his recollections of TR at Harvard, Laughlin speculates that it was Lodge who persuaded TR to stay with the party and Blaine. J. Laurence Laughlin, "Roosevelt at Harvard," *American Review of Reviews*, October 1924, 393.

8. "Interview in the Boston *Herald*," July 20, 1884, in *Works*, 14: 41–42 at 41.

9. "Address before the Young Republican Club of Brooklyn, N.Y.," October 18, 1884, in *Works*, 14: 39–40, at 40; even before the Blaine nomination, Roosevelt proudly defended the reputation of the Republicans as the "party of moral ideas," "Address at a Mass-Meeting of Republicans of the 21st Assembly and Aldermanic Districts," October 28, 1882, in *Works*, 14: 13–15, at 14.

10. "Machine Politics in New York City," November 1886, in *Works*, 13: 76–98, at 81–82; also, "Phases of State Legislation," January 1885, in *Works*, 13: 47–75, at 54–55; Alexander Hamilton, James Madison, and John Jay, *The Federalist Papers*, ed. Clinton Rossiter, with an Introduction and Notes by Charles R. Kesler (New York: A Mentor Book, 1999), *Federalist* No. 72, 405.

11. "The Manly Virtues and Practical Politics," in *Works*, 13: 27–35, at 28, 33. They were, in the memorable words of George Washington Plunkitt, "dudes that part their names in the middle." Cited in Richard Hofstadter, "'Idealists, Professors, and

Sore-Heads': The Genteel Reformers," *Columbia University Forum* 5, no. 2 (Spring 1962): 4–11.

12. "Address at the Harvard Union," February 23, 1907, in *Works*, 13: 564; also Roosevelt, *Autobiography*, 57.

13. Why the best men do not go into politics was a question that the British political thinker and diplomat James Bryce asked in his *American Commonwealth*, which was first published in 1888, and to which Roosevelt contributed information on municipal government.

14. Review of *The Law of Civilization and Decay*, January 1897, in *Works*, 13: 242–260.

15. "American Ideals," February 1895, in *Works*, 13: 3–12.

16. *Federalist* No. 11, 53; *Federalist* No. 12. See also Alexis de Tocqueville, "Some Considerations on the Commercial Greatness of the United States," in *Democracy in America*, trans. Harvey Mansfield and Delba Winthrop (Chicago: University of Chicago Press, 2000), 384–390. Unlike Tocqueville, Roosevelt saw no heroism in the sea captain who risked all to sell his tea for one penny less. "Manly Virtues," in *Works*, 13: 27–35, at 29; "American Ideals," in *Works*, 13: 11.

17. "American Ideals," in *Works*, 13: 9, 11.

18. "The Reunited People," April 9, 1902, and "North and South," October 18, 1905, in *Works*, 14: 26–35; "Address at the Harvard Union," February 23, 1907, in *Works*, 13: 564.

19. Roosevelt praised Grant on numerous occasions, but see especially his speech delivered at Galena, Illinois, April 27, 1900, in *Works*, 13: 430–441.

20. "Address at the Quarter-Centennial Celebration of Statehood in Colorado," August 2, 1901, in *Works*, 13: 455; *The Winning of the West*, in *Works*, 9: 18–19.

21. "Manly Virtues," July 1894, in *Works*, 13: 27–35, at 32.

22. "Machine Politics," November 1886, in *Works*, 13: 76–98, at 82.

23. Harvey Mansfield, *Manliness* (New Haven, Conn.: Yale University Press, 2006), 95, notes the recurrence of "shirk" and "shrink" in Roosevelt's vocabulary, to which he might also have added "flinch."

24. "The American Boy," May 1900, in *Works*, 13: 401–407, at 407. "Athletics, Scholarship, and Public Service," February 23, 1907, in *Works*, 13: 559–570. John J. Miller, *The Big Scrum: How Teddy Roosevelt Saved Football* (New York: Harper, 2011).

25. Arthur Lee, Introduction to *Oliver Cromwell*, in *Works*, 10: 183.

26. Mansfield, *Manliness*, esp. ch. 4.

27. Of course, he could and did imagine that society might become so over-refined that these virtues would wither away. But this, he thought, would unquestionably spell decline. Review of *The Law of Civilization and Decay*, January 1897, in *Works*, 13: 247.

28. "Manly Virtues," in *Works*, 13: 28, 32.

29. Roosevelt, *Autobiography*, 75–76.

30. "Phases of State Legislation," January 1885, and "Machine Politics in New York

City," November 1886, in *Works,* 13: 47–98. Ironically, in warning against civic lethargy, Roosevelt here sounded very much like the Jefferson he so "cordially despised."

31. What is more, although he acknowledged that the term "machine" was usually employed in a derogatory sense, he thought the machine was "often a very powerful instrument for good." "Machine Politics," in *Works,* 13: 76.

32. "Machine Politics," in *Works,* 13: 79.

33. "Machine Politics," in *Works,* 13: 79–80.

34. Benjamin Franklin, "Information to Those Who Would Remove to America," in *The Writings of Benjamin Franklin,* 11 vols., ed. Albert Henry Smyth (New York: Macmillan Company, 1907), 8: 603–614, at 607.

35. TR to HCL, August 10, 1899, in *Selections from the Correspondence of Theodore Roosevelt and Henry Cabot Lodge 1884–1918,* 2 vols. (New York: Charles Scribner's Sons, 1925), 1: 416.

36. Ibid., 79–80.

37. *Federalist* No. 72, 405; Lincoln, "Temperance Address Delivered before the Springfield Washington Temperance Society, February 22, 1842," in *Abraham Lincoln: His Speeches and Writings,* ed. Roy P. Basler (Cambridge, Mass.: Da Capo Press [orig. pub. Cleveland: World Publishing, 1946]), 131–142, at 137.

38. "True Americanism," April 1894, in *Works,* 13: 13–26, at 25; Roosevelt, *Autobiography,* 192. Nevertheless, while denouncing anti-Catholic sentiments, Roosevelt seemed unaware that the animus against parochial schools stemmed largely from the same prejudice.

39. *Winning of the West,* in *Works,* 9: 36. Roosevelt was clearly fascinated with ethnic differences. In an article published in 1897 after Roosevelt had stepped down as president of the New York City Police Board, he noted approvingly that "men of Irish blood" had demonstrated their soldierly virtues in the Civil War. "The Ethnology of the Police," in *Works,* 14: 226–235, at 228.

40. "Diary of Five Months in the New York Legislature," in *The Letters of Theodore Roosevelt,* 8 vols., ed. Elting E. Morison et al. (Cambridge, Mass.: Harvard University Press, 1954), 2: 1469–1471.

41. Nevertheless, he was encouraged by the progress some had made toward manliness. "The outdoor Jew who has been a gripman, or the driver of an express-wagon, or a guard on the Elevated, or the indoor Jew of fine bodily powers who has taken to boxing, wrestling, and the like, offers excellent material for the force." Like the native American, he is "very intelligent," though he also shares with him a tendency to be either "very good or very bad." "Ethnology of the Police," June 1897, in *Works,* 14: 233.

42. "Fifth Annual Message," December 5, 1905, in *Works,* 15: 270–341, at 320.

43. Joshua David Hawley, *Theodore Roosevelt: Preacher of Righteousness* (New Haven, Conn.: Yale University Press, 2008), 36. Hawley calls this neo-Lamarckianism.

44. Reviews of *Social Evolution,* July 1895, and *National Life and Character,* August 1894, in *Works,* 13: 223–241, at 240; 200–222, at 216.

45. Racial differences were, however, exacerbated by economic considerations.

The willingness of Asian laborers to work for less also justified "stringent immigration laws." Review of *National Life and Character*, in *Works*, 13: 213.

46. Review of *National Life and Character*, in *Works*, 13: 213. Ironically, Roosevelt shared with Jefferson, the founder he most despised, the belief that religion posed no obstacle to assimilation, only race, but this was because, like Jefferson, he believed that the Enlightenment had succeeded in taming fanaticism and reducing religion to a moral code.

47. *Thomas Hart Benton*, in *Works*, 7: 103.

48. Review of *National Life and Character*, in *Works*, 13: 213.

49. For a discussion of Wilson's *Congressional Government*, see R. J. Pestritto, *Woodrow Wilson and the Roots of Modern Liberalism* (Lanham, Md.: Rowman & Littlefield, 2005), ch. 4. On the likelihood of TR's acquaintance with the work, see John Milton Cooper, Jr., *The Warrior and the Priest: Woodrow Wilson and Theodore Roosevelt* (Cambridge, Mass.: The Belknap Press of Harvard University Press, 1983), 60–61.

50. "College Graduate and Public Life," in *Works*, 13: 36–46, at 42–45.

51. TR renewed his attack on Americans who sought to ape the British system in "A Colonial Survival," December 1892, in *Works*, 12: 300–316.

52. TR to James Brander Matthews, February 10, 1890, H. W. Brands, ed., *The Selected Letters of Theodore Roosevelt* (New York: Cooper Square Press, 2001), 71–72.

53. "The Vindication of Speaker Reed," December 1895, in *Works*, 14: 169–180. For a discussion of Reed's rule changes, 174. When Reed balked at Roosevelt's proposal to build more ships after he was appointed assistant secretary of the navy, their relationship began to cool. Reed's opposition to the Spanish-American War further strained relations between them. But for the time being, Reed was his idol.

54. Pestritto, *Woodrow Wilson*, 167.

55. Woodrow Wilson, "The Study of Administration," first published in 1887 and reprinted in *Woodrow Wilson: The Essential Political Writings*, ed. Ronald J. Pestritto (Lanham, Md.: Lexington Books, 2005), 231–248. On the other hand, it is possible that a Congress paralyzed by procedural hurdles might be tempted to redirect its energies toward administrative oversight at the committee level.

56. "The Spoils System in Operation," speech at the meeting of the Civil Service Reform Association, February 23, 1889, in *Works*, 14: 88–92, at 88.

57. "Merit System," February 1890, in *Works*, 14: 99–112, at 99–100.

58. On Roosevelt's low estimation of reformers, see "Machine Politics," and "Six Years of Civil Service Reform," August 1895, in *Works*, 13: 76–98, at 82; 99–117, at 105, 108–109. On his practicality: "Spoils System in Operation," in *Works*, 14: 88; on Taft: TR to Walter C. Camp, March 11, 1895, in Brands, *Selected Letters*, 100.

59. Jeremy Rabkin, "Bureaucratic Idealism and Executive Power," in *Saving the Revolution: The Federalist Papers and the American Founding*, ed. Charles R. Kesler (The Free Press, 1987), 185–202, 309, n. 57.

60. "Six Years of Civil Service Reform," in *Works*, 13: 99–117, at 99.

61. "Merit System," in *Works*, 14: 99–112, at 99, 104, 101.

62. "Merit System," in *Works*, 14: 99.

63. "Merit System," in *Works*, 14: 109–110.

64. "Merit System," in *Works*, 14: 99, 109.

65. Or at least give the appearance of being above parties. Not for nothing did TR describe Jefferson in *Thomas Hart Benton* as "shifty." Also, Ralph Ketcham, *Presidents above Party: The First American Presidency, 1789–1829* (Chapel Hill: University of North Carolina Press, 1987).

66. *Federalist* No. 57, 318; also No. 10, No. 51.

67. *Federalist* No. 68, 414.

68. Jeremy Rabkin, "Bureaucratic Idealism"; Sidney M. Milkis, *The President and the Parties: The Transformation of the American Party System since the New Deal* (New York: Oxford University Press, 1993), 25. On the other hand, Herbert Storing, "Political Parties and the Bureaucracy," in *Toward a More Perfect Union: The Writings of Herbert J. Storing*, ed. Joseph Bessette (Washington, D.C.: The AEI Press, 1995), 307–326, sees a closer connection between the founders' antipathy to party spirit and the civil service reformers, though he remains critical of the whole idea of a completely neutral civil service. James Q. Wilson, "The Bureaucracy Problem," *The Public Interest* (Winter 1967), and reprinted at http://www.nationalaffairs.com/publications/detail/the-bureaucracy-problem (accessed April 30, 2012).

69. "Speech in the New York Assembly," April 9, 1883, in *Works*, 14: 23–24, at 23.

70. *Federalist* No. 72, 405.

71. "Six Years of Civil Service Reform," in *Works*, 13: 117. Also, Storing, "Political Parties and the Bureaucracy," 311.

72. "Political Assessments," July 1892, and "Address at a Dinner of the Boston Civil Service Reform Association," February 20, 1893, in *Works*, 14: 134–139, 156–168.

73. Stephen Skowronek, *Building the New American State: The Expansion of the National Administrative Capacities, 1877–1920* (New York: Cambridge University Press, 1982), 74–75; Richard D. White, Jr., *Roosevelt the Reformer: Theodore Roosevelt as Civil Service Commissioner 1889–1895* (Tuscaloosa: University of Alabama Press, 2003).

74. "Civil Service Reform: A Report of Stewardship," "Address at a Dinner of the Boston Civil Service Reform Association," in *Works*, 14: 156–168, at 160. In *The Winning of the West*, which he was completing at the same time, TR went so far as to venture that the Indians would be better off if the reservations were broken up and the lands parceled out individually, *Winning of the West*, in *Works*, 8: 80.

75. "Civil Service Reform," in *Works*, 14: 156–168.

76. "Civil Service Reform," in *Works*, 14: 162–165.

77. TR to James S. Clarkson, April 22, 1893, in Brands, *Selected Letters*, 84–85.

78. "Six Years of Civil Service Reform," in *Works*, 13: 99–117, at 102. See also Skowronek, *Building the New American State*, 74–84.

79. Nathan Miller, *Theodore Roosevelt: A Life* (William Morrow, 1992), 208, 216–217; Skowronek, *Building the New American State*, 77–78.

80. Roosevelt, *Autobiography*, 155. Here the remark is attributed to "Tom Reed," i.e., Thomas Brackett Reed of Maine, Speaker of the House from 1889–1891 and

again from 1895–1899. See also "True Americanism," April 1894, in *Works*, 13: 13; "Address before the Liberal Club," in *Works*, 14: 192–206, at 197.

81. Cited in Kathleen Dalton, *Theodore Roosevelt: A Strenuous Life* (New York: Alfred A. Knopf, 2002), 148.

82. "The City in Modern Life," April 1895, in *Works*, 12: 223–231, at 223. In this respect, the essay seemed to extend the argument of his review of Pearson's *National Life and Character* the previous year, where he praised the "race selfishness" of the whites in claiming the most temperate parts of the globe for themselves.

83. "The City in Modern Life," in *Works*, 12: 225–226. Dalton, *Theodore Roosevelt*, sees this review as evidence of TR's emerging progressivism, but notes that he did not campaign on these issues in the 1896 election, 162.

84. Roosevelt, *Autobiography*, 64, 197. For a recent assessment of his service as police commissioner, Richard Zacks, *Islands of Vice: Theodore Roosevelt's Doomed Quest to Clean Up Sin-Loving New York* (New York: Doubleday, 2012).

85. "Administering the New York Police Force," September 1897, in *Works*, 13: 118–138, at 133.

86. "Speech in the New York Assembly," January 24, 1884, in *Works*, 14: 26–32, at 27.

87. "The Pigskin Library," in *Works*, 12: 337–346.

88. Roosevelt, *Autobiography*, 175–176, cf. *Federalist* No. 72, 437; No. 70, 423, 427.

89. "Speech before the American Republican College League," October 15, 1896, in *Works*, 14: 258–274, at 260.

90. Roosevelt, *Autobiography*, 172–173.

91. *Review of Reviews*, September 1896, in *Works*, 13: 139–156; "Speech before the Commercial Travellers' Sound-Money League," September 11, 1896, in *Works*, 14: 251–257, at 257.

92. "The Menace of the Demagogue," October 15, 1896, in *Works*, 14: 258–274. For the discussion of the differences between hard and soft demagogues, see James W. Ceaser, *Presidential Selection: Theory and Development* (Princeton, N.J.: Princeton University Press, 1979), 166–167.

93. Debs, who would later run for president of the United States five times on the Socialist ticket, was imprisoned for his role in the Pullman Strike. As governor of Illinois, Altgeld pardoned three men jailed for murder during the Haymarket Riot in 1886. "Pitchfork Ben" Tillman was a racist governor and senator from South Carolina who backed a radical economic program that he claimed would benefit the poor white farmer.

94. See the exchange between Thomas E. Watson and TR, *Review of Reviews*, January 1897, as well as the original article in the *Review of Reviews*, September 1896, that prompted it, in *Works*, 13: 139–167, at 159.

95. Ibid., 160.

96. In his essay, Turner emphasized how as the pioneers moved westward they tended to shed the vestiges of their European ways, becoming ever more democratic and developing a distinctive American character. Turner explicitly denied the "germ

theory" that located American liberty in the forests of Germany. For Turner, the new American democracy "came from no theorist's dreams of the German forest," but rather "from the American forest." Roosevelt, by contrast, could not decide whether it was Teutonic or Anglo-Saxon "blood" that was decisive for the frontiersmen or geography. See Frederick Jackson Turner, "The Problem of the West," orig. pub. *Atlantic Monthly*, September 1896; also "The Significance of the Frontier in American History," originally delivered at the American Historical Association in 1893, in http://xroads.virginia.edu/~Hyper/TURNER/ (accessed November 3, 2006).

97. Turner, "Problem of the West."

98. TR to James S. Clarkson, April 22, 1893, in Brands, *Selected Letters*, 84–85.

99. Essay on the Monroe Doctrine, March 1896, in *Works*, 13: 168–181, at 172, 179, 177.

100. TR to Harvard *Crimson*, January 2, 1896, in Brands, *Selected Letters*, 113–115.

101. The review appeared in October 1890, in *Works*, 12: 264–272.

102. To some extent, the address could be seen as a muscular response to Cleveland's invocation of Washington's Farewell Address advising Americans to avoid entangling alliances.

103. "The Monroe Doctrine," March 1896, in *Works*, 13: 168–181, at 180.

104. "Address as Assistant Secretary of the Navy, before the Naval War College," June 1887, in *Works*, 13: 182–199.

105. Aristotle, *Nicomachean Ethics*, trans. Martin Ostwald (Englewood Cliffs, N.J.: Library of Liberal Arts, 1962). In Book 3, Aristotle observes that courage is the first of the virtues, for without it all the others are unavailing, but it is not the highest virtue.

106. *The Rough Riders*, in *Works*, 11: 3.

107. TR to W. W. Kimball, November 19, 1897, in Morison, *Letters*, 1: 716–718, at 717.

108. Dalton, *Theodore Roosevelt*, defends TR against charges that he acted impetuously in his orders to Dewey, arguing that "Long did not countermand the order when he returned to the office, and it was actually consistent with navy war plans," 169.

109. TR to Dr. Sturgis Bigelow, March 29, 1898, in Morison, *Letters*, 2: 801–803; also to C. Whitney Tillinghast, II, March 19, 1898, 1: 792.

110. Henry F. Pringle, *Theodore Roosevelt: A Biography* (New York: Harcourt, Brace and Company, rev. ed. 1955), 122. In fairness, Pringle sees two different motives at work: a legitimate concern with military preparedness and a "lust for war."

111. TR to Douglas Robinson, April 2, 1898, in Morison, *Letters*, 2: 809.

112. As this latter suggests, Roosevelt believed that expansion could not succeed by fostering the manly virtues alone. Women, too, had a role to play in "the strenuous life." Although not a major part of his address to the Hamilton Club, he sounded a theme to which he would return many times with ever more urgency: the refusal of American women, especially of fine old New England stock, to have large families, or even any children at all. Roosevelt chalked this up to a kind of

female timidity: a fear of motherhood and of the duties of a wife. Just as men must cultivate the manly, fighting virtues, women must accept their duties as housewives, homemakers, and "wise and fearless mother[s] of many healthy children." "The Strenuous Life," April 10, 1899, in *Works*, 13: 319-331, at 320-321.

113. "Strenuous Life," in *Works*, 13. The unnamed poet is James Russell Lowell.

114. Review of *National Life and Character*, in *Works*, 13: 206-208.

115. "Strenuous Life," in *Works*, 13: 330.

116. "Expansion and Peace," in *Works*, 13: 332-340, at 337. Undated in the National Edition, the essay was published in the *Independent*, December 21, 1899.

117. "Strenuous Life," in *Works*, 13: 328.

118. "Strenuous Life," in *Works*, 13: 329.

119. "Strenuous Life," in *Works*, 13, also TR to Rudyard Kipling, November 3, 1904, in Brands, *Selected Letters*, 369-370.

120. "Strenuous Life," in *Works*, 13: 328; also, TR to Henry Cabot Lodge, April 29, 1896, in Brands, *Selected Letters*, 117-118.

121. "Expansion and Peace," in *Works*, 13: 336.

122. "Expansion and Peace," in *Works*, 13: 339; "Strenuous Life," in *Works*, 13: 331.

123. "Expansion and Peace," in *Works*, 13: 337; "Address at the Quarter-Centennial Celebration," in *Works*, 13: 450-459, at 450.

124. At Akron, Ohio, September 23, 1899, as cited in Thomas W. Handford, *Theodore Roosevelt: The Pride of the Rough Riders* (Chicago, 1899), 190-191.

125. Review of *National Life and Character*, in *Works*, 13: 214-216.

126. "Address at the Minnesota State Fair," September 2, 1901, in *Works*, 13: 469-480, at 479.

127. On this point, see also James W. Ceaser, *Reconstructing America: The Symbol of America in Modern Thought* (New Haven, Conn.: Yale University Press, 1997), 158-160.

128. Although the Constitution followed the flag into Louisiana, the common law did not.

129. "Address at the Minnesota State Fair," in *Works*, 13: 469-480, at 477; Richard Boyd, "Tocqueville's Algeria," *Society* (September/October 2001): 65-70.

130. "Address at the Lincoln Club Dinner in New York City," February 13, 1899, in *Works*, 14: 314-318, at 317; cf. the Supreme Court's rulings in *The Insular Cases*.

131. *Federalist* No. 6, 27.

132. In a similar vein, Roosevelt's political science took its bearings in part from natural science, while the political science of *The Federalist* was guided by political philosophy, history, and experience. James W. Ceaser, *Liberal Democracy and Political Science* (Baltimore: Johns Hopkins University Press, 1990), esp. ch. 1.

133. Alexander Hamilton, "Report on Manufactures," December 5, 1791, in *Selected Writings and Speeches of Alexander Hamilton*, ed. Morton J. Frisch (Washington, D.C.: American Enterprise Institute for Policy Research), 277-318, at 290-292.

134. Alexander Hamilton, "First Speech of June 21 in the N. Y. Ratifying Convention," in Frisch, *Selected Writings and Speeches*, 205-212, at 210.

135. *Federalist* No. 6, 27.

136. Karl-Friedrich Walling, *Republican Empire: Alexander Hamilton on War and Free Government* (Lawrence: University Press of Kansas, 1999), 300–301, n. 30. After careful consideration, Walling finds little merit in Jefferson's charge that Hamilton regarded Caesar as the greatest man who ever lived, even though he gives some credit to the remarks of Hamilton's son that his father loved to read Caesar's works to his children, and that his father had a soldier's temperament. But Walling concludes that even though Hamilton possessed the capacity to be a Caesar, he "preferred to be the American Publius, which is arguably an ambition far greater than to be a Caesar. Such an ambition, however, might well have to rely on many of Caesar's virtues (speed, decisiveness, industry, careful administration, and so on)." In this connection, it is worth noting that Hamilton called his greatest political enemy, Aaron Burr, an "embryo-Caesar," which was not meant as a compliment. See also Stephen F. Knott, *Alexander Hamilton and the Persistence of Myth* (Lawrence: University Press of Kansas, 2002), 87–92.

137. During the Revolutionary War, Hamilton condemned wartime profiteering and confided to his friend Dr. John Laurens that he hated "money-making men." But, as Peter McNamara has wisely observed, wartime inevitably brings out both the best and worst in human nature. In ordinary circumstances, Hamilton was more at home with businessmen and financiers than TR, even though he too understood that profit and honor did not automatically coincide. The task of the republican statesman was to try to bring them together. For two different views, see Peter McNamara, *Political Economy and Statesmanship: Smith, Hamilton, and the Foundation of the Commercial Republic* (DeKalb: Northern Illinois University Press, 1998), 95–151. Cf. Richard Loss, *The Modern Theory of Presidential Power: Alexander Hamilton and the Corwin Thesis* (Westport, Conn.: Greenwood Press, 1990), 1–42, at 5.

138. TR to Henry Cabot Lodge, December 6, 1898, in *Selections from the Correspondence*, 1: 366.

139. Walling, *Republican Empire*, 114–116.

140. Review of *National Life and Character*, in *Works*, 13: 215.

4. INTRODUCTION TO EXECUTIVE POWER

1. As noted in the previous chapter, it should be emphasized that although Roosevelt gave the order, he was not acting impetuously, but in accord with established naval plans, Kathleen Dalton, *Theodore Roosevelt: A Strenuous Life* (New York: Alfred A. Knopf, 2002), 169.

2. *The Rough Riders*, in *The Works of Theodore Roosevelt*, 20 vols., ed. Herman Hagedorn (New York: Charles Scribner's Sons, 1924), 11: 8–11 (hereafter cited as *Works*).

3. *The Rough Riders*, in *Works*, 20: 40, 64.

4. *The Rough Riders,* in *Works,* 20: 89.

5. See especially his letter to the secretary of war, *The Rough Riders,* in *Works,* 20: 164–169; also Theodore Roosevelt, *An Autobiography* (New York: Da Capo Press, 1985 [orig. pub. Macmillan, 1913], 231.

6. Roosevelt, *Autobiography,* 255–256.

7. Political scientist Stephen Skowronek casts Roosevelt's concern with balance in terms of the people and the leaders, rather than between the poor and the rich, or the oligarchs and the democrats. To be sure, oligarchic interests found much of their support among the leaders of the Republican Party, but in developing his typology, Skowronek blurs Roosevelt's explicit appeal to the different classes in society. Skowronek, *The Politics Presidents Make: Leadership from John Adams to George Bush* (Cambridge, Mass.: The Belknap Press of Harvard University Press, 1993), 228–259, esp. 247.

8. "Civic Helpfulness," *The Century,* October 1900, in *Works,* 13: 369–380, at 379.

9. The problem was, as Roosevelt had already hinted in his 1895 review of Albert Shaw's book on municipal life in Britain, that he saw no principled point at which to draw the line. Consequently, he would find it difficult to know where to stop.

10. Unless otherwise noted, all citations in the preceding paragraphs are from Roosevelt's "First Annual Message," January 2, 1899, in *Works,* 15: 5–29.

11. "Gubernatorial Message to the Legislature," March 27, 1899, in *The Roosevelt Policy: Speeches, Letters, and State Papers, Relating to Corporate Wealth and Closely Allied Topics,* ed. William Griffith (Honolulu, Hawaii: University Press of the Pacific, 2001 [reprinted from the 1919 edition]), 2.

12. TR to T. C. Platt, May 8, 1899, in *The Selected Letters of Theodore Roosevelt,* ed. H. W. Brands (New York: Cooper Square Press, 2001), 221–226, at 221. For a full discussion, G. Wallace Chessman, *Governor Theodore Roosevelt: The Albany Apprenticeship, 1898–1900* (Cambridge, Mass.: Harvard University Press, 1965), ch. 7. Richard Hofstadter, *The Age of Reform: From Bryan to F.D.R.* (New York: Vintage Books, 1955), esp. 234–236. Hofstadter argued that Roosevelt was the first major politician to grasp that the only way the public would agree to enlarge the powers of the state was if it remained scrupulously neutral with regard to the various competing economic interests. Though he does not say it, Hofstadter's analysis may owe something to Herbert Croly's criticism of the liberal state in *The Promise of American Life.* According to Croly, the state should not be neutral; rather it should actively discriminate in favor of its friends. Herbert Croly, *The Promise of American Life* (Boston: Northeastern University Press, 1989 [orig. pub. 1909]).

13. "Second Annual Message," January 3, 1900, in *Works,* 15: 30–78, esp. 37–39.

14. "Second Annual Message," in *Works,* 15; also "Latitude and Longitude among Reformers," June 1900, in *Works,* 13: 341–354, at 351.

15. TR to Elihu Root, December 7, 1899, and December 15, 1899; TR to Henry Cabot Lodge, August 10, 1899, in which he confided to Lodge that Root was already "disgruntled" with him over the taxation of franchises, in *The Letters of Theodore*

Roosevelt, 8 vols., ed. Elting E. Morison et al. (Cambridge, Mass.: Harvard University Press, 1954), 2: 1105–1106, 1110, 1047; Chessman, *Governor TR*, 167 ff.

16. "Second Annual Message," in *Works*, 15: 41.

17. "Second Annual Message," in *Works*, 15: 46. According to Chessman, *Governor TR*, the measure failed, and after Roosevelt left Albany the publicity proposal was quietly shelved, 175. It is also worth keeping in mind that not all of these giant enterprises were incorporated.

18. "Second Annual Message," in *Works*, 15: 53–54.

19. "Machine Politics," in *Works*, 13: 76–98, at 79–80.

20. "Latitude and Longitude among Reformers," and "Civic Helpfulness," in *Works*, 13: 341–354, at 342; 369–380, at 375.

21. "Fellow Feeling as a Political Factor," "Civic Helpfulness," "Latitude and Longitude among Reformers," "The Labor Question," "Christian Citizenship," in *Works*, 13: 341–380, 481–499. Speaking before the YMCA, Roosevelt would emphasize Christian brotherhood, but for the most part, he tended to use the more secular phrase "fellow feeling." Only later would the two become completely merged in his mind.

22. "The Eighth and Ninth Commandments in Politics," May 12, 1900, in *Works*, 13: 387–394.

23. Privately, Roosevelt acknowledged that there was "a good deal of misery and injustice," but that it was mainly due "to the individuals themselves or to the mere operation of nature's laws," but his public statements had softened. TR to HCL, August 10, 1899, in *Selections from the Correspondence of Theodore Roosevelt and Henry Cabot Lodge 1884–1918*, 2 vols. (New York: Charles Scribner's Sons, 1925), 1: 415–418, at 416.

24. "Promise and Performance" and "Character and Success," *Works* 13: 395–400, at 396; 381–386.

25. "Promise and Performance," *Works*, 13: 400. The quote is from the last paragraph of Book 8 of Aristotle's *Politics*, in the translation by Benjamin Jowett. The quote was obviously a popular one, as Nicholas Murray Butler cited it in his commencement address at the University of Michigan, on June 22, 1899, which was reported the next day in *The New York Times*.

26. Howard K. Beale, *Theodore Roosevelt and the Rise of America to World Power* (New York: Collier Books, 1956), 102–104.

27. Introduction to *Oliver Cromwell*, in *Works*, 10: 169–171.

28. Introduction to *Oliver Cromwell*, in *Works*, 10: 183. In this connection, it is telling that the one correction Lodge offered upon reading the first installment was "when you revise the book you ought to correct your quotation from Macauley. It is not 'general of the Lord,' but 'servant of the Lord.'" HCL to TR, December 22, 1899, in *Selections from the Correspondence* 1: 431. Cf. Machiavelli's discussion of David going up against Goliath in chapter 13 of *The Prince*.

29. *Oliver Cromwell*, in *Works*, 10: 215, 300–301, 219–220, 315, 268, 320, 331.

30. The question of why Roosevelt was open to the vice presidency is an interest-

ing one, since that office had not served as a path to an elected presidency in seventy-four years. But especially after Vice President Hobart's death in November 1899, Lodge was convinced that "the V.P. was becoming stronger and more desirable" for TR than he had thought possible. A short time later, he cast it as "the true stepping stone toward either the Presidency or the Governor Generalship of the Philippines." In addition to these counsels of friendship, Roosevelt also received advice from Boss Platt, who warned him that he would be fortunate to get through one term in Albany without "irretrievably" ruining his political prospects; he should not "tempt Providence" by seeking another term. And by February, Roosevelt understood that the "big monied men" were scheming to push him out of the governorship by backing him for the vice presidency. Thus, despite the objections of his wife and sister, and his own worries that "for a young man there is not much to do," Roosevelt eventually came around and accepted the nomination at the Republican Convention in June. TR to HCL, July 1, 1899; HCL to TR, December 19?, 1889; HCL to TR, February 2, 1900; January 22, 1900; TR to HCL, February 3, 1900; TR to HCL, December 11, 1899; in *Selections from the Correspondence* 1: 403–405, 430–431, 437–438, 449, 426–427.

31. *Oliver Cromwell,* in *Works,* 10: 288, 275.

32. *Oliver Cromwell,* in *Works,* 10: 215.

33. *Oliver Cromwell,* in *Works,* 10: 215, 219–222, 254.

34. *Oliver Cromwell,* in *Works,* 10: 248. The founders would not have denied that culture matters, but creed, that is, the dedication to the natural rights of all men and women, came first.

35. *Oliver Cromwell,* in *Works,* 10:, 190.

36. *Oliver Cromwell,* in *Works,* 10: 308–309.

37. *Oliver Cromwell,* in *Works,* 10: 306.

38. *Oliver Cromwell,* in *Works,* 10: 304–305.

39. *Oliver Cromwell,* in *Works,* 10: 331, 315, 299. But cf. Jeffrey Tulis, who argues that the Cromwell study persuaded TR of the need for statesmen to preserve constitutional forms, even as they are forced to violate them in emergencies. Roosevelt paid lip service to the idea, but increasingly violated it in practice. Jeffrey Tulis, *The Rhetorical Presidency* (Princeton, N.J.: Princeton University Press, 1988), 115.

5. EXECUTIVE POWER AND REPUBLICAN GOVERNMENT

1. TR to Nicholas Murray Butler, November 4, 1903, in *The Letters of Theodore Roosevelt,* 8 vols., ed. Elting E. Morison et al. (Cambridge, Mass.: Harvard University Press, 1954), 3: 641–644, at 642.

2. Cited in Edmund Morris, *Theodore Rex* (New York: Random House, 2001), 137.

3. TR to Philander Chase Knox, August 21, 1902, in Morison, *Letters,* 3: 323.

4. TR to Henry Cabot Lodge, September 27, 1902, ibid., 331–332; also TR to Marcus Alonzo Hanna, September 27, 1902, 329–330; October 3, 1902, 337–338.

5. TR to Winthrop Murray Crane, October 22, 1902, ibid., 359–366, at 360.

6. HCL to TR, September 27, 1902, in *Selections from the Correspondence of Theo-dore Roosevelt and Henry Cabot Lodge 1884–1918*, 2 vols. (New York: Charles Scrib-ner's Sons, 1925), 1: 531–532.

7. TR to Grover Cleveland, October 5, 1902, in Morison, *Letters*, 3: 338–339.

8. TR to Marcus Alonzo Hanna, October 3, 1902, ibid., 338.

9. TR to Winthrop Murray Crane, October 22, 1902, ibid., 359–366, 362.

10. In framing this argument, I am happy to acknowledge the assistance of Jer-emy Rabkin, James Stoner, James Y. Stern, and Richard E. Morgan.

11. TR to Oswald Garrison Villard, October 9, 1902, in Morison, *Letters*, 3: 345–346.

12. TR to J. H. Woodard, October 19, 1902, ibid., 356–357. For the "evil" prec-edent, see TR to Crane, ibid., 362.

13. Indeed, as Nathan Miller points out, although TR briefly ordered federal troops to suppress violence during a copper miners' strike in Arizona in 1903, he withdrew them when they were used to intimidate the workers. At the same time, he refused to intervene in another strike in Colorado, where mine owners called in the state militia to restore order. In neither case did he propose that the govern-ment take over and run the mines as he did in the coal strike. Nathan Miller, *Theo-dore Roosevelt: A Life* (New York: William Morrow, 1992), 377–378.

14. Theodore Roosevelt, *An Autobiography* (New York: Da Capo Press, 1985 [orig. pub. Macmillan, 1913]), 479, 372.

15. Ibid., 372.

16. Ibid., 378.

17. As TR later put it, his presidency would be judged more by who he was, rather than what he did. TR to George Otto Trevelyan, June 19, 1908, in Morison, *Letters*, 6: 1085–1090, at 1087.

18. Harvey C. Mansfield provocatively asks, "Who is more manly, George Wash-ington, a man of dignity not to be trifled with, or Teddy Roosevelt, steward of the people, who sees humiliating constraint in the Constitution but not in popular favor?" Harvey C. Mansfield, *Manliness* (New Haven, Conn.: Yale University Press, 2006), 97.

19. Raymond Tatalovich and Thomas S. Engeman, *The Presidency and Political Science: Two Hundred Years of Constitutional Debate* (Baltimore: Johns Hopkins University Press, 2003), 77–82. But cf. Stephen Skowronek, *The Politics Presidents Make: Leadership from John Adams to George Bush* (Cambridge, Mass.: The Belknap Press of Harvard University Press, 1993), 244, who accepts Roosevelt's assertion that the stewardship theory was nothing new.

20. *Thomas Hart Benton*, in *The Works of Theodore Roosevelt*, 20 vols., ed. Her-man Hagedorn (New York: Charles Scribner's Sons, 1924), 7: 156–157, 75–79, 48 (hereafter cited as *Works*).

21. TR to Winthrop Murray Crane, October 22, 1902, in Morison, *Letters*, 3: 359–366.

22. As cited in William Henry Harbaugh, *Power and Responsibility: The Life and Times of Theodore Roosevelt* (New York: Farrar, Straus and Cudahy, 1961), 177.

23. Abraham Lincoln to Albert G. Hodges, April 4, 1864, in *Lincoln: Selected Speeches and Writings*, ed. Don E. Fehrenbacher (Vintage Books/The Library of America, 1992), 419–421. Also, Allen C. Guelzo, *Lincoln's Emancipation Proclamation: The End of Slavery in America* (New York: Simon & Schuster, 2006), and Benjamin A. Kleinerman, "Lincoln's Example: Executive Power and the Survival of Constitutionalism," *Perspectives on Politics* (December 2005): 802–816.

24. William Howard Taft, *Our Chief Magistrate and His Powers*, with a Foreword and Introduction by H. Jefferson Powell (Durham, N.C.: Carolina Academic Press, 2002 [orig. pub. 1916]), 145–148; see also the discussion in Tatalovich and Engeman, *Presidency and Political Science*, 92.

25. Taft, *Our Chief Magistrate*, 146.

26. Morison, *Letters*, 3: 345, n. 1.

27. As Knox explained, "the sugar decision [the *Knight* case] directly bars the case in point unless it can be shown that there is a pool for transportation; and that if it did apply (bar the case of the pool) proceedings might have to be taken up against the labor union exactly as we would have to proceed against the syndicate." TR to Seth Low, October 3, 1902, in Morison, *Letters*, 3: 336–337, at 337; 337, n. 2, 3.

28. William H. Harbaugh, "The Constitution of the Theodore Roosevelt Presidency and the Progressive Era," in *The Constitution and the American Presidency*, ed. Martin L. Fausold and Alan Shank (Albany: State University of New York Press, 1991), 63–82, at 67. On a related matter, it is worth noting that Roosevelt, speaking of common law doctrine on restraint of trade in 1908, explicitly dismissed its adequacy for modern industrial conditions. "Special Message to Congress," January 31, 1908, in Morison, *Letters*, 6: Appendix, 1588.

29. Taft, *Our Chief Magistrate*, 147.

30. Harbaugh, "Constitution of the Theodore Roosevelt Presidency," 67. TR to Dr. Lyman Abbott, September 5, 1903, in Morison, *Letters*, 3: 590–593, at 592.

31. From "Address Delivered October 4, 1906, at the Dedication Ceremonies of the New State Capitol of Pennsylvania, in Harrisburg," in *Works*, 16: 69–75.

32. "Considerations on the Bank of North America," in *The Works of James Wilson*, 2 vols., ed. Robert Green McCloskey (Cambridge, Mass.: The Belknap Press of Harvard University Press, 1967) 2: 824–840, at 829.

33. "Harrisburg Address," in *Works*, 16: 70. But cf. Wilson's letter to George Washington, December 31, 1791, in http://books.google.com/books?id=igMOAA AAIAAJ&pg=PA387&lpg=PA387&dq=james+wilson+to+george+washington,+ dec.+31,+1791&source=web&ots=VPfVvwf4-m&sig=ofsABLs_v6KeAsCnDP68IJY jIas&hl=en&sa=X&oi=book_result&resnum=10&ct=result#PPA389,M1 (accessed January 19, 2009).

34. "Harrisburg Address," in *Works*, 16: 70.

35. "Harrisburg Address," in *Works*, 16. Skeptics might object that there is really no difference between inherent powers and implied powers, since both lead to the

unlimited expansion of federal power. (And this would explain why Wilson did not repeat his doctrine of inherent power after the Constitution was adopted.) But it is worth noting that at the time Roosevelt made his argument, critics believed that there was in fact a principled difference between the two. See, e.g., Westel Woodbury Willoughby, *The Constitutional Law of the United States,* vol. 1 (New York: Baker, Voorhis & Company, 1910), 1: 66–68. Note, however, the contrasting view, which tends to run together Wilson's jurisprudence and Marshall's, in James De Witt Andrews, "James Wilson and His Relation to Jurisprudence and Constitutional Law," *American Law Register* (1898–1907), vol. 49, no. 12, vol. 40 New Series (December 1901): 708–728, http://www.jstor.org/pss/3306951 (accessed August 23, 2008).

36. "Harrisburg Address," in *Works,* 16: 70.

37. Perhaps he was thinking of something like Burgess's argument, although Burgess distinguished sharply between the State and the government, attributing sovereign power only to the former.

38. This would be precisely Herbert Croly's argument in *The Promise of American Life* (Boston: Northeastern University Press, 1989 [orig. pub. 1909]), 178–180.

39. 206 U.S. 46; 27 Sup. Ct. Rep. 6555; 51 L. ed. 956. And see also the contemporary discussion of inherent powers by Willoughby, *Constitutional Law,* 1: 47–51, 66–69, especially n. 25, 69–70, citing Justice Brewer's forceful rejection of inherent power in *Kansas v. Colorado.* Nevertheless, as Willoughby notes, the doctrine of inherent power did not completely wither on the vine after the ratification of the Constitution. Justice Bradley referred to it in an *obiter dictum* in the *Legal Tender Cases,* and supporters of the Spanish-American War invoked inherent power to justify the right of the United States to acquire its new possessions. In the *Insular Cases,* the inherent power argument was urged, but the Court declined to recognize it, 67, n. 21; 68, n. 23.

40. "Transcript of Sherman Anti-Trust Act (1890)," http://www.ourdocuments .gov/doc.php?flash=true&doc=51&page=transcript (accessed August 17, 2007).

41. Martin J. Sklar, *The Corporate Reconstruction of American Capitalism, 1890–1916: The Market, The Law, and Politics* (New York: Cambridge University Press, 1988), 105–117.

42. Robert H. Bork, *The Antitrust Paradox* (New York: Basic Books, 1978), 3–32.

43. Alfred H. Kelly, Winfred A. Harbison, and Herman Belz, *The American Constitution: Its Origins and Development,* 7th ed., 2 vols. (New York: W. W. Norton), 1: 379–380; Charles W. McCurdy, "The Knight Sugar Decision of 1895 and the Modernization of American Corporate Law, 1869–1903," *Business History Review* 53, no. 3 (Fall 1979): 304–342, at 330, n. 97. That the states chose not to go after the trusts for a host of economic reasons was the point that Roosevelt would emphasize.

44. As the foregoing discussion makes clear, *Northern Securities Company v. United States* did not present the Court with the opportunity to revisit the *Knight* decision directly, since it was not concerned with the distinction between "manufacture" and "commerce." Unlike the Sugar Trust, the railroads linking Chicago and Duluth to San Francisco and Seattle were manifestly engaged in interstate com-

merce. Moreover, the precise legal question did not concern the railroads themselves, but whether holding shares in the Northern Securities Company constituted
an illegal combination in restraint of commerce within the meaning of the Sherman Act. Kelly, Harbison, and Belz, *American Constitution*, 1: 379, 420–421.

45. Morris, *Theodore Rex*, 316. Not surprisingly, Holmes saw matters differently.
Roosevelt, he opined, "couldn't forgive anyone who stood in his way."

46. For Holmes's dissent, see http://www.law.cornell.edu/supct/html/historics/
USSC_CR_0193_0197_ZD1.html (accessed August 1, 2008). Albro Martin, *Enterprise Denied* (New York: Columbia University Press, 1971), 181; John Morton Blum,
The Republican Roosevelt (New York: Atheneum, 1974 [orig. pub. Harvard University Press, 1954), 119–120.

47. Martin, *Enterprise Denied*, 17–21.

48. Roosevelt, *Autobiography*, 465.

49. Roosevelt made the same point, only more forcefully, in each of the Annual
Messages of his second term.

50. TR to Arthur B. McFarquhar, August 11, 1911, in Morison, *Letters*, 7: 326.

51. Peri E. Arnold, *Remaking the Presidency: Roosevelt, Taft, and Wilson, 1901–
1916* (Lawrence: University Press of Kansas, 2009), 47; Sklar, *Corporate Reconstruction of American Capitalism*, 342.

52. Kelly, Harbison, and Belz, *American Constitution*, 1: 373–376.

53. See especially "The Controversy with E. H. Harriman," October 8, 1906, in
Works, 16: 425–435. In his influential discussion of the Hepburn Act, John Morton
Blum states that TR opposed a general ratemaking authority, omitting Roosevelt's
qualification "at present." "Theodore Roosevelt and the Hepburn Act: Toward an
Orderly System of Control," in Morison, *Letters*, 6: Appendix 2, 1558–1571, at 1560.

54. "Address Delivered before the Union League Club," Philadelphia, January
30, 1905, in *The Roosevelt Policy: Speeches, Letters and State Papers, Relating to Corporate Wealth and Closely Allied Topics*, 2 vols., ed. William Griffith (Honolulu,
Hawaii: University Press of the Pacific, 2001), 239–245. Also, "Fourth Annual Message," in *Works*, 15: 225.

55. For a full account of the complex legislative and public relations maneuvers,
Lewis L. Gould, *The Presidency of Theodore Roosevelt* (Lawrence: University Press
of Kansas, 1991), 147–165.

56. Jeffrey Tulis, *The Rhetorical Presidency* (Princeton, N.J.: Princeton University Press, 1988), 19, 95–109. More recently, Colleen J. Shogan has challenged this
view, arguing that Roosevelt's moralizing initially generated public support, but in
the end, made his compromises with the Old Guard in the Senate look unprinci-
pled. But this was only to the progressives on his left. Gould, *Presidency of Theodore
Roosevelt*, 163, argues that his shifts did not hurt him with the larger public. Shogan,
The Moral Rhetoric of American Presidents (College Station: Texas A&M University
Press, 2006), 64–66. Skowronek, *Building a New American State*, 257, also takes a
less sanguine view, arguing that Roosevelt paid a high price for presidential leadership, driving a wedge between the two wings of the Republican Party.

57. "Address at the Laying of the Corner-Stone of the Office-Building of the House of Representatives," popularly known as "The Man with the Muck-Rake," April 14, 1906, in *Works*, 16: 415–424. At first glance, this might appear to be another of Roosevelt's signature attempts at "balance," but buried in the speech were calls for a progressive tax on inherited wealth and greater "supervision" of all corporations engaged in interstate business, 421.

58. Gould, *Presidency of Theodore Roosevelt*, 20–21.

59. "Inaugural Address," March 4, 1905, in *Works*, 15: 267–269, where Roosevelt speaks of "devotion to a lofty ideal," 269.

60. "Fifth Annual Message," in *Works*, 15: 270–341, at 280.

61. "Address at the Laying of the Corner-Stone," in *Works*, 16: 415–424, at 421. Perhaps he thought they might act more like selfless colonial administrators in the Philippines and Cuba.

62. "Sixth Annual Message," December 3, 1906, in *Works*, 15: 364.

63. "Special Message to Congress," January 31, 1908, in Morison, *Letters*, 6: Appendix 2, 1572–1591, at 1575ff.

64. Sklar, *Corporate Reconstruction of American Capitalism*, 222–223.

65. Thus, I disagree with John Morton Blum's assertion in *Republican Roosevelt*, 107, that "after his fortieth year [1897], Roosevelt experienced no major change of thought." For Blum, the constants in Roosevelt's thinking were "power" and "order." Given this overbroad conceptual framework, he argues that Roosevelt's actions as president were "inherent in his early thinking." The difference is that, while president, "he came better to understand himself."

66. "Special Message to Congress," in Morison, *Letters*, 6: Appendix 2, 1572–1791, at 1587, 1584.

67. John Milton Cooper, Jr., *The Warrior and the Priest: Woodrow Wilson and Theodore Roosevelt* (Cambridge, Mass.: The Belknap Press of Harvard University Press, 1983), 115.

68. Alexander Hamilton, James Madison, and John Jay, *The Federalist Papers*, ed. Clinton Rossiter, with an Introduction and Notes by Charles R. Kesler (New York: A Mentor Book, 1999), *Federalist No. 6*, 59.

69. Blum, "Theodore Roosevelt and the Hepburn Act," in Morison, *Letters*, 6: Appendix 2, 1558–1571, at 1561. Blum argues that TR was not interested in discriminations between short and long hauls or among different commodities. What angered him was exorbitant rates, which he regarded as immoral, but cf. Martin, *Enterprise Denied*, 354–355, and TR, "Fifth Annual Message," in *Works*, 15: 281, where TR called for a ban on discounts to shippers who provided specialized cars.

70. "Special Message to Congress," March 25, 1908, in *A Compilation of the Messages and Papers of the Presidents*, 20 vols. (New York: Bureau of National Literature, [1917?]), 16: 7341–7347, at 7342–7343.

71. TR recognized that it would be difficult and complicated for government bureaucrats to establish maximum rates, but he was confident that men of "lofty probity" were up to the task. "Fifth Annual Message," in *Works*, 15: 281. For an

outline of his additional regulatory proposals, see "Special Message to Congress," in Morison, *Letters*, 6: 1572–1591.

72. Martin, *Enterprise Denied*, xii, 150–154, 176, 354–355. Cf. Kolko, who sees the Hepburn Act as little more than a tool of the railroads, in that they were able to avoid more stringent regulation by the states. Gabriel Kolko, *Railroads and Regulation, 1877–1916* (Princeton, N.J.: Princeton University Press, 1965). See also Blum, *Republican Roosevelt*, 104, who praises the Hepburn Act for substituting "informed, expert decisions" for the "artificial configurations of a market that had long since ceased, in the classic sense, to be free."

73. Martin, *Enterprise Denied*, 354.

74. "First Annual Message," in *Works*, 15: 81–138, at 91.Though he did not say it here, Roosevelt was already gathering statistics on the Chicago meat-packing industry, the anthracite coal industry, and the Colorado mining industry, Kathleen Dalton, *Theodore Roosevelt: A Strenuous Life* (New York: Alfred A. Knopf, 2002), 210. "Fourth Annual Message," December 6, 1904, in *Works*, 15: 224.

75. First Annual Message, in *Works*, 15: 81–138, at 91.

76. *Federalist* No. 10, 47. See also John Adams Wettergreen, "Capitalism, Socialism, and Constitutionalism," in *To Secure the Blessings of Liberty: First Principles of the Constitution*, ed. Sarah Baumgartner Thurow (Lanham, Md.: University Press of America, 1988), 248–268, who argues that the Framers intended a middle way between socialism and laissez-faire. However, that "third way" emphatically was not the progressive "third way."

77. "First Annual Message," in *Works*, 15: 81–138, at 92. Also McCurdy, "Knight Sugar Decision," 304–342.

78. Address delivered in Providence, Rhode Island, August 23, 1902, and Address delivered in Symphony Hall, Boston, Mass., August 25, 1902, in Griffith, *Roosevelt Policy*, 1: 31–49. In the Hebrew Bible, Jeshurun is a poetic term for Israel.

79. Cited in Ron Chernow, *The House of Morgan: An American Banking Dynasty and the Rise of Modern Finance* (New York: Atlantic Monthly Press, 1990), 111.

80. This discussion of the Bureau of Corporations draws heavily on Arthur M. Johnson's seminal essay, "Theodore Roosevelt and the Bureau of Corporations," *Mississippi Valley Historical Review* 45, no. 4 (March 1959): 571–590.

81. In response, the meat packers sued in federal court and won, invoking inter alia the Fifth Amendment's protections against self-incrimination. Roosevelt then had to go back to Congress to get an amendment to the Hepburn Act, providing immunity only to "natural persons," and not corporations, ibid., 582.

82. For a discussion of the provisions of the Hepburn bill amending the Sherman Act, see Sklar, *Corporate Reconstruction of American Capitalism*, 238–253.

83. Johnson, "Bureau of Corporations," 589.

84. Sklar, *Corporate Reconstruction of American Capitalism*, 246–247, 201–203, 238, 196, 251–252, 348–351, 328–332; also Blum, *Republican Roosevelt*, 116–118.

85. Wettergreen, "Capitalism, Socialism, and Constitutionalism," 253–254. Peter McNamara, *Political Economy and Statesmanship: Smith, Hamilton, and the Foun-

dation of the Commercial Republic (DeKalb: Northern Illinois University Press, 1998), 111–143. McNamara's analysis of Hamilton's policies makes clear that there was considerable leeway for the republican statesman to direct the economy, especially a developing economy, in the service of classical liberal ends. McNamara emphasizes Hamilton's concern for the protection of individual property rights.

86. *Federalist* No. 10, 47.

87. Wettergreen, "Capitalism, Socialism, and Constitutionalism," 254–257, 265–268. Also, Uhlmann, "Taming Big Government," 38–43.

88. Sklar, *Corporate Reconstruction of American Capitalism*, 195, 203, 246. Sklar underscores Wettergreen's point, by observing that what Roosevelt proposed was more than regulation because corporations would now be controlled and "governed" by the state.

89. Johnson, "Bureau of Corporations," 589; Sklar, *Corporate Reconstruction of American Capitalism*, 283.

90. *Federalist* No. 72, 405.

91. Roosevelt for once was happy to quote his old antagonist, Senator Robert M. La Follette, who made the connection between conservation and progressivism explicit when he praised TR for inaugurating a "world movement for staying terrestrial waste and saving for the human race the things upon which, and upon which it alone, a great and peaceful and progressive and happy race life can be founded," Roosevelt, *Autobiography*, 407.

92. Gifford Pinchot, *Breaking New Ground* (Seattle: University of Washington Press, 1947).

93. TR to Gifford Pinchot, February 24, 1910, in Morison, *Letters*, 6: 1535–1536, which would explain his dismay in learning that Taft had fired Pinchot. TR included in this "peculiar intimacy" James Garfield, who had served him in the Bureau of Corporations and later as secretary of the interior. Roosevelt, *Autobiography*, 409.

94. First Annual Message, in *Works*, 15: 102–103. This was not simply a question of efficiency, for the Land Office and the Division of Forestry had fundamentally different philosophies and histories. The Land Office pursued a policy of privatizing public lands, which Pinchot regarded the source of waste and abuse. The Land Office stood out as the exception in the Department of the Interior, which was generally concerned with managing public resources.

95. The idea itself was sensible as a principle of public policy, but what was the statutory authority for such a move? Roosevelt had been down this road before when his first attorney general had advised him that he could not, without express congressional authorization, ban hunting in the reserves. But this time Pinchot had carefully prepared the ground, getting Attorney General William H. Moody to sign off on fees for a fish saltery in remote Alaska, without raising any opposition. Thus, when the more explosive question of fees for grazing in the western forest reserves came up, the legal precedent was already in place. In his autobiography, Pinchot candidly acknowledged how calculated his legal strategy was, see Pinchot, *Breaking New Ground*, 268–272.

96. Roosevelt, *Autobiography*, 420–421, 416–417, 378.

97. 220 U.S. 506.

98. Gould, *Presidency of Theodore Roosevelt*, 111. Also "History of Pelican Island National Wildlife Refuge," http://www.eoearth.org/article/History_of_Pelican_ Island_National_Wildlife_Refuge (accessed October 4, 2008), 8. In this respect, the law authorizing the creation of the forest reserves the following year (1891), which prevented the president from banning hunting, fishing, and trapping in the reserves without explicit Congressional authorization, was the exception to the otherwise broad executive power over public lands.

99. "History of Pelican Island National Wildlife Refuge," 7.

100. Roosevelt, *Autobiography*, 378. Emboldened by his success with Pelican Island, Roosevelt established a handful of additional bird refuges before Congress enacted a law in 1906 protecting birds and their eggs in game and bird preserves, lending additional legitimacy to his actions. Because Roosevelt chose these sites carefully, their creation sparked no great outcry, apart from the millinery industry and the nefarious plumers and eggers.

101. For the most recent celebratory treatment, see Douglas Brinkley, *The Wilderness Warrior: Theodore Roosevelt and the Crusade for America* (New York: HarperCollins, 2009), 14–19, 492.

102. Roosevelt, *Autobiography*, 436; W. Todd Benson, *President Theodore Roosevelt's Conservation Legacy* (Haverford, Pa.: Infinity Publishing, 2003), 64, 43. And see the helpful chart in Brinkley, *Wilderness Warrior*, 828–829. Surprisingly, Brinkley does not comment on the number of refuges that were withdrawn, though the numbers speak for themselves. In all, Benson claims nineteen, while Brinkley's chart suggests that seventeen were withdrawn for water reclamation or recreation priorities, or because private/state claims took precedence.

103. Libertarians object that the government had no business using taxpayer monies to encourage agriculture in an area that was so naturally unsuited to it. But in fact, the irrigation projects turned the West into one of the great agricultural regions of the country, suggesting that there are indeed times when government intervention serves the common good, Jim Powell, *Bully Boy: The Truth about Theodore Roosevelt's Legacy* (New York: Crown Forum, 2006), ch. 6.

104. Western settlers resisted having to pay back the loans, Roosevelt, *Autobiography*, 413. See also Samuel P. Hays, *Conservation and the Gospel of Efficiency: The Progressive Conservation Movement, 1890–1920* (Cambridge, Mass.: Harvard University Press, 1959), 110.

105. Hays, *Conservation*, 62–63, 70–71, 272–273.

106. Ibid., 14, 135–36.

107. Pinchot, *Breaking New Ground*, 298.

108. Joshua David Hawley, *Theodore Roosevelt: Preacher of Righteousness* (New Haven, Conn.: Yale University Press, 2008), 176. After James Garfield replaced Ethan Allen Hitchcock as secretary of the interior in 1907, Pinchot would find a dependable ally in the streamlined department.

109. "Address before the Deep Waterway Convention at Memphis, Tennessee," October 4, 1907, in *Works*, 16: 109–118, at 117.

110. Roosevelt, *Autobiography*, 433–434.

111. Pinchot, *Breaking New Ground*, 328, incorrectly states that Newlands chaired the committee. As John Milton Cooper, Jr., pointed out to me, Newlands did not become chair until 1913. At the time, Republicans controlled the Senate, and the chair of the committee was Stephen B. Elkins of West Virginia.

112. Hays, *Conservation*, 109–113.

113. John Milton Cooper, Jr., "Gifford Pinchot Creates a Forest Service," in *Leadership and Innovation*, ed. Erwin Hargrove and J. W. Doig (Baltimore: Johns Hopkins University Press, 1990), 83–95.

114. "Address at the Opening of the Conference on the Conservation of Natural Resources, at the White House, May 13, 1908," in *Works*, 16: 119–126, at 119; also, "Seventh Annual Message," in *Works*, 15: 410–488, at 443.

115. "Address at the Opening of the Conference," in *Works*, 16: 125–126.

116. Roosevelt, *Autobiography*, 423.

117. Pinchot, *Breaking New Ground*, 357.

118. Roosevelt, *Autobiography*, 432.

119. Roosevelt, *Autobiography*, 432–433, emphasis added. TR also praised the bureau's work in investigating waterpower and recommending that rental prices for waterpower sites be set, not by the market, but on a par with fuel power. In his discussion of the Bureau of Corporations, Martin J. Sklar, *Corporate Reconstruction of American Capitalism*, 277, noted that Smith had certain reservations about Roosevelt's creeping statism, but his comments on the timber industry make clear just how much he shared the president's fundamental outlook.

120. As Hays, *Conservation*, 261ff, points out, contrary to the narrative of earlier progressive historians, who focused solely on class struggle, Roosevelt's policies often favored the large stockmen and timber interests to the detriment of smaller farmers.

121. TR to George Otto Trevelyan, June 19, 1908, in Morison, *Letters*, 6: 1085–1090, at 1087.

122. Here I sidestep the debate between William E. Leuchtenburg and John Milton Cooper, Jr., over whether progressivism and imperialism were intertwined, since both agree that they were for Roosevelt. William E. Leuchtenburg, "Progressivism and Imperialism: The Progressive Movement and American Foreign Policy, 1898–1916," *Mississippi Valley Historical Review* 39, no. 3 (December 1952): 483–504. But cf. John Milton Cooper, Jr., "Progressivism and American Foreign Policy: A Reconsideration," *Mid-America* 51 (October 1969): 260–277.

123. *Federalist* No. 11, 58; "First Annual Message," in *Works*, 15: 81–138, at 116. And see also Henry Cabot Lodge, *Alexander Hamilton* (Boston: Houghton Mifflin Company, 1898), 151, where Lodge credits Washington's Proclamation of Neutrality, defended by Hamilton in the "Pacificus" papers, with laying the foundation for the Monroe Doctrine and national greatness. Nevertheless, at the time Monroe

announced his policy, the United States had no naval power to enforce it and had to rely on the Royal Navy.

124. "First Annual Message," in *Works*, 15: 116.

125. TR to Herman Speck von Sternberg, July 12, 1901, in Morison, *Letters*, 3: 115–117, at 116.

126. "Third Annual Message," in *Works*, 15: 169–214, at 183–185. Despite Roosevelt's earlier warnings that America should never rely primarily on international arbitration to preserve peace, as president he came to see that arbitration could sometimes be a useful tool. Nevertheless, he remained convinced that it really only worked if backed up by the willingness to use force. In this case, Roosevelt had shown extraordinary tact in confronting the Kaiser, making it easier for him to back down, but he also left him in no doubt that if he refused, he would have to face Dewey's warships. As a general matter, international arbitration was most likely to be successful where the parties were on friendly terms or the issues were relatively unimportant. On vital American interests, it would be foolish, if not worse, to submit to international arbitration. See especially Frederick W. Marks, *Velvet on Iron: The Diplomacy of Theodore Roosevelt* (Lincoln: University of Nebraska Press, 1982).

127. TR to Elihu Root, May 20, 1904, in Morison, *Letters*, 4: 801; also "Fourth Annual Message," in *Works*, 15: 215–266, at 257.

128. Cited in Miller, *Theodore Roosevelt*, 384.

129. Roosevelt blamed "conservative" and "reactionary" Republicans unhappy with his assault on the trusts. But he also did not help his case with southern Democrats by mentioning in his Fourth Annual Message that America had enough to do at home with, among other things, "brutal lawlessness and violent race prejudices." *Works*, 15: 215–266, at 258.

130. Roosevelt, *Autobiography*, 524; also, "Address at the Harvard Union," February 27, 1907, in *Works*, 13: 559–570, at 568.

131. Roosevelt, *Autobiography*, 536, and see a draft of the Message Roosevelt prepared for Congress, 544–546.

132. Samuel Flagg Bemis, *The Latin American Policy of the United States: An Historical Interpretation* (New York: W. W. Norton, 1943), 150, observes that the Panamanians granted even more rights to the Americans. Within the ten-mile zone, the United States could act "as if it were sovereign."

133. In one form or another, that criticism has persisted. On both the left and the right, the Panama Canal is still regarded as an act of raw imperialism, where a more powerful nation interceded by force to gain an area of strategic importance, which it then administered for its own purposes. Blum, *Republican Roosevelt*, 130–131. See also Leuchtenburg, "Progressivism and Imperialism," 483–504, at 487–488. Bemis, *Latin American Policy of the United States*, 151, does not use the word "imperialist," but he calls the intervention of 1903 "the one really bad mark in the Latin American policy of the United States." Powell, *Bully Boy*, 70–76. One recent notable exception is Andrew Roberts, *A History of the English-Speaking Peoples since 1900* (New York: HarperCollins Publishers, 2007), 19–20.

134. Roosevelt, *Autobiography*, 526.

135. TR to William Howard Taft, October 18, 1904, in Morison, *Letters*, 4: 985–986. Taft was then head of the Isthmian Canal Commission.

136. Roosevelt, *Autobiography*, 542–543.

137. "Address at the Exercises Held in Memory of Joseph H. Choate at the Century Association," January 19, 1918, in *Works*, 11: 267–272, at 271.

138. See especially the assessment of Harbaugh, *Power and Responsibility*, 210–211. Bemis, *Latin American Policy of the United States*, 151.

139. "Third Annual Message," December 7, 1903, in *Works*, 15: 212.

140. "The Panama Blackmail Treaty," February 1915, in *Works*, 18: 414–441; Bemis, *Latin American Policy of the United States*, 151.

141. "First Annual Message," in *Works*, 15: 81–138, at 111–112.

142. TR to Rudyard Kipling, November 1, 1904, in Morison, *Letters*, 4: 1007–1008. Kipling's poem, "The White Man's Burden," had been composed in 1899 in defense of American imperialism in the Philippines.

143. TR to Silas McBee, August 27, 1907, in Morison, *Letters*, 5: 772–776, at 774.

144. Ibid., TR to William Howard Taft, August 21, 1907, ibid. 761–762. For the clearest discussion of Roosevelt's retreat from imperialism, see Stephen Wertheim, "Reluctant Liberator: Theodore Roosevelt's Philosophy of Self-Government and Preparation for Philippine Independence," *Presidential Studies Quarterly* 39, no. 3 (September): 2009, 494–518.

145. "Eighth Annual Message," December 8, 1908, in *Works*, 15: 489–545, at 537–539. By 1913, with Wilson in power and the Democrats calling for Philippine independence, Roosevelt acceded to the inevitable, with two caveats. First, he considered it imprudent to set a definite timetable for independence from which it would be difficult to depart, even if circumstances warranted a reconsideration. And second, he thought that the United States should either retain control or relinquish all responsibility for the islands. "Any half and half course," he warned, would be both "foolish and disastrous." What the United States should not do was to establish a protectorate, in which it continued to exercise responsibility, but had relinquished power, Roosevelt, *Autobiography*, 516–518.

146. TR to William Howard Taft, August 21, 1907, in Morison, *Letters*, 5: 761–762.

147. TR to Elihu Root, July 13, 1907, ibid., at 717.

148. Roosevelt, *Autobiography*, 563 and cf. *Federalist* No. 70.

149. Roosevelt, *Autobiography*, 568.

150. Ibid., 563; Miller, *Theodore Roosevelt*, 482.

151. Karl-Friedrich Walling, *Republican Empire: Alexander Hamilton on War and Free Government* (Lawrence: University Press of Kansas, 1999), 146.

152. In addition to the Lodge biography, the probate inventory of Roosevelt's books at Sagamore Hill in 1919 listed Frederick Scott Oliver, *Alexander Hamilton: An Essay on American Union* (1906), and William Smith Culbertson, *Alexander Hamilton: An Essay* (1911). The inventory also lists *Writings*, Hamilton, 9 vols. Nei-

ther Oliver nor Culbertson discussed the theory of executive power set forth in "Pacificus." In his 1904 edition of Hamilton's *Works*, Lodge called the "Pacificus" papers "indispensable" and authoritative, but offered no analysis. *The Works of Alexander Hamilton*, ed. Henry Cabot Lodge, 12 vols. (New York: G. P. Putnam's Sons, 1904), 4: 489, n. 1.

153. Just as the Constitution does not spell out precisely what is meant by "executive power," neither did *The Federalist* address the matter. Only after the Constitution was ratified did Hamilton attempt to explain the meaning of this pregnant silence.

154. "Pacificus" I, in *Selected Writings and Speeches of Alexander Hamilton*, ed. Morton J. Frisch (Washington, D.C.: American Enterprise Institute for Public Policy Research, 1985), 396–404, at 402; see also Walling, *Republican Empire*, 148–149, and Clement Fatovic, "Constitutionalism and Presidential Prerogative: Jeffersonian and Hamiltonian Perspectives," *American Journal of Political Science* 48, no. 3, July 2004): 429–444, esp. 435–439.

155. Here, Jefferson followed Locke. Although recognizing that the executive might be forced to take extraordinary measures in extreme circumstances, he insisted that such actions were always illegal. An executive compelled to take such steps would then have to plead his case to the public, frankly acknowledging that he broke the law. Thomas Jefferson to John B. Colvin, September 20, 1810, Jean M. Yarbrough, *The Essential Jefferson* (Cambridge, Mass.: Hackett Publishing Company, 2006), 208–210. See also Fatovic, "Constitutionalism and Presidential Prerogative," 429–444.

156. Harvey C. Mansfield, Jr., *Taming the Prince: The Ambivalence of Modern Executive Power* (The Johns Hopkins University Press, 1993) 269–271, 275–278.

157. *Federalist* No. 72, 437.

158. "Fifth Annual Message," in *Works*, 15: 288. Closer to home, he might have noted Hamilton's observation in *Federalist* No. 15 that government exists precisely because the passions refuse to conform to the dictates of justice and reason without constraint.

159. TR to Arthur Hamilton Lee, December 26, 1907; TR to George Otto Trevelyan, January 1, 1908, in Morison, *Letters*, 6: 874–875, 880–883.

160. Blum, *Republican Roosevelt*, 123, makes a similar suggestion. Of course, the separation of powers put in place by the Framers imposed a formal constraint, against which Roosevelt increasingly chafed. And in an impersonal way, so also did markets, from whose discipline TR also sought to escape.

161. TR to Arthur Hamilton Lee, December 26, 1907, in Morison, *Letters*, 6: 875.

162. "Sixth Annual Message," in *Works*, 15: 342–409, at 348–350; "Eighth Annual Message," in *Works*, 15: 489–545, at 507–516.

163. TR to Arthur Hamilton Lee, December 26, 1907; TR to George Otto Trevelyan, January 1, 1908, in Morison, *Letters*, 6: 874–875, 880–883. Cf. "Speech in the New York Assembly," March 12, 1884, in *Works*, 14: 33.

164. "The Puritan Spirit and the Regulation of Corporations," August 20, 1907, in *Works*, 16: 76–85, at 84; "Sixth Annual Message," in *Works*, 15: 370.

165. TR to Arthur Hamilton Lee, December 26, 1907, in Morison, *Letters*, 6: 874–875.

166. TR to George Otto Trevelyan, June 19, 1908, ibid., 6: 1085–1090, at 1088.

167. "Address at the Dedication of the New State Capitol Building at Harrisburg, Pa.," October 4, 1906, in *Works*, 16: 69–75, at 70; TR to George Otto Trevelyan, June 19, 1908, in Morison, *Letters*, 6: 1085–1090, at 1086.

168. McNamara, *Political Economy and Statesmanship*, 93–151, esp. 113, 136, 151; Harvey Flaumenhaft, *The Effective Republic: Administration and Constitution in the Thought of Alexander Hamilton* (Durham, N.C.: Duke University Press, 1992).

169. Walling, *Republican Empire*, 23, 164, 170. On whether Hamilton's principles lead to the indefinite expansion of the executive in domestic matters, cf. Hadley Arkes, *The Return of George Sutherland: Restoring a Jurisprudence of Natural Rights* (Princeton, N.J.: Princeton University Press, 1994), 114, who argues that Hamilton's method of moral reasoning imposed limits on what the federal government should do, and Kleinerman, "Lincoln's Example," 802–816, who remains more skeptical.

170. "Socialism I—Where We Cannot Work with Socialists," *The Outlook*, March 20, 1909; "Socialism II—Where We Can Work with Socialists," *The Outlook*, March 27, 1909, at http://www.theodore-roosevelt.com/treditorials.html (accessed July 27, 2011). The file names are 072 and 090, respectively.

6. PROGRESSIVE CRUSADER

1. Alexander Hamilton, James Madison, and John Jay, *The Federalist Papers*, ed. Clinton Rossiter, with an Introduction and Notes by Charles R. Kesler (New York: A Mentor Book, 1999), *Federalist* No. 72, 406. Strictly speaking, Roosevelt was not barred from seeking another term. Nevertheless, the strong tradition established by Washington discouraged him from seeking a third term, though it did not absolutely prohibit it.

2. TR to George Otto Trevelyan, June 19, 1908, in *The Letters of Theodore Roosevelt*, 8 vols., ed. Elting E. Morison et al. (Cambridge, Mass.: Harvard University Press, 1954), see also November 6, 1908, 6: 1085–1090, at 1086; 1328–1330.

3. TR to HCL, March 1, 1910, in *Selections from the Correspondence of Theodore Roosevelt and Henry Cabot Lodge 1884–1918*, 2 vols. (New York: Charles Scribner's Sons, 1925), 2: 361.

4. TR to Kermit Roosevelt, November 22, 1908, in which TR informs his son that he has already completed the Romanes lecture and the Sorbonne address, in Morison, *Letters*, 6: 1375–1376.

5. Theodore Roosevelt, *African and European Addresses*, ed. Lawrence F. Abbott (New York: G. P. Putnam's Sons, 1910), xv–xvi. In his Introduction, Abbott observes that the Cairo and Guildhall addresses were prepared in advance, while his speeches at the Sudan, the University of Christiania, and University of Cambridge were extemporaneous.

6. "The Conditions of Success," an address at the Cambridge Union, May 26, 1910, in ibid., 143–154, at 151. As Abbott notes, the speech before the Cambridge Union and a talk to students in Christiania on the evening of his Nobel Prize acceptance speech were both taken down in shorthand. Extemporaneous remarks in other European cities were not recorded, but it seems safe to assume that they repeated the central message of his prepared addresses, all of which, no matter what the regime, emphasized the need to foster those virtues, both homely and heroic, that would be necessary to meet the challenges of a new century.

7. "Citizenship in a Republic," an address delivered at the Sorbonne, Paris, April 23, 1910, in ibid., 31–71, at 33.

8. Ibid., 38–39.

9. Ibid., 44–45.

10. Review of *The Law of Civilization and Decay*, in *The Works of Theodore Roosevelt*, 20 vols., ed. Herman Hagedorn (New York: Charles Scribner's Sons, 1924), 13: 242–260, at 247 (hereafter cited as *Works*). The theme was also brought home in Owen Wister's 1902 popular novel, *The Virginian*. However, TR did not perhaps appreciate the extent to which the decline in the birthrate resulted from the shift from an agricultural to an industrial economy, a development he otherwise applauded.

11. "Citizenship in a Republic," 47–48.

12. See the introduction by Abbott, xxiv, in Roosevelt, *African and European Addresses*. Sidney M. Milkis, *Theodore Roosevelt, the Progressive Party, and the Transformation of American Democracy* (Lawrence: University Press of Kansas, 2009), 32, adds that Roosevelt delivered this part of his speech in French for emphasis.

13. "Citizenship in a Republic," 55. Consider also TR's sympathy with the goals of Italian socialism, if not their methods. TR to George Otto Trevelyan, October 1, 1911, in Morison, *Letters*, 7: 348–399, at 359.

14. "Citizenship in a Republic," 57. Also, "Socialism and Social Reform," first published in two parts in 1909 and then updated and republished in *Foes of Our Own Household* (1917), in *Works*, 19: 96–112.

15. Perhaps this is because the Declaration does not specifically mention property rights, but there is no doubt that Jefferson, along with the rest of the founders, understood property in a Lockean way. Jean M. Yarbrough, *American Virtues: Thomas Jefferson on the Character of a Free People* (Lawrence: University Press of Kansas, 1998), chs. 1 and 3.

16. It is possible that TR meant to call into question only the sanctity of property rights, rather than the trilogy of rights in the Declaration. But if this is so, how far was he willing to go? Did he mean, as Henry Cabot Lodge asked him after reading reports of the speech, to challenge the general right to property or only industrial combinations and corporate wealth? According to Milkis, the latter was Lodge's objection to the speech. Milkis, *TR and Transformation*, 33.

17. Here again, Roosevelt seems muddled, speaking in one sentence of "equal opportunity to show the stuff that is in him by the way in which he renders service"

and then insisting, "reward must go to the man who does his work well." "Citizenship in a Republic," 59.

18. "The World Movement," an address delivered at the University of Berlin, May 12, 1910, in Roosevelt, *African and European Addresses*, 99–139, at 117.

19. Review of *The Law of Civilization and Decay*, in *Works*, 13: 242–260.

20. "The World Movement," 125, 135.

21. Ibid., 137–138, emphasis added.

22. William James, "The Moral Equivalent of War," 1906, at www.constitution .org/wj/meow.htm (accessed April 9, 2012), and see also Wilfred M. McClay, "The Moral Equivalent of War?" *National Affairs*, no. 5 (Fall 2010): 134–144, at 136, and William E. Leuchtenburg, "The New Deal and the Analogue of War," in *Change and Continuity in Twentieth-Century America*, ed. John Braeman, Robert H. Bremner, and Everett Walters (New York: Harper Colophon Books, 1964), esp. 120–127.

23. "An Address before the Nobel Peace Prize Committee," delivered at Christiania, Norway, May 5, 1910, in Roosevelt, *African and European Addresses*, 75–83, at 76. TR offered qualified approval of arbitration treaties among the "really civilized communities," though he was careful to insist that no nation should enter into arbitration on vital matters affecting the national interest or national honor. Surprisingly, he also called for arms limitation, especially on naval armaments, though he stipulated that this be done by international agreement and not unilaterally. Finally, he proposed for the first time a league of peace among the great powers, with the critical provision that its decisions be backed up by force.

24. Ironically, it was at that moment that Roosevelt seemed most to agree with Hegel that war represented a higher ethical moment in the life of a state because it demanded the sacrifice of lives and property for the sake of something nobler.

25. Milkis, *TR and Transformation*, 33, regards the lecture as further evidence of Roosevelt's political ambition, but since the speech was written while he was still in the White House, this would mean that he was already plotting his return, even before the disappointments of the Taft presidency.

26. "Biological Analogies in History," Oxford, June 7, 1910, in Roosevelt, *African and European Addresses*, 175–236, at 177, 186.

27. Without actually saying so, Roosevelt seemed to be hinting that the Social Darwinists' attempt to explain social change solely by natural selection and survival of the fittest was unwarranted.

28. "Biological Analogies," 208–210.

29. Ibid., 222–224.

30. Ibid., 227.

31. "The Colonial Policy of the United States," an address delivered at Christiania, Norway, on the evening of May 5, 1910, in Roosevelt, *African and European Addresses*, 87–96, at 88–93.

32. Ibid., 94.

33. "Biological Analogies," 223.

34. Ibid., 225.

35. Ibid., 231, 229, 230, 223.

36. Kathleen Dalton, *Theodore Roosevelt: A Strenuous Life* (New York: Alfred A. Knopf, 2002), 362; George E. Mowry, *Theodore Roosevelt and the Progressive Movement* (Madison: University of Wisconsin Press, 1946), 146. For an illuminating comparison of social welfare policies in Germany, Denmark, England, and the United States, see Daniel Levine, *Poverty and Society: The Growth of the American Welfare State in International Comparison* (New Brunswick, N.J.: Rutgers University Press, 1988), esp. parts 2 and 3.

37. "Natural Resources," speech before the National Conservation Congress, September 6, 1910, at St. Paul, Minnesota,. in *The New Nationalism*, ed. William E. Leuchtenburg (Englewood Cliffs, N.J.: Prentice-Hall, Inc., 1961), 74.

38. Had he paid more attention to Tocqueville, this phenomenon would not have been so mysterious. Alexis de Tocqueville, *Democracy in America*, trans. Harvey C. Mansfield and Delba Winthrop (Chicago: University of Chicago Press, 2000), esp. vol. 2, part 2, chs. 1 and 10.

39. TR to George Otto Trevelyan, October 1, 1911, in Morison, *Letters*, 7: 348–399, at 385, 390.

40. For an early discussion, see Lord Charnwood, *Theodore Roosevelt* (Boston: The Atlantic Monthly Press, 1923), 175. For a more recent statement, Milkis, *TR and Transformation*, 30.

41. *The Outlook*, ed. Lyman Abbott et al., vol. 93, September-December 1909, 788–789, http://books.google.com/books?id=QFAAAAAYAAJ&printsec=frontco ver&dq=the+outlook+1909&source=bl&ots=jtURexFlf6&sig=ebNWEow3VQOP-JA7dYvPLmIoNKY&hl=en&ei=R-ijTPSpCY7MswaMtKC8CA&sa=X&oi=book_ result&ct=result&resnum=4&sqi=2&ved=0CB8Q6AEwAw#v=onepage&q= the%20outlook%201909&f=false (accessed September 29, 2010).

42. David W. Levy, *Herbert Croly of the New Republic: The Life and Thought of an American Progressive* (Princeton, N.J.: Princeton University Press, 1985), 136–138. Levy offers the following anecdote as evidence that Roosevelt had actually read Croly's book with care. In October 1910, the journalist Roy Stannard Baker visited Roosevelt at Sagamore Hill and was shown into the library to await the Colonel's return from riding. Baker later recorded in his diary that he found a copy of *The Promise of American Life* "with many passages heavily scored & pages on the fly-leaf with references. I understand T.R. has been confirmed in his 'New Nationalism' by this book." According to information supplied by Susan Sarna, Sagamore Hill administrator, TR's copy of *The Promise of American Life* is listed in the probate inventory of 1919, but is no longer among the books in the Sagamore Hill library.

43. Croly had actually dropped out of Harvard several times. On the strength of the book, Harvard finally awarded Croly his degree in 1910. Levy, *Herbert Croly*, 141.

44. In his 1890 history, *New York*, Roosevelt praised Hamilton as "the most brilliant American stateman who ever lived, the loftiest and keenest intellect of his time," in *Works*, 10: 485.

45. Herbert Croly, *The Promise of American Life* (Boston: Northeastern University Press, 1989 [orig. pub. 1909]), 21–22, 27–51, 214.

46. Ibid., 169, 170.

47. Ibid., 174.

48. Ibid., 278–279.

49. Ibid., 175.

50. See, e.g., John Milton Cooper, Jr., *The Warrior and the Priest: Woodrow Wilson and Theodore Roosevelt* (Cambridge, Mass.: The Belknap Press of Harvard University Press, 1983), 145–149; John Morton Blum, *The Republican Roosevelt* (New York: Atheneum, 1974 [orig. pub. Harvard University Press, 1954]), 107, 122; William E. Leuchtenburg, Introduction, *The New Nationalism: Theodore Roosevelt* (Englewood Cliffs, N.J.: Prentice-Hall, 1961), 11–17; Eric F. Goldman, *Rendezvous with Destiny* (Alfred A. Knopf, 1952), 189; and Levy, *Herbert Croly*, 139–140.

51. This is also the conclusion of Levy, *Herbert Croly*, 139–141, who has more at stake in this dispute than historians who focus on TR and New Nationalism. Yet even Goldman, after initially stating, "it is doubtful whether Roosevelt read many of Croly's 454 pages, which include a good deal of labyrinthine analysis and even more tedious writing," went on to note the ways in which Croly deepened Roosevelt's nationalism. Goldman, *Rendezvous with Destiny*, 189, but cf. 204–207. Something similar, if less dramatic, can be found in Cooper, *Warrior and Priest*, 194; Leuchtenburg, *New Nationalism*, 15–17.

52. Croly, *Promise*, 180.

53. Ibid., 18, 22.

54. Ibid., 194.

55. Ibid., 180–181.

56. Ibid., 181. One hundred years later, after many of the programs Croly supported have long been enacted, the magazine Croly helped to establish continues to trumpet this line. Writing in *The New Republic*, Jonathan Chait maintains that the United States still has not achieved a genuine equality of opportunity, and that "there is no realistic plan to make it anything remotely close to equal." Jonathan Chait, "The Death of Facts," *New Republic*, October 28, 2010, 32–35, at 34. More recently, the magazine made "The Inequality Issue" its principal focus, March 1, 2012.

57. Croly, *Promise*, 202, 209. For a sketch of Croly's industrial and labor policies, see ch. 12.

58. Ibid., 189.

59. Ibid., 207–208.

60. As Croly put it, his program was "not so much socialistic as unscrupulously and loyally nationalistic," 209. I leave aside here the interesting question of Croly's fascination with fascism in the 1920s and the possible implications for Roosevelt, who died in 1919. For a discussion, see John P. Diggins, "Flirtation with Fascism: American Pragmatic Liberals and Mussolini's Italy," *American Historical Review* 71, no. 2 (January 1966): 487–506; more recently, Jonah Goldberg, *Liberal Fascism*

(New York: Broadway Books, 2007, 2009), ch. 3. Edward A. Stettner, *Shaping Modern Liberalism: Herbert Croly and Progressive Thought* (Lawrence: University Press of Kansas, 1993), 155–157, defends Croly against these charges.

61. Croly, *Promise*, 418.

62. On his westward swing, Roosevelt steered clear of Wisconsin and La Follette.

63. After the trip, Roosevelt wrote that, based on his conversations with "Regulars" and their opponents, his campaign swing had been "a very material help" in trying to reunite the party. TR himself did not think they were "entirely insincere." TR to HCL, September 12, 1910, in *Selections from the Correspondence*, 2: 391–392. He had also campaigned for Lodge in Massachusetts and Warren Harding in Ohio.

64. Cooper, *Warrior and Priest*, 145; Mowry, *Theodore Roosevelt and the Progressive Movement*, 144. Dalton, *Theodore Roosevelt*, 365–366.

65. Writing to Roosevelt days after the speech, Henry Cabot Lodge gently suggested that it was not "helpful" to single out particular decisions because such criticism tended to undermine respect for the law. He also worried that his friend had given the *Lochner* decision "a meaning that it will not bear." In Lodge's view, there was "a broad distinction" between a state's efforts to protect workers by regulating working conditions and limiting the number of hours they could work. HCL to TR, September 5, 1910, in *Selections from the Correspondence*, 2: 388–390, at 389.

66. Leuchtenburg, *New Nationalism*, 40–49. At the same time that Roosevelt threw down his challenge to the courts, he insisted, once again, that he was trying to steer between "the Scylla of demagogism" and the "Charybdis of corruption and conservatism." Note, however, that this time one of the evils to be avoided was "conservatism." As Cooper, *Warrior and Priest*, 149, has observed, Roosevelt claimed to be the moderate and sane voice, but his intemperate attacks stirred up the insurgents within his own party.

67. "Address to Germans in Cincinnati, Ohio," February 12, 1861, in *Abraham Lincoln: His Speeches and Writings*, ed. Roy P. Basler (Cambridge, Mass.: Da Capo Press [orig. pub. Cleveland: World Publishing, 1946]), 572–574. These brief and somewhat cryptic remarks on the eve of the Civil War appear to be in response to a question about what Lincoln's policy on secession and/or slavery would be, which he declined to answer. The Germans were generally pro-Republican and anti-slavery.

68. "Reply to a Committee from the Workingmen's Association of New York," March 21, 1864, in Abraham Lincoln, *Complete Works, Comprising His Speeches, Letters, State Papers, and Miscellaneous Writings*, 2 vols., ed. John G. Nicolay and John Hay (New York: The Century Co., 1894), 2: 501–503. As the full text makes clear, Lincoln is quoting from his First Annual Message in the first of these comments. The second selection combines ideas from the First Annual Message and his address directly to the workers at the end of the speech. The third "Lincolnlike sentence" is the last line of his address to the workers. Lincoln made essentially the same arguments when addressing farmers in Wisconsin and workers in New York.

69. In his "Annual Address before the Wisconsin State Agricultural Society, at Milwaukee, Wisconsin," September 30, 1859, in Basler, *Abraham Lincoln,* 493–505, at 500, Lincoln associated this position with the "mudsill theory," which argued that the slave and laboring classes existed principally to support the higher classes that made up civilization. It was first expounded by the South Carolina senator James Henry Hammond in 1858.

70. See especially Lincoln's speech on the *Dred Scott* decision, which TR cited in his Sorbonne address, though he omitted the section in which Lincoln spoke of the "natural right" of the slave "to eat the bread she earns with her own hands without asking leave of anyone else," Basler, *Abraham Lincoln,* 360.

71. Here in capsule form is Lincoln's response to Croly's footrace analogy: through their own efforts, men may improve their economic circumstances. Even if they do not win the race, they are farther along at the end than when they started.

72. "Reply to a Committee from the Workingmen's Association of New York," Basler, *Abraham Lincoln,* 503; see also "Annual Address before the Wisconsin Agricultural Society," and Annual Message to Congress, December 3, 1861, 493–505, 616–635. And see the discussion in Harry V. Jaffa, *A New Birth of Freedom: Abraham Lincoln and the Coming of the Civil War* (Lanham, Md.: Rowman & Littlefield, 2000), 243, 320. For a contrasting view, more sympathetic to Roosevelt, see Milkis, *TR and Transformation,* 39–40, 45, who suggests that Lincoln's views were no longer applicable in 1910 when "economic lines were hardening."

73. "The New Nationalism," in Leuchtenburg, *New Nationalism,* 21–39, at 26.

74. Ibid., 30, 33.

75. Ibid., 30, emphasis added.

76. Ibid., 33–34. Locke's view is far more nuanced than Roosevelt allows. In the *Second Treatise,* Locke had argued that the "regulating and preserving of property" was the end of government, but that all this was for "the public good." Locke's view of the "public good" was at odds with Roosevelt's, however. John Locke, *Second Treatise of Government,* ed. Richard Cox (Arlington Heights, Ill.: Harlan Davidson, 1982), ch. 1, para. 3, p. 2.

77. *Realizable Ideals,* in *Works,* 13: 615–674, at 666. Once the axiom that property no longer belonged fundamentally to the individual was planted, there were no principled limits on how far government could go in regulating or redistributing it. Roosevelt tried to strike a balance, but the line was constantly shifting.

78. "New Nationalism," in Leuchtenburg, *New Nationalism,* 30. It also assumed that wealth was a "zero sum" game, in which one person could only prosper at another's expense, and thus required the government to intervene to spread the wealth around more evenly.

79. Here, he was not being completely candid, as TR did and would again in "The Progressives, Past and Present" call for the ICC to be given general rate-making powers, as well as setting schedules and controlling all terminals.

80. "New Nationalism," in Leuchtenburg, *New Nationalism,* 34.

81. Perhaps in anticipation of this charge, Roosevelt would later that fall insist on

the importance of the old virtues and old moralities. Unlike the old political principles, which had clearly been rendered obsolete by changing economic conditions, Roosevelt asserted that the new qualities he called for could "only supplement, and never supplant, the old, homely virtues; the need for the special and distinctive pioneer virtues is as great as ever." "The Pioneer Spirit and American Problems," September 10, 1910, in *Works*, 16: 20–25, at 21. But cf. Woodrow Wilson's response, "Freemen Need No Guardians," in *The New Freedom: A Call for the Emancipation of the Generous Energies of a People*, ed. William E. Leuchtenburg (Englewood Cliffs, N.J.: Prentice-Hall, 1961), 47–58.

82. "The New Nationalism and the Old Moralities," in Leuchtenburg, *New Nationalism*, 165–173.

83. TR to Henry Cabot Lodge, September 21, 1910, in Morison, *Letters*, 7: 134–137, at 134. It was an error for a public man to state his position in such a way that good men could misconstrue it.

84. HCL to TR, September 5, 1910, and see TR to HCL, September 12, 1910, where TR thought it "a curious thing" that the most incendiary part of the speech was his quotation from Abraham Lincoln, in *Selections from the Correspondence*, 2: 388–390.

85. Theodore Roosevelt, "The Progressives, Past and Present," http://www .theodore-roosevelt.com/treditorials/html (accessed October 15, 2010). The file name is 0160. Because the online version does not give page numbers, this will be the only reference to the essay that I shall cite. All future references to the essay are from this version.

86. Labor Day Speech, Columbia County, New York, September 5, 1917, as reported in the *New York Times*, September 6, 1917 at http://www.theodore-roosevelt .com/trspeeches complete.html (accessed October 15, 2010). The file name is 876. Also, Robert H. Bork, *The Antitrust Paradox: A Policy at War with Itself* (New York: Basic Books, 1978). Bork focuses specifically on antitrust policy, but the regulatory regime Roosevelt wished to install faced the same paradox: the policies that spared the small competitor imposed hardships on the consumer, and vice versa.

87. As William Voegeli has recently argued, this is a question that progressives and liberals still have not answered, William Voegeli, *Never Enough: America's Limitless Welfare State* (New York: Encounter Books, 2010). Voegeli is, however, also critical of conservatives and libertarians who are unwilling to make compromises with the modern welfare state.

88. For a useful discussion of the 1910 midterm elections, see Andrew E. Busch, *Horses in Midstream: U.S. Midterm Elections and Their Consequences, 1894–1998* (Pittsburgh, Pa: University of Pittsburgh Press, 1999).

89. "The Radical Movement under Conservative Direction," address before the Chamber of Commerce, New Haven, Conn., December 13, 1910, in *Works*, 16: 86–99, at 89, 98.

90. See, especially, "The Rights and Duties of Labor," speech in Freeport, Ill., September 8, 1910, in *Works*, 16: 159–163.

91. As he elsewhere observed in all seriousness, he was a progressive, but he did not see this as a partisan issue at all. "Rights and Duties of Labor," in *Works*, 16: 162.

92. "Progressive Nationalism; Or What?" January 14, 1911, in *Works*, 17: 49–52.

93. "Nationalism and Popular Rule," January 21, 1911, in *Works*, 17: 53–65. See the exchange between TR and HCL, December 13, 1911, and HCL's reply, December 18, 1911, in *Selections from the Correspondence*, 2: 416–418.

94. "Nationalism and the Judiciary," in *Works*, 17: 74–99, at 93. The essay, as reprinted in *Works*, appeared in three installments on February 25, March 4, and March 11, 1911, in *The Outlook*.

95. Ibid., 84, 86–87.

96. "Justice Moody," November 5, 1910, in *Works*, 11: 259–263, at 262. But cf. Lincoln, especially his "Address at Cooper Institute," February 27, 1860, and "Fragment: The Constitution and the Union (1860?), in which he likens the principles of the Declaration of Independence to an "apple of gold," and the Constitution to a "picture of silver," in Basler, *Abraham Lincoln*, 517–536, 513.

97. "Nationalism and the Judiciary," in *Works*, 17: 88–89.

98. Oddly, the fourth installment of "Nationalism and the Judiciary," dated March 18, 1911, is not included in the National edition of Roosevelt's *Works*. It can be found at http://www.theodore-roosevelt.com/treditorials.html (accessed December 13, 2010). The file name is 064.

99. Howard Gillman, *The Constitution Besieged: The Rise and Demise of* Lochner *Era Police Powers Jurisprudence* (Durham, N.C.: Duke University Press, 1993), 4–5, 208–210, n. 10. More recently, David E. Bernstein, *Rehabilitating* Lochner: *Defending Individual Rights against Progressive Reform* (Chicago: University of Chicago Press, 2011). For one thing, the law limiting the number of hours bakers could work was upheld by the New York courts. For another, the decision ignored the fact that unionized bakers supported the law, not for health reasons, but in order to deprive their nonunion competitors of what they saw as an unfair economic advantage.

100. "The Conservation of Womanhood and Childhood," October 20, 1911, in *Works*, 16: 181–207; with minor changes, the October speech was reprinted December 23, 1911, in *The Outlook*, "Judges and Progress," January 6, 1912 at http://www .theodore-roosevelt.com/treditorials.html (accessed November 12, 2010). The file name is 021. But cf. Jeremy Rabkin, "Is It Unnatural to Shun Foreign Precedent?" in *Freedom and the Rule of Law*, ed. Anthony Peacock (Lanham, Md.: Rowman & Littlefield, 2010), 155–178.

101. As he himself later conceded, his remedy was not based on "a library study of constitutional law," but on his own experience using governmental power "to redress social and industrial evils." "The Right of the People to Rule," March 20, 1912, in *Works*, 17: 151–171, at 164–165. Roosevelt perhaps thought that he was following Lincoln, who in his First Inaugural observed that "if the policy of the government upon vital questions, affecting the whole people, is to be irrevocably fixed by decisions of the Supreme Court, the instant they are made, in ordinary litigation

between parties, in personal actions, the people will have ceased to be their own rulers, having to that extent practically resigned their government into the hands of that eminent tribunal," but his recall proposal was far more radical than what Lincoln was suggesting. Basler, *Abraham Lincoln*, 585–586.

102. Roosevelt devoted very little attention to these problems. One of the few speeches to deal with it is "The Meaning of Free Government," March 28, 1912, in *Works*, 17: 172–176, at 174.

103. Martin J. Sklar, *The Corporate Reconstruction of American Capitalism, 1890–1916: The Market, The Law, and Politics* (New York: Cambridge University Press, 1988), 288. Sklar also notes that Herbert Knox Smith, who continued to serve as head of the Bureau of Corporations in the Taft administration, raised objections to Roosevelt's call for a federal licensing power, and thought that the administration should wait to see how the new line of Supreme Court decisions would work before pushing ahead with more regulatory legislation, 292–293.

104. On Taft's overall regulatory policy, see ibid., 285–287, 297ff.

105. "The Trusts, the People, and the Square Deal," November 18, 1911, at http://www.theodore-roosevelt.com/treditorials.html (accessed November 1, 2010). The file name is 065. Mowry, *Theodore Roosevelt and the Progressive Movement*, 192.

106. Lewis L. Gould, *Four Hats in the Ring: The 1912 Election and the Birth of Modern American Politics* (Lawrence: University Press of Kansas, 2008), 56.

107. John J. Dinan, *Keeping the People's Liberties: Legislators, Citizens, and Judges as Guardians of Rights* (Lawrence: University Press of Kansas, 1998), 82–84.

108. Even so, the Pinchots, who had read a draft of the speech, criticized it for, as TR put it, "not taking a sufficiently well-defined radical position." TR to Amos Pinchot, February 15, 1912, in Morison, *Letters*, 7: 505–506.

109. "A Charter of Democracy," address before the Ohio Constitutional Convention, February 21, 1912, in *Works*, 17: 119–148, at 134.

110. Cf. Croly, *Promise*, 22, 196.

111. "Charter of Democracy," in *Works*, 17: 123.

112. By empowering the state to take sides, it replaced natural selection with a superior "artificial selection." It was, as Croly wrote, "the business of the state to see that its friends are victorious." Croly, *Promise*, 190, 192; cf. Gillman, *Constitution Besieged*, 6–10; Hadley Arkes, *The Return of George Sutherland: Restoring a Jurisprudence of Natural Rights* (Princeton, N.J.: Princeton University Press, 1994), 114.

113. "Charter of Democracy," in *Works*, 17: 135–136. In support of this last criticism, he could have cited Hamilton's observation in *Federalist* No. 78 that the judiciary was "the least dangerous branch" so long as it refrained from making the law.

114. "Right of the People to Rule," in *Works*, 17: 151–171, at 157–158, 163.

115. "Charter of Democracy," in *Works*, 17: 138–143; for the two-year waiting period, "Right of the People to Rule," in *Works*, 17: 161; "The Recall of Judicial Decisions," April 10, 1912, in *Works*, 17: 190–203, at 195.

116. TR to Henry Lewis Stimson, February 5, 1912; TR to Herbert Croly, February 28, 1912, in Morison, *Letters*, 7: 494–495, 512.

117. Mowry, *Theodore Roosevelt and the Progressive Movement*, 213.

118. HCL to TR, February 28, 1912, in *Selections from the Correspondence*, 2: 422–423; for Root, Morison, *Letters*, 7: 122, n. 3, and 507, n. 2.

119. Cooper, *Warrior and Priest*, 140–141; Milkis, *TR and Transformation*, 87. For a fine discussion of Taft's constitutionalism, see Milkis, 86–97. However, Milkis exaggerates when he writes that Taft's "sober view of human nature betrayed the depth of his conservatism," 89. Taft's view of human nature could more accurately be described as realistic.

120. "Recall of Judicial Decisions," in *Works*, 17: 190–203, at 202.

121. "Recall of Judicial Decisions," in *Works*, 17; also, "Right of the People to Rule," in *Works*, 17: 151; "Meaning of Free Government," in *Works*, 17: 172–176, at 174.

122. "Duty and Self-Control," speech in Madison, Wisconsin, April 15, 1911, in *Works*, 13: 593–595.

123. *Oliver Cromwell*, in *Works*, 10: 217.

124. "Women's Rights; and the Duties of Both Men and Women," February 3, 1912, in *Works*, 16: 208–219, at 216. Among the works TR admired was *The College Man and the College Woman*, by William DeWitt Hyde, president of Bowdoin College.

125. "Race Decadence," Review of *Racial Decay*, by Octavius Charles Beale, April 8, 1911, in *Works*, 12: 184–196.

126. *Realizable Ideals*, in *Works*, 13: 611–674, at 636–637.

127. "Women's Rights," in *Works*, 16: 208–219, at 215.

128. "Sixth Annual Message," in *Works*, 15: 377–378. Citing the census reports of 1890, 1900, and 1910, Allan Carlson notes a threefold increase in the number of divorced Americans. Between 1880 and 1920, the birth rate toppled by 30 percent, with the steepest declines in the Northeast. "Theodore Roosevelt's New Politics of the American Family," at http://www.profam.org/pub/fia/fia_1510.html (accessed December 10, 2010).

129. *Realizable Ideals*, in *Works*, 13: 631, 637.

130. *Realizable Ideals*, in *Works*, 13: 632.

131. "Women's Rights," in *Works*, 16: 218.

132. "The Woman and the Home," address before the National Congress of Mothers, March 13, 1905, in *Works*, 16: 164–171, at 166–167.

133. For a discussion of mothers' pensions and the move toward social security, see Levine, *Poverty and Society*, 162–163. See also the recommendations of the White House Conference on the Care of Dependent Children, January 25, 1909, at http://www.libertynet.org/edcivic/whoukids.html (accessed January 7, 2011).

134. "Women's Rights," in *Works*, 16: 219, 215–216. Emphasis in original. Also, "Socialism I—Where We Cannot Work with Socialists," *The Outlook*, March 20, 1909, where he attributed this position to the socialists, http://www.theodore-roosevelt.com/treditorials.html (accessed July 27, 2011). The file names are 010 and 072, respectively.

135. Dalton, *Theodore Roosevelt*, 393, 418.

136. "Woman and the Home," in *Works,* 16: 165.

137. "Women's Rights," in *Works,* 16: 209–210.

138. Ibid., 209, 214–216. Emphasis in original.

139. As Dalton, *Theodore Roosevelt,* 373, notes, TR would later embrace the movement enthusiastically in a bid for votes.

140. "Woman and the Home," in *Works,* 16: 168.

141. Eldon Eisenach, *The Lost Promise of Progressivism* (Lawrence: University Press of Kansas, 1994), 81–84. For a discussion of the larger world of progressive intellectuals, Eisenach's work is most helpful.

142. "New Nationalism," in Leuchtenburg, *New Nationalism,* 32.

143. "Conservation of Womanhood and Childhood," in *Works,* 16: 181–207, at 184–185.

144. But as Thomas Sowell has argued, immigrants often chose to live and work in these cramped quarters to save money to move into better surroundings. Thomas Sowell, *The Quest for Cosmic Justice* (New York: The Free Press, 2001), 128–129.

145. "Conservation of Womanhood and Childhood," in *Works,* 16: 188, 192.

146. "The Conservation of Business—Shall We Strangle or Control It?" in *The Outlook,* March 16, 1912, at http://www.theodore-roosevelt.com/treditorials.html (accessed December 1, 2010). The file name is 057.

147. John Adams Wettergreen, "The Regulatory Revolution and the New Bureaucratic State," Parts 1 and 2, Heritage Foundation Lectures, February 11, 1988, and August 10, 1988.

148. "The Word of Micah; The Religion of Service," in *Works,* 19: 132–139, at 135.

149. "The Welfare of the Farmer," April 20, 1912; also "Progressive Democracy: Country Life and Conservation," September 7, 1912 at http://www.theodore-roose velt.com/treditorials.html (accessed November 27, 2010). The file names are 068 and 029, respectively.

150. "What a Progressive Is," April 3, 1912, in *Works,* 17: 177–189.

151. Ironically, in making this argument, Roosevelt sounded very much like the much-despised Jefferson, who 100 years earlier, had a similar vision of Whigs and Tories.

152. "The Case against the Reactionaries," speech at the Auditorium, Chicago, Ill., June 17, 1912, in *Works,* 17: 202–231, at 222–231.

153. As Levine, *Poverty and Society,* 174ff, who is sympathetic to the modern welfare state notes, almost all of organized labor, employers, and doctors opposed social insurance, except for workers' compensation. There was no conspiracy that prevented its implementation. Americans did not adopt social insurance programs during the Progressive Era because they did not want them or believe that the country needed them.

154. "Case against the Reactionaries," in *Works,* 17: 229–231, and cf. Lincoln, in Basler, *Abraham Lincoln,* 133; *Oliver Cromwell,* in *Works,* 10: 306. Here too, compare with Lincoln, who in one of his fragments on slavery wryly observed, "Certainly

there is no contending against the Will of God; but still there is some difficulty in ascertaining and applying it, to particular cases," Basler, *Abraham Lincoln*, 477–478.

155. The situations were not exactly parallel because this time Roosevelt himself was the aggrieved candidate.

156. Historian Michael Barone takes the threat of socialism seriously, see "The Return of the Jeffersonian Vision and the Rejection of Progressivism," in *The American: The Journal of the American Enterprise Institute*, July 13, 2010, at http://www.american.com/archive/2010/july/the-return-of-the-jeffersonian-vision-and-the-rejection-of-progressivism (accessed August 15, 2010).

157. "Socialism and Social Reform," in *Works*, 19: 96–112, at 108.

158. "Socialism and Social Reform," in *Works*, 19: 110; also, "Socialism II—Where We Can Work with the Socialists," http://www.theodore-roosevelt.com/treditorials .html (accessed July 27, 2011). The file name is 090.

159. In "Social Justice: The Brotherly Court of Philadelphia," Roosevelt would later explain that the term meant protecting women and children from "evil and brutality" and as far as possible from "grinding misery" and "open[ing] the doors of fair dealing to men who would otherwise find them closed." May 1917 in *Works*, 19: 84–95, at 84. Among other things, social justice required courts that applied common sense and were not sticklers for legal technicalities.

160. Levine, *Poverty and Society*, 135, 168.

161. "A Confession of Faith," August 6, 1912, in *Works*, 17: 254–299, at 269.

162. Social security would prove more difficult than Roosevelt imagined, however, as not even Samuel Gompers, head of the AFL, could endorse these measures, warning that they would undermine unions and erode individual freedom. Levine, *Poverty and Society*, 156, 173.

163. "Confession of Faith," in *Works*, 17: 276.

164. "Confession of Faith," in *Works*, 17: 295.

165. Charles Willis Thompson, "Recollections of Roosevelt," *New York Times*, January 12, 1919.

166. TR to Julian La Rose Harris, August 1, 1912, in Morison, *Letters*, 7: 584–590; "The Progressives and the Colored Man," August 24, 1912, in *Works*, 17: 300–305. On the paradoxes and contradictions of his position, see John A. Gable, *The Bull Moose Years: Theodore Roosevelt and the Progressive Party* (Port Washington, N.Y.: The Kennikat Press, 1978), 66–72.

167. For further analysis, see Milkis, *TR and Transformation*, 166–176, 193–198; Gould, *Four Hats*, 133–136; Dalton, *Theodore Roosevelt*, 393–385.

168. But cf. Gould, *Four Hats*, 162; Cooper, *Warrior and Priest*, 140–141, 211–221.

169. Cooper, *Warrior and Priest*, 140–141, 193, 213. On Wilson's idealism, 254, 260.

170. But cf. Ronald J. Pestritto, *Woodrow Wilson and the Roots of Modern Liberalism* (Lanham, Md.: Rowman & Littlefield, 2005), who persuasively argues that Wilson the academic had long been an adherent of progressive thought.

171. Gould, *Four Hats*, 167; Cooper, *Warrior and Priest*, 194.

172. "The Limitation of Government Power," September 14, 1912, in *Works*, 17: 306–314.

173. "The Leader and the Cause," October 14, 1912, in *Works*, 17: 320–330, at 328. It is true that the Democratic Party platform placed a heavier emphasis on the role of the states in controlling the trusts and favored breaking them up to promote competition, but Wilson was no admirer of Jefferson.

174. "Roosevelt Favors Recall of President," special to The *New York Times*, September 20, 1912.

175. "How I Became a Progressive," October 12, 1912, in *Works*, 17: 315–319. See in particular his statement, "We recognize in neither court, nor Congress, nor President, any divine right to override the will of the people, as expressed with due deliberation in orderly fashion and through the forms of law." "The Purpose of the Progressive Party," October 30, 1912, in *Works*, 17: 334–340, at 337.

176. "The Purpose of the Progressive Party," in *Works*, 17: 334–340; also Mowry, *Theodore Roosevelt and the Progressive Movement*, 277.

177. Jason R. Jividen, *Claiming Lincoln: Progressivism, Equality, and the Battle for Lincoln's Legacy in Presidential Rhetoric* (DeKalb: Northern Illinois University Press, 2011).

178. "1. *Resolved,* That we believe this truth to be self-evident, that when parties become subversive of the ends for which they are established, or incapable of restoring the government to the true principles of the Constitution, it is the right and duty of the people to dissolve the political bands by which they may have been connected therewith, and to organize new parties upon such principles and with such views as the circumstances and exigencies of the nation may demand. 2. *Resolved,* That the times imperatively demand the reorganization of parties, and, repudiating all previous party attachments, names, and predilections, we unite ourselves together . . . pledged to bring the administration of the government back to the control of first principles."

179. "The Heirs of Abraham Lincoln," February 12, 1913, in *Works*, 17: 359–378, at 359, 360–361, and compare with Lincoln's remarks in his Cooper Institute speech, February 27, 1860, cited in the epigraph, in Basler, *Abraham Lincoln*, 525.

180. "The Foreign Policy of the United States," August 22, 1914, http://www .theodore-roosevelt.com/treditorials.html (accessed December 7, 2010). The file name is 0124. Emphasis in original.

181. "Progressive Democracy," November 18, 1914, in *Works*, 12: 232–239.

182. The image is from Cooper, *Warrior and Priest*, 225.

183. Mowry, *Theodore Roosevelt and the Progressive Movement*, 332–333; Cooper, *Warrior and Priest*, 248–250, 306. Patricia O'Toole, *When Trumpets Call: Theodore Roosevelt after the White House* (New York: Simon & Schuster Paperbacks, 2004), 247. Most recently, Edmund Morris, *The Colonel* (New York: Random House, 2010), 391, 393, 446, 457. But cf. Dalton, *Theodore Roosevelt*, 474–482, 493–511.

184. *America and the World War*, in *Works*, 18: 185.

185. Dalton, *Theodore Roosevelt*, 474, 520, stands out among historians for hav-

ing called attention to this, though she goes too far in crediting him for having overcome "the bigotry of his own time," 524.

186. "Socialism and Social Reform," in *Works*, 19: 96–112, at 106.

187. "The Soul of the Nation," in *Fear God and Take Your Own Part*, in *Works*, 18: 442–452. Also, John Milton Cooper, Jr., *Woodrow Wilson: A Biography* (New York: Alfred A. Knopf, 2009), 350–351.

188. "The Men Who Pay with Their Bodies for Their Souls' Desire," in *The Great Adventure*, in *Works*, 19: 248–259, at 253.

189. Dalton, *Theodore Roosevelt*, 442, 501.

190. TR to Hugo von Munsterberg, February 8, 1916, in Morison, *Letters*, 8: 1017–1018, at 1018.

191. Theodore Roosevelt, *An Autobiography* (New York: Da Capo Press, 1985 [orig. pub. Macmillan, 1913]), 487–488.

192. "Industrial Justice; The Tool-Owner and the Tool User," in *Foes of Our Own Household*, in *Works*, 19: 71–83, at 78–80.

193. Labor Day Speech, Columbia County, New York, September 5, 1917, as reported in the *New York Times*, September 6, 1917 at http://www.theodore-roosevelt.com/treditorials.html (accessed November 5, 2010). The file name is 876.

194. "A Square Deal in Law Enforcement," in *Works*, 19: 62–69, at 68. See also Morris's comparison of Wilson's handling of the railroad strike of 1916 with Roosevelt's more evenhanded mediation of the coal strike of 1902. However, Morris omits that Roosevelt was prepared to send in the army to run the mines if his mediation efforts failed. Morris, *The Colonel*, 466.

195. "Industrial Justice; The Tool-Owner and the Tool User," italics in original, in *Works*, 19: 82. Also, Theodore Roosevelt, "The Problems of Peace—Part II," Roosevelt R052.R67m8, Theodore Roosevelt Collection, Houghton Library, Harvard University.

196. Speech to the Maine Republican Convention, March 28, 1918, at http://www.theodore-roosevelt.com/treditorials.html (accessed November 13, 2010). The file name is 714.

197. Roosevelt, "The Problems of Peace—Part II."

198. "Washington and Lincoln: The Great Examples," in *Works*, 19: 48–61, at 59–60.

199. For a similar approach, see "Socialism and Social Reform," in *Works*, 19: 96–112.

200. "Industrial Justice; The Tool-Owner and the Tool User," in *Works*, 19: 81.

201. *America and the World War*, in *Works*, 18: 131, 130. For a more recent statement of the progressive infatuation with autocracy, see Thomas Friedman, "Our One Party Democracy," September 8, 2009, *New York Times*.

202. "The Men Who Pay with Their Bodies," in *Works*, 19: 248–259, at 255.

203. "The Farmer: The Corner-Stone of Civilization," in *Works*, 19: 113–131, at 126.

204. "The Parasite Woman; The Only Indispensable Citizen," in *Works*, 19: 140–151 at 143, 149.

330 NOTES TO PAGES 256–263

205. "Birth Reform, from the Positive, Not the Negative Side," in *Works*, 19: 152–167, at 155, 157. Emphasis in original.

EPILOGUE: THE "HEIRS" OF THEODORE ROOSEVELT

1. Roosevelt helped to cinch his renomination when he declared that he wanted "Perdicaris alive or Raisuli dead," after a Moroccan bandit had kidnapped Perdicaris, whom TR mistakenly believed (as did Raisuli) was an American citizen. See also Burt Solomon, "The Cult of TR," *National Journal*, February 15, 2002, 452–459.

2. David Brooks, "A Return to National Greatness: A Manifesto For a Lost Creed," *The Weekly Standard*, March 3, 1997, 16–21; "Bully for America: What Teddy Roosevelt Teaches," *The Weekly Standard,* June 23, 1997, 14–22; William Kristol and David Brooks, "What Ails Conservatism?" *The Wall Street Journal*, September 15, 1997; "Politics and Patriotism: From Teddy Roosevelt to John McCain," *The Weekly Standard,* April 26, 1999, 16–23; "National Greatness: Teddy Roosevelt's Vision for the Twenty-First Century," *American Experiment Quarterly*, Winter 1998–99 at http://www.google.com/#hl=en&&sa=X&ei=v9iWTbPOK0K8lQfXm-nmBw&sqi=2&ved=0CBIQBSgA&q=david+brooks+on+Theodore+roosevelt&spell=1&fp=9221d319c6f86414 (accessed February 12, 2011); "The Coming Activist Age," *The New York Times,* July 18, 2008. For a dissenting view, see Christopher Caldwell, "Tagging after Teddy," March 22, 2000, at http://www.theatlantic.com/past/docs/unbound/polipro/pp2000-03-22.html (accessed February 12, 2011). With the release of the chairmen's report of the presidential fiscal commission immediately after the 2010 midterm elections, Brooks revived his calls for "national greatness," but without explicit reference to TR, "National Greatness Agenda," *The New York Times*, November 12, 2010.

3. Harvey C. Mansfield, "The Manliness of Theodore Roosevelt," *The New Criterion*, March 2005, 4–9; Harvey C. Mansfield, *Manliness* (New Haven, Conn.: Yale University Press, 2006), 90–99.

4. Robert Kagan, *Dangerous Nation: America's Place in the World from Its Earliest Days to the Dawn of the Twentieth Century* (New York: Knopf, 2006); Robert Kagan and William Kristol, "Toward a Neo-Reaganite Foreign Policy," *Foreign Affairs*, July/August 1996, 18–32. Although TR takes a backseat to Ronald Reagan, the authors admire Roosevelt's international engagement.

5. http://www.slate.com/id/2202950/pagenum/2 (accessed February 12, 2011).

6. "The Children of the Crucible," in *Foes of Our Own Household*, in *The Works of Theodore Roosevelt*, 20 vols., ed. Herman Hagedorn (New York: Charles Scribner's Sons, 1924), 19: 30–47, at 30 (hereafter cited as *Works*).

7. *Time* Magazine, July 3, 2006, at http://www.time.com/time/magazine/0,9263,7601060703,00.html (accessed February 12, 2011). Additional web entries by Newt Gingrich, Karl Rove, and Andrew Ferguson attempt to redress the imbalance of the print version.

8. Kathleen Dalton, *Theodore Roosevelt* (New York: Alfred A. Knopf, 2002) brings out the radical character of TR's proposals, but she muddies the water by using the terms "liberal," "radical," and "reformist" interchangeably.

9. "Socialism I—Where We Cannot Work with Socialists," *The Outlook*, March 20, 1909; "Socialism II—Where We Can Work with Socialists," *The Outlook*, March 27, 1909, at http://www.theodore-roosevelt.com/treditorials.html (accessed July 27, 2011). The file names are 072 and 090, respectively. Theodore Roosevelt, *An Autobiography* (New York: Da Capo Press, 1985 [orig. pub. Macmillan, 1913]), 514–515; "Socialism and Social Reform," in *Works*, 19: 96–112.

10. For a survey of liberal comments on the gradual transition to socialism, see Jonah Goldberg, "What Kind of Socialist Is Barack Obama?" *Commentary*, May 2010, 9–15.

11. FDR's "Commonwealth Address," in which he makes essentially the same point, is often regarded as a great innovation, but in fact the ground was prepared by TR.

12. John Dewey, "Theodore Roosevelt," *The Dial* 66, no. 783 (February 8, 1919): 115.

13. The extent of Croly's infatuation with fascism is disputed. John P. Diggins, "Flirtation with Fascism: American Pragmatic Liberals and Mussolini's Italy," *American Historical Review* 71, no. 2 (January 1966): 487–506; more recently, Jonah Goldberg, *Liberal Fascism* (New York: Broadway Books, 2007, 2009), ch. 3. Edward A. Stettner, *Shaping Modern Liberalism: Herbert Croly and Progressive Thought* (Lawrence: University Press of Kansas, 1993), 155–157, argues that Croly's admiration for fascism has been exaggerated.

14. Dalton, *Theodore Roosevelt*, 522.

15. William E. Leuchtenburg, "Progressivism and Imperialism: The Progressive Movement and American Foreign Policy, 1898–1916," *Mississippi Valley Historical Review* 39, no. 3 (December 1952): 483–504. But cf. John Milton Cooper, Jr., "Progressivism and American Foreign Policy: A Reconsideration," *Mid-America* 51 (October 1969): 260–277.

16. Arthur M. Schlesinger, Jr., *The Imperial Presidency* (Boston: Houghton Mifflin, 1973).

17. Alexis de Tocqueville, *Tocqueville on America after 1840: Letters and Other Writings*, ed. Aurelian Craiutu and Jeremy Jennings (New York: Cambridge University Press, 2009), 396.

18. "The 2009 Index of Dependence on Government," The Heritage Center for Data Analysis, The Heritage Foundation, at http://www.heritage.org/research/reports/2010/03/the-2009-index-of-dependence-on-government (accessed February 22, 2011).

19. As cited in *The Bully Pulpit*, ed. H. Paul Jeffers (Dallas: Taylor Publishing, 1998), 65.

20. Alexis de Tocqueville, *Democracy in America*, trans. Harvey Mansfield and Delba Winthrop (Chicago: University of Chicago Press, 2000), 661–673.

Index

CPSIA information can be obtained
at www.ICGtesting.com
Printed in the USA
JSHW020322130123
36170JS00001B/5

9 780700 619689